The Gulf Crisis

&

The New World Order

By

Hazrat Mirza Tahir Ahmad
Supreme Head of the Ahmadiyya Muslim Jamaat

*Behind-the-scene motives
and hidden causes*

*An enlightened analysis of the
contemporary situation*

A genuine solution to the crisis

"The Gulf Crisis and the New World order"
First Published in Canada in 1992
Reprinted in U.K. in 1993

© Islam International Publications Limited

All Rights Reserved

Published by:
Islam International Publications Limited
"Islamabad",
Sheephatch Lane,
Tilford, Surrey GU10 2AQ, U.K.

Printed by Unwin Brothers Ltd., The Gresham Press, Old Woking, Surrey GU22 9LH

Canadian Cataloguing-in-Publication Data

Tahir, Hazrat Mirza Tahir Ahmad, Khalifatul Masih IV, 1928-
 The Gulf crisis & the new world order.
 xi, 396 p. : ill. ; 22 cm.
 17 Friday sermons of the Supreme Head, Ahmadiyya Muslim Jamaat.
 Translated from Urdu by Mubarak Ahmad Nazir.
 Includes index.
 Bibliography: p.375]378

1. Persian Gulf war, 1991
2. Iraq-Kuwait crisis, 1990-1991
3. Persian Gulf war, 1991 – Moral and ethical aspects.
4. Persian Gulf war, 1991 – Religious aspects.
5. Persian Gulf war, 1991 – Economic aspects.
6. Persian Gulf war, 1991 – Diplomatic history.
7. Islam and world politics.
8. United States – History – Persian Gulf war, 1991.
I. Ahmad, Mirza Tahir. II. Nazir, Mubarak Ahmad. III. Ahmadiyya Muslim Jamaat, Canada. IV. Title: The Gulf crisis and the new world order.

DS79.72T3   1992   956.70536 7 – 20dc.

A catalogue record for this book is available from The British Library

ISBN: 1-88249 400 8 (Canada)

ISBN: 1 85372 506 4 (U.K.)

Love For All
Hatred For None

"Scientific thought is the Common Heritage of all Mankind."
(Dr Abdus Salam Sahib)

A brief Profile of the author:

HAZRAT MIRZA TAHIR AHMAD

Hazrat Mirza Tahir Ahmad, born on December 18, 1928 at Qadian, India is the fourth successor of the Promised Messiah[as]. He is the spiritual and administrative head of the Ahmadiyya Muslim Jamaat, and a grandson of the Founder, Hazrat Mirza Ghulam Ahmad, the Promised Messiah[as]. The official title of the Supreme head of the Ahmadiyya Muslim Jamaat is: **"Hazrat Khalifa-tul-Massih IV"** - fourth vicegerent to the Promised Messiah[as].

A graduate of "Jamia Ahmadiyya", a missionary college of the organization, Hazrat Ahmad attended the School of Oriental and African Studies, University of London, England, from 1955-57. Upon his return from England, he volunteered to dedicate his life to the cause of Islam and thus became involved in the Jamaat as a full time worker.

He served the organization in various capacities, including from minor roles to leading important institutions. In 1982, he was elected to head the Ahmadiyya Muslim Jamaat in the capacity of **"Khalifa-tul-Massih IV"**.

Hazrat Mirza Tahir Ahmad is a widely travelled man and a keen observer of other cultures, groups and societies. Outstanding scholar, blessed with extraordinary understanding of the Holy Quran, he is an orator par excellence and keeps his audience spellbound. His most inspiring Friday sermons are tape-recorded and distributed to all Ahmadiyya Muslim Communities in some 120 countries regularly every week. In dozens of European and the former USSR countries, these sermons are seen live through T.V. satellite networks. He conducts very interesting and highly educative "Question- Answer" sessions with the young and old which are recorded and distributed all over the world. Until now, he has recorded over 500 Friday Sermons and numerous "Question- Answer" sessions in both English and Urdu. These serve as an excellent guide to Ahmadi Muslims to conduct their lives on Islamic principles.

Hazrat Mirza Tahir Ahmad is an avid reader and takes keen interest in modern scientific knowledge. He is also an acclaimed writer and poet. His book, "Murder in the name of Allah" published by Lutterworth Press, London, England in which he very forcefully projected the peaceful posture of Islam, gained wide acclamation.

His Holiness is a good sportsman, a squash player, and a specialist in Homoeopathic medicine.

HAZRAT MIRZA TAHIR AHMAD

CONTENTS

Profile of the author - **Hazrat Mirza Tahir Ahmad,**
Supreme Head of the Ahmadiyya Muslim Jamaat
A note from the translator xi
Foreword 1
Quotations from Sermons 5
FIRST FRIDAY SERMON **August 03, 1990** 31
The Quranic procedure of settlement of conflicts 31
The Islamic world constantly in the grip of problems 31
The Quranic solution of any conflict 32
Clear violation of the instructions of the Holy Quran 33
The necessity of reverting to the teachings of Islam 34
The basic analysis of the problems faced by Muslims 36
The cause of these recurring problems 37

SECOND FRIDAY SERMON **August 17, 1990** 39
The fatal consequences of the Gulf Crisis 39
The painful situation in the Middle East 39
Politics devoid of justice and piety 40
Iraqi occupation of Kuwait: reaction and dreadful dangers . . . 40
Double standard of justice and mischievous propaganda 42
Havoc wrought by politics, deprived of morality 44
Fatal implications of the present situation 45
A deep conspiracy against the world of Islam 48
A survey of the world of Islam in its historical
perspective 48
Attack on Islam 51
Respectful appeal and humble advice 52
Ahmadi Muslims should offer earnest supplications
before Allah 54

THIRD FRIDAY SERMON **August 24, 1990** 57
**The real cause of protracted period of restlessness
in the Middle East** 57
Gemal Abdul Nasser of Egypt 58

i

Contents

Saddam Hussein 58
Sick minds: the real cause of the disease 58
Wrong diagnosis and wrong reaction 59
Intrigues of the Western Powers in Iran 60
The U.S. Dilemma 61
Saddam Hussein - a product of the West 62
Reaction of the West 63
Freezing of assets 64
The greatest blunder 64
The real duty of Islamic leadership 66
Occupation of Arab land by Israel 67
The Muslims continue to be stung from the same orifice 67
The remedy prescribed by the Holy Quran 68
The Jamaat of the Muhammadan Messiah and
its responsibilities 69
Appeal to members of the Ahmadiyya Muslim Community ... 71

FOURTH FRIDAY SERMON **October 26, 1990** 73
An alarming conspiracy hatched against the Muslim World 73
New challenges emerging in the changing circumstances 73
Expected confrontation of Islam with racial prejudice 74
Rising trends of nationalism and racism in Europe 75
The Russian empire on the verge of disintegration 77
Islamic concept of national ideology 78
Evidence of rising racial prejudice in Europe 81
The real nature of the differences between USSR and China .. 84
A deep-rooted and dreadful conspiracy against the Muslims .. 84
The essence of the great conspiracy 85
Appeal to pray for the World of Islam 88

FIFTH FRIDAY SERMON **November 09, 1990** 89
The need to offer solemn and heart-rending prayers 89
Reminder to pray for the welfare of the Muslim World 89
The argument presented against Iraq 90
The historic deceptions of those presenting this argument 91
Plunder of the African continent 91
Naive logic of the Western thinkers 93

A futile attempt to advice Iraq 94
The geographical change in India 95
Happenings in India are a reaction of injustices
in Pakistan 97
Valiant stand of Mr. V.P. Singh 99
The need and importance of a pious reaction by Muslims 100
God and his Apostles will eventually prevail 102

SIXTH FRIDAY SERMON **November 16, 1990** **105**
The greatest danger facing mankind today **105**
Prejudices and selfishness 105
Dangers of racial prejudices in Russia 109
The deplorable conditions in Africa 110
Some further examples of national prejudices 111
Occupation of Tibet by China/ occupation of
Kuwait by Iraq 114
The rule of selfishness on the world 115
Duties of the Ahmadiyya Muslim Jamaat 117
Launch a Holy-War for the establishment of Peace 118

SEVENTH FRIDAY SERMON **November 23, 1990** **121**
**The Quranic command of holding fast to the
"Rope of Allah"** **121**
Two Quranic commands 121
The importance of a balanced reaction under all
situations 122
What is meant by fulfilling the demands of *Taqwa* 124
The importance of allegiance to *Khilafat* 127
The flames of war are flared by discord 129
The consequences of disobeying Quranic commands 130

EIGHTH FRIDAY SERMON **January 11, 1991** **135**
Contradictory attitude of the Western Powers **135**
An essential explanation - Islam allows no prejudice 135
Nature of my criticism 136
The current international situation 137
History stands as an incriminating witness against
Western powers 138

iii

Contents

- Double standards of Western Powers 141
- Strange and shaky standpoint of Muslim countries 143
- Saddam Hussein has only one option open to him 147
- Prayerful obligations of Ahmadis 149
- The duty of the Muslim countries in the present situation 150
- Selfishness of Saudi government 151
- A forceful appeal for prayers 153

NINTH FRIDAY SERMON January 18, 1991 155
A war sowing sinister seeds of extreme unrest 155
- Extremely painful reality 155
- The stance of the Ahmadiyya Muslim Jamaat on Iraq 156
- A judicious advice to Iraq 157
- An extremely painful situation for the Muslim World 160
- A war giving birth to a dreadful aftermath 163
- Comprehensive prayers for the victory of Truth 165
- An important advice 166

TENTH FRIDAY SERMON January 25, 1991 171
Fundamental difference between political wars and *Jihad* .. 171
- A basic principle : Islam has no territorial boundaries 171
- A question of loyalty to ones's faith or to one's country 173
- Definition of *Jihad* 175
- The reasons behind the labelling of political wars as *Jihad* 177
- Antagonism between the East and West 177
- Has the U.N. the right to create new countries? 178
- Israeli excesses and the American veto 179
- The United Nations - does it merit this name? 179
- Israeli attack on Iraq's nuclear plant 180
- Muslim impression is based on facts 180
- Israel persuaded to wait until U.S. has liquidated Iraq 181
- U.S. preaching humanity and morality to the world 181
- Are these attacks intended to punish Saddam or the innocent people of Iraq? 182
- No Muslim ruler is justified to term this war as an *Islamic Jihad* 183
- Hate begets hate 184

iv

The Gulf Crisis & The New World Order

Unprejudiced comments 185
Verdict of destiny 187

ELEVENTH FRIDAY SERMON **February 01, 1991** 191
The attitude of the Muslim countries in the Gulf War   191
Present war has its roots in the conspiracies
hatched a century ago........................... 191
Real solution to the crisis lies in true teachings
of Islam 191
High treason against Islamic interests 191
Egypt and Saudi Arabia 192
The relationship between the U.S. and Saudi Arabia 192
Who are the "British agents" and the "Jewish agents"? 193
Economic misery may have forced certain nations to
barter their faith 193
Commendable behaviour of Iran 194
An unpardonable crime of Saudi Arabia and Egypt 195
The war as evaluated by Western commentators 196
The long drawn plan of Jewish domination 198
The Jewish plan will never succeed. 200
A frightful era of dreadful conspiracies against Islam. 202
The mystery: the richest land but the most poorly
defended 203
The West distorts a just stand 204
The need for a detailed assessment of the situation 206
Promise to present the Islamic solution 207

TWELFTH FRIDAY SERMON **February 08, 1991** 209
**The reality of the new world order of President
George Bush**................................... 209
The significance of the Gulf War 209
The background to the Palestinian issue 211
Conflicts of interest 216
Premeditated action against Egypt 218
Wars of Jewish expansionism 220
President Bush's dream of peace 225
The nature of U.S. - Israel relations. 227
Another shady aspect of President Bush's dream 230

v

Contents

Hands stained with the blood of the oppressed 231

THIRTEENTH FRIDAY SERMON February 15, 1991 .... **233**
Latest situation of the Gulf War **233**
Determining the responsibility for war 235
Historical perspective and the sad indifference
of the Muslims 239
The gains and losses of the war 243
The psychological perspective of the war 247
The historical perspective 248
Jews - victims to tyranny and persecution in Europe 249
Promise to offer advice 252

FOURTEENTH FRIDAY SERMON February 22, 1991 .... **255**
Optimism of the United States and its allies **255**
The wrong thinking of the U.S. and its allies 255
Hate always begets hate 256
Israeli motives 257
Saddam - pictured as a new Hitler 258
What is happening & why it is happening 259
The status of Israeli promises 261
Horrendous cruelties inflicted on Palestinians 263
The fate of the United Nations resolutions against Israel 264
The difference between the resolutions passed against
Israel and those passed against Iraq 265
The United Nations 266
Deep animosity of the West against the World of Islam 267
The Jewish tribes of Banu Qunkah, Banu Nazeer
and Banu Qariza 268
The Jews never forget to avenge themselves 269
Psychological repercussions of defeat in Vietnam 271
United States was humbled 272
U.S. sets the most dangerous precedent in the
history of wars 272
Mercenaries and war 274
The land of Iraq: minarets of death, made of human scull ... 275
The most critical time in human history 276
Offer prayers 277

The Gulf Crisis & The New World Order

FIFTEENTH FRIDAY SERMON March 01, 1991 279
Advice to the world of Islam & to the
Third world countries 279
The current situation of the Gulf War and its background ... 279
Shouts of Kuwait - Kuwait - Kuwait 280
Three basic principles of secular politics 281
The greatest tragedy of the Muslim World 283
This is not a battle between Truth and Falsehood 284
The real culprit 285
The remedy for the heartbreak of Muslims 286
Lessons of history 287
Advice to the Allied Powers 288
Muslim countries should establish Islamic system of
Justice 289
Three vicious viewpoints 289
The obligation of Muslim Statesmen 291
The real danger for the Muslim countries 293
Meaningless shouts of *Jihad* without adequate preparation ... 295
"God does not change the fate of those who do not
attempt to change themselves" 296
Advice to the Muslim World 297
The need for self reliance 298
There is always humiliation in a beggar's life 298
Advice to the Third world 300
Raising the standard of living of the lower classes 301
Who will derive benefit from this advice? 302

SIXTEENTH FRIDAY SERMON March 08, 1991 305
Comprehensive advice to transform the dream of
World Peace into reality 305
Another tale of horrifying atrocities 305
Humiliation in Vietnam 305
3,000 Iraqi villages turned to dust 307
Some valuable suggestions for the Arab nations 307
The need of establishing an Economic Commonwealth 311
Danger for the Third World 311
The need for economic cooperation and for resolving
mutual problems 312

Contents

The curse of begging 313
The need for self-sufficiency 313
The curse of military aid 314
The Third world - a dumping ground of obsolete weaponry
of the West 315
Similarities between military aid and the disease 'AIDS' 315
Insurgency and counter insurgency measures 316
Harmful effects of foreign aid 317
Establishment of a new Islamic system of assistance 318
Food used to enslave poor nations 318
The need to resolve the Kashmir dispute 319
A humble advice to Pakistan 320
The results of trampling upon descent human values 322
The need of a new Organisation of the oil
producing countries 323
Association of non-oil producing countries 324
The need to protect the interest of the workers from
other countries 324
Equilibriums and Justice 325
The need of a new United Nations for the Third World 326
Muslims and non-Muslims pitched against each other 327
Contradictions in the charter of the U.N. 328
U.N. takes decisions which it cannot implement 329
An important advice to Israel 331
Prophecy about the affliction of "AIDS" 336
Compassion for the Jews, if they change their ways 338
Advice to Western Christian nations 339
My humble supplications 340
Terrorism should be erased from the dictionary of Muslims .. 340

SEVENTEENTH FRIDAY SERMON *(extract)* **March 15, 1991** .. 343
A special appeal for prayers for peace in the
Muslim world 343

SAMPLING OF PUBLIC OPINION ON THE GULF WAR 349
Bibliography English 375
Bibliography Arabic 378
Index & Notes 379

A note from the translator:

As I listen to the Urdu audio recordings of these sermons and compare them with this translation, my heart sinks at observing how much force and eloquence has been lost. The fact is that the dimension of the spiritual rhetoric of His Holiness is such that it defies all attempts at translation. Despite all possible efforts to maintain the unique style of Hazoor, I must admit that the book remains only a translation.

I am aware that my shortcomings prevented me from doing justice to this work. May Allah forgive me. I assume personal responsibility for all errors of facts and mistaken interpretations. If in any doubt, readers should check the original text in Urdu which has been published in the form of a similar booklet.

The name of Muhammad, the Holy Prophet of Islam, has been followed by a symbol [sas] for the salutation *"Sallal laho alaihe wa alehi wa sallam"* (May the peace and blessings of Allah be upon him and upon his progeny). Similarly the names of all other Prophets are generally followed by the abbreviation [as] *"Alaehis salam"* meaning 'on whom be peace'. All arabic words used have their translation in the text.

The translation and publication of this book is not my solo effort. I have been assisted by a team of most dedicated and selfless workers including Saleem-ur-Rahman, Mian Muhammad Afzal, Chaudhry Abdul Qadir, Dr. Mohammad Aqeel Athar and Waseem A. Sayyed. Nasir A. Shah assisted in the proof-reading. Khalil Nazir worked for hundreds of hours in preparing its camera-ready format while Majid Ahmad Javed was the Urdu/Arabic calligrapher. Mr. Malik Khalil-ur-Rahman, Mr. Munir Ahmad Javed and Mr. B. A. Rafiq offered vital support and advice from our offices in London U.K. The entire work was done under the guidance of Mr. Naseem Mahdi.

Mubarak Ahmad Nazir
Calgary, Canada

Foreword

The radical changes occurring on the global scene and the complicated and furious problem facing the Muslim World in the aftermath of the Gulf War, are the burning topic of the day. The spiritual Head of The Ahmadiyya Muslim Community, His Holiness, Hazrat Mirza Tahir Ahmad, delivered a series of 17 Friday Sermons on the Gulf War. 14 of these sermons were delivered while the war was in progress and the events were still unfolding. The remaining 3 sermons were delivered in March 1991, when the war had just come to a tragic end.

In these sermons, he put political posturing and policy manoeuvring in its religious and historical perspective; highlighting various hidden motives and offering vivid glimpses of their far-reaching consequences. He has presented a profound analysis of the situation in its entirety and offered proposals for the establishment of the genuine New World Order that is predicated upon the system of absolute JUSTICE proclaimed by the Holy Quran. This alone will guarantee a lasting peace in the world and insure a bright future for humanity.

He said:
"I declare on behalf of Jamaat Ahmadiyya that the comments I make are based on truth and I do so honestly and impartially. They may appear bitter to some. But no matter how bitter they may appear to be, the world, if not today then in the near future, will accept the truth of what I say and will agree to this truth that I have made them without any trace of prejudice, bigotry or ulterior motives."

"Since I will represent Islam, therefore, I firmly believe that the solution put forth by Ahmadiyya Muslim Jamaat is inherently undeserving of contempt. If you will accept it, it will be to your own benefit and the benefit of mankind at large. But if

Foreword

you turn it down then remember that you remain unable to eliminate transgression from the world, and one effort after another on your part will fail. And one war would follow another war, and one instability after another will cause the human society to become awash with blood, and rob the peace and tranquillity of mankind. This is my faith that since I will present the Islamic Solution, by the Grace of Allah, therefore, what I have stated above will come to pass. Either you will accept it and benefit from it or you will reject it and then you will have to suffer the damaging consequences."
(Friday Sermon Feb 01, 1991)

"Our unassuming appeal in this respect is a humble word of advice. If someone wants to listen to it in earnestness, understands it and then acts upon it, then he will benefit from it, because what I am presenting is the Quranic teaching. But if this word of advice from us is rejected with scorn and arrogance then I warn you today that the Muslim world will sink into such grave dangers that the entire world of Islam will lament for a very long time to come. It may go on lamenting but it will amount to nothing more than bashing its head against the wall. It will gain nothing, and will not be able to regain its lost strength and dignity, as it is now or as it could attain in future."

"If a message of truth provokes anybody's anger against us then let it be known that our sanctuary is in our God. We entrust Him with our affairs, and we are not fearful of any worldly political fallout."

The study of these sermons is thought-provoking and very informative for any person who wishes to have a better future for his posterity.

The Gulf Crisis & The New World Order

One wonders how His Holiness could stand for over an hour with just a few scraps of notes and deliver such marathon sermons on a topic which may never have been tackled to such depth by any Muslim scholar. These sermons portray his deep yearning for peace in the world. Many of his predictions and apprehensions are now unfolding. No doubt this book will remain as a guideline to the Muslims and the world in general for many decades. During the war, Muslim nations were shuffling to side with the victor even if it meant the slaughter of their brethren in faith. There were others who were standing as silent spectators while the genocide was in progress. None spoke out. But here was the spiritual successor of the Promised Messiah[as] who spoke with such foresight, coupled with unmatched bravery and candour that the world was astonished. He criticized the West for their double standards and when the need arose never hesitated to lash at the East including the Muslims for forsaking the excellent teachings of the Holy Quran and for being repeatedly bitten from the same hole. One message which he constantly emphasized in all these sermons was that the Muslims should revert to prayers and supplications to God, since this was the weapon that would shield the world from the intrigues of the deceptionist.

I thank my colleague Mr. Mubarak Ahmad Nazir who headed the team that translated these sermons into English. He must have spent countless hours on the translation and compilation of this work. He was most ably assisted by Mr. Saleem-ur-Rahman who devoted his valuable time in translations and review.

August 27, 1992

Naseem Mahdi
President & Missionary In-charge,
Ahmadiyya Muslim Jamaat,
Toronto, Canada

Quotations from Sermons:

"I feel that this period of adversity and decline and these repeated miseries are the consequence of the Muslim denial of his Holiness - the Promised Messiah[as]. There is no doubt about it. Therefore my message to you is that you should submit yourselves to the 'Imam of the Age'. Accept that one, who was sent by God. He is the one who has the ability to lead you. Without him, separated from him, you are like a body which has no head. There may be apparent signs of life and the limbs may flutter. There is much painful fluttering, but the head which God has created for the guidance and leadership of the body is missing. So, turn back and establish your contact with the Divine Leadership. After denying the leadership established by God, no path of peace and prosperity is left open for you. The period of adversity has been long and painful. You should turn to God, repent, and seek His forgiveness. Let me assure you that to whatever extent the matters may have worsened, if you submit today before the leadership established by God, then not only will you rise as a great power in the world, but such a great movement of the new supremacy of Islam will be set in motion that no power in the world will be able to confront it and the progress which appears to spread over centuries will become a matter of years."
(August 03, 1990)

"When you omit the word 'Islam' from the context of this conflict and portray an 'Islamic problem' as a regional problem, then God withdraws His helping hand. In the Quranic injunction there is no mention of any particular nation or group. The guidance which the Holy Quran has given, mentions the Muslims as a whole, and declares all of them as brothers of one another. Therefore, it is certainly not just an Arab problem. It is a problem which concerns the Islamic world."
(August 03, 1990)

"The Islamic world has not followed the guidelines as enunciated in this verse of the Holy Quran regarding mutual disputes. If the Muslim states had tried to settle their mutual differences in light of this clear injunction of the Holy Quran, then the bloody and protracted war of attrition between Iraq and Iran could have been brought to a speedy end. The difficulty is, that decisions are taken on the basis of alliances, without giving consideration to the spirit of righteousness."
(August 03, 1990)

"The non-Muslim nations are busy making tall claims in the name of justice, as if they have been appointed the sole custodians of justice in the world, and that justice would become extinct but for the might of these nations. On the other hand, Muslim countries are making tall claims in the name of Islam; but when you hold these claims - being made on either side - up for scrutiny, you discover that these are equally devoid of the elements of justice that are laid down by the Holy Quran."
(August 17, 1990)

"But Iraq, too, is not fulfilling the obligations placed by the Islamic principles of justice. Islam does not allow, under any circumstances, to take hostages from among those foreign nationals who are living in your country, with whom you may even be at war. Nor does Islam allow you to use them as bargaining chips in any way; any act of wrongdoing against them is prohibited by Islam."
(August 17, 1990)

"On the one hand they accuse Iraq of having an immoral position - and we agree that it is a violation of the Islamic principles of morality - but then, in the same breath, they themselves are being guilty of a glaring act of immorality that is only thinly disguised by diplomatic euphemisms. But, in reality, the cruelty that Iraq is being subjected to by the joint efforts of Britain and U.S., constitutes a crime whose horror exceeds the hypothetically feared potential execution of a few thousand Britons and Americans held in Iraq."
(August 17, 1990)

"Where is justice? The Western world has adopted their own style of diplomacy - which in Islamic terminology would be called "duplicity" - reaching the utmost limits. They have promoted duplicity under the guise of diplomacy and politics to a degree that is unparalleled in human history. So their crimes are always in disguise, their language has lucidity, and their presentation - aided by propaganda - carries a semblance of rationality."
(August 17, 1990)

"My apprehension is that Iraq will be subjected to horrific revenge and it may be blown to bits. The fire of their revenge will not quench until they annihilate this up-and-coming Muslim country which is an exceptional force in this region. These ill-intentions were first conceived in Israel. I am convinced as a result of various Israeli statements that they were the harbinger of the current state of affairs. **God alone knows how Iraq was lured into occupying Kuwait and then the whole sinister development ensued.** But such incidents are seldom accidental. There are some underlying motives and some subterranean intrigues at work. There are the CIA agents and then there are indigenous traitors who meticulously perform the cryptic and surreptitious assignments designed to fulfil the wishes of Super Powers."
(August 17, 1990)

"What is that disease? It is the founding of Israel and after that it is the continuous preferential treatment given to Israel by the West. Whenever there were two paths, and a question facing the West was whether to tread the path that led to the interest of Israel or to follow the path that led to the interest of the Arab Muslim world, then without exception, the West always followed the path which gave preference to Israel and discarded the interest of the Islamic world. The essence of this disease has been expressed by an Arab poet in a simple couplet saying that:

"A man who dresses his dog well, but for me he thinks that my bare skin is enough to cover me.
Without doubt, for him the dog is better than me, but for me, the dog is better than him."

This is exactly the ultimate diagnosis of the disease. This attitude of the West has sunk into the heart of the Arab world and their analysis is based on facts that the West will no doubt prefer to clothe even its dogs but will keep the Arabs nude and this situation is very true when you make a comparison between Israel and the Arab States."
(August 24, 1990)

"So long as one does not cast a glance at the fundamental cause which gives rise to the development of the so-called "Nazism", "Nasserism" or "Saddamism" - so long as the disease is not correctly diagnosed and attention is not paid to its treatment; such 'heads' will continue to surface one after the other. These 'heads' will continue to be severed and will continue to be a justification for the dismembering of other heads, and this sore will continue to ripen till that time when it might spill out of the control and power of the governments of the West! In fact the power which Saddam Hussein now brandishes is just a reflection of the past injustice and unprincipled stand of the West."
(August 24, 1990)

"But Alas!, no attention was paid to our advice. The other Muslim Arab countries also failed to pay the least consideration to our plea. Little did they realise that they were acting in liaison with non- Muslim powers, bearing all the expenses of this cruel endeavour, to completely destroy and decimate a Muslim power, to entail elimination of peace for all times from this part of the world! It is besides the point, whether the peace of the world is threatened, but I can say with certainty to these

States which are about to bear the expense of this war and those who have brought in mercenaries, that they will never be able to return to their past. Their condition will deteriorate, from bad to worse and peace in this region will vanquish for all times to come."
(November 9, 1990)

"Therefore, the nations which see a danger in Iraq today, I can show them thousands of dangers spread throughout the world. If they are truly desirous of world peace then in accordance with my advice, they should become established on fairness; on the fairness of Islam which differentiates neither between East and West nor between North and South. Rather, keeping God in view it puts forward a concept of justice and fairness. If they will try to resolve their conflicts and the conflicts of the world according to this fairness then I assure you that the world can achieve peace. But this peace can be achieved through the affectionate hand of the Holy Prophet Muhammad[sas] because he is the only Prophet who has been declared "a mercy" for all creation and who has been sent by God for the whole universe. So long as you do not extend your hand toward him; so long as you do not benefit from him, you cannot grant peace to the world."
(November 16, 1990)

"So, whatever criticism has originated from me or will emanate from me, would be predicated on the noble moral principles of Islam. And it will be directed towards whoever is deserving of it - not with a view to hurting anybody's feeing but in order to bring out the fact and illuminate the issues involved. In view of the aforesaid,

whenever I deliver a critical commentary, I check out my innermost feelings and make it a point to never level criticism rooted in any prejudice. Rather I cleanse my heart, feeling the presence of God, and try to present the facts and state the truth. Such a dose of truth tastes bitter, to one group of people or another, at times, but it is involuntary on our part. We cannot give perpetually biased support to anyone. We shall always side with the truth and constantly lean towards the Word of God and the 'Practice' of the Holy Prophet of Islam. Whoever seeks our eternal friendship must befriend the Word of God, the Sunnah of The Holy Prophet, righteousness and the truth. In so doing, he will always find us by his side."
(January 11, 1991)

"These Western nations are the same who present themselves as great animal-lovers, and use their news-media to raise concern about certain endangered species of animals, and make appeals to save them from extinction. But they themselves killed the Red Indian nations that spread throughout the continent, with such savagery that many of these nations are now completely annihilated. There is but a handful of these nations whose mention we now find in the Western history or in their literature. Now they are confined to the realm of their movies or their literature; otherwise most of the tribes are no longer in existence. The atrocities committed against them would need a long narrative. Then the plunder and pillage and colonization of the African Continent by the European nations is a case in point. How heinous were the atrocities committed against the African nations; how the hundreds of thousands of them were enslaved and sold as chattel!

How forcibly slave labour was extracted from them. The U.S. had the greatest demand for these enslaved Africans who were sold as slaves to the American customers. The population profile of the U.S. today presents a grim reminder of this history of the U.S. in the form of existing generations of Black Americans. So, imagine a nation with such historical record to be clamouring today that it is motivated by its humanity and high morals to come to the help of the weak and restore the land of Kuwait to its people! It is claiming that it is forced to react against cruelty to humans because of its deep sense of "humanity and high moral values". And if it did not intervene - it claims - then humanity would disappear from the face of the earth, and there would not remain any guarantee of peace for any poor and weak country in the world.If such sentiments are genuine, and if America has awakened to a new sense of sublime values - even though much too late - then why not apply these same values at home and relinquish the Red Indian land in their favour and return to your old country which was your ancestral land? If you say that to them, they will reply: What are you talking about? It was "another matter altogether". Have you lost your mind? Obviously, one cannot argue with this 'it-was-another-matter' attitude."
(January 11, 1991)

"Now, if the people of Iraq are going to be brutalized and punished for the wrong steps taken by President Saddam, then which decent citizen of this world, whether Muslim or not can be happy over this misery? Nobody who loves humanity and Islam can, in any case, be happy over this. But one is shocked to watch on the T.V., the lazy-rich

Kuwaitis and Saudis, with their vaults full of money, listening to the radio bulletins of Iraq's destruction, and gloating over it and laughing at it aloud."
(January 18, 1991)

"As I pondered over the contemporary difficulties of the world of Islam, my attention was diverted to the hungry millions of the African continent who span vast areas and several countries. Humanity is dying of hunger in Ethiopia, Somalia, Sudan, Chad and many other countries; and mankind is not mindful of this problem as a very human problem."
(January 18, 1991)

"The weapon that Jesus Christ[as], gave to the Christian was that if he is slapped on one cheek then he should offer the other. This is the approach that was prescribed to wage spiritual battles. In practice, however, the Christians failed to grasp the meaning of this precept. As it was impracticable in every day life, they discarded it altogether............When it is said that Islam was created to triumph over all other religions in the world, this does not imply that one should pick up the sword and behead those who reject Islam. It does not mean that the promise of peace is only in favour of those who bow their heads and accept Islam, and for the rest, the Muslims become a message of war and disorder. This principle does not appeal to wisdom, neither is it practicable in the world nor will it ever succeed. The Ahmadiyya Muslim Community should always have sight of this important principle. When we talk of striving for and aiming to establish the supremacy of Islam over all mankind, we talk in the

terminology taught to us by the Holy Quran and by Muhammad[sas]. It is unrelated to the military terminology of the world."
(January 25, 1991)

Defination of *Jihad*:
"The second question which is being frequently raised at the present time is about *"Jihad"*. Ahmadi Muslims from various countries ask me what reply should they give. Is this war a *Jihad* i.e Holy-War according to the teachings of Islam? As far as the definition of the concept of *Jihad* in Islam is concerned, the most comprehensive definition has been given in the Chapter Al-Haj of the Holy Quran in the verse which I have mentioned a number of times.
"Permission to fight is granted to those against whom war is made because they have been wronged." (Al-Haj:40)
That is, those people are granted permission to raise their sword against those who are engaged in fighting against them. They can raise their swords only against those who first commenced hostilities against them, not because of any justifiable cause but because they are oppressed and have been wronged. This verse develops this subject further and it is not possible to give a finer or more perfect definition of *Jihad* than this. If we apply this definition to the present situation then it is definitely not *Jihad* in the Islamic sense. It is a political war. A political war, whether it be between Muslims and non-Muslims or between one Muslim nation and another Muslim nation, does not become a *Jihad*. Only the war of an oppressed group which is being prevented from declaring its faith in God or which is fighting against religious persecution on itself can be called *Jihad*." (January 25, 1990)

"What programmes are the U.S. and the West preparing? On what powers do they rely? They talk of *desert storm*! Little do they know that the real and dreadful storms are in the hands of God. I do not know what the decree of Allah will be but I do know for certain that the decree of Allah will eventually cause the destruction of the arrogant and the boastful. If not today, then tomorrow, this over bearing arrogance will be utterly destroyed. This is so, because to God belong the Kingdom of heaven and God's Kingdom will certainly be established on earth also. So if not today, tomorrow, if not tomorrow then the day after, you will see that this arrogance will be destroyed and erased from the world. The storms they started will turn on them, and in fulfilment of God's decree, those storms will be so violent and ferocious that their combined collective forces will be annihilated and crushed into oblivion. Existing unjust system will be destroyed. You must remember this and remain steadfast. Remember and do not ever forget that these obsolete powers which in effect constitute what is known as the United Nations today use means and pursue policies which cannot last. These nations will disappear and become national relics of bitter memories from which lessons can be drawn. It is from their ruins, that YOU O' worshipper of the Unity of Allah, Yes, it is YOU! who will build a new structure; YOU will erect a magnificent and lofty building for a new United Nations which will reach up to the heavens. O' servants of Messiah of Muhammad[sas], it is YOU to whom has been granted this task. You will see it, if not today, then tomorrow; if you see it not, your future generations will certainly see it. These are the words spoken by Allah and His decree cannot be altered in the

world. You are the workers who have to build these new structures. The foundation of the new United Nations have already been laid in heaven. It is YOU - who have to build from the foundation and raise the building to a great height. You must not ever erase names of those workers i.e Hazrat Abraham[as] and Hazrat Ishmael[as] from your hearts. Always remember them and continue to exhort your future generations as follows: O' workers in the cause of Allah remain firm in the path of righteousness, honesty, sincerity and the Unity of Allah. Let that Unity enter into every vein and fibre of your being and continue this glorious work of construction; if necessary continue it into the next century, and into the century after that, until this building reaches its completion. **I assure you that, whether you can see it with your worldly eyes or not, the eyes of my soul see these events today. My eyes see these great changes as if they are happening before me.** After our deaths our souls will be made aware of them."
(January 25, 1991)

"**Mr. Edward Heath**, the former Prime Minister of U.K. is among the greatest living personalities in Britain who are endowed with foresight and political acumen as well as extensive political experience. He has consistently held that our present political leadership is practising deception upon us, and that this war is extremely selfish, brutal and foolish for, according to him, it will produce horrifying evil consequences in the post-war era."
(February 01, 1991)

"This historical background shows that the Western powers accepted the right of the Jews to carry out terrorism and that these activities of the Jews were not to be termed as "Jewish Terrorism". On the other hand, the Muslim countries are not even allowed to retaliate to protect their territorial and political interests, and if they do so then not only are they censured but even Islam is slandered and such efforts are maliciously termed "Islamic Terrorism". The other rights and privileges which appear to have been accorded to the Jews are that:

1. The Jews have the right to defy the Security Council resolutions and they even have the right to regard these resolutions with contempt, reject them or toss them into the proverbial trash can. Yet no country has the right to condemn this behaviour.

2. Israel has the right to alter the geographical boundaries of its neighbouring countries on the pretext of its security considerations.

3. Israel has the right to produce and stockpile atomic bombs and other nuclear devices. It can even manufacture chemical and biological weapons of mass destruction.

No one seems to have the right, particularly the Muslim countries, even to criticize Israel for indulging in such activities."

(February 08, 1991)

"But Syria is in real danger and may likely be the next victim of their designs. This country has recently emerged as a military power. It would be a colossal misconception, indeed a folly, on the part of Syria if it thinks that it would be spared because of its alignment with the Western powers in the current war against Iraq. As long as Israel stands as a power at its borders, Syria cannot be secure." (February 08, 1991)

"The prime responsibility of this war thus lies with the U.S., although Saddam has only been made a tool. As for Saddam's share of responsibility for this war, there are certain elements in view of which we are obliged to admit that he had little or no other choice. The responsibility of the allies is quite obvious, and the worst part of it is that this has been done to achieve certain petty objectives. All the allies had a vested interest in this war. The Israeli part of responsibility for this war is that the entire plot was hatched by Israel, and as I have pointed earlier, from the Israeli point of view, there couldn't possibly have been a better time. A rapidly expanding Muslim force which could have proven a great threat to Israeli interests during war was intended to be pulverised in such a classic manner that the instruments of destruction were partly financed by Muslim countries and partly by some allies. The manpower being happily provided by the Americans, the British or the Arabs - all this to achieve the objectives of Israel. As a by-product of this War, Israel may also have the excuse to occupy certain other parts or parcels of land and later collect a "booty" of many billions of dollars. Israel further reserves the right to target a half-dead Iraq, (God forbid) and extract vengeance at its convenience. So Israel has been the greatest beneficiary of this war and therefore it must assume the greatest responsibility. The United Nations is also responsible for it. When members of Parliament were being purchased in Pakistan, then a political term gained currency, it was

called "**horse-trading**". What was happening was indeed horse-trading but one wondered what was the origin of this term which meant the purchasing of votes of the Members of Parliament to gain political advantage. But looking at the behaviour of the U.S. government one can easily see that the idea must have originated in America, for the way they have purchased votes in the United Nations is clearly horse-trading. They have indeed done a great deal of horse-trading. So if the United Nations has degenerated into an Organization which can be easily bought by rich nations to serve their interests then it becomes a heinous crime. Indeed it is suicidal and it robs this Organization of International trust for ever."
(February 15, 1991)

"It is sheer emotionalism and ignorance that you should hate the British or hate the Americans. These are only the ravings of madmen. Hate can never triumph in this world. It is the high virtues which eventually emerge as victorious. The code of conduct of the Holy Prophet[sas] succeeds, because that is the conduct of the best behaviour. If the Muslims were to adopt that code of conduct it would be an exemplary charter for the whole world. Such a code of conduct is invincible. No power on earth can eclipse the code of conduct of the Holy Prophet Muhammad[sas]. So revert to that code of justice and adopt that precept, then the entire problems of this world can be resolved, and that genuine new revolution can start, creating a heaven on earth! If you do not accept that, then you would continue to fight and this world would continue to face trials and tribulations."
(February 15, 1991)

"Twenty five million African people are on the brink of death, as a result of hunger. And this is an estimate made by the United Nations. If it costs two dollars per day to provide food for one African person to keep him or her alive then only 1.5 billion dollars are needed to keep 25 million Africans alive for one whole year. Now you imagine that those who have no mercy for 25 million people - those who are raining down death and destruction on 16 million Iraqis by spending tons of money are raising hue and cry at the death of a few birds! This is nothing but mere deception and mischief. If the allies had an iota of human compassion, they would first attend to the human lives. They would have attended to the poor Africans and people of other countries who are dying of hunger and attempted to remove the economic imbalance. These 25 million starving Africans could have had two hearty meals for one complete year for only 1.5 billion dollars. But they continue to spend one billion dollars each day to rain down death and destruction upon human beings and cannot spend this one billion dollars for a period of nine months to promote life - and imagine that this amount will sustain the life of 25 million people!!......"

"They have lost the sense of balance of their values, and this has been going on for a long time. They are willing to mortify human beings in favour of dogs. They are unwilling to sacrifice their petty self-interest for the welfare of humanity. So they are completely and fully involved in the criminal responsibility of this war. If they would not be held accountable today, then definitely tomorrow would hold them to account."

(February 15, 1991)

Jews - victims to tyranny and persecution in Europe
"....But the fact remains that the Jews were certainly justified in saying that the Christian Western world subjected the Jews to such sustained horrifying cruelties that have no parallel in history. The crusades which began in the year 1095 started from France and it was probably Lord Godfrey of Bouillon who took the lead. When he and other French monarchs embarked on this campaign or the first crusade they thought of performing an act of "charity" before embarking upon such a momentous task. So Godfrey of Bouillon put forward the idea that the best charity is to avenge the crucifixion of Jesus Christ[as] by slaughtering all the Jews. Just as the Muslims have an institution of offering animal sacrifice or charity before they proceed to accomplish important tasks, similarly their idea took the form of a Jewish genocide in France. We do not find many examples of an unarmed nation being subjected to such extreme cruelties in the entire human history. So this was the so called "act of charity" that they performed before embarking upon the first crusade. Then this became a common practice, and for the next two hundred years that before embarking on each crusade, the Jews would be randomly slain as an act of charity!"
(February 15, 1991)

"From another angle it would be more accurate to say that Israel, and not President Bush brought the world to heel, and that the United States itself has joined the pack, at the heel of the hunter. This gives a more accurate picture and the world views the recent events in this perspective."
(February 22, 1991)

"Thus in destroying an imaginary Hitler in Saddam, the Americans and their allies are in fact fostering the state of Israel which has assumed the posture of a real Hitler. How ignorant and devoid of inner vision is the West? Does it not realize that it was Israel which in the first place called Saddam and the Palestinians as Hitler? By raising the Hitler-bogey, the West is patronizing a "Hitler" and if they do not realize, the future will reveal what Israel's motives are and how Israel will treat the United States and the West."
(February 22, 1991)

The United Nations
"I ask the Muslims, the Arabs and the world: What is the use of this United Nations? The United Nations only serves the interest of the rich and powerful nations. What is the use of such a U.N., the constitution of which permits the powerful nations to make others the victims of their cruelty and yet not allow them to raise their voice of protest. If they somehow manage to introduce such a resolution, it is vetoed and the big powers, through their tout, continue perpetrating cruelty. They virtually rule the world and govern the destinies of the nations. In the name of the United Nations, the rich and the strong punish the Arabs and Muslims with impunity and inflict cruelties and atrocities on them. But when the friends of these powerful nations transgress, no punishment is meted out and only weak and ineffectual protest resolutions are passed."
(February 22, 1991)

"In Vietnam, the greatest and strongest world power was humbled by a small and poor country which was a great psychological blow to this Super Power. The United States was determined at any cost to redeem its honour and to restore its self respect and pride and its image as the world's greatest military power. But the truth is that a broken back seldom gets fully restored and cured. To date, the U.S. has rained four times as many bombs upon Iraq as in Vietnam and the fight still goes on."
(February 22, 1991)

"What is happening today is a repetition of that mournful tale of sordid history. I don't know what the future will bring or when the tide of history will turn and the arrogant and the mighty humbled, but I do know that Allah will in due course, humiliate and humble the arrogant. I can assure the United States of America that it cannot restore its back that was broken in Vietnam by inflicting indignities and atrocities on Iraq. The back of United States of America broken in Vietnam will remain broken. The United States can gouge great and deep craters in the earth by exploding 2,500,000 tons of explosives. In those deep craters and ditches the reputation and good name of United States of America will remain buried in disgrace for ever. As time goes on, these barbaric deeds will become more and more manifest and the reputation of United States will be sullied and stained beyond redemption. It may well be that because of the overwhelming might of United States of America at the present, few critics may venture to proclaim their misdeeds and atrocities for fear of reprisals. However, these acts against humanity will not disappear or fade, but

with the passage of time these will become more obvious and pronounced, and future generations will read with horror and abomination that a so-called civilised nation could commit and condone such dark and wicked deeds. The United States must see itself as others see it and take great care to avoid becoming the moral outcast of the 20th century."
(February 22, 1991)

"One good aspect of the U.S. in Vietnam war was that this time it did not go around with a begging bowl for financial support to wage a war. In Vietnam, the U.S. spent $120 billion to fight that war for eight and a half years, and for this it relied entirely on its own resources. $120 billion is a vast sum. But the present war is being waged entirely on foreign money - money collected from other parties. When such an example has been set of waging a war that is entirely financed by others, there remains no guarantee of world peace. It is as if, the United States has leased out its armed forces. It smacks of a mercenary force. That could mean that the destiny of poor countries will be solely in the hands of the rich ones. The rich and the powerful nations can demand contributions and financial resources from the poor ones and hire mercenaries to wage war on them, killing, maiming and destroying them. This precedent is indeed dangerous. Besides, an element of greed is associated with this type of war. When its results are made known, the other European nations too, will be motivated to reap benefits by waging a similar war. Great havoc and damage has been inflicted on Iraq and Kuwait. The U.S. has been paid vast sums of money to bring about such destruction,

and it will be paid huge sums of money for repairing the damage done by its forces. The U.S. is paid to destroy and then paid to repair and re-construct. Thus the U.S. plays two roles, the demolisher as well as the restorer. Paid for destruction - and paid much more for restoration."
(February 22, 1991)

"So long as the Islamic world does not establish the system of Islamic Justice, it does not adopt the Quranic concept of Justice, it can neither present Justice to the world nor should *expect* Justice from the world!"
(March 01, 1991)

"The solution of all the problems of today is the revival of this spirit in politics. This will bring back to life a dying humanity. If this spirit survives, wars will be doomed. But if this spirit is allowed to die, fire of wars is sure to get rekindled, and then there will be no power on earth to extinguish them."
(March 01, 1991)

"Muslims claim one set of rules for themselves and a completely different set of rules for non-Muslims. Superior rights are reserved for the Muslims while the non-Muslims are deprived of every such right! If God forbid, this is the Quranic principle, the whole world would naturally loathe it and would consider the Muslims as a threat to world peace. Therefore, it is not fair to blame only the others for their excesses on Muslims. We should look inwards as well and see why these excesses are being committed and see how a shrewd

enemy is using the very weapons manufactured by Muslims themselves against them. It is a fact that factories of such lethal weapons are functioning in Muslim countries and are being run by the Mullahs. These weapons are being 'exported' in large quantities to other countries where in turn these are used against the Muslim countries."
(March 01, 1991)

"**Which ears will listen to this advice?** Which hearts will be moved and triggered into action? If the entire moral, economic and political foundation is unstable, if the very ideology is deteriorated, if the motives are rotten, no correct advice will produce healthy effects on anyone. I have given advice to affluent nations, that for the sake of God, they should safeguard their motives, which have demons and wolves lurking in their intentions. The decision on the fate of the world is decided by such motives. Their diplomatic craftiness cannot subjugate their motives, rather they stimulate them; so on the other hand I advise Muslim countries and those of the Third world that for the sake of God, search into your motives."
(March 01, 1991)

"History's view of Vietnam has always been and shall always be that in this modern age, the United States of America, donning the cloak of civilization, unjustly attacked an extremely weak and poor nation, and continued raining death and destruction upon it for eight and a half years. Such hideous bombardment was rained down upon them, that village after village and entire regions were made desolate. They cannot, therefore, ever

erase the memory of Vietnam because the world will not permit them to forget it. And now to this has been added the tyranny perpetrated upon Iraq."
(March 08, 1991)

"The advanced or developed nations, outwardly profess that dictatorship must be brought to an end. But in reality it is dictatorship alone which suits them in enslaving the Third world countries because wherever there is dictatorship, internal dangers start developing. To safeguard against such dangers external allies have to be found and these external allies are found just as I have already mentioned. Then, so long as things are done in accordance with their wishes, they provide the needed support. When something is done against their wishes, this 'support' crumbles by itself. This is the ignominy to which the Third world is prey. It is high time that we make use of our wits. Now that a new era of imperialism has started posing extreme dangers, it is essential for the preservation of our national independence, freedom, self respect and for leading a life of dignity amongst the comity of nations, that we reflect deeply on all such matters, and act with swiftness."
March 08, 1991)

"When nations become prey to such vices, then why lament that we are dying and that vultures are sitting next to us, awaiting our death. A disease develops from within you, for your death, and that disease invites bacteria. It is true that diseases develop from bacteria, but it is a fact that bacteria can do no harm to a healthy body. Therefore, a disease develops from within and not from

the outside. When a body no longer has any power left to resist a disease then these bacteria thrive and take control of the body and when their control becomes complete, death becomes inevitable, and the flocking of vultures to chew upon the carcass is a natural sequence of events which has to happen afterwards. The truth of the matter is, that this is a law of nature from which no power can safeguard you, if you do not decide to change yourself today. Thus, before you reach this stage, where your corpses are left in the open fields for others to draw lessons from, or are interred in graves, if you decide today that you will make the moral values and the teachings, as expounded by the Holy Master Hazrat Muhammad[sas], as your plan of action and you resolve to protect human values and strive to restore and re-establish those lost values, then this is the only way of salvation for you from a life of disgraceful enslavement by others. Besides this, there is no other way."
(March 08, 1991)

"No evil should ever be perpetrated in the name of Islam in the future. The concept of terrorism should be removed from the vocabulary of the Muslims. To do mischief and to cause pain to others just to keep some issues alive is a despicable act. These things have nothing to do with Islam. Become peaceful yourselves. Rectify your own relations first. Build up your relationships with the other nations and wait with patience. Then you will see how the plans of God will frustrate the evil designs of every other nation."
(March 08, 1991)

An Appeal

"I appeal not only to the Muslim countries but to the Eastern world, Africans and South Americans, that after you have experienced all this, I implore you to please become aware and take a decision to change your own fate. The period of humiliation and degradation has been long. Now come out of this nightmare. For your enemies and the Super Powers there could be a cheerful conception of a New World Order, but for the Third world nations no other nightmare could be more dreadful. If you want to be the builders of the New World Order, then start caring for, and fashioning your own dreams. Try to learn the noble ways of transforming your dreams into deeds and actions. No nation can be free until it is economically free. The first step towards economic advancement is to safeguard your ego and self-respect. This will not be possible until and unless a campaign for austere lifestyle is adopted in the Third world countries."

(March 01, 1991)

In the name of Allah, the Gracious, the Merciful

FIRST FRIDAY SERMON

AUGUST 03, 1990

THE QURANIC PROCEDURE OF SETTLEMENT OF CONFLICTS

After reciting the Opening Chapter of the Holy Quran, Al-Fatiha, Hazoor recited the following verses:

$$\text{وَإِنْ طَآئِفَتٰنِ مِنَ الْمُؤْمِنِيْنَ اقْتَتَلُوْا فَأَصْلِحُوْا بَيْنَهُمَا ۚ فَإِنْ بَغَتْ اِحْدٰىهُمَا عَلَى الْاُخْرٰى فَقَاتِلُوا الَّتِىْ تَبْغِىْ حَتّٰى تَفِیْءَ اِلٰٓى اَمْرِ اللّٰهِ ۚ فَاِنْ فَآءَتْ فَأَصْلِحُوْا بَيْنَهُمَا بِالْعَدْلِ وَاَقْسِطُوْا ۚ اِنَّ اللّٰهَ يُحِبُّ الْمُقْسِطِيْنَ ۝ اِنَّمَا الْمُؤْمِنُوْنَ اِخْوَةٌ فَأَصْلِحُوْا بَيْنَ اَخَوَيْكُمْ وَاتَّقُوا اللّٰهَ لَعَلَّكُمْ تُرْحَمُوْنَ ۝}$$

(Holy Quran, Chapter 49 Al-Hujurat Verses 10 & 11)

Hazoor then went on to say:

THE ISLAMIC WORLD CONSTANTLY IN THE GRIP OF PROBLEMS

It has been more than ten years since the Islamic world has been faced with many problems and afflictions. If these sufferings and miseries were being inflicted on Islam by the outsiders, it would no doubt have been painful, but far more painful is the fact, that the Islamic world is responsible for creating trouble for itself and as a result it has been split into two halves - each continuously creating problems and difficulties for the other.

The oil-wealth has been of a great boon for many Muslim countries but it has also caused some harm. The most serious harm of this oil-wealth has been that the Muslims gradually lost sight of the essence of righteousness (*Taqwa*). The oil-wealth diverted their inclination entirely towards materialism. This fact has also been documented by many historians, that as long as the Islamic nations were impoverished, they possessed the noble quality of righteousness (*Taqwa*), but the oil-wealth seems to have torched this noble trait. Thus, the Muslim governments that sprang up, were essentially materialistic. It was incumbent upon them to adhere to the trait of *Taqwa* (righteousness) and impress upon their citizens to follow the guidelines of *Taqwa*. Mutual relations between the Islamic countries should have been established on the basis of righteousness. Disputes should also have been decided by following the guidelines of righteousness. Unfortunately, this has not been done.

THE QURANIC SOLUTION OF ANY CONFLICT

The teaching of the Holy Quran is not only universally practical but the Quran has also touched upon every cause of conflict that can possibly arise, along with the suggestions for reaching an appropriate solution. For instance, the Holy Quran accepted this possibility that disputes between various Muslim countries might reach a point of one Muslim country attacking another Muslim country. Discussing this possibility, the Holy Quran states:

$$وَاِنْ طَآئِفَتٰنِ مِنَ الْمُؤْمِنِيْنَ اقْتَتَلُوْا فَاَصْلِحُوْا بَيْنَهُمَا$$

That it is possible that some Muslim powers may be drawn into such a confrontation with other Muslim powers which might culminate in an all-out war. In such a situation, it is the joint responsibility of the entire **Muslim nations** to establish peace among them.

$$فَاِنْ بَغَتْ اِحْدٰىهُمَا عَلَى الْاُخْرٰى$$

And if one Muslim nation insists on a defiant posture against the other and does not stop its aggression, then the solution is that the entire world of Islam should unite and subdue the aggressor. When the aggressor is inclined to submit itself to the Divine commands based on **justice**, then the operation must stop forthwith and efforts be made to establish peace between the warring factions. It should be borne in mind, that in the effort of reconciliation, *Taqwa* (righteousness) and justice must always be kept in view. The Holy Quran admonishes once again that you must follow the principle of fairness, because God loves those who are impartial.

It further says:

إِنَّمَا الْمُؤْمِنُونَ إِخْوَةٌ

That you must remember that **all believers are like brothers among themselves.**

فَأَصْلِحُوْا بَيْنَ اَخَوَيْكُمْ وَاتَّقُوا اللهَ لَعَلَّكُمْ تُرْحَمُوْنَ

So it is essential that you should establish peace between your brothers and adopt righteousness so that you are shown mercy.

CLEAR VIOLATION OF THE INSTRUCTIONS OF THE HOLY QURAN

In light of these verses, one thing becomes very clear, that the Islamic world has not followed the guidelines as enunciated in this verse of the Holy Quran regarding mutual disputes. If the Muslim states had tried to settle their mutual differences in light of this clear injunction of the Holy Quran, then the bloody and protracted war of attrition between Iraq and Iran could have been brought to a speedy end. The difficulty is, that decisions are taken on the basis of alliances, without giving consideration to the spirit of righteousness. As such, for eight long years these Muslim countries were antagonized and remained in a state of war with each other, while the Super Powers took sides.

The Muslims disregarded the Islamic principle that they should take a unified decision and get together and declare war against the aggressor. If this was done, then it would not have been the question of an Arab-Iran war. Rather all the Muslim countries, including Pakistan, Indonesia, Malaysia and the countries of North Africa, as a united body, should have intervened in this conflict and by using their combined strength should have stopped the aggression of the aggressor.

Now, another painful situation has arisen before us. It is no longer a war between Iran and the Arabs but the Arabs themselves have become fragmented, and one Muslim Arab state has attacked another Muslim Arab state. In this regard there is the 'Arab League' which has been established to consider such matters. When I heard the statement of one of its representatives in a T.V. programme, I was amazed that despite this long-drawn and painful experience, they have not used their intelligence and instead of following the Quranic principle, they are proposing other ways of reconciliation. The greatest outrage is that those countries that have no association with Islam, have become united and are ready to intervene in this conflict. There are some Muslim countries that are even appealing for their intervention.

I watched a television interview of a Western expert who declared that as a result of the current war between Iraq and Kuwait, two concentric circles have been established; one is a smaller circle, i.e. the circle of the Islamic world, and the other larger circle is the circle of the whole world. He said that they were waiting and hoping that the Islamic world would direct its attention to the core of this conflict and succeed in mediation, although he could not foresee this happening and noted that the larger circle of the whole world may well have to intervene in this conflict.

THE NECESSITY OF REVERTING TO THE TEACHINGS OF ISLAM

Through this brief sermon, I want to draw the attention of the Islamic world to the fact that if they turn to the teaching of Islam, it can solve all their problems. It is a most outrageous and damaging matter that the outside world should interfere in the internal affairs of the Muslim countries and then toy with them as though they were *pawns in a game of chess* - using one against the other, as has been their past practice. The fact of the matter is that at present some Muslim countries are using their wealth against their own brothers. This oil was granted by God as a blessing to the Islamic world. Oil has brought a means of unprecedented advance for the outsiders whose industry is benefitting from its discovery. All kinds of sources of energy found in the Muslim countries are creating a fortune that is benefiting the outsiders. Alas! the Muslim countries are using this very oil to incinerate each other's homes and reduce each other's countries to ashes. As a matter of fact this is the ultimate analysis of the predicament of Muslims.

There is still some time left! If the Islamic world were to follow the standards of righteousness and resolve to act upon the teachings of the Holy Quran, then there would be no chance for any non-Muslim power to interfere in the affairs of the Islamic world. It is essential that in the light of these two verses of the Holy Quran, this conflict which has erupted in an extremely shocking form should not be handled by the Arab-world alone.

When you omit the word 'Islam' from the context of this conflict and portray an 'Islamic problem' as a regional problem, then God withdraws His helping hand. In the Quranic injunction there is no mention of any particular nation or group. The guidance which the Holy Quran has given, mentions the Muslims as a whole, and declares all of them as brothers of one another. Therefore, it is certainly not just an Arab problem. It is a problem which concerns the Islamic world. In this, Indonesia should be involved in the same way as Pakistan. Malaysia should be involved in this, as should Algeria or other Muslim countries. And a committee should be formed comprising all these countries which should force the conflicting parties into mutual reconciliation. But if they are not ready to reconcile then the entire power of the Islamic world should be used against the rebellious party. They should send a strong message to all the non-Muslim powers that they should withdraw their hand and not meddle in the internal affairs of Muslims. According to the teaching of the Holy Quran, we are capable of solving our own problems and settling our own disputes. But unfortunately, we see no signs of them acting upon this teaching.

The episode of the war between Iraq and Kuwait or the attack of Iraq on Kuwait has, as its background, much dishonesty and breach of faith. There are disagreements not only between the Arabs, but there are other Muslim oil-producing countries that are also involved in this. For instance there is Indonesia, she has bitter complaints against her Arab Muslim brothers that they secretly violate the OPEC oil production quota and, as a result, whatever financial advantage could have been gained through a united effort, is transformed into a loss. Each country tries secretly to sell its oil, in its own way, to amass the greatest possible amount of wealth. As such, in this case too they lack the element of righteousness (*Taqwa*). It is not only a matter of the war between Iraq and Kuwait but it is also a matter of the lack of fair-play and piety in their mutual dealings.

Whatever international organization is established to resolve the problems resulting from the war between these two countries, it will be its duty to get to the crux of this conflict and examine all those causes as a result of which, time and again, such dangerous situations develop. In this, Iran should also be included on an equal basis and no Muslim country should be excluded. If they can do this then as the

Holy Quran has said, *"Allah loves those who are just"*, which means that God's favour will be granted to you and you will certainly succeed in your efforts. The Holy Quran, as a further reminder states:

اِنَّمَا الْمُؤْمِنُوْنَ اِخْوَةٌ فَاَصْلِحُوْا بَيْنَ اَخَوَيْكُمْ وَاتَّقُوا اللّٰهَ لَعَلَّكُمْ تُرْحَمُوْنَ

That you should establish peace between your brothers, who are brothers to one another and follow the path of righteousness, because it is those who follow the path of righteousness that are shown mercy. So any matter that concerns Islam or the Holy Quran, cannot be resolved without *Taqwa* (righteousness).

THE BASIC ANALYSIS OF THE PROBLEMS FACED BY MUSLIMS

The Promised Messiah[as], Hazrat Mirza Ghulam Ahmad, has given a brief analysis of the problems facing the Muslims. It is such an analysis which encompasses all situations. He says:

"The path of *Taqwa* (righteousness) has been lost. Mere name of Islam remains, but the path of righteousness is no longer there, it has been lost." When the path of righteousness is lost, then nothing remains, besides wandering aimlessly in the wilderness.

So as the leader of the Ahmadiyya Muslim Community, I give emphatic but humble advice to all our Muslim brothers; no matter whether they consider us brothers or not, that the *Ummah* (brethren in faith) of the Holy Prophet Muhammad[sas] should cling to the path of righteousness because they face very grave dangers. The powers opposed to the Islamic world are seeking lame excuses to interfere even in your minor internal affairs. A long period has elapsed but you continue playing in their hands like powerless and helpless **pawns** - grievously injuring one another. Therefore, you should hold fast to the principle of *Taqwa* (righteousness). Today, the blessed *Ummah* of the Holy Prophet Muhammad[sas] is looked down upon, and treated with disdain. All the great powers look at the Islamic world with great contempt. They feel the Muslim countries are in their clutches like a mouse is in the clutches of a cat. They feel they can play with Muslims whenever they want and in whatever manner they like. Their dealings are extremely humiliating - it is a shame that the image of the Islamic world is repeatedly tarnished and falls into disrepute. The very honour and prestige of Islam is at stake. Therefore, have fear of God and return to the teaching of Islam. Beside this there is no other shelter.

THE CAUSE OF THESE RECURRING PROBLEMS

I feel that this period of adversity and decline and these repeated miseries are the consequence of the Muslim denial of his Holiness -the Promised Messiah[as]. There is no doubt about it. Therefore my closing message to you is that you should submit yourselves to the 'Imam of the Age'. Accept that one, who was sent by God. He is the one who has the ability to lead you. Without him, separated from him, you are like a body which has no head. There may be apparent signs of life and the limbs may flutter. There is much painful fluttering, but the head which God has created for the guidance and leadership of the body is missing. So, turn back and establish your contact with the Divine Leadership. After denying the leadership established by God, no path of peace and prosperity is left open for you. The period of adversity has been long and painful. You should turn to God, repent, and seek His forgiveness. Let me assure you that to whatever extent the matters may have worsened, if you submit today before the leadership established by God, then not only will you rise as a great power in the world, but such a great movement of the new supremacy of Islam will be set in motion that no power in the world will be able to confront it and the progress which appears to spread over centuries will become a matter of years. Whether you join us or not, the Ahmadiyya Muslim Community is in any case, staking its body, soul and its resources as it has always done in this path. It is doing it today and will continue to make these sacrifices tomorrow and the honour of this final triumph will be written only in the destiny of the Ahmadiyya Muslim Jamaat. So, come and be included in this blessed and historical good fortune. May God enable you to do so and may God enable us to serve you. You have been given most excellent servants who, in the name of God, for the sake of God, and in the love of the Holy Prophet Muhammad[sas] are ready and eager to give sacrifices for you in difficult times but you have taken no advantage of them and have thus been deprived of their service. It is the greatest misfortune of the Islamic world at the present time. May God grant them wisdom and intelligence.

As far as Ahmadiyya Muslim Jamaat is concerned, it is my advice that whether they take advantage of your service or not, whether they count you as their brothers or not; through prayers you should continue to help the *Ummah* of the Holy Prophet Muhammad[sas] and you should never forget this teaching of his Holiness the Promised Messiah[as] when he said in one of his persian poems:

اے دل تو نیز خاطر ایناں نگاہ دار

کافر کنند دعویٰ حب پیمبرم

"O my heart, you must always keep this in view and must always consider that your opponents, i.e., those among the Muslims who are opposing you, they at least claim to belong to your beloved Messenger, The Holy Prophet Muhammad[sas]".

So, for the sake of the love of this beloved Messenger[sas], you should always continue to treat them with kindness." May God enable us to do so.

Amen.

In the name of Allah, the Gracious, the Merciful

SECOND FRIDAY SERMON

AUGUST 17, 1990

THE FATAL CONSEQUENCES OF THE GULF CRISIS

After reciting the Opening Chapter Al-Fatiha, of the Holy Quran, Hazoor said:

THE PAINFUL SITUATION IN THE MIDDLE EAST

The situation in the Middle East is worsening day by day. Since there is a preponderance of Muslims in this region, therefore, it is but natural for the Muslims in the world at large to have grave concerns about it. Moreover, those sacred places which are dearer to the Muslims than anything else in the world i.e., Mecca and Medina, the soil which the Holy Prophet of Islam once walked upon and the very atmosphere which was once permeated with the aroma of his blessed breath, that holy land is surrounded by dangers and intrigues. Although at present the entire Muslim world feels deep pain and there is an extreme restless feeling among the ordinary Muslims but as an organised Community, Ahmadiyya Muslim Jamaat holds a unique position. It is free of all kinds of politics and is exclusively dedicated to serve Islam. For this reason, among those who feel sympathy for Islam, it is indeed the Ahmadiyya Muslim Jamaat that is experiencing the greatest agony. This Community alone is the true and sincere representative of Islam in the world today. When I say this, perhaps the uninformed would construe it as an empty boast: an unsubstantiated claim that will invite the disdain of the other Islamic sects who would regard it as a blurb on our part to be claiming as the sole standard-bearers and "monopolists" of Islam who do not have genuine sympathy with Islam. But as I analyze the situation, it would become evident that if there is any entity in the contemporary world that genuinely feels concern for Islam, it is none other than the Ahmadiyya Muslim Jamaat.

Second Friday Sermon Aug 17, 1990

POLITICS DEVOID OF JUSTICE AND PIETY

Contemporary politics has become vitiated. It is devoid of justice and the spirit of righteousness. Those among the Muslim states who claim moral superiority, in the name of Islam, are themselves not loyally attached to the Islamic moral principles. Their loyalty is not with the lofty Islamic principles of justice but, instead, with their petty self-interests. It is for this reason that we observe inconsistent and self-contradictory behaviour on the part of the Muslim world.

With the single exception of the Ahmadiyya Muslim Jamaat, the rest of the Muslim sects have parochially aligned themselves with one Islamic country or another, for their show of support; although the spirit of righteousness would dictate that they should have been loyal to none other than the **Islamic values**. If one has the true love of Islam, then one must show loyalty to the demands placed by Islam and the Holy Quran, as well as the requirements laid down by the moral precept of the Holy Prophet of Islam. In the light of these prerequisites, when we scrutinize the contemporary politics, of Muslims as well as of non-Muslims, we find that in either case, it is not predicated upon the moral precept of the Holy Prophet of Islam.

The non-Muslim nations are busy making tall claims in the name of justice, as if they have been appointed the sole custodians of justice in the world, and that justice would become extinct but for the might of these nations. On the other hand, Muslim countries are making tall claims in the name of Islam; but when you hold these claims - being made on either side - up for scrutiny, you discover that these are equally devoid of the elements of justice that are laid down by the Holy Quran.

IRAQI OCCUPATION OF KUWAIT: REACTION AND DREADFUL DANGERS

I would now like to speak, with reference to the current situation in the Gulf. Iraq, due to some grievance it had nursed, attacked a small neighbouring state and, before the world could take note of it, secured its total occupation. This caused a sudden commotion in the whole world, and those who would normally remain unmoved in the face of similar events, nor would they become perturbed and rush to offer any extraordinary help, their sympathies for Kuwait have acquired such dimensions and the intensity of their consternation is so intense that the like of it may not be found in recent history. I do not wish to elaborate upon the events that have taken place so far - those who follow the news are aware of what is happening - but I would like to put before you the issues involved from the standpoint of how far the Islamic principles of justice are being followed, and to what extent the practice of modern politics is devoid of them.

When the U.S. and its allies initiated various measures to render the government of Baghdad completely ineffective, and eventually to bring it down to its knees, it became increasingly obvious that this great Muslim country is heading towards such a perilous situation that it would be beyond its capacity to cope with this challenge. For this reason, I certainly grew more and more concerned and started keenly to observe the direction taken by the continuing parleys and the various solutions that are being put forth.

Recently, when King Hussein of Jordan visited the U.S. it was initially conjectured that he is bearing a letter for the U.S. administration, but it was subsequently held that there is no letter as such but he has some messages and some proposals to discuss. In this context the language used in the communication between the Presidents of the U.S. and Iraq that has surfaced in the context of mutual accusations and is carried by the television, radio and newspapers, is indicative of how inflamed the situation really is, and how the Heads of great nations in the world are capable of stooping down, from their normally dignified posture, to the infradig prattle. These statements amaze one as to the indecency of the language in which they are labelling each other as liars, wretched and deceitful etc.; all such display of indecency is occasioned by the simple fact that a bigger Muslim state has occupied a smaller Muslim state. There are numerous events of much greater severity and of far greater horror that have taken place in the world - and still continue today - that the significance of this event would pale before them, by comparison.

But there are, necessarily, many ulterior motives at work in this case, which caused such extraordinary publicity to be given to this event. At any rate the occupation of Kuwait is a *fait accompli*; what lies ahead is the question of giving permanence to this assimilation. In view of the strong reaction shown by the world, the Iraqi President Saddam Hussein sent a message to the U.S. that if you are really interested in justice to prevail then let it prevail in the entire Middle

Second Friday Sermon Aug 17, 1990

Eastern region; we are ready and willing to restore the government of our little brotherly state to the same dynasty that had been ruling it.

Their restoration would cover everything as it existed prior to the outbreak of hostilities. But this region is characterized by similar other precedents - there are similar other unlawful occupations here, which were either condoned by you or were achieved as a result of your support or patronage - you should arrange for them to be set free from their present illegitimate subjugation. For instance, the Jewish occupation of Jordan's West Bank which they have been strengthening progressively, and where they are busy settling the Russian expatriates. He said: even in this region there is occupation by aliens; such aliens who do not even share their religion. This land is under the occupation of those who have been antagonists with the Arabs for long; yet they have been given a free reign to give permanence to their usurpation. Why did the Western sense of justice remain a silent spectator? The Western morality exhibited no reaction to these happenings. Let this case be also included in the dispensation of justice.

Then, there is the example of Syria - an Islamic country - which invaded Lebanon and subjugated it. It has since made a practice of frequent military interventions in that country, and of acting out its wanton will; Syria must also be prevented from doing so and pressurized to withdraw its forces from Lebanon. Similar other events that are endemic to this region, must be approached uniformly and in this perspective.

This particular stand taken by Saddam Hussein is quite rational; if the purpose of justice is to be served then we must necessarily view the events taking place in this region, in total perspective.

<u>DOUBLE STANDARD OF JUSTICE AND MISCHIEVOUS PROPAGANDA</u>

Something else should also be pointed out in this context. If we view Saddam Hussein's invasion of Kuwait, in the light of justice and *Taqwa*, then we find no legitimate justification for it. But, as we have pointed out earlier, the Jews have even lesser justification for perpetuating their occupation of Jordan's West Bank and retaining this part forever.

The Western press has attributed some other atrocities to Saddam Hussein, e.g., they gave much publicity to the news that an

Englishman who was attempting to flee Iraq, was shot and killed at the border. This is one incident, but how about the persistent reign of terror let loose on the people of Lebanon and adjacent territories? And how about Israel's unilateral air-attack on Iraq's nuclear power-plants in broad daylight, that resulted in the total destruction of these installations? The Western world has turned a blind eye to all these events and not once pointed an accusatory finger in this regard. Imagine the whole Western media raising a clamour over a single casualty - described as the ultimate act of cruelty - and then look at the thousands of people of all ages, elderly, young and infants, who are helplessly languishing in camps. They are killed mercilessly; the skulls of infants are cracked open with rocks; children are brutally murdered in front of their wailing mothers, and the mothers themselves soon follow their children on the death trail. These horrors of a Lebanese camp are real, but no one raised a voice against it! So the question is whether all this was justice, or was it something else? If your motives are based on justice then you must know that justice calls for equal treatment of everyone. The yardstick of justice remains invariant.

The alleged rape and brutal treatment of some white air-hostesses by Iraqi soldiers was also propagandized against Iraq. This caused a great uproar. Yet, in Kashmir, for the past several months, impoverished Muslim men, women and children are being brutalized. Reported instances of rape are so numerous, and the reports of torture so disquieting, that they make my hair stand on end in horror, and it makes my heart tremble that human beings are capable of such beastliness and tyranny. Tell me, which Western news and information media has exposed these crimes to the rest of the world, and which Western countries have condemned India for this? Dozens of such atrocities are being committed daily in the world, but the West has closed its eyes to them; yet an alleged act of brutality in Iraq - which, by the way, was later proven to be no more than a rumour - caused such uproar!

But Iraq, too, is not fulfilling the obligations placed by the Islamic principles of justice. Islam does not allow, under any circumstances, to take hostages from among those foreign nationals who are living in your country, with whom you may even be at war. Nor does Islam

Second Friday Sermon Aug 17, 1990

allow you to use them as bargaining chips in any way; any act of wrongdoing against them is prohibited by Islam.

HAVOC WROUGHT BY POLITICS, DEPRIVED OF MORALITY

The entire lifetime of the Holy Prophet of Islam, and all the battles in which he himself took part, bear testimony to the fact that not a single incident of any excess committed against non-Muslim residents occurred, with whose nation the Muslims were at war. They were totally free, and had the liberty to lead their life the way they wanted. Not even a single individual ever acted cruelly towards them. As a matter of fact, Islam directs us to grant sanctuary, if requested, even to your enemy. But Iraq, in complete disregard of this principle of Islamic morality, announced that all British and U.S. nationals who were living in Iraq and Kuwait in any capacity are not allowed to either leave the country or even stay in their current residences, instead, they should gather together in a designated hotel. Similarly, foreign nationals from other Islamic countries were restricted in like manner. It is obvious that the way things are moving now, these people will be used as **hostages**. This conduct is abhorrent even to the commonly accepted norms of morality in the world, not to speak of the injunctions of Islamic morality. So, where is morality? In politics today, is there any country in the world - Islamic or otherwise - about which one can say that it passes the strict test of righteousness, or meets even the minimum criteria of Islamic morality? There is laxity everywhere.

Recently, under cover of the U.N. resolutions, an all-out **blockade of Iraq** was put into effect i.e., a total ban on Iraqi imports and exports of any kind was militarily enforced. It involves two kinds of moral violations and excesses that are very serious.

Firstly, the U.N. in its resolutions had not included food-supply and the flow of other necessities of life in the proposed boycott. Secondly, it had not originally intended to forcibly secure the participation of any country in this boycott of Iraq.

In both these matters, U.S. as well as U.K. are indulging in wanton excesses. On the one hand they accuse Iraq of having an immoral position - and we agree that it is a violation of the Islamic principles of morality - but then, in the same breath, they themselves are being guilty of a glaring act of immorality that is only thinly disguised by diplomatic euphemisms. But, in reality, the cruelty that Iraq is being subjected to by the joint efforts of Britain and U.S., constitutes a crime whose horror exceeds the hypothetically feared potential execution of a few thousand Britons and Americans held in Iraq. For instance, the scope of this jointly sponsored crime has now been extended to include even Jordan as a target.

East Jordan is a country that has perpetually been loyal to the West, unabashedly so - and, for the West, it has been the most loyal state in the region. Then consider the Kingdom of Saudi Arabia, even more than Jordan, which perhaps has the dubious distinction of having the greatest loyalty to the West. But in its case, it is no longer a case of loyalty alone: all the interests of the Kingdom of Saudi Arabia have become synonymous with the interests of the U.S. So it is not a case of mere loyalty with the U.S.

However, East Jordan, which is a small state, is widely known to be loyal to the Western world. It has deep friendly, even fraternal, relations with Britain and the U.S., and has always ranked with them at the top of their list of friends. The problem with Jordan is that its participation in the economic boycott against Iraq would ruin Jordan's own economy, its own survival is put on the line; and the possibility of reprisals from Iraq - to annex it by force - threatens it militarily. Jordan is not strong enough to withstand such an onslaught even for a few hours. So, Jordan is in a tight spot; but, disregarding its precarious balance, the West has decided to extend the arena of its criminal activity to include Jordan.

Jordan is being threatened that if it did not join the West in the boycott of Iraq then Jordan too would have to face a similar blockade which includes a ban on the transmission of food-supply, and that amounts to a sinister plan to starve multitudes of people. This is calculated to humiliate Jordan to the point where it decided to retreat from its present resolve. And that is not all; there are many other sinister plans which one cannot visualise without shuddering.

FATAL IMPLICATIONS OF THE PRESENT SITUATION

So, the question is: where is justice? The Western world has adopted their own style of diplomacy - which in Islamic terminology would be called "duplicity" - reaching the utmost limits. They have promoted duplicity under the guise of diplomacy and politics to a

Second Friday Sermon Aug 17, 1990

degree that is unparalleled in human history. So their crimes are always in disguise, their language has lucidity, and their presentation - aided by propaganda - carries a semblance of rationality.

Anyhow, this crisis is deepening day by day. Many dangers have become quite obvious and there are many more that are still hidden from a cursory glance, but a profound look would reveal them. It reminds me of a *fish-pond* we had. The first glance would show nothing more than water-surface; then slowly the fish that floated up to the water-surface would become visible, and finally a careful and penetrating look would reveal lower strata of fish that were not visible in the first or second glance. The political affairs of the world are quite similar. People usually have a cursory perception of events; with a little more effort they may see the fish near the surface. **But to the inspired vision of a true believer, the view is crystal-clear all the way to the bottom.** There are many dangers that have not yet become apparent to you; time will bring them out. I pray, and I would like to include you in this prayer, that God may lift these dangers from the Muslim world. Now as far as the Muslim groups are concerned and their reaction is concerned it is a most painful and regretful reaction.

I had fully elaborated this point in an earlier sermon and issued press-releases. Whether they were published or not, but I did arrange for the gist of that advice to be sent to the Muslim Heads of State. In gist, I invited them to make a recourse to the teachings of the Holy Quran in this regard. The Holy Quran says:

فَاِنْ تَنَازَعْتُمْ فِیْ شَیْءٍ فَرُدُّوْهُ اِلَی اللّٰهِ وَالرَّسُوْلِ

"If you differ in anything, refer it to Allah and His Messenger"
(Holy Quran 4:60)

It means that you should take the lead of the Holy Quran and Sunnah; this alone would guarantee your peace and survival. So, instead of trying to solve your problems through intrigue with other politicians, you should revert to the teachings of the Holy Quran and draw the guiding-light from it.

Simply put, the teaching is this: whenever two Muslim countries are at war with each other, it is incumbent upon **all** Muslim countries to collectively put pressure on the party that they unanimously believe to be the transgressor. Then judiciously listen to either side and try to bring about reconciliation between them. If the reconciliatory efforts fail to produce the desired result, and one country continues its belligerence, then it is incumbent upon the Muslim countries to collectively counter the violator of peace-effort. **Notice, that there is no mention of seeking assistance from non-Muslim countries!** If this teaching was adhered to, this ever-deepening and dangerous crisis would not have taken this turn.

In view of this teaching of the Holy Quran, I am convinced that no matter how big a Muslim country may be, if all Muslim countries collectively oppose it, they would always be strong enough in the aggregate to forcibly nip the stubbornness of this country and to force it to swallow its pride. If it were not possible then the Holy Quran would not have taught us so.

This is such a clear-cut and definitive teaching: if a Muslim country, no matter how strong - shows recalcitrance and if you, i.e., other Muslim states, try to resolve the matter in accordance with the teachings of the Holy Quran - and that particular country remains adamant and rebels against you - then your collective force will bring it down to its knees. In fact this is a glad-tiding given to us by the Holy Quran, and it is applicable today if someone wants to benefit from it. But, unfortunately, the Kingdom of Saudi Arabia asked its patrons i.e. Britain and the U.S., for immediate intervention. And they not only sent their own forces but also persuaded all other powerful governments to contribute some measure of their forces - even Far Eastern naval units, air-force units and troops arrived on the scene - so as to achieve the complete isolation of Iraq, and its partner Jordan, from the rest of the world.

The propaganda so far is that all these measures are defensive in nature, and are designed to contain the threat of war from spreading far and wide. Another unfortunate aspect of the situation is that most of the Muslim countries, either because of their own selfish interests or because they are unable to withstand the pressure of the big powers, have willingly come forward to send their troops to the theatre of war. Pakistan has touched the limits of folly by agreeing to send its forces to Saudi Arabia to fight Iraq, shoulder to shoulder with the U.S. and British forces.

Second Friday Sermon Aug 17, 1990

A DEEP CONSPIRACY AGAINST THE WORLD OF ISLAM

This situation is becoming increasingly grim, and it is the height of foolishness to think that such massive efforts are under way only for ensuring Saudi security. It is really naive if someone thinks that all these upheavals that are taking place in the world, these naval blockades from all directions, and the most lethal fighter-planes - which have so far never been used in any part of the world - being sent to the already amassed most modern arsenal, all this is a mere attempt to fortify Saudi Arabia against Iraq!

My apprehension is that Iraq will be subjected to horrific revenge and it may be blown to bits. The fire of their revenge will not quench until they annihilate this up-and-coming Muslim country which is an exceptional force in this region.

These ill-intentions were first conceived in Israel. I am convinced as a result of various Israeli statements that they were the harbinger of the current state of affairs. **God alone knows how Iraq was lured into occupying Kuwait and then the whole sinister development ensued.** But such incidents are seldom accidental. There are some underlying motives and some subterranean intrigues at work. There are the CIA agents and then there are indigenous traitors who meticulously perform the cryptic and surreptitious assignments designed to fulfil the wishes of Super Powers. Such activities are mentioned in the *Chapter Al-Naas* of the Holy Quran where these forces are referred to as *Khannaas* i.e., those forces which sow the seed of mischief and then secretively withdraw from the scene, leaving others to ponder as to how and why it all started. If a blunder was committed then where does the responsibility lie? In reality there are great forces behind these happenings. So, from this angle, the current state of affairs has taken a very ominous turn.

A SURVEY OF THE WORLD OF ISLAM IN ITS HISTORICAL PERSPECTIVE

If you put the Muslim world in its historical perspective, you would realize that no Islamic power could ever be damaged without securing the participation of some Muslim countries. The entire Islamic history bears witness to the fact that whenever the Western powers have succeeded in suppressing an emerging Muslim power, or otherwise crushed it with the help of some overt or covert military action, the conspiratorial support of some Muslim countries was invariably involved.

I would like to give you a few pointers from this history, summarily. *Hazrat Musleh Maood* who was among the pioneers in the exegesis of the expression **"Alif-Laam-Meem-Raa"** of the Holy Quran, states in his *Tafseer-e-Kabeer* (Commentary of the Holy Quran) that according to the Holy Prophet of Islam, the numerical value of this expression in the verses i.e. 271, bears some connotation for Islamic history. Two hundred and seventy-one years cover three generations i.e. the generation of the Holy Prophet himself, and two following generations, about whom the Holy Prophet had foretold that they would remain in peace. The completion of 271 years marked that dangerous year when the foundation of the Muslim world's downfall was laid; and whatever the Muslim world witnessed by way of mutual rifts and enervation later on, its inception can be traced to this particular year. Two main events were selected by *Hazrat Musleh Maood*, for illustration.

First, in the year 271 A.H., the Muslim government of Spain entered into an agreement with the Pope that he will have the co-operation of the Muslim government of Spain in his attempt to demolish the government of Baghdad. The Pope exercised unusual political influence in the Western world at that time, and in some respects he was the *de facto* sovereign; so this treaty was potentially devastating in its implications. It was as if, today, the Saudi government were to conspire with all the Western powers to destroy a Muslim country which, yet again, has **Baghdad** as its capital.

Secondly, Baghdad entered into a treaty with the *Caesar* of Rome, in the year 272 or 273 A.H., that called for the joint effort of the two governments to overthrow the Muslim government of Spain. So, this was the year which let loose the disruptive forces that subverted the peace of Muslim states for all times to come. Following this, whenever Muslim states had to undergo major upheavals, it was always the consequence of some Muslim countries giving conspiratorial support to the non-Muslim powers.

In the year 1258 A.D. destruction was wreaked on Baghdad through the fateful instrumentality of *Halaku Khan*. The last Abbasid Caliph, *Al-Mostasim*, who was a weakling, was ruling at that time. He had taken some anti-Shiite initiatives which, being the coercive

Second Friday Sermon Aug 17, 1990

measures as they were and quite unjustifiably introduced by *Al-Mostasim*, invited the ire of his prime-minister who was of Shiite persuasion. The prime-minister avenged himself by inviting Halaku Khan in, who was on a whirlwind victory foray but was afraid to take on Baghdad - thinking it to be an unwise move which might bring about undesirable consequences.

The prime-minister of Baghdad sent him a message saying that the state had only outward trappings of power but, in reality, its power-base had eroded. The prime-minister saw to it that the forces are far too thinly deployed to be effective; he further caused the deployment of forces along the least-threatening borders, and even caused the retrenchment of a portion of the army under the pretext that it was a burden on the national exchequer. At any rate, Halaku Khan was invited in, and the catastrophic destruction of Baghdad and the Muslim government ensued. This is not the occasion to go into the details of this destruction; many people have heard some description of this well-known historical event which has been the subject of some very moving works of fiction as well.

This event took place in 637 A.H. Later, in 1386 A.D., once again the mutual rifts and destructive squabbles presented an opportunity to *Tamerlane* to smash Baghdad into pieces and destroy this state completely.

The third time around, the Muslim government of Turkey was used to destroy the Muslim government of Baghdad. In 1638 A.D. the Turkish government, however, was itself not spared: the British conspired with the clan that currently rules Saudi Arabia, and enlisted the support of the religious faction of this clan i.e., the *'Wahabiyya sect'*, which were aided by the tribes living in, what now is known as, Kuwait. If the alliance of the current ruling dynasty of Saudi Arabia, the *'Wahabiyya sect'* and the tribes of Kuwait had not helped the British, the Turkish Empire would not have been wiped out.

The idea of 'Arabism' was given publicity, and many other sinister steps were taken; it is a very long story. But anyhow, even at that time, a foreign power used Muslim governments as stooges to destroy a great Muslim power i.e., first Turkey was used to cause the destruction of the government of Baghdad, then the Muslim tribes that inhabited the area that is currently known as Kuwait and Saudi Arabia, were used as the instruments of destruction against the government of Turkey.

Now, once again the same kind of circumstances have come to prevail. Once again a great Muslim state is facing a very great threat which has materialized with the help of Saudi Arabia and adjoining Muslim states. As far as I can see, these Western nations have decided to administer such a horrible punishment to Iraq this time that it may be impossible for any Muslim country, for decades, to dream even of standing up against them or to shake off their yoke. The state of Israel is the prime-mover of this plan; because Israel, for some time now has been clamouring that it faces the threat of a chemical attack from Iraq, which would obliterate the tiny state of Israel.

ATTACK ON ISLAM

Without getting into the detail as to whether the threat was real or fictitious, it is in fact an attack on Islam. Who was responsible for it? At least this much is clear that Israel and its interests provide the greatest motivation behind the present array of events.

At present the entire Muslim world has arrayed itself as if it stands ready to defend the interests of Israel, and has decided to aid in the destruction of a Muslim country which, though it did indulge in some ventures that are un-Islamic, does not deserve to be obliterated for that.

Injustice is prevalent in many places around the world; it is present to a far greater extent in many other places in the world. No Super Power does as much as move its little-finger in protest of that. So, whatever they are doing now, it can be for the sake of anything, but justice. There are many deep-seated enmities behind it; some plans of revenge are pending. This tightening of the noose around a Muslim country, which has itself not exhibited any Islamic morality, is not just an attack on this individual Muslim country - it is in fact an attack on Islam! These animosities are very profound and historical in origin; and these recent decisions have been taken at the highest level to contain the rising force of Iraq in the region which, they thought, might consolidate its influence over the neighbouring Middle Eastern states, to present a unified Islamic-front in the region, with a sizeable portion of world's oil-resources providing an economic backbone to

Second Friday Sermon Aug 17, 1990

enable it, in time, to become self-sufficient in other respects and emerge as a remarkable military force. This is the stuff that their apprehensions are made of. Whatever their apprehensions, the real danger that should be visible to the Muslim world is that it has been decided that a Muslim state would be eliminated from the face of this earth, and that too with the help and full co-operation of Muslim countries. No doubt, the leadership of that country itself has called it upon themselves. What can be done in a situation like this? I still think that the time elapsed so far is not so much as to put the situation beyond any hope of being normalized. But there is little hope for the deliverance of Muslims except if they return to God and the Holy Prophet of Islam.

RESPECTFUL APPEAL AND HUMBLE ADVICE
As for Iraq, the foremost among its responsibilities is to not hurt Islamic morality any further and not to make Islam the laughing-stock of the world any further. Those foreign nationals who are under Iraqi control now, whether they be of British, American or of Pakistani origin, let them have the freedom of choice as to where they want to go, without any hinderance. Let them know that if Iraq is at war with their country, this would be dealt as a separate matter, but they are innocent and are an inviolable trust. **As a matter of fact, every foreign national visiting a Muslim country is a trust, even if a war breaks out subsequently between his country and the Muslim country. The embezzlement of this trust will bear very ugly fruit: their fire of revenge which is already leaping up will then flare up out of control and consume millions of Muslims who are completely innocent.**

Members of the government are but a handful of individuals to lose their lives, if at all; but it is the innocent Muslim civilians who will get killed, and those who survive will face the reprisals in the post-war era. Therefore the only way to peace, open to the government of Iraq, is to return to the teachings of Islam, in a spirit of *Taqwa*. It should take this step and then inform the Muslim world as to its readiness to bow before whatever collective decision is reached, and guarantee the withdrawal of its forces from Kuwait. Peace would then return. **But the condition is that the decision-making must be done by the Muslim world alone, without allowing the non-Muslim**

world to participate in it. This campaign must be pushed forward vigorously.

If Iraq can patch up things with Iran after a protracted and bloody war, in which millions were killed or seriously injured, and can agree to return the captured Iranian territory, then why cannot Iraq show this spirit before the outbreak of hostilities now? So, Iraq should withdraw from Kuwait and assure the Muslim world saying that 'just as I had made peace with Iran, I now want to make peace with all of you in order to cope with the impending repression of the anti-Islamic forces, because this repression will not be limited to Iraq in its scope, rather it will engulf all of you in turn.' Otherwise the strength of Muslim countries would be set on a backward course for decades and they will be abjectly dependent on the aid of other countries.

The thunderclaps resounding at the moment are so deafening and the lightening is flashing so fiercely that if these are not visible to the Muslims, then it is beyond comprehension. They are oblivious of the dangers lurking on the horizon, and they have fallen into two camps and are arraying themselves against each other like fools.

It is therefore necessary for Iraq to broadcast such a message extensively to the Muslim world, and declare that Iraq wants to withdraw and accept the unanimous verdict of the Muslim world, provided non-Muslim powers are not allowed to be a part of this process. This appeal would cause the universal Muslim public opinion to rise up in favour of Iraq, and those powers who, for the sake of keeping up appearances, even with latent ill-intentions, are bound to keep good relations with Muslim countries, would inevitably have to respond positively to such an appeal; if they did not, then since such an initiative by Iraq to follow the Islamic teachings would be for the sake of God and His Word, God would afford His Protection to Iraq from those dangers that are currently hovering over its soil.

> Our unassuming appeal in this respect is a humble word of advice. If someone wants to listen to it in earnestness, understands it and then acts upon it, then he will benefit from it, because what I am presenting is the Quranic teaching. But if this word of advice from us is rejected with scorn and arrogance then I warn you today that the Muslim world will sink into such grave dangers that the entire world of Islam will

lament for a very long time to come. It may go on lamenting but it will amount to nothing more than bashing its head against the wall. It will gain nothing, and will not be able to regain its lost strength and dignity, as it is now or as it could attain in future.

To all intents and purposes, Muslim countries have now reached a stage that if they continue their thrust forward - unobtrusively, cautiously and without getting involved in any way to attract attention - they can become a sizeable force in a decade or so, such that their enemies will not be able to cast an evil glance at them, no matter how much they wish to. But if the Muslim countries erred today, they would stumble over a precipice of disaster that may spell a point of no return for them.

AHMADIS SHOULD OFFER EARNEST SUPPLICATIONS BEFORE ALLAH

At the same time I advise the Jamaat to earnestly pray and supplicate before God. Whatever excesses were committed against our Community by the Muslim countries in the past - and whatever they would do in the future - it is a matter between them and God, for which they are answerable to Him. But, as I have always pointed out, we are certainly loyal to Islam and Islamic values.

We are not afraid to point out the errors of a Muslim country, from the Islamic viewpoint, and put a request in our humble way for it to reform itself. Even if that country turns against us, or may think of victimizing us later on, we are not worried about it at all; because we are acting this way purely for the sake of God.

We know that the spirit of Islam is enshrined in the Holy Quran and the Sunnah of the Holy Prophet of Islam; if we love these then we must guard the spirit of Islam. And Ahmadi Muslims, everywhere in the world, are ready to offer all kinds of sacrifices for the sake of the spirit of Islam. They would not flinch from telling the truth - and no power on earth can constrain them from telling the truth. **If a message of truth provokes anybody's anger against us then let it be known that our sanctuary is in our God. We entrust Him with our affairs, and we are not fearful of any worldly political fallout.**

Let me give you a glad-tiding as well, regarding this word of advice to the Muslim world. I was destined to administer this advice;

it was pre-planned by God that it should so transpire. The Promised Messiah[as] wrote:

ان ربى قد بشرنى فى العرب والهمنى ان امونهم و اربهم طريقتهم و اصلح لهم شئونهم و ستجدونى فى هذا الامر ان شاءالله من الفائزين ۔

> "My God has given me a glad-tiding in respect of the Arabs, and has instructed me through His Revelation to look after them, guide them on the right path, and set their affairs straight. And God willing, you will find me successful and victorious in this task."
> (*Hamamatul Bushra* Page 7, *Roohani Khazain* Volume 7 Page 182)

So, the mission with which the Promised Messiah[as] was divinely entrusted, is now being addressed by me as his representative and humble servant.

Therefore, in view of this revelation, I give this glad-tiding to the Muslim world that if they act upon my humble and simple word of advice, they will be victorious and they will prosper in this world as well as in the Hereafter. But if, unfortunately, they remained slaves to their selfish interests and threw away the interests of Islam to the winds - and disregarded the teachings of Islam - then no worldly power would be able to shield them from the wrath of God.

May God give us good news from the Muslim world, bring peace to the restless and grieving hearts of Ahmadi Muslims all over the world.

Amen.

In the name of Allah, the Gracious, the Merciful

THIRD FRIDAY SERMON

AUGUST 24, 1990

THE REAL CAUSE OF PROTRACTED PERIOD OF RESTLESSNESS IN THE MIDDLE EAST

After reciting the Opening Chapter of the Holy Quran, Al-Fatiha, Hazoor said:

For the past several centuries, the region of the Middle East has been constantly in a state of deterioration. It has been plagued by wars, discontent and many kinds of hardships and suffering. But especially, for the past 40 years, not only have these afflictions and sufferings persisted but have been on the increase. It is not difficult to find its cause, but despite the knowledge of the root causes, neither the East nor the West is paying any attention to it. The fact is that in the last 40 years, the peace of the region was shattered a number of times resulting in a threat to world peace. On every such occasion, the reaction of the West was such that it could only cause greater dangers for the future, instead of diminishing such possibilities.

Unfortunately, after repeatedly passing through such bitter experiences, the Muslims living in the Middle East showed the same erroneous reaction as a result of which they had repeatedly suffered losses and thus continued in their agony.

It does not behove an intelligent people to go through the same experience over and over again and relive the same disastrous consequences. But apparently there are intelligent people on both sides. Therefore, there must be some other reason for this situation to be getting worse instead of getting any better. A summary diagnosis of the problem is that the root cause of all restlessness is the State of Israel.

The West presented an analysis of each conflict in its aftermath, placing the entire responsibility of the war and its ensuing losses upon the people in the Middle East and their leaders while ignoring the root cause of this problem and never paying any attention to rectifying their own policies.

GEMAL ABDUL NASSER OF EGYPT

For instance, there was a time when the West used to label General Gemal Abdul Nasser as a "mad man" who had lost his mental balance. He was depicted as a person who did not comprehend the overwhelming powers arrayed against him as compared to his own, or even the combined strength of all the Arab powers. He was portrayed as a man who, whenever he went to war, would always suffer ignominious defeat and would revert to an even worse condition than before. Therefore according to the analysis of the Western world, a "mad leader" rose to fame, whose rhetoric swayed the whole Arab nation to his side. Yet he was devoid of intelligence and thus failed to instil wisdom in his nation. Consequently, every action which he took against his enemy eventually recoiled on him and on his friends and each time he went to war he not only failed to achieve his objective but continued to suffer substantial losses. The same was their view about the other leaders who followed him. So the analysis of the West for the earlier period was that Nasser was just a zealot and mad leader who inspired the Arabs.

SADDAM HUSSEIN

They are now presenting the same analysis about Saddam Hussein. They are calling the whole world to attention: "look, another mad leader has risen. Such a mad leader, whose roots are to be found not only on 'Nasserism' but also in the ideas of Hitler and 'Nazism'". So, in the Western world, films about the Hitler-period are constantly being shown on T.V. these days, and they present such scenes and incidents of that war, which would revive the memories of the time of Hitler and link Hitler's era and his motives with the present period of Saddam Hussein and his motives.

SICK MINDS: THE REAL CAUSE OF THE DISEASE

This is the analysis of the West, but no Western scholar has ever considered that if these were truly sick minds who rose as leaders, then what was the disease in the Middle East which created these sick minds, and little do they realise that even if these diseased heads are cut off, even then as long as the disease persists it will continue to produce an abundance of such diseased heads. Never will they become free of that disease and from the ill effects of that disease. What is that disease? It is the founding of Israel and after that it is the continuous preferential treatment given to Israel by the West. Whenever there were two paths, and a question facing the West was whether to tread the path that led to the interest of Israel or to follow the path that led to the interest of the Arab Muslim world, then without exception, the West always followed the path which gave preference to Israel and discarded the interest of the Islamic world. The essence of this disease has been expressed by an Arab Poet in a simple couplet saying that:

من كان يلبس كلبه ثيبا و يقنع لي جلدي   فالكلب خير عنده مني و خير منه عندي

"A man who dresses his dog well, but for me he thinks that my bare skin is enough to cover me. Without doubt, for him the dog is better than me, but for me, the dog is better than him."

This is exactly the ultimate diagnosis of the disease. This attitude of the West has sunk into the heart of the Arab world and their analysis is based on facts that the West will no doubt prefer to clothe even its dogs but will keep the Arabs nude and this situation is very true when you make a comparison between Israel and the Arab States.

<u>WRONG DIAGNOSIS AND WRONG REACTION</u>
On such occasions, the response of the West has always been that in order to protect themselves from the "unenlightened" Arabs and to safeguard the world from their harm, there is only one solution that Arabia and the Arabs should be torn apart, thus eliminating the possibility of their ever emerging as a power. This analysis of the West is similar, though not as dreadful or as criminal as was the one enforced after the First and Second world wars. In both cases that analysis was proved wrong. So long as one does not cast a glance at the fundamental cause which gives rise to the development of the so-called "Nazism", "Nasserism" or "Saddamism" - so long as the disease is not correctly diagnosed and attention is not paid to its treatment; such 'heads' will continue to surface one after the other. These 'heads' will continue to be severed and will continue to be a justification for the dismembering of other heads, and this sore will

continue to ripen till that time when it might spill out of the control and power of the governments of the West! In fact the power which Saddam Hussein now brandishes is just a reflection of the past injustice and unprincipled stand of the West.

INTRIGUES OF THE WESTERN POWERS IN IRAN

Prior to this it was the Western nations which laid the foundation of "Khomeneism". France is that Western country where Imam Khomenei had sought shelter and where he lived under their protection for a long time. With the influence and help of France, a propaganda campaign was launched which eventually brought about the revolution in Iran which still continues. Until that time, the West was faced with the dilemma, that if "Khomeneism" or the religious revolution did not triumph, then there would be a Communist revolution in view of the deep rooted hatred of the people for the Shah of Iran. So it was not the love of "Khomeneism" or the concept of Islam as practised in Iran, but rather, a fear of the bigger enemy which had forced them to feel that they should nourish "Khomeneism". When "Khomeneism" was firmly established, the religious junta, who were well aware that they had come to power simply as a result of religious passions, felt that in order to maintain that tempo of religious frenzy, the hatred of the nation had to be diverted into another direction.

The first revolution was also based upon hatred. Hatred against the Shah of Iran and in its background, and against his powerful ally and patron - America. So they used the same weapon of hatred to gain religious benefit and portrayed the U.S. as the 'Great Devil' thus keeping alive, those religious sentiments of the nation that are associated with hatred. The repercussion of such a policy was that "Khomeneism" was further strengthened. Thus, whatever lawlessness prevailed in the region before Imam Khomeini, or the dreadful wars, disturbances, murders and injustices that followed, its responsibility too basically lies with the West. The West has a fundamental responsibility because they supported the oppressive measures of the Shah of Iran.

It is inconceivable that America, which has the most sophisticated surveillance and intelligence network that is capable of gaining knowledge of events that even escape the observation of the natives of a country, would have no prior knowledge of the atrocities unleashed against his own people by the Shah, or its reaction brewing among the masses! It is amusing that in our country (Pakistan), after some military *coups*, the ousted leaders bitterly complained to the U.S. later, that the U.S. intelligence networks never gave them advance warning of the simmering unrest. The leader of a country or a political party is overthrown, and the Americans are reproached for failing to give forewarning! You govern a country without the in-depth knowledge of that country and expect others to lend you that information!

So, as the East becomes indifferent to its own affairs, so is the West becoming more keenly aware and sensitive to the happenings in the East. The foremost responsibility of patronizing the tyranny of the Shah rests on America and no sane person in the world can absolve America of this responsibility. This observation is not reflecting a feeling of hatred nor it is due to an emotional outburst; it is such an obvious fact that even a person of ordinary intelligence would admit. Monarchy of Iran was nurtured by America and, as a result, the responsibility of all the ensuing reactions lies squarely on the U.S.

THE U.S. DILEMMA

And whatever action America took to contain that reaction in Iran, against the Shah, was necessary to protect their own interest or, according to them, was essential to protect the interest of the world. They felt that now only two powers could benefit from this reaction. Either the power of religion, as symbolized by Khomeneism, or the power of Communism. And since Communism was a worse enemy, they grudgingly extended their tacit support to Khomeneism. If at that juncture, Communism had gained the upper hand in Iran, the present climate of peace between the U.S. and Russia was totally out of question. Then "Saddamism" would also not have been born and there would have been a great danger in the Middle East from Russia and the Communist-dominated Iran; a challenge against which the U.S. would have no counter response. Therefore it was in their interest and, as they claim, in the interest of the whole world, that they created Khomeneism and nourished it. When it gained power, the Iranians used their foresight and attempted to follow a middle course between the Super Powers for the continuation of their system and to protect it from the evil influence of the U.S. A middle path, in the sense, that it lay in-between Russia and America. However, according to the principle of Islamic justice it was not the middle course because they indulged in a spree of murders and executions, making it the order of the day. Alas! they did it all in the name of Islam.

SADDAM HUSSEIN - A PRODUCT OF THE WEST

The world of Islam suffered many setbacks due to these events and then to take their revenge from Iran, the Americans created Saddamism encouraging Iraq in every way. They asked the Arab powers which were under their influence to help Iraq and they directly helped it as well. On one occasion, when Iraq faced extreme danger and it was clearly visible that the Iranian Army would overrun Baghdad, the U.S. openly declared that they will not allow this to happen. So they rapidly boosted Iraq's defensive capability to the level of an offensive one. These days, the West is carrying out a propaganda campaign against Saddam Hussein that he is such a tyrant and such an insensitive person that he has no hesitation in using poisonous nerve gases against his adversaries, which cause blisters and suffocation and that it is therefore necessary to free the world from this tyrant.

Until recently, these very nations were helping Iraq in acquiring the capability of producing these lethal gases!! It was all in their knowledge, and chemical plants were being established before their very eyes and it was they who gave Iraq the technical know-how. They did all that because, at that time, they were faced with a bigger enemy, i.e. Iran. For these nations to say today that they did not know about it and that Iraq did all these things secretly, on its own, is an utter lie. When the chemical plants that manufacture nerve gas were started in Libya, they bombed that country and declared to the world that they would never allow these plants be established at any cost because they would pose a threat to the world peace. They presented details of these plants which were later found to be precisely correct to an amazing degree. They said that if Libya continues to claim that it was not making any chemical weapons and was rather manufacturing fertilizers or some other chemicals, we could reveal the photographs of the interior of these plants. They laid before the world the very detailed plans of chemical weapon production by Libya. They were indeed aware of every minute detail!.

Then, how can their eyes fail to observe what was happening in Iraq while they were actively supporting it? At that time they wanted that at no cost should Iran gain supremacy over Iraq, or achieve dominance over the Arab world: that Iran must be denied the victory of any kind. They feared lest the whole region slip out of their control and dominance. At that time, it was Iran that was screaming that the use of chemical weapons was an outrage and injustice, and was even supporting its claim with the help of photographs of the victims of gas attacks. After showing a few glimpses, the West stopped showing those horrible pictures to the world.

Now that they have decided to disgrace and humiliate this 'sick and mad man' who was the product of their own creation to begin with, they have started showing those gruesome pictures which were once shown by Iran. They are now showing these photographs and orchestrating before the world saying: 'how could they expect decency and fair play from such a tyrant? How could the world remain unharmed from the atrocities of such a tyrant who did not show sympathy or mercy even towards his own kinsmen or towards his Iranian Muslim brothers.'

REACTION OF THE WEST

So the reaction and methodology of the West is the same as before, paying no attention to the disease which produces such sick minds. They disregard those forces and powers - and indeed they constitute the very powers which produce, sustain and help the production of such sick minds. They ignore the ailment which gives rise to such births and continue to suckle them to their ultimate maturity. In the end, they only focus the attention of the world towards those diseased heads, because it is these heads which they have decided to sever.

This is done to show to the world that a 'diseased head' has again surfaced which is destined to be dismembered, otherwise it will pose a threat to the other 'heads' of the world. *The ultimate question remains:* why do such diseased minds continue to be created? It is because of the aggressive, repressive and cruel attitude of the West towards the Muslims, especially the Arab and Iranian Muslims. This was despite the fact that the West won the friendship of many of these countries whom they backed and apparently even helped.

Third Friday Sermon Aug 24, 1990

FREEZING OF ASSETS

But their ultimate motives were very pragmatic and it was clear that the best way to benefit from them was to befriend them. They had them to deposit their entire oil-wealth in their banks and thus derived a two-fold benefit. Firstly, the Western countries got control over huge stockpiles of wealth that benefitted them by boosting their investment capabilities and secondly, they acquired the leverage and power to freeze and seize their assets at the slightest indication of any discord. In normal circumstances, they brag about their standards of trust, but their *concept of honesty* changes as soon as it affects their interests. They preach that when a citizen of one country goes to another country, he becomes a *trust* and that there should be no breach of that trust... Then what right do they have to seize and seal the assets of a country even in adversarial situations. A country that trusted them in the time of peace and friendship and in accordance with the rules of international monetary system deserves better treatment, even if it turned out to be an error to deposit its wealth in their vaults. How can they justify the posture of seizing a country's assets for the welfare of humanity.

How many Eastern countries there are whose total assets were frozen every time there was an apprehension of war. Even now, Kuwaiti funds have been frozen with the intension of releasing them later on, because of their acknowledged friendship. All the wealth of Iraq in various foreign countries has been seized.

These are the intricate forms of deceit. The Western countries skilfully present these injustices before the world in an extremely polished and civilized language! Contrary to this, the ill-fated Islamic nations have always attempted to counter and fight the intelligence of the West with sheer passion and each time the emotions were pitched against intelligence, the emotions were routed and torn to bits, thus further disgracing and humiliating the Muslim world!

THE GREATEST BLUNDER

The greatest blunder which the Arab world made, and continues to repeat, is the lack of awareness that, in political causes and worldly matters, the reaction of selfish nations is always the same, irrespective of the differences in their religions. Rather than dealing with these issues at the political level where they belong, the Arabs unnecessarily converted these into a religious frenzy, and the hatred that was thus generated was all attributed to the religion of Islam. As human beings you do have the right to fight those nations who attack your national interests. But, by switching an ordinary political war into an Islamic *Jihad* (holy-war), without any justification, they give the West an additional opportunity to attack Islam as a religion, whereas previously they attacked only the Islamic world. They now tell the whole world that the real disease is Islam and not Israel. The West does not consider its own injustices, but portrays Islam as a religion which breeds crookedness. Also, they contend that Islam is an unjust religion which spreads prejudiced thought and trace all the related maladies to the *Muslim way of thinking*.

For instance, the turmoil in Iran that followed the departure of the Shah, consisted of totally un-Islamic reactions which were not even remotely connected with Islam; but if it had have been presented in secular terms then the world could have been pacified to a considerable extent that they were taking revenge after decades of continued oppression. The world would have understood it to some extent, if they had said that 'we are helpless to stem the tide of this violent reaction. That, behind this reaction lie centuries of injustice and hatred for the monarchy. That, our reaction is similar to the reaction of a weak man, overcome with rage, that when he gets hold of a brick, he hurls it at his opponent, oblivious of the repercussions or the fury of his stronger opponent.' Instead of presenting this state of affairs with righteousness, truthfulness and in a straightforward way, according to the teachings of Islam, which would have provided them with great benefits, the Muslim countries once again faltered and provided the West with an opportunity to attack Islam. It was as if the Muslims had first invited the West to attack their **body** and them beckoned them to attach their very **soul**! They presented the Islamic teachings in such an unjust way, by twisting and confounding it, that all intelligent people in the world knew that it was not a religious reaction. However, the intelligentsia felt that if the Muslims persist in calling this reaction a "religious reaction", then they will have no alternative but to criticize their religion and tell the world that it is their crooked religion which is to be blamed and not our own way of thinking.

Third Friday Sermon Aug 24, 1990

THE REAL DUTY OF ISLAMIC LEADERSHIP

So the leaders whom the West had been presenting before the world as 'sick heads', and who, in fact were sick because of the West inflicted ailments, the same Muslims provided the West with a further opportunity to blame the religion of Islam for their malady. An incorrect diagnosis - blaming Islam - was thus re-introduced in the world. The world believed this wrong diagnosis because a patient's description of his own sickness is always given more credence. If the patient says that he has a headache and attributes this headache to certain foods he had eaten or his other activities, then even if the doctor says otherwise, no one is fully convinced. Therefore, when these diseased heads are presented to the world, it is also stated that the 'sick man' has himself given an excellent diagnosis of his ailment. This sick man says "my religion is illogical. My religion forces me to commit atrocities against women and children and thus redress my grievances, and that it is my religion of Islam which gives me the right to take revenge in this way." You are free to indulge in acts of sabotage, you can disrupt the peace in the cities by planting bombs. You can take revenge and relieve your anguish in whatever way you want and Allah's support is with you. Islam stands behind you and teaches you that you should do it in the name of the religion.....!! Such actions are utterly wrong. There is not the remotest justification for these.

> If my analysis is presented to the world, the world will necessarily begin to see why there are 'diseased heads' and what has caused the disease. But these unjust Muslim fanatics not only allowed the world to attack them, but also presented the religion of Islam to become the target of their wrath!

This is a summary and background of the tyranny and injustice that is unfolding before us today. It is imperative that the Islamic leadership understand the real causes of their sickness and turn all its attention to the real disease and persuade others to focus their attention on it. This analysis must be clearly presented before the world. It should be stated that we have been forced to join you against Saddam Hussein, but in no way does it mean that you are absolved, and in no way does it mean that the removal of Saddam or the ruin of Iraq is the remedy for the Muslim world. Failure to act in this manner, will further result in the ravage of Islamic nations and those causes will continue to operate and those diseases will remain as a result of which, time and again, the peace in the Middle East is disturbed, and time and again the world feels endangered from the Muslims.

OCCUPATION OF ARAB LAND BY ISRAEL

It certainly did not serve the purpose of justice that, after each war, Israel occupied additional Muslim territory and the West always supported Israel to make those occupations permanent. There was not an inch of land which Israel had to evacuate except some Egyptian territory. When Israel was made to give up its occupation of the Sinai desert they first forced Egypt to submit to their humiliating conditions. Egypt was forced to finalize such a treaty with Israel as a result of which it was hoped that Egypt would be cut-off from the Islamic world for good, and would become a target of their animosity and after this its continued existence would depend on the West. As long as the West would give its support, it would survive, otherwise it would be torn to pieces. These were their expectations based on which they restored those desert areas to Egypt which had been occupied by the Jews. But besides that, no land has been recovered anywhere else. That is to say, Israel has not been made to return the land of those who did not stoop so low as to accept a treaty of humiliation. How long has Jordan been a friend of the West? Even now when they speak of Jordan in the news they refer to it as a friend. But now they say: Look at how much we depended upon Jordan. How insane of us! How unfaithful a friend she has proved to be. And they do not see how they have reciprocated towards Jordan for this long friendship? All this time, a part of your friend's territory remained in the possession of its enemy and all the while you strengthened the enemy to continue with its unlawful occupation. Despite all that, it remained your friend.

THE MUSLIMS CONTINUE TO BE STUNG FROM THE SAME ORIFICE

When the Holy Quran admonishes not to befriend the enemy, some people created a misunderstanding about this statement and, as a result, certain Muslim scholars of the medieval period engendered a bad name to Islam. When Islam advises that you should never befriend such a non Muslim it means: do not befriend outsiders at the cost of compromising the principles of Islam and Justice. This is the context of this teaching. At the same time the Holy Quran states that those who do not show enmity towards you, or those who have not done you any injustice, Allah does not stop you from befriending them. Rather Islam teaches you to have kind and cordial relations with them. This is Islam; but the principles of Islam which appeal to commonsense have always been discarded by them. Instead, they followed a version of this teaching that they themselves distorted, and which was contrary to Islam. Alas! when they were admonished not to befriend a certain type of people, they developed keen friendships with them but where they were advised to cultivate friendly relationships - in fact taught ways of approach to such desirable type of friendships - they neglected those opportunities.

> Therefore the ultimate analysis of their disease is that they have moved away from righteousness and the teaching of Islam. The Holy Prophet[sas] said that a believer is never stung twice from the same hole but how many times have they been stung! They push their fingers in the same hole and get repeatedly stung. To this day, they have not learned any lesson from this.

If you analyze the policies of the prudent West, you will observe that it too is ignorant and imprudent. Despite repeated setbacks, it has not been able to discover what the true disease is. As long as this disease persists, the dangers and threats will continue to hover over the world. On the other hand, the Muslim countries, despite repeated sufferings, have not learnt their lesson and continue to repeat the same mistakes. What is its remedy?

<u>THE REMEDY PRESCRIBED BY THE HOLY QURAN</u>

There is but one remedy which was taught to us by the Holy Prophet Muhammad[sas], about which I reminded you earlier, and wish to remind you once again. The Holy Prophet, referring to the *latter days*, prophesied (I will quote only an excerpt of this long prophecy):

> "gog and magog will rule the world and they will rise wave after wave and the whole world will be overwhelmed by the waves of

their power. At that time the Messiah will be raised in the world and the Messiah with his followers will try to fight them, and will attempt to counter them. Allah will then speak to the Messiah saying:
that no man in the world has been granted the power to fight these two nations which We have created - not even you! There is only one way, that you seek shelter on a mountain and pray to God. It is only the weapon of prayer that can subjugate these nations."

THE JAMAAT OF THE MUHAMMADAN MESSIAH AND ITS RESPONSIBILITIES

What is meant by the mountain in this context? I believe that the Holy Prophet[sas] is that mountain which has been mentioned here. Because, while speaking about the Holy Quran, Allah says that:

لَوْ اَنْزَلْنَا هٰذَا الْقُرْاٰنَ عَلٰى جَبَلٍ لَّرَاَيْتَهٗ خَاشِعًا مُّتَصَدِّعًا مِّنْ خَشْيَةِ اللّٰهِ

"if We had revealed this Quran even on a mountain it would have dreaded and would tremble due to its majesty and would have been shattered to pieces"(Al Hashr 22).

But in this, there are lessons and signs for those who are inclined to reflection. It means that the Holy Prophet[sas] had a supremacy over all the mountains. The Holy Prophet[sas] was the greatest of the mountains. The mountains of the world did not have the power to encompass the greatness and majesty of this revelation but it was the Holy Prophet Muhammad[sas] who was the highest of the mountains and was the strongest of the mountains. So what it means is that you should revert to the lofty principles of the Holy Prophet[sas] and seek refuge and gain fortitude in the teaching of this great Prophet. If you will return to the lofty ideals of the Holy Prophet[sas] and after taking shelter in them you will supplicate before God, then the prayers that are thus nourished will never go waste. Then, with your prayers you will also share in his greatness.

And the other message in this prophecy is that apart from all other Muslim sects, the instructions by Allah to offer prayers has been given only to the Jamaat of the Messiah. (Ahmadiyya Muslim Community) It also signifies that, at that time, all other Muslims will forfeit faith in the power and importance of prayer. Therefore, it would have been useless to suggest the recipe of prayers for those who had lost hope in the power of prayer. You may scan the statements of Muslim leaders suggesting that we must run towards America to implore for help and shelter. Someone else is advising to make peace with Iran or is talking of other plans for his own reassurance. But no one, not even a single country, has said anything about going into the shelter of Allah and the shelter of Muhammad[sas], the Messenger of Allah! No one has reminded them that 'O Muslims! this is the time of prayer, the hour of supplications, because it is only through prayer that you will achieve victory over the enemy.'

There is only one Jamaat - and indeed only the Jamaat (Community) of the Messiah of the Holy Prophet Muhammad[sas] - about whom Allah had so decreed that if the world of Islam was ever to be saved, it would be through the prayers of this Community. But there is one condition, that they should seek refuge in the eminence of Muhammad[sas] and should seek guidance from his teachings, his character and his noble practices.

So, even if a temporary solution for this whole predicament is proposed, then one thing is certain, the solution will make the people living in the Middle East, and for that matter, the whole world, worse off. An extremely dreadful situation is in the offing, and as far as the real diseases and the afflictions are concerned, they will find no solution. If a solution does exist, it is with you, i.e. with the Jamaat of the Messiah of Muhammad[sas].

You should supplicate and continue to supplicate because this period of agony is bound to be protracted. The situation will have many reversals and will enter into many new phases. Therefore, it is still not too late to pray. We are a Community who pray in any case, but in view of the world situation today, in view of the analysis that I have presented before you, I assure you that besides prayer there is no panacea for the afflictions of the world, and of the Muslim *Ummah*. You should also pray for the Western nations, that Allah may grant them wisdom. They have repeatedly tried to solve the problems of the world through clever political maneuverings and high-level diplomacy; yet they failed on every occasion. Not once have their crafty moves been of any benefit to the world. This is so because their cleverness is motivated and guided by purely selfish interests. True wisdom is associated with righteousness. The world has not understood this, to this day. The Holy Quran lays emphasis that righteousness begets wisdom, it assists the believer to see with the help of Divine illumination. True wisdom and righteousness are in fact synonymous. All crafty moves, because they are devoid of righteousness, are ultimately bound to fail. You may call such a move 'cleverness' but you can never call it as an act of intelligence. So the world today, whether it be the East or the West, is stripped of true intelligence because it is dispossessed of righteousness!!

APPEAL TO MEMBERS OF THE AHMADIYYA MUSLIM COMMUNITY

O, the Community of Muhammad Mustafa[sas], O, the Community of the Promised Messiah[as] of the Muhammadan[sas] dispensation! You have been entrusted with the wealth of righteousness, so fulfil the obligations of this trust and as long as you continue to be worthy of this trust, Allah will always grant you victory and you will continue to transform the impossible into possible. May Allah enable us to do so.

Amen.

In the name of Allah, the Gracious, the Merciful

FOURTH FRIDAY SERMON

OCTOBER 26, 1990

AN ALARMING CONSPIRACY HATCHED AGAINST THE MUSLIM WORLD

After the reciting the Opening Chapter of the Holy Quran, Al-Fatiha, Hazoor recited the following verses:

يَٰٓأَيُّهَا ٱلنَّاسُ إِنَّا خَلَقْنَٰكُم مِّن ذَكَرٍ وَأُنثَىٰ وَجَعَلْنَٰكُمْ شُعُوبًا وَقَبَآئِلَ لِتَعَارَفُوٓا۟ إِنَّ أَكْرَمَكُمْ عِندَ ٱللَّهِ أَتْقَىٰكُمْ إِنَّ ٱللَّهَ عَلِيمٌ خَبِيرٌ ۝

"O mankind, We have created you from a male and a female; and We have made you into tribes and sub-tribes that you may recognize one another. Verily, the most honourable among you in the sight of Allah is he who is the most righteous among you. Surely, Allah is All-Knowing- All-Aware."
(Holy Quran, Chapter 49 Al-Hujurat verse-14)

Following the recitation of these verses Hazoor said:

<u>NEW CHALLENGES EMERGING IN THE CHANGING CIRCUMSTANCES</u>
During the course of my previous sermon I had called the attention of the Jamaat towards the changing circumstances that have opened up new fields of struggle for the Ahmadiyya Muslim Community, where the values of Islam will be pitted against those of the non-Islamic forces. New challenges will have to be confronted. The fact is that, historically, such conflicts have occurred all along, but during certain era these battles arise too conspicuously and appear unusually significant compared to other periods. In the present era, Islam will be confronted with the rival social values. The Western world, which predominantly consists of Christians, is bound to divert the attention

Fourth Friday Sermon Aug 24, 1990

of the world from the ideological contrast to social differences, with the intent of keeping the Western nations away from Islam.

EXPECTED CONFRONTATION OF ISLAM WITH RACIAL PREJUDICES

Racism is another aspect of this subject, which is making an upsurge at a phenomenal pace. Although one frequently hears the voice of the Western world against racism, so that calling anyone a racist is considered to be an abuse, but all this is superficial. Whatever movement against racism is observed in the Western world, it mainly emanates from the Jewish camp, with the sole purpose of eliminating opposition to Jewish racism. This movement is not meant to deter the Jewish racial tendencies but instead, it is a well orchestrated propaganda campaign beamed at Europe and the U.S. to silence all such movements which occasionally rise to denounce Jewish racial trends. In the pursuit of this objective they give prominence to race-oriented atrocities of the *Nazi era* by way of stage-dramas, pictorial presentations and by holding occasional seminars in the Western hemisphere. In this manner the world is being cautioned that it must never again commit such a blunder. Along with this propaganda campaign, prosecution and punishment for old war crimes still continues, sending a strong message to the world that any recurrence of the past racial hatred against the Jewish people would never be forgiven.

So whatever movement you find here against racism, in fact pertains to the benefit of this limited circle. The tendency towards racism is actually on the increase in these nations. But the prime target of this racism is the Eastern world, the African nations or Islam. Sometimes Islam is portrayed as 'nationalism' and racial sentiments are aroused against it. At other times, racism is presented in the form of religion and society, and sentiments are aroused against other races.

Whatever has happened, or is still happening, in the Soviet Union, or the changes which were brought about following the fall of the Berlin Wall and its global repercussions have already been briefly mentioned by me in my concluding address at the Ahmadiyya Annual convention in July. I had explained that the upsurge of racial prejudice is a very crucial factor which will be in direct conflict with Islam. It is only the Ahmadiyya Muslim Community which has been established to defend Islamic values and by the Grace of God, is fully capable of doing so. Therefore the Community should fully comprehend these inherent dangers and must remain adequately informed of its minutest details, so that whatever course is chosen by the adversary to launch an attack, the Community is prepared to swiftly counter such attacks with intelligence.

RISING TRENDS OF NATIONALISM AND RACISM IN EUROPE

In the wake of recent developments in Europe, as I mentioned earlier, nationalism will gain momentum in Europe and will be followed by racism. In fact, nationalism and racism are deeply interlinked. They differ only in their areas of scope and influence.

First of all you must remember that the Soviet Union is not composed of one nation. The world consists of various types of states. Some of them emerged on the basis of nationalism and then adhered to it, while the others were established on the basis of some ideology. Israel is a case in point where both these elements coexist. But in the case of most countries, the concept of a state based on nationalism is quite ambiguous. In fact these states are inhabited by more than one nation, and they always keep trying to distract the attention of their people from the fact of national diversity to forestall their disintegration. For instance, these days, the United Kingdom is in the grip of this problem. Geographically it has Scotland in its north, Wales in the West, then further deep in the West is Ireland. Some differences between the north and the south are reaching national proportions. Of all their conflicts, the prominent differences are between the Scottish and the English, the Welsh and the English, and between the Irish and the English. On the surface, Great Britain, or the United Kingdom, appears to be one nation, and when faced with any external danger they all get united for common interest and in such eventuality, a wider national interest prevails. But during peace time the same old sub-national trends surface and the nature of national danger changes. They start giving vent to mistrust against one another, and display selfishness in their mutual relations. Their differences, then, make them look distinctly as separate nationalities, and then their mutual relationship is measured by the regional yardstick. Selfishness at national level creates division, because the inhabitants of the south start saying that they have to protect the interest of the south, the English give priority to their interest over that of the Scottish. In the same way the Welsh think that they are being subjected to injustice and exploitation and that the English are depriving them of their legitimate rights. This was just an example to illustrate the fact that most of the states in the world, whether they be America, England, Germany or others, are not composed of one nation. The scholars in this field are of the opinion that if there is any country that may be called a nation, it is *Turkey*. But this too may not be entirely correct because the *Kurds* call themselves a distinctly separate nation from the Turks. Their values, language, and temperament are entirely different from those of the Turks, and it is for this reason that a great hatred and mistrust exists between them. The Kurds have been protesting for long that they continue to be subjected to atrocities and injustices by the ruling Turks. Only God knows how far this is true. Nevertheless it appears correct that if any country is entitled to being called one nation then, barring the Kurdish area, it is the Turks. In fact, comparatively speaking, it can be said about them that they are one nation and one country. But it is surprising that the number of Turks living outside Turkey is much more than those living in Turkey; there is a ratio of 3:2. Although Turks live in all parts of the world yet their greatest number is settled in the Soviet Union, where they are known as 'Turkman'. Even there, they are fragmented and various movements are emerging in them. One Turk dominated state exaggerates its apprehensions against the other state, thus creating barriers between the two. But at the same time, a popular sentiment is developing that since basically they are all Turks, their eventual identification with mainland Turkey is essential. Turkey, at one stage can exploit this feeling and link the overall interest of the Turks with the formation of a single greater Turkey. The historical entity of the Ottoman Empire - a concept that applied to vast areas of the world at one time - is bound to be resurrected. And Islam would have to play a crucial role in this development. At this point those who may be classified as Turks linguistically, will be attracted towards Iran because of their Shiite faith and their Iranian roots. Then there are those nations which adhere strictly to the Sunni school of thought - they may speak the Turkish language, the Oi-ghar dialect or any other language - they will be coaxed by the Sunni Muslim world through its economic power.

THE RUSSIAN EMPIRE ON THE VERGE OF DISINTEGRATION

The Soviet Union has reached a point where it is on the verge of a breakup and awaits a complete disintegration. Only an extraordinary power can avert this catastrophe which is in the offing. As far as I have contemplated over this matter, there appears no such external or internal powers to keep the Soviet Union intact; and the major cause of its disintegration lies in its erroneous conception of laying the foundation of nationhood on ideology, a situation analogous to that of Pakistan where ideology was confused with nationality. The emergence of the Soviet Union was not due to the geographical settlement of one nation, but owed its existence to the ideology of Communism. In earlier times, the occupation of large adjoining territories by the Czars, was a type of 'colonialism' where a European power held on to a large number of Muslim states. This was similar to the era of the Muslim *Khawaneen* who, much earlier in history, occupied areas which now constitute the Soviet Union and other neighbouring European lands. So this was in a way, a reversal of that position. During the revolution of 1918 a new concept emerged in Russia, i.e. instead of a country based on nationality, the foundation of an ideological state was laid. Russia started making a forceful propaganda throughout the world that countries are best created by an ideology rather than by nationalities. Further they claimed that since their concept was universal, therefore a universal Communist nation would now emerge in the world. With the help of this ideology they succeeded in causing a rift among smaller countries. Wherever this concept took root, a movement against nationalism was set in motion. But in some regions a strong stand was taken against this ideology. At this juncture it was also claimed that Islam too wants to establish an ideological state and that it recognizes no other concept of nationhood. A limited version of this concept took the shape of the "Two Nation Theory" that resulted in the creation of Pakistan. At present I do not have enough time to elaborate upon the correct position as to how far the Two Nation Theory was workable or unworkable, and how far it was realistic, and why the Muslims of India undertook such a great struggle for the establishment of Pakistan and what were the real motives lurking in its background. Whether the establishment of Pakistan was a result of the concepts of *Allama Iqbal*, the Pakistani poet and thinker, or were there some entirely different reasons for it. This is a separate subject. But, at present, I intend to explain to you that Russian ideology of Communism was playing a pivotal role and its satellite nations were spinning around this ideology. When the nucleus of this concept got dislodged, the nations revolving around it will fall apart and no power on earth can stop this from happening. It is possible that at a later stage, as a result of external pressure these nations may consider it in their own long term interest to stay together. But the concept of common interests which had unified the North American States is presently non-existent in Russia. The reason is that although all these Russian nations were consolidated under the Communist concept, but with the exception of the European stock, the other ethnic groups were treated unjustly.

As far as Russia's economic system is concerned, or as to the question of mutual relationship between various constituent nations of the Soviet Union, the fact is that the Muslim nations and some other underdeveloped nations have not been treated at par with the other nations in Russia. These nations were kept undeveloped in their economic growth and industrial development. So, instead of making efforts to keep them together in the wider national interest, the actual situation has taken the opposite turn. Now these nations are ready to go their separate ways not only due to the demise of the Communist doctrine but also because of the bad memory of injustices done to them in the past. This is inciting them to secede.

ISLAMIC CONCEPT OF NATIONAL IDEOLOGY

Islam, as a religion, cannot be of any help to these Muslim groups under the present circumstances, for the reason that a large majority of the population of these states have practically become faithless, even though they continue to be called Muslims. Not to speak of their younger generation, even their religious leaders are unaware of the real concept of God except that they follow some vague concept. To worship God in the real sense, to make sacrifices in this way, or to bring about a spiritual change in themselves demands a constant effort. Islam will have to be gradually re-introduced to them. This is quite a challenge that the Ahmadiyya Muslim Jamaat will have to meet. But Islam is influencing them in another way, i.e. by way of the relationship Islam has with nationalism. The same Two Nation Theory, a version of which was once put forth by Allama Iqbal, may be invoked by these states for winning freedom from the United Republics of Russia. This theory can even be exploited for a revolt but not because the others do not offer 'Salat' prayers, a Jihad is called for. Nor would it be done due to the apprehension that their freedom of religion would be curtailed in the emerging set-up, but for entirely different reasons. Actually, the situation is quite the opposite of restraint right now, and a measure of religious freedom is being granted under the new set of circumstances. But separate nation theory will spring up nonetheless. The freedom of faith is not just for the Muslim dominated areas but in the European dominated states as well, and the laws are being relaxed for the sake of Christianity; a situation that will benefit the Muslim-populated states.

So if there were any reaction in the name of Islam, one would have observed some intervention in Islamic matters. When there were many restrictions actually imposed on the Muslims no reaction was displayed by them. At that time, no Muslim segment of the country had the power to take any initiative to get rid of the Soviet Union for the sake of Islam. The present feelings of revolt rising in the new younger generation against Russia, is not for the sake of Islam. Although most of the younger people do not even know what the Islamic prayer is; they know nothing about the Quran, yet the affection for Islam is undoubtedly rekindling in their hearts, and it is this affection that we will have to streamline and develop. But to think of this affection being transformed, overnight, into action is an illusion, and it has nothing to do with reality. So far, this affection has taken the form of racial consciousness or, one might say, a nationalistic awareness, and this is causing the feelings of revolt against Central Russia. In such conditions, the external vested interest would get activated. The Sunni Muslims would try to get involved and attempt to win them over; the Shiite Muslims would also attempt to sneak in to win their favour, and similarly the other factions and national groups of the Muslims from the outside world would come in and try to compete with each other to take advantage of this fluid situation.

So a new battle ground is in the offing, and if the Ahmadiyya Muslim Jamaat did not despond quickly and introduce these nations to the real Islam, which has nothing to do with racial or national ideologies, then Islam can get a great setback. Islam has a universal message which is based on the negation of the regional or racial

Fourth Friday Sermon Aug 24, 1990

tendencies. Islam has suffered, in the past, due to the presence of such ideologies which, in fact, were alien to Islam. The verses I recited before you clearly present the Islamic point of view on this subject:

يَاأَيُّهَا النَّاسُ إِنَّا خَلَقْنَاكُمْ مِنْ ذَكَرٍ وَّ أُنْثَى وَجَعَلْنَاكُمْ شُعُوْبًا وَّقَبَآئِلَ لِتَعَارَفُوْا

"O mankind We have created you from a male and a female, and We have made you into tribes and sub-tribes so that you may recognize one another."

By saying that We have created you from a male and a female, God implies that you are one species, irrespective of the regional or racial attachments. The difference lies only in your being a male or a female. This distinction cannot be erased by you, nor can you base your national or racial identities on such considerations. If you were to try that, you would realise your mistake. The human race cannot exist in the absence of bilateral cooperation between the male and the female. By saying that, وَجَعَلْنَاكُمْ شُعُوْبًا وَّقَبَآئِلَ لِتَعَارَفُوْا

"We have made you into tribe and sub-tribes so that you may recognize one another", connotes that division into tribes and sub-tribes is made for the sole purpose of your identification, just as we recognize and identify different people by their personal names. But, merely on the basis of names, people are never divided into separate groups. For instance, all persons by the name of *Nasir* should get together, and so persons by names *Tahir* should form a separate group, or all persons whose name is *Khalil* may get together and form a group against all persons whose name is *Mubarak*. It would be a ridiculous thing to do. So the names are only for the purpose of identification and have no further significance. Specifically, they should not give rise to any prejudice and common sense dictates that this be so. So the word "recognition" in the verse cited, implies that if you exceed these limits it would be a wrong and foolish act. The division of nations must be confined to the extent of their personal recognition. There would be no harm if recognition covers their temperamental identity but this division must not go beyond this limit.

The verse:

إِنَّ أَكْرَمَكُمْ عِنْدَ اللَّهِ أَتْقَاكُمْ

"The most honourable among you is the most righteous" signifies that Islam permits the distinction between individuals or among nations only on one consideration, and that is the criterion of *Taqwa* or righteousness. If anyone is more righteous, irrespective of his nationality or religious affiliations, colour or creed, geographic or regional attachments, he or she should be respected without the consideration of these differences. So based on this criterion of righteousness an Englishman can be at par with the Welsh, the Welsh can join the Scottish and a Scottish person may combine with the Irish. This principle would create their harmony with the African people, the Arabs, the Russians, the Chinese, the Americans and with the people of all nationalities in the world. Eventually all the righteous people would be linked together. This criterion of righteousness (*Taqwa*) is the only national concept presented by Islam. Islam accepts no rival concept. Respect would be on the basis of righteousness and it would be righteousness alone taken into consideration. People who will be so unified would create a "nation" of the righteous people, but this grouping would not conform to the political divisions or political attachments.

EVIDENCE OF RISING RACIAL PREJUDICE IN EUROPE

New developments are now shaping up in the Soviet Union and perverse new national concepts are on the rise. At the same time, new tendencies of racial hatred are emerging in Europe as well as in the Western world, which have a bearing on their internal as well as external matters. In Europe, feelings of distrust of one nation against the other are mounting and an atmosphere of lack of confidence is growing. Today, if there exists a feeling of envy, tomorrow it will be transformed into jealousy. So, whereas on the one hand Europe appears to be getting united, on the other hand the seeds of division have already been sown in this drive for the so called unity, and it appears certain that the new unifying states in Europe will face internal differences, which will be further intensified in the atmosphere of jealousy and mistrust. Now consider the case of

Fourth Friday Sermon Aug 24, 1990

Germany, which is re-emerging as a big power in Europe. Some nations of Europe are apprehending a great danger from this rising state, but are not expressing their feelings openly at present, yet internally they are realizing its inherent dangers. As to the government of the U.K., it has, on many occasions, expressed such apprehensions that Germany would rise as a big power and then there is a possibility that it may repeat its previous mistakes which had culminated in a World War. Some time ago a Deputy Minister of England had to resign on this account. He had expressed such apprehensions during his visit to Germany, where he expressed certain views which were taken by the Germans to be the policy stance of the British Cabinet, although he had expressed them as his personal views. The British Cabinet confirmed that this was his personal opinion and even though he said that it was his honest opinion he was compelled to resign. But the matter does not end with this incident. Such voices are being raised repeatedly. Recently a British scholar, Mr. Anthony Burgis had appeared in a T.V. interview in Sweden. Probably, the report of the interview was published by the local papers also. He was introduced as a prominent British scholar who possessed a deep knowledge of Islam, and had vast and long-standing relations with some Muslim countries. It was stated that he had stayed in some Muslim countries for quite a long time, and had developed such a great desire to gain knowledge of Islam that it was feared that he might convert to Islam, but God saved him from this folly after the reality (of Islam) was dawned upon him. As if, narrowly escaping and coming back from the precipice. Now he was here and being presented as a great scholar who was fully conversant with the Muslim politics and possessed profound knowledge of Islam. So the real intention behind his returning to Europe and expressing his views on different occasions, was to paint a very dire and tyrannical picture of Islam, and that the gist of his message was that, today if there was any religion inimical to human rights and to the freedom of conscience, it was Islam, and that today the greatest danger to the world in the matter of freedom of conscience was from Islam. After having said this he at last spoke his mind on a question that is presently agitating the minds of the English people, that is, their apprehensions about the way Germany was going to rise as a great power. In this context, he forcefully stated that just as Germany's rise constitutes a great danger for Europe, so does Islam spell a great danger to the freedom of human conscience. On this occasion a member of the panel, who was a representative from Eastern Europe took a strong exception to his statement. While agreeing with his statements about Islam, the panel member found Mr. Burgis in error regarding Germany and maintained that Germany would pose no danger to anyone. He stressed that he understood the present generation fully and that this was merely a propaganda against them. In fact, it was not merely a matter of propaganda, rather it concerns human psychology. The nations who are basically selfish, and where the concept of justice rests on the type of nationality or is based on regional ideology, always keep their concepts of nationalism fluctuating and let them be guided by the expediency of their mutual dealings. But when confronted with other countries, then the Welsh, the Irish or the Scottish all merge and a wider British concept emerges. Similarly in the case of Germany, the *Bavarian concept* or any other German concepts are sidelined and a wider combined German concept surfaces in which all distinctions between the East German concepts and the West German concepts are vanished as do those of the north and the south. At this point, nationalism gradually transforms into racism. Racism, in the first place, spreads within its geographical boundaries. Then, instead of one nation, two or four nations get together at a common platform against two or four other nations. And when their collective interests clash with those of the rest of the world, the whole national ideology concept transforms into a racial doctrine. Then the confrontation starts between the white and the black and between the red and the yellow. In this process the dark complexioned people, like us, also get entangled into this situation and become victims of one prejudice or another. In such a situation the people of Indo-Pakistan sub-continent, now settled in America come to be looked upon as a separate nationality by the local Blacks and are labelled as colonists. So is the case with the white people. Similar dangers are looming large in the African continent where the Pakistani settlers have a somewhat fairer complexion compared to the locals, so they are also counted as aliens, as if they had gone there from outside to rule over them. In short, these prejudices which, in fact, are a product of a concept of nationalism, ultimately pass into hatred based on skin-colour.

Fourth Friday Sermon Aug 24, 1990

THE REAL NATURE OF THE DIFFERENCES BETWEEN USSR AND CHINA

The long-standing disputes between Russia and China are said to be mostly based on their divergent views on the ideology of Communism. That is to say, the concept of Communism in the Soviet Union is at variance with that of China. They disagree with each other in their philosophies of Communism. Their interpretations of the application of this concept are also far apart and, therefore, no common ground has developed between the two nations. But the fact of the matter is that, these differences are quite superficial. Their basic difference is that the people of Russia during its period of power and pomp had never tolerated that the yellow coloured nations of communist China should prevail upon the world. On the other hand, China was not prepared to tolerate that the white European Communists should have much to say in the matter of yellow coloured world. So, in fact, the real differences between them lay in their colour based jealousy, i.e. it was really a question of a yellow coloured nation versus a red or white race, but it surfaced in different forms before the world in the past, and its real face was never revealed. But the people who know their national psyche are aware that these disputes were actually not over Communism but it was a colour-based prejudice between the yellow complexioned China on one side and the white or red complexioned Russian on the other, which was fanning other minor differences. A situation of distrust which is a natural consequence of this, did develop. So these are fluid situations and these differences are likely to widen still further. These are the challenges which will have to be addressed by the Ahmadiyya Muslim Jamaat.

A DEEP-ROOTED AND DREADFUL CONSPIRACY AGAINST THE MUSLIMS

Now, once again, I prompt you for prayers for the general welfare of the people of Iraq, the Arabs and for the Muslims in general. I have already shed light, in detail, on this issue and need not repeat it. The new emerging situation indicates that the Western powers are totally caught up in the trap of an Israeli plan, and are now bent upon causing total destruction of the Iraqi power, and in the same momentum they want other Muslim states to be weakened and fragmented. They want this mission to be achieved covertly so as not to make it look like a confrontation between the Christians and the Muslims, or appear as a dispute between the Western nations and the Eastern nations. A plan has been drawn to drag Japan into this conflict. For this purpose a resolution is being put up in the Japanese Assembly to bring about an amendment to a special constitutional provision in Japan to facilitate its participation in the destruction of Iraq. This provision of non intervention was actually proposed by the Western nations for Japan and it binds Japan not to take part in any war away from its country and to not get involved in any military activity outside its own territorial boundaries. A similar law was promulgated for Germany but that has already been changed. This law was enforced in Japan so that the Japanese nation may never think of participating in any future world war.

So in pursuit of their animosity with the Muslims they are now involving Japan in this conflict to bring about a total annihilation and destruction of a rising Muslim power so that no one may be able to say that it was only a Western plot. In this way, neither the East and West would be divided, nor Islam and anti-Islamic division would appear. A few Arab states and some Muslim countries are also involved in it to create an impression that the East, the West, and the other world nations were allied together in this activity. Since Japan is a great economic power and its industrial interests are deeply linked with oil-producing countries, therefore they were apprehensive that if Japan stayed aloof then, in the aftermath of this war, if any feelings of hatred arose, the West would be the lone target of such resentments. It was for this purpose that Japan is being brought into the war. In short, Japan has been embroiled in it quite cunningly under a well prepared conspiracy.

THE ESSENCE OF THE GREAT CONSPIRACY

Conferences are being held in the Western countries and their scholars are expressing opinions which indicate that a dreadful conspiracy has been hatched to cause an immense damage, not only to the Muslim world, but also to some other Eastern countries; a situation as a result of which, many of these countries may not survive. For long, these countries would keep licking their wounds - not knowing what to do. In the first place, a big war is being thrust upon this area and it involves a huge cost. How would they defray such voluminous expenses of war? How would harm done to the industries in Europe and other Western countries due to the rising oil prices be rectified? How would all these losses be recouped? Seminars are being held in various countries to sort out these questions. I don't have their full details with me but whatever reports are reaching me, in bits and pieces, I am passing on to you for the sole purpose of prompting you for prayers.

In a nutshell, they are planning to recover these costs from the Muslim nations for which their agreement had been secured. All expenses of this war, would be billed to and received primarily from Saudi Arabia and partly from Kuwait and the other participant nations. Saudi Arabia would be specially pressurized to become the principal contributor. The wealth of Saudi Arabia is mostly in the hands of America, so there is no question of its running away from its commitments.

Secondly, as a result of the rise in oil prices, the losses sustained by the Western powers shall also be recompensed by the Muslim states and agreements to this effect have also been reached with, because this escalation in oil prices has taken place in consequence of the present conflict. One cannot say with certainty as to the exact nature of their agreements, but we have inferred it from the public speeches delivered by their scholars at various conferences, otherwise we do not have any direct proof. These statements have been published by the media to reassure their people that no harm would come to their economy, because they have secured the agreements in advance that, they will be reimbursed with the higher price of Oil that is caused by the war. In the present circumstances they cannot reduce the price, as this would then deprive the West of receiving higher price from the rest of the world. Therefore a formula has been worked out according to which, only a pre-determined Arab share of the profit out of the gross earnings would be remitted to them. As to their own profit earned from the escalation in oil prices, it would in any case accumulate in their own banks. It has also been decided that not only Kuwaiti territory shall be retrieved but the rising power of Saddam Hussein shall be destroyed by all means at their disposal. You may have heard of a new rumour that Iraq possesses not only the capability of waging a nuclear war but it also has the means of carrying out biological warfare and possesses a delivery system. It has further been said that it has developed a technology to spread the most dreadful germs to the other countries and that, at present, it is very difficult to counter such an eventuality. For example "Anthrax" is such a bacterium which can cause dreadful sours on the body, causes blood poisoning that result in a painful death. The fact of the matter is that the use of Anthrax as an instrument of war was initiated by the West, although it is being alleged that Iraq too has acquired this technology. Similar is the case with the germs of typhoid, cholera and many other diseases against which curative injections have been invented for long, yet the Western thinkers are propagating that Iraq would spread various types of chemicals and that it may not be possible to readily find out antidotes to such weapons.

As far as I know, such developments were never disclosed to the world until a few days ago, nor was it heard of Iraq having ever posed such a threat. But it appears that such rumours are aimed at winning over the world sympathies, and for this purpose, a propaganda campaign has been launched. Only God knows how far is it right or wrong, but their purpose seems to be to use it as a pretext for the total destruction of Iraq. Then later it could be explained that it was due to this horrifying Iraqi weaponry that we resorted to this deterrent action. When the allies talk of such plans, in Europe or in the Western hemisphere, assuring their people that they have secured agreements to this effect, they in fact do not divulge any secret. Rather, their intention is to propagate such things in justification of their nefarious plans. Because, if the Western people understood how tremendous a loss, a real war can cause to their industry and population, they would never permit their politicians to undertake this venture. Thus these are their constraints, and not any secrets which have now been divulged by a secret agent. In fact these are their devices to arouse the sentiments of their people and yet retain their unity. They, in fact mean to convey a message that they are fully prepared for this war and that in this operation, even a part of the Muslim world would be made to stand up against its own brethren. One cannot conceive a more horrifying idea than that of inflicting such a destruction. In this conspiracy many Muslim countries, including Pakistan, are being aligned to help the Western world and accept the full responsibility of their evil designs of causing destruction, and elimination of a rising Muslim power from the surface of the earth.

Fourth Friday Sermon Aug 24, 1990

APPEAL TO PRAY FOR THE WORLD OF ISLAM

We posses no weapon except the weapon of prayer, and I had earlier drawn the attention of the Community towards it. I am also praying and believe that you would also be remembering me in your prayers.

This danger is, in fact, for the whole Muslim world and that, it does not constitute an ordinary danger. It conceals a much greater catastrophe in the waiting. There will be other repercussions giving rise to further renewed racial ideologies. The future map of the world will take shape only after the present one is obliterated through complete destruction. There is still some time left before the formation of this new map. To counter these looming dangers effectively, if we remain steadfast - seeking help through prayers - exercising our mental abilities and with the commitment to give every sacrifice for the survival of Islam, then I can assure you that our prayers, coupled with our concerted efforts will bring about a positive change in the world. We, by the Grace of Allah, will never allow any conspiracy against Islam to succeed.

May Allah help us in our endeavour.   Amen

In the name of Allah, the Gracious, the Merciful

FIFTH FRIDAY SERMON

NOVEMBER 09, 1990

THE NEED TO OFFER SOLEMN AND HEART-RENDING PRAYERS

After reciting the Opening Chapter of the Holy Quran, Al-Fatiha, Hazoor said:

REMINDER TO PRAY FOR THE WELFARE OF THE MUSLIM WORLD

The situation which the Muslim world is currently faced with is a matter of grave concern to all Ahmadis, more so because the dangers continue to escalate rather than recede. As I had urged the Jamaat on many earlier occasions, to revert in supplications to Allah, I am again reminding all Ahmadis, through this Friday sermon, to offer prayers with solemnity, affection and deep concern that Allah may remove the dangers facing Islam and the Muslims. Although very ominous dark clouds are hovering over the Muslims, yet we believe that the decree of Allah can change the direction of these clouds. For the present, there seems to be no region in the world, where either directly or indirectly the Muslims do not feel threatened. In reality, the Muslims all over are totally ill-prepared to face up to such dangers. Nowhere in the world do we observe that the Muslims are countering these perils with the intelligence and foresight expected of them.

It is therefore our obligation that we advise, admonish and guide the Muslims; irrespective of whether anyone pays heed to our plea. It is our duty to render whatever advice is necessary - but we must not limit ourselves only to advice, because if such an advice is offered to ears which are not ready to listen; or placed before such eyes which are not inclined to perceive or to convey this message to such hearts which are sealed with the seal of stubbornness then whatever effort is made would never achieve the desired results. Therefore prayers are most essential to produce the desired effect of advice. Prayers areessential even to make your advice effective and meaningful and to

Fifth Friday Sermon Nov 9, 1990

beseech Allah to change the direction of attitude of the rest of the world.

Your prayers should be two pronged: Firstly, that Allah may create intelligent leadership among the Muslims and may grant foresight and wisdom to the Muslim leaders who now exercise authority, may He bless them with the incandescence of *Taqwa* (righteousness) and may He help them to appraise the present predicament. The second aspect of your prayers should be that Allah may turn the tide upon those external oppressors who are causing harm or are poised to attack Islam. Also that Allah may totally nullify and frustrate all sinister designs of the enemies of Islam from within who pose themselves as Muslims.

THE ARGUMENT PRESENTED AGAINST IRAQ

I now place before you, briefly, the current situation. In fact I had earlier thrown light on this subject from various angles in my previous addresses. As you are well aware that the present confrontation with Iraq is based on its occupation of Kuwait. I had mentioned one or two motives behind the mobilization of all world powers against Iraq. There are very deep diabolic motives which I shall elaborate later to reveal the real hands that control the reigns of these conspiracies.

Anyway, the gist of this conflict is that a Muslim country occupied an adjoining territory which it considers to be a part of its main-land which the British had severed from its parent body and then established an independent government therein. **This is the claim of Iraq.** In response, it is being argued that if today we allow a country to occupy a territory based on its belated historical claim, this would result in complete chaos and world peace would be seriously threatened. So we would, under no circumstances condone such vicious action. At the same time, the Western leaders are repeatedly dispelling this notion that they have a vested interest in the **Oil** wealth of this land.

They contend that if at all they have any interest, it is the peace of the world. Further, it is totally absurd to justify the occupation of a territory merely on an historical claim; they would never allow this to materialize.

THE HISTORIC DECEPTIONS OF THOSE PRESENTING THIS ARGUMENT

Now let us cast a cursory glance on the history of this region to find out what has been happening in the past and analyze the true nature of this dispute. In the world of Islam, the land of Palestine has always been reckoned as a Muslim territory. Now on a large part of this area, the state of Israel is now established and it continues to extend its territory creeping up to the West bank of the River Jordan. This was in fact a matter of historical dispute. Thousands of years earlier, this land was occupied by the Jews who had built synagogues there. So, to the Jews, this land had extraordinary importance. Keeping this ancient history in view, the Western powers have now changed the geography of this region. They showed extreme stubbornness and boldness. They paid no heed to the hues and cries of the Muslim nations and went ahead to establish the State of Israel in Palestinian land. Other nations stood up in support of the Muslim nations questioning the right of these Western powers to plunge into three or four thousand years of history and rekindle a splinter which had been buried in heaps of ash. What right have you, they asked, to accept this ancient claim and change the current geographical boundaries of the world? But the same world powers which are now ganged up and are poised to destroy Iraq, were the very powers that were once united on a self-styled principle that changes in geographical boundaries is an on-going process.

Cast a glance at the situation in Kashmir, in Junagharh or in Hyderabad Deccan (India), in fact, there are many such countries which can be cited as witnesses, where as a result of historical claims or even without any claims, geographical boundaries have been altered causing no agitation or threat to the political stability of the world. Non of the international political movements protested against these geographic alterations or cried before the world to join hands and restore the original boundaries.

PLUNDER OF THE AFRICAN CONTINENT

Not only this, but when we glance at the history of the African continent, even a more strange and frightful spectacle emerges. I will put before you some excerpts from a magazine called "The Plain Truth" stating as to which nations have the right to change the geography of the world and which nation do not have such a right. It writes:

"In November 1884, representatives of 13 European nations and the United States met in Berlin. Having partitioned out Africa among themselves, they agreed to respect each other's 'spheres of influence'. Soon only Ethiopia and Liberia remained independent nations." (The Plain Truth October 1990)

"In actuality the division of Africa was done with mainly European interests in mind ...... in most black African states south of the Sahara the standard of living is falling, the people hungry, bewildered and disillusioned. A part of the blame must be placed on the way the continent was, and is, divided. Only a divine power could reverse this tragedy peacefully."
(The Plain Truth October 1990)

This article in essence states the reasons for the assembly of 13 European nations and the U.S. in Berlin, i.e for the unfair division of Africa. As such, they shared among themselves the entire African Continent in such a way that certain portions came under the influence of one nation while others in the influence of other nations. In effect, all the European nations agreed to pick up the portions of their choice to be under their respective control and agreed not to interfere in the affairs and areas of influence of the others. This division was made for the sole benefit of the European states.

Details of this seizing and grabbing have been described in this article, and can as well be observed in the documented history. In short, while splitting the African Continent, the interest of the African nations was never once considered. Nations were divided neither on the basis of territorial jurisdiction, linguistic uniformity, nor on the basis of the peoples interests. Even their economic interests were not kept in mind, nor was it seen as to where the natural wealth or minerals were located. No consideration was given that certain states would become too small to be able to sustain themselves economically. It was not visualized either that certain states would become so large that as result of their sheer size, they could endanger and compromise the interests of the smaller neighbouring states. This is the gist of events we find in history, so beautifully described in this article. The entire African Continent was split-up into either smaller or bigger portions with the sole purpose of funnelling all wealth of this land, now and later, to the benefit of the people of the West. Most of the problems facing African nations, after their independence, have their roots in these unfair divisions. The concept of national unity gives rise to linguistic unity and then a person finds unacceptable such geographical barriers which conflict with linguistic boundaries. Then there is the problem of protracted historical animosities between various African tribes. Take the case of **Liberia** as an example, where serious bitterness exists between different tribes.

Such enmities not only exist within nations but are widespread over large territories. Some of such nations have been split up in such a way that stronger nations have established hegemony over comparatively weaker nations. In effect many such conflicts have emerged. Consequently the whole of Africa is in the grip of insecurity, mistrust and prejudice. No one has ever thought of eliminating these injustices, nor has anybody considered it to be of any importance. By now, the situation has deteriorated to such an extent that it is considered that even if all of these injustices are removed and Africa is divided all over again, the threat to the peace of this continent would far exceed the present dangers. This, as such, is the summary of the relationship between history and geography.

<u>NAIVE LOGIC OF THE WESTERN THINKERS</u>
Now when we revert to the case of the occupation of Kuwait by Iraq, it seems that, if a non-Muslim country occupies the territory of a Muslim country and thus changes the geography, it poses no danger to world peace. So to say, if a Western power or powers jointly alter the geography of a vast continent; wreck its economy and carry out such unfair and unjust divisions, turning it into a active volcano ready to erupt any moment - then such an action would pose no danger to world peace. On the contrary, if a Muslim country occupies the territory of another Muslim country, it threatens the peace of the whole world! This "threat to world peace", the Western powers contend, cannot be tolerated! This is their ultimate logic which we have been able to understand, after making this analysis.

This history is based on well known facts and is not such a thing that I have now discovered, or with whom the Muslim scholars or

Fifth Friday Sermon Nov 9, 1990

historians are unfamiliar. All the realities are wide open before them and yet they prefer to be oblivious. **Whatever is happening in the Middle East or is about to happen will hurt Islam and the Muslims, and all the gains will go to the non-Muslim states and non-Muslim religious powers.** The entire financial burden will be borne by the Muslim countries. This massive troop movement from one continent to the other, involves voluminous costs. It requires mountains of wealth; but these mountains are already piled up by Saudi Arabia and other Sheikdoms in the Western countries. These treasures will be transferred to them in a 'lawful' way abandoning all rights to this wealth, in reward for the total annihilation of an emerging Islamic country and thereby engraving in the minds of all Muslim nations that the very thought of an independent action, even for safeguarding their honour and self-respect would in future be considered a crime!

A FUTILE ATTEMPT TO ADVICE IRAQ

We tried our best to convince Iraq and sent them several messages through different channels saying that:
"for God's sake, for the sake of your own interests and for the sake of that Islamic cause which you claim to defend, retract these unjust steps, explaining that it in no more possible to alter the geographical boundaries on the pretext of historical support. It is now impossible to do so, even in Africa or for that matter in any other part of the world. As such, it is in your own interest; it is in the interest of Kuwait; in the interest of the entire Islamic world; that you withdraw your step and consolidate your strength and strive to unite the Islamic world."

But Alas!, no attention was paid to our advice. **The other Muslim Arab countries also failed to pay the least consideration to our plea. Little did they realise that they were acting in liaison with non- Muslim powers, bearing all the expenses of this cruel endeavour, to completely destroy and decimate a Muslim power, to entail elimination of peace for all times from this part of the world!** It is besides the point, whether the peace of the world is threatened, but I can say with certainty to these States which are about to bear the expense of this war and those who have brought in mercenaries, that they will never be able to return to their past. Their condition will deteriorate, from bad to worse and peace in this region will vanquish for all times to come.

Therefore, after offering all these advices, what else is our option, except to offer supplications to God. May God, The Almighty, have mercy on them and may He grant them wisdom. May He bless our advice, however insignificant it may appear to be, with Divine strength and thus incline their hearts to accept it. It is God alone, who can change these circumstances. How well this writer has projected his views:

"Only a divine power could reverse this tragedy peacefully".
(The Plain Truth October, 1990)

THE GEOGRAPHICAL CHANGE IN INDIA

Now let us consider the situation in India. Whatever happened there in the past is on records. What is currently happening in Kashmir is also a matter of concern, but the biggest tragedy is that, even in India an attempt is being made to bring about a geographical change on the pretext of historical claims. It is said that about four hundred years earlier, a temple in Ajodhiya known as **"The Temple of Rama"** was demolished by the Muslim Emperor Babar and a mosque called the **"Babri Masjid"** was erected in its place. The authenticity of this claim is still under investigation by an Indian court of law. It is said that a Muslim mystic once saw in a dream that the body of Rama, a Hindu deity, was buried under this mosque and hence it could be assumed that there must have been a Hindu temple at that site where this mosque now stands. As such, supposedly it is the place where Rama lies buried. This is a very old dream and on this reference, Hindus have attempted to strengthen their court case. They have also presented many other similar documents which in fact have no historical relevance. At any rate, for the present this is a matter under proceedings in an Indian court of law.

Regardless, whether or not this claim is true, if an attempt is made this day, to bring about a change based on a four hundred year history, it could only be considered valid, if it is based upon the same principles of the Western powers i.e, if it is initiated by non-Muslims, then it is perfectly legitimate but if it is attempted by Muslims then it

Fifth Friday Sermon Nov 9, 1990

becomes totally wrong. It was neither legitimate for Muslims then, nor is it now, to assign this building to themselves on this ground, but it becomes valid for the Hindus to change its occupancy and to change its geography on the pretext of historic references.

As such, today there is a grave threat to the Muslims in India but this danger is far substantial than those of a geographical nature in other regions. Here, the glory of Muslims and the unity of Islam is threatened, the glory of Almighty God and the unity of God is endangered.

At a place where ONE God was worshipped, might end up into a temple where idols, attributed to non-existent gods, would be worshipped. As such, to transform a place of worship of ONE God which is the emblem of the Unity of God, into places of idol-worship, is no minor an incident, for it is an attack on the very foundation of Islam. The reverberations of this act would be far and wide in India. As a result, the fragile peace for the Muslims in India would disappear and a series of terrible, uncontrollable riots would ensue. In any event, this a very extraordinary and highly sentimental matter pertaining to our faith, which the Islamic world must understand, but any counteraction must be compatible with the Islamic traditions.

I am pained to observe that, the sequence of events in this incident are similar to the ones prevailing in Iraq. As a result of the attacks on the Babri Mosque by many thousands of Hindus, and their entry into the premises, and the worship of a deity already installed there; some Muslim fanatics in Bangladesh destroyed and burnt down many Hindu temples, killed and looted their properties. *Is this an Islamic reaction? Certainly not.* It is impossible to declare such a reaction justified on the basis of Islamic teachings. Islam stands to protect the glory and sanctity of all religions of the world. Protection and sanctity, not in the sense of bowing down before them in matters of faith but in the sense of legally protecting the adherents of those religions. Because they are at liberty to consider anything glorified to their reckoning, however false it may be in reality. Islam safeguards the sanctity of all religions in such a way, that a Muslim is not allowed to desecrate the places of worship of others even with the aim of building a Mosque or for any purpose whatsoever.

HAPPENING IN INDIA ARE A REACTION OF INJUSTICES IN PAKISTAN

Whatever is happening in India is in fact a reaction to some of the incidents which have taken place in Pakistan. The way, there was a reaction in Bangladesh and in parts of Sind, as a result of happenings in India, on the same analogy the Indians justify that whatever they are doing in India is no different from what happens in Pakistan. The Hindus contend that in Pakistan also, the fanatic Mullah claims to wield his influence on others in the name of religion. On this plea, the Hindu extremists in India say that if the Mullah of Pakistan has the right to suppress the human rights of those who, according to him, are non-Muslims then why can't the Hindu faith allow us to suppress the basic rights of all Muslims for the sake of the Hindu religion and its glory. On one such occasion, during the last elections, one Hindu leader had announced that he would advice the Muslims that if they need to survive in India, they should bow down their heads in complete submission to the Hindu religion or else pack-up and leave this country. In other words there was now, no place for Muslims in India! This statement is identical to the one made by the Pakistan Mullah against the Ahmadi Muslims. But there is one difference which makes the declaration by the Pakistani Mullah even more unreasonable. In India, it was a Hindu leader who passed a verdict, though totally unreasonable, but it was against non-Hindus. However unfair be this statement, but there appears some fairness of their principle, in stating openly their feelings about non-Hindus. They did not make their views mandatory upon the people who called themselves Hindus. They passed such remarks upon Muslims who obviously have nothing in common with the Hindus.

But the high-handedness and unfairness in Pakistan was a step further. In Pakistan, those who would sacrifice their lives for Islam, who would swear allegiance to the Holy Prophet Muhammad[sas], recite the **Kalima**(declaration) of the Unity of God and apostleship of Muhammad[sas], have been declared non-Muslims by law, and then subjected to such extreme oppression which are totally forbidden in Islam. But since they did it after unilaterally declaring Ahmadi Muslims as "non-Muslims", the non-Muslim world got the excuse that if the Mullah of Pakistan can use, a so-called, Islamic injunction to mistreat others whom they consider non-Muslims, then why can't the non-Muslims (e.g. the Hindus) treat the Muslims in India or

Fifth Friday Sermon Nov 9, 1990

elsewhere in the same manner. In Pakistan, the mosques of Ahmadi Muslims were demolished and people of all the four Provinces of Pakistan had witnessed this spectacle. The places of worship (Mosques) of the ONE and the only God, where the Ahmadi Muslims used to gather five times a day to worship their Creator, were demolished and rendered desolate - where the recitation of the Kalima (Declaration) of God's Unity by Ahmadi Muslims was declared tantamount to "hurting their feelings" - at that point, why did they not consider that such an action may invoke the wrath of Allah and punish them for this cruelty in God's own way and thus unveil before them, their own dirty conduct by paying them back in their own coins.

Therefore, the foundations of the unfortunate happenings in India, and the cruelty to which the Muslims of that country are being exposed, were actually laid by the Mullah of Pakistan! The Mullah is the real culprit who will ultimately be answerable to God. You will behold that, a day will come, in this world as well, when this Mullah will be apprehended because of his injustice and cruelty. If he does not repent, he is bound to stand condemned and humiliated on the Day of Judgment.

As such, whatever is happening in Pakistan, has its repercussions on other parts of the world and similarly what happens in one region of the world reflects on the other regions as well. Incidents happening in the non-Muslim world are bound to affect the Muslim world and *vice versa*. So in essence, this world is not formed of islands which remain separated from each other. The reverberations of actions in one area are bound to have a reaction in other areas, resembling waves of the ocean. Cruelty begets cruelty.

Therefore, if justice has to be established in the world and indeed, we have to establish it, then we shall have to stand up against such cruelties, we shall have to wage a **holy-war** to establish justice, peace and truth on this earth - The Holy Prophet Muhammad[sas] has said:

اُنْصُرْ اَخَاكَ ظَالِمًا اَوْ مَظْلُوْمًا

"Help your brother, whether he be the oppressor or the oppressed" When asked, 'O Prophet of God, we understand that we have to support our oppressed brother, but how do we support the brother who is the oppressor?' The Prophet replied : "support him by stopping his hands from cruelty." Therefore, whenever, the Muslims countries have shown this reaction and have done such detestable things in the name of Islam or have destroyed and looted the Hindu temples, it is our duty to stop them from committing this cruelty and that would be the way to 'support' them. Wherever, or whenever the Muslims are oppressed or are being subjected to injustices by others, to help them in any possible way is the true teachings of Islam, as taught to us by the Holy Prophet[sas]. Therefore, the Ahmadi Muslims should be in readiness to 'fight' in this holy-war on both these fronts!

VALIANT STAND OF MR. V.P. SINGH

In the first place, a correct reaction from all Muslims countries should have been, to get prepared to safeguard the places of worship of other religions and should have learnt a lesson from the former Prime Minister of India, Mr. V.P. Singh, a great leader, who though no longer in power, yet it is only fair to praise his truthfulness. It is a great misfortune for India, indeed a historical misfortune, that it has lost the leadership of this great statesman who could have restored to them their past glory. In the present world, a nation cannot hope for a better leader than the one, who is unbiased and is willing to sacrifice his own interests for the sake of his principles. For two reasons I have a great respect for Mr V.P. Singh and I prayed that God may cause other leaders of the world to become fair minded like him. Firstly, he stood up all alone for hundreds of thousands of oppressed people, the so-called **"Untouchables"** and challenged the opposition and even the whips of his own political party opposed to this stand, and he passed a law in the whole country safeguarding their interests and creating jobs for the "Untouchables", who were subjected to injustices for thousands of years. He earmarked a percentage in accordance with their numerical ratio, and so jobs were reserved by the government for these "Untouchables". This was indeed, an exceptionally bold step, worthy of praise, especially in a country like India, which has been dominated by the higher castes for a long period, where even their religion proclaims that the "higher-caste" Hindus have dominant rights, thereby, practically denying any rights for the "lower-castes". This type of boldness by a politician was a rare example. Besides this,

Fifth Friday Sermon Nov 9, 1990

when serious protests erupted as a result of his stand, he bravely stood up to this pressure in support of his stand, caring the least, even if this would cost him to loose power. This noise had hardly died down, when those who were previously conspiring against him, started to drum up the issue of the **Babri Mosque**. Hundreds of thousands of Hindus got prepared to march towards the Babri Mosque to destroy it and to reconstruct in its place, the historic or otherwise Temple of Rama. It is not an ordinary thing to face such a huge challenge and to persuade the army which is Hindu-dominated that even if people belonging to their own religion attempted to forcibly invade the Mosque premises they must be fired upon, and that the sanctity of the mosque and the sanctity of the laws of India be safeguarded at all costs. Undoubtedly, many Hindus got killed in their efforts to occupy the mosque at the very hands of the Hindu army, many were roughed up at the hands of the Hindu police, in addition many were injured and imprisoned. Their militant Hindu leader supporting the intruders, who is quite powerful and with whose help and cooperation the government was in power, was imprisoned. As such, knowing full well that, he was cutting the very branch on which he was perching, this great leader accepted this fall from his high office, not because of any idiocy on his part but solely out of sheer greatness and bravery to uphold his principle. He cared the least, even if this political set-back would seal his political career for good.

THE NEED AND IMPORTANCE OF A PIOUS REACTION BY MUSLIMS

Islam teaches us to recognise and laud all such leaders, wherever they may be, who remain ready to offer such valiant sacrifices in the cause of justice. The Holy Quran states:

$$\text{تَعَاوَنُوْا عَلَى الْبِرِّ وَالتَّقْوٰى}$$

"Cooperate with one another in acts of goodness and righteousness"

In this Quranic injunction, religion is not made the criterion for cooperation, rather, it is justice, righteousness and good deeds. Only the future will tell, as to how much the Indian nation learns from such incidents and upto what extent they possess the ability to distinguish between their real friends and foes. The Islamic world should have been grateful for the efforts of Mr Singh. The Islamic world, instead of criticising the Indian government in vain, should have encouraged and strengthened his bold stand. They should have proclaimed that although we do not accept this cruelty by Hindu extremists, yet we support in every possible way those Indian leaders who, in spite of their political weakness, have stood up for a justifiable settlement of this issue. This is the voice of justice, which in fact, is the true voice of Islam. Regarding the threats of some Muslim countries, it must be remembered that no sensible nation is scared of such hollow threats. Instead, all Muslim countries should have consulted and sent firm messages to the government of India, stating that its vital interests are hinged on good relations with the Islamic countries, and if they allow this sort of thing to happen, their own interests would be jeopardised. Economic boycott with an aggressor nation does not negate the principle of honesty. So to say, there are a number of diplomatic ways to discipline an aggressor, and an economic boycott would have been a legitimate weapon to stop this injustice. If, in Kuwait alone, five hundred thousand Indian workers were forced to return to their homeland abandoning their economic interests, you can well imagine how many Hindu and Indian interests would be in the whole Islamic world. The present economic situation in India could not, at any cost, sustain such huge economic pressure. In that case, any government by any name, would have been forced, to respect the Islamic sanctuaries.

As such, abandoning a fair and legitimate method of redress, and to resort to the burning down of temples in order to defame and tarnish the religion of Islam, and to create a precedence as if, it makes no difference to demolish someone's place of worship is totally wrong and un-acceptable. If demolishing of other temples makes no difference, then what difference would the destruction of one mosque in India make? In essence, these are such matters which can only be resolved by reverting to the Islamic principles and judging with the light of righteousness. The Islamic world, instead of exhibiting an ignorant and sentimental reaction, should have reacted purely on the basis of righteousness, which would have carried moral strength, and instead of bringing a bad name to Islam, would have helped restore the glory of Islam.

Fifth Friday Sermon Nov 9, 1990

GOD AND HIS APOSTLES WILL EVENTUALLY PREVAIL

Regarding the present government in Pakistan, many Ahmadis seem to be worried and write letters to me expressing concern that the present government is composed of elements which were, and are the bitter antagonists of Ahmadiyyat. But the government leaders who are at the helm of affairs have a different claim. The fact is that, when this new government took control and the authority came in their hands, misgivings and dangers were expressed from many quarters, but the leaders gave the assurance that they were gentlemen. They promised to reciprocate decent behaviour and reassured all law-abiding citizens that they had nothing to fear. On the other hand, the Ahmadis were listening to another voice, and that was the voice of the Mullah, who was, as if saying 'do not be misled by the voice of the government. No matter, whoever has the apparent power, but the real power and the ability of exercising oppression continues to be in our hand. We possess the ability to use the sword to swipe off the neck of anybody we choose. This sword is now in our hands." It seems that the Ahmadis heard this message and perceived many apprehensions in their hearts. They nurtured numerous fears and scepticism, and at the moment, this appears to be their thinking.

I wish to remind them of an incident in the life of the Holy Prophet Muhammad[sas] which serves as an excellent gist of the advice I wish to give. During one campaign, the Holy Prophet[sas] was separated from his companions and was resting under the shade of a tree. He was awakened by the shout of an enemy who had managed to sneak up to the spot where the Prophet was resting. He grabbed the Prophet's sword and brandishing it over his head, enquired: "O' Muhammad! Who can save you from my sword now?" The Prophet remained in his reclining position and replied with impeccable confidence: *"My Allah"*. **What an excellent reply! The Holy Prophet's reply to this opponent, is the one, and only reply, to all such challenges and trials that may befall humanity till the end of days.** Believers will continue to give this reply to all tyrants. If a believer does not give this answer, then there is no guarantee of his survival on this earth. So, do not look at the hands which have a grip of the sword today, rather fix your eyes on that God, in whose control, those hands are. Watch that Divine Power, controlling those shoulders which brandish the sword at your head.

Our opponents think that their sword will be the first to smite, but our Lord is aware, and indeed He is our witness, that the wrath of Allah will always precede their intended swipe. Such hands that rise today, or may rise in future, with the ill intention of wiping out Ahmadiyyat from the surface of the earth, will themselves be paralysed. No power will ever alter this decree of Allah. Many obstacles will be encountered and many trials will come, so says the Holy Quran. You will be confronted with various types of spiritual and emotional shocks, but if you remain steadfast and cling to this response of the Holy Prophet Muhammad[sas] with trust and absolute sincerity and challenge the opponent saying: O' my adversary who stands poised with the sword, remember that just as my God, in the past, shielded and protected Godly men from the evil of your sword, do not forget that even today, That God is a Living God. We swear by the name of His Majesty that the same God will deliver us from your oppression and cruelty. Therefore, if some members of the Ahmadiyya Muslim Community have been pained by the threats of our opponents, I have been equally distressed by the reaction of some Ahmadis who consider that God-forbid the sword of oppression has been handed over to such hands which will eventually end-up by destroying Ahmadiyyat. I swear to God, this will never happen! The opposition of such tyrants has always resulted in the progress of Ahmadiyyat, opening new vistas of advancement. The last eleven years of **Zia-ul-Haq**'s tyrannical rule were such that he endured every moment of this period in extreme anguish and frustration and could not stem the progress of Ahmadiyyat in the world, and later bid farewell to this world, in total ignominy, failure and disappointment. Thus, how can your faith fluctuate with the swapping of swords. Guard your faith and exhibit steadfastness. Put your trust in God and have firm faith that, that God who has vowed that **He, and His apostles will eventually prevail**, will see to it that He and His apostles prevail - they will certainly prevail - will certainly prevail - will certainly prevail!

In the name of Allah, the Gracious, the Merciful

SIXTH FRIDAY SERMON

NOVEMBER 16, 1990

THE GREATEST DANGER FACING MANKIND TODAY

After reciting the Opening Chapter of the Holy Quran, Al-Fatiha, Hazoor said:

PREJUDICES AND SELFISHNESS

The greatest threat to world peace today emanates from prejudices and selfishness, which, unfortunately, reigns over the minds of most of the politicians of the world. A politician, whether from the East or the West, white or black, generally coordinates his politics with his cunning moves in such a way that the question of tangibility of moral values and politics does not arise. It is only Islam where politics is free of deceptive moves and that is what constitutes true Islamic politics. Otherwise to profess that Islam is our faith and our politics and then to detach political values from Islamic values is inconsistent. At the moment, the ideal system of Islamic politics is not seen anywhere in the world. The mode of politics is the same in countries that are Islamic and in those that are non-Islamic, and selfishness is ruling politics. Prejudices, as opposed to principles, are ruling it. As such, the greatest threat to the world is from prejudice and selfishness.

At the start of the new revolutionary period of peace between Soviet Union and America the politicians of the world looked at the future with great hope. They started to say that now a new period of peace had begun. In actuality, this is a thought found only in dreams; in ignorant dreams. There have been certain benefits as a result of these revolutionary changes. However, there have also been certain setbacks and among the setbacks, the greatest one is that as a result of the ideological division of the East and the West, the prejudices that were hitherto suppressed, have now emerged before us in clear terms.

Sixth Friday Sermon Nov 16, 1990

Day by day, they are going to become more manifest and are going to create a variety of threats in different regions. When great dangers are faced, and the world is divided between two large blocks, smaller dangers either disappear under the shadow of the greater dangers or get suppressed. Similar is the case of illnesses. When one is suffering a major illness, minor illnesses do not develop and the entire attention of the body is directed toward the major illness.

Therefore, the dangers which have now arisen for mankind, are so widespread and so dreadful that if we do not analyze them at length and do not begin a holy-war against them, right from today, and live with the deception that we are being ushered into a cradle of peace, will be totally erroneous. In fact it will be tantamount to jumping into the fire; blind-fold! I want to put a few examples before you so that the Ahmadiyya Muslim Communities located in every country, convey these messages to the intelligentsia and try to explain to them. The members of the Ahmadiyya Muslim Community should exert moral pressure on them as far as possible, so that the intelligentsia would raise their voice against these dangers in their respective countries. They would thus enlighten the public in their countries and alert the masses as to the kind of dangers facing the world of today. If today, the world pays no attention to these dangers; tomorrow it might be too late! That which has come to light, quite clearly, in the Iraqi dispute is not that the whole world has become united against aggression. Rather, it is only being presented before the world in such a way, so that it would appear that as a result of peace between Soviet Union and America or as a result of the coming closer of the two blocks, the whole world is now taking notice of such dangers and that wherever world peace is threatened the entire world will unite to face this threat. This is not at all correct.

I will put before you, examples of some of the dangers which are far more dreadful than the Iraqi situation and which are facing the world. They are not only closing their eyes to these dangers but have been keeping their eyes closed for a long time. They will keep their eyes closed in future also, until such time when the selfish interest of some nations will force these nations to divert their attention to these dangers.

There are nationalist and racial dangers and the dangers of the linguistic differences as well as of the religion and historical disputes and there are many other similar areas in which we can catalogue the various dangers. When we consider these examples, we are amazed to see how explosive and how volcanic these issues are. They remain buried in various places and they can be resurrected at any time. I will put a few examples before you.

Religious and political dangers in India is one example. First of all, the **Sikh nation** has adopted a separate identity on the basis of religion demanding separation from other nations in India. This demand is somewhat similar to the one having to do with the concept of the creation of Pakistan. It was not purely a political demand. Rather, religion and politics together created prejudice and as a result of it, a tendency was developed for separation from other nations. On the contrary prejudices have also emerged to suppress this demand. Neither side in this conflict has asked that we should put our heads together and should settle these differences in the light of justice and see as to what extent these matters should be subservient to the demands of justice. If the Sikhs are in fact faced with threats then these threats should be removed. But the same voice is being heard from both sides. The Sikhs say that we face a danger in living in India and living in India will destroy our religious and national identity; India says that if we accept this demand, the country will then become fragmented into factions to such an extent that there will be no stopping it. Both voices appear to carry a lot of weight but as I have said, if you look for the ultimate cause, you will see that there is selfishness and prejudice on both sides. Prejudices have played a major role in the way India has treated the minorities since partition of the country. Hindus are in a large majority and despite the fact that the State of India was not established on the basis of religion, Hindus have adopted a nationhood and because of their large numbers and majority, the power is in their hands and the smaller nations do not share that power. All the authority for decisions have remained entirely in the hands of the Hindus. Even if they continue to call India a secular state, the fact remains the same. These powers (of decision making) have not only remained in the hands of the Hindus but in the hands of only one cast of the Hindus, known as the **Brahmins** or the higher caste. These are the prejudices which have then given birth to further disputes. Fundamentally, politics was at work but prejudices were buried under that apparent foundation. This

Sixth Friday Sermon Nov 16, 1990

was bound to make the edifice crooked as it was being built on prejudices. As such, many of the dangers which we see in India today, the ultimate cause of them is prejudice. The tendency is to make decisions away from justice and on the basis of selfishness. For instance you can see the differences which have now begun to develop between the Muslims and the Hindus in which deep rifts have developed. Its basis, according to the Hindus, is the prejudices of the Muslims, while the Muslims claim quite the converse. Similarly, the dangers which are arising because of the linguistic differences in India, are due to prejudices as well.

South India is developing a feeling of deprivation, in that the races living in the north of India who are more familiar with the Hindi language, or have some knowledge of Sanskrit, are ruling all of India, and are not treating with fairness those who speak one of the other 1500 languages spoken in India. Thus selfishness and prejudice is apparent behind all the divisiveness in India. It may have different names. In some places linguistic conflicts are seen, in other places religious and national conflicts are seen while in still others, racial conflicts and the conflicts of castes are seen. For instance, the lower caste Hindus have been a target of oppression by upper caste Hindus for thousands of years and they are being ground in the mill of atrocities. They have never been able to gain any human respect. It is such an unjust treatment, but there is such a psychological and ideological division that the lower castes are not considered worthy of any human dignity. **The government of V.P. Singh which has recently collapsed and the reason of its collapse, in essence, was that he had raised voice against these prejudices; he had hoisted a banner in support of justice.** Despite the fact that he belonged to the higher caste of the **Rajputs**, he started a great movement to restore the rights of the minorities. Similarly, he protected the sanctity of the Muslim religion. In short, the strife which has now started in India (you will hear different names for it, and the different names will be based on various kinds of differences), is due to lack of justice and due to the height of prejudice. It is this fundamental reality which is emerging as a danger for the whole of India and this danger is increasing by the day.

In a country like **Britain** which at the close of 20th century is regarded as being among the distinguished developed nations of the world, prejudices have been at work until this day and its politics has not been able to free itself from prejudices. In **Ireland**, religious prejudice mixed with politics is showing its true colours. Despite the fact that the historical practice of colonialism appears to have ended, it is still being practised. The rule of the British may have shrunk and is now practically confined to its own territory but the economical muscle and political influence stretches throughout, in many places of the world. This prejudice gives them the feeling that they have the right to rule the world and to rule its economy and its geography and to control the making and breaking of the relations with other countries. This attitude is showing its effect and they still consider that the smaller countries should not have the final and full authority about their foreign policy but in fact Britain should formulate their foreign policy. On the surface, the world does not observe any desire on the part of the developed nations to exercise any influence on the developing countries but in reality they have a strong urge to dictate the fundamental and major foreign policies to the smaller nations. This is the time when smaller nations realize that their foreign policies are not independent. What happens in practice is that, the stronger nations formulate the foreign policy of the smaller nations in such a way that they draw certain lines for the smaller nations. If these smaller nations develop contact with other nations or make changes in their policy while remaining within those "boundaries", then there is no objection but as soon as they venture to cross those lines, these developed nations find some pretext to interfere in their policies. Thus, they are not allowed to follow any independent policy.

DANGERS OF RACIAL PREJUDICES IN RUSSIA

For instance in the way of racial prejudices at the moment, we can see many kinds of dangers in the Soviet Union. Turkish nation is now passing through such a historic period from the racial prejudice that new thoughts and new hopes are being born among it. The fact is that this nation is likely to take certain steps in the next few years which could result in significant worldwide changes, or it might as well have an impact on world peace. In the last sermon I had said that the majority of the Turks live outside Turkey and that more than half of them live in the Soviet Union. As such the number of Turks living in Turkey is 44,000,000 and in the Soviet Union they are 42,000,000. Similarly, in China there are 7,000,000. Therefore the total number of Turks living in those two communist countries is more than those living in Turkey. But they are not sentimentally affiliated with their countries of residence. Rather, they are inclined towards Turkey itself. Turkey is also watching them and inclined towards them. When I toured Portugal and Spain, the Ambassadors of Bulgaria in both those countries wished to see me. During my talk with them, I learnt that both were apprehensive of a danger from Turkey. Upon further research, I realized that they were fearful of Turkey, because of the past excesses committed against the Turkish people. Now that they do not have the protection of the Soviet Union, they fear that they will be left at the mercy of Turkey; and the Turkish nation will extract its historical revenge against them. At that time I did not know much about this subject but when I returned from my tour and investigated further, I understood the reason of the worry of Bulgaria. In 1989 i.e., last year, Bulgaria committed such atrocities against the Turks living there, that within one year three hundred thousand immigrated from Bulgaria to Turkey. As such, not only the national prejudices exist at the present time but they are escalating as a result of the revolutionary changes in the Soviet Union.

It will indeed be an extremely ignorant man who says that the world has entered a period of peace and the danger of wars has disappeared. In fact, these suppressed dangers are only now raising their head. Similarly, there are old enmities between Armenia and Turkey and also between Armenia and Azarbaijan, a state in the Soviet Union. There have been historical conflicts between them. The Turks who live in the Soviet Union also have differences between themselves. Uzbic Turks are demanding a separate identity from the rest of the Turks. They fear that if they are lumped together with the rest of the Turks, they will lose their identity and will be overwhelmed by the other Turks. For long, there have been fights with continuing conflicts between **Uzbekistan** and the adjoining Turkish States.

THE DEPLORABLE CONDITIONS IN AFRICA

As far as the racial prejudices are concerned, we should now look at Africa. In fact whatever conflicts and dangers exist in Africa, their background, as I had mentioned in my previous sermon, is the past colonial rule of the Western nations in Africa which took various shapes and divided the African nations. People who spoke common language were divided. Tribes were divided in such a way that instead of down playing them, the differences were made to emerge more prominently. Previously as a result of hostility between the Soviet Union and America some nations had gained protection against other nations. Now, this protection cannot continue so that after a time their internal conflicts will start to surface. Whatever has happened in Liberia is in actual fact due to the above mentioned reasons. Previously, the Western nations were keenly interested in Liberia and had thus kept Liberia's national differences under some control but when the tension between Soviet Union and America ended, those dangers suddenly re-emerged. Now, in the name of democracy, voices are being raised to install a multi-party system throughout Africa. So, from the point of view of politics also, Africa is facing many dangers. By politics I mean the type of political system that would finally take shape there. From this point of view and with regard to the boundary differences and unfortunately from the religious point of view as well, they face many kinds of dangers. The difficulty is that no collective attempt has been made so far to eliminate those dangers. From this, one can conclude that when the Western nations say that they have united the whole world and made them aware of the danger of Iraq, and that it is a splendid achievement for the protection of world peace, they are talking about unreal things and are making false claims which have no truth. All these dangers which I have put before you constitute only a few examples. There are untold dangers which are buried in various places like Volcanic material. Some are giving out hissing sounds and are, as if, ready to explode. Some will eventually explode after a while. But the divisions which are national, linguistics, and religious are all, but ready to play their lethal hand. I will put a few more examples before you.

SOME FURTHER EXAMPLES OF NATIONAL PREJUDICES
The old enmity between the Greek and Turkish nations, had been suppressed because of **NATO** (North Atlantic Treaty Organization). Since Greece was a Western country and Turkey was also a member of NATO as one of its region is in Europe, the interest of the Western

Sixth Friday Sermon Nov 16, 1990

nations demanded that as long as the threat of the Soviet Union remained, these two countries ought not be allowed to fight one another. These dangers did not come to an end but for a time they were ignored because of other immediate concerns. Similarly I have mentioned Armenia to you. In India there are linguistic quarrels. In Sri Lanka there are serious quarrels because of linguistic and national differences. With regard to "racial superiority", the whole world faces the same danger from the Jews today, as it has faced for thousands of years. On surface, the Jewish nation is performing a front line role in erasing the concept of racial superiority from the world. The Jews are doing a lot of propaganda in the world that we should erase the racial divisions and the racial prejudices. This is being done merely because the Jews are afraid that some nation may make the Jewish nation the target of their wrath in the name of racism. **But as far as the concept of superiority of Jews over other races is concerned, this concept is in no way less than the Nazi concept of Hitler.** I have studied their historical literature, not merely their contemporary literature. From ancient times, from the time of the Prophet David[as], we find material in their literature as though this nation was created to overwhelm the world and enslave it and until the whole world is not brought under the Jewish rule, peace cannot be achieved. *They also talk of peace but a peace according to their own definition.* From the point of view of the rest of world, however, it appears as tyranny and oppression! Similarly the concept of superiority is showing its effect in America even today. Although as far as the legal protection is concerned the blacks of America have been given equality with the whites but the racial prejudices do not get eliminated as a result of such laws. Whatever laws there may be, the racial prejudices have their own *"law"* which continues to operate and overwhelm the rest of the laws. Whatever the present situation of the black people might be in America, to consider them equal to the whites, will be the height of insanity. They do not have equality in any respect. They have become so backward in every way and have been so oppressed that it is giving rise to hatred. When I visited America, some one said to me that your Community is spreading rather slowly among the black people while some other Muslim sects are becoming popular among these people quite rapidly. Why don't you adopt similar tactics. I said to them that I have come here to launch a holy-war against the methods which ignite hidden hatred in the name of religion thus transforming these cinders into flames. This may suit the temperament of some sects. If Ahmadiyyat starts preaching hatred, taking advantage of their inferiority complex and fanning these cinders into flames, then the Ahmadiyya Muslim Community which is an organised Community, can out-class all other Communities in the field. The Ahmadiyya Muslim Community can then win-over all the blacks in America within ten to fifteen years. **But we do not need a victory of numbers, we do not care for such a victory of numbers, as a result of which nations hate other nations and peace transforms into flames of war. The concept of our Community is totally different. If we do not triumph today we may triumph after 200 years, 400 years or after 1000 years but we will achieve a victory on the pattern of the victory of the Holy Prophet Muhammad^{sas}. A victory of his morals, a victory of his teaching, and that of the Holy Quran. Such is the only victory which carries respect and value in our heart. The rest of the victories are of injustice, cruelty and of satanic powers. We have no interest in such victories. Rather we have been raised to oppose them and to confront them.**

So, these racial prejudices are found in America, in the North as well as in the South and as far as the Red Indians of America are concerned, they have practically been eliminated from the surface of the earth. However, in South America, Red Indians still exist in very large numbers. They are being oppressed in such a way and their rights are being violated in such a way that day by day they are getting more and more inclined toward violence. Movements which intend to take revenge, are rising among them as a result of which either today or tomorrow there will be explosive outcries. As a result of these tendencies they explode bombs in various places taking the life of innocent citizens and disturbing public peace. No matter how much you condemn it and speak against it, as an outsider you will not be able to solve these problems with large scale condemnations and criticism. You will not achieve anything as long as you do not pay attention to the causes which develop these tendencies. As such, the dangers which exist because of the racial divisions, are spread far and wide in the world. Take for instance **Yugoslavia** which has six federal republics and each one of them is feeling restless with the others and is trying to distance itself from the others. Two of the republics are independent; two other republics follow catholic beliefs and despite a long rule of Communism, Catholicism is still very strong. It does exist as a political force but we don't know how far it exists as a religion. **Slovenia and Croatia** are the two large republics which are the wealthiest. Their preference to be separate independent states is becoming quite evident. In the south there is the **Muslim province of Serbia**, and similarly there is another province of **Kosoro Metohija**. The regions that are Albanian speaking have a large majority of Muslims. In these regions, religion plus nationalism and the past oppression is creating a feeling of independence, and movements toward this objective are starting there. The central government of Yugoslavia is presently facing such threats from these Muslim regions that they are putting an ever greater restriction on them and making it more difficult for the foreigners to visit these regions. In other areas where there is comparatively more freedom, we recently sent a delegation to take part in a book fair. The members of our delegation told us that they could not go to the Muslim areas. They could only develop contacts in other areas where there are fewer Muslims. The reason is that they are putting a lot of restrictions in these areas.

In Spain, as a result of regional tensions, bomb explosions are going on for a long time and these conflicts have taken the shape of a running sore which is continuously festering like the running sore of Ireland.

Then there are international boundary conflicts. Also there are such conflicts in which some nations have occupied other nations, and have absorbed them in their own territory. Even if we do not touch upon the old historical disputes and look only at the recent events, we find that there is a potential danger to world peace from these conflicts.

OCCUPATION OF TIBET BY CHINA/ OCCUPATION OF KUWAIT BY IRAQ

There is the situation regarding the occupation of Tibet by China. China has occupied Tibet by force. India made a lot of noise and tried to force China out of Tibet, but the superior strength of China did not allow the Indian moves to succeed. If the pictures of Tibet which are shown here on television, are true, and are not just propaganda, then the Chinese have also committed many atrocities against the Tibetan nation.

Now if you reflect and ponder, if Iraq occupies Kuwait, then why don't they compare this occupation with the Chinese occupation of Tibet. The fact is that in the case of Tibet there are national differences, racial and religious differences, as well as many other differences which have been trampled upon and a nation has been crushed. Here is a Muslim country which has occupied a neighbouring state on the basis that in practice, there is no difference between them. They are both Arabs and Muslims but historically, (and it is not a very old history either) Kuwait was a part of Iraq and the British government had sliced it off and separated it. I am not advising here that these old graves should be dug up, all I am showing is that the uniting together of mankind against Iraq, is not based on any righteousness or on the principles of justice. When Israel occupied the West Bank of Jordan River, no one paid any attention and no one thinks that this action poses a great threat to the world peace.

THE RULE OF SELFISHNESS ON THE WORLD

So it is only selfishness which rules the world today and it is the selfishness which creates dangers. The strong and bigger nations are inclined to suppress many a danger for the sake of their political gains. They take enjoyment in the thoughts that if such and such person or such and such leader or nation acts against our interests then we will incite the latent danger in that region and will unleash the volcanic material to teach them a lesson for such actions.

Now you can see that when Iran treated America unfairly, The Ahmadiyya Muslim Community which is based on justice did not support Iran or its occupation of the American Embassy and the seizing of their diplomatic personnel. The sanctity established for the Ambassadors by the Holy Prophet Muhammad[sas] and the splendid teaching which he has given in this regard, is such that it does not behove any Muslim country to ignore these teachings. Therefore we never supported them. But it is wrong to think that it was a one sided oppression. For a long time America, through the Shah, had unleashed atrocities against the people of Iran and had made them a target of such cruelty and oppression that one's mental balance can be

Sixth Friday Sermon Nov 16, 1990

disturbed with such happenings. As such, when passions and revenge are excited, how could one channel these in the right directions. Revenge, then, does not see a balanced course of action. It rises like a flood and it is not possible for the flood waters to keep within the river banks. Flood is the very name of that water which over-flows the river banks. So the passion and revenge spills over the limits and as a result of it, excesses which you have witnessed, are committed. But then the revenge that was taken against Iran, was to use Iraq against that country. They used Iraq in this way that there was a historical conflict of borders between Iran and Iraq and the two nations had never agreed as to where the Iranian borders end and Iraq's borders begin; or where Iraqi borders end and the Iranian borders start. These differences were always kept in view by these advanced and clever nations and they exploited these differences on this occasion. They encouraged and coaxed Iraq and promised to offer help.

When I wrote in my book: *"Murder in the Name of Allah"* that Saudi Arabia had also helped the Iraqis, and that it was Saudi Arabia, which had incited them; some people asked, as to what proof I had and that I was simply conjecturing. Now the proof has become evident. Saudi Arabia is now saying openly that Iraq is an unjust country, since it was Saudi Arabia that gave Iraq the means to fight with Iran and now it is giving us a menacing look. So the fact has now become open before the world. What I am saying is that many dangers are suppressed at the moment in various places and these suppressed dangers have numerous forms, the conflict of Kashmir is also one of them and there are many other conflicts.

These powerful Western nations take notice of these suppressed dangers and as one makes maps to show the mineral deposits, similarly they make political maps indicating areas of possible conflict. These smart, advanced and educated countries have such official maps and they know, when to rouse certain danger and explode certain "bombs". These intentions remain dormant and only come to the surface, when their selfish interests force them to execute them; otherwise they remain in their minds and constitute a part of "Western diplomacy". The sad part is that Muslim countries as well as the Hindu and Buddhist countries have also become involved in the same politics. This unjust politics has overwhelmed the whole world today. On this, as I have said earlier, rules, selfishness; and injustice. As long as one does not destroy these tendencies, the world cannot enter peace, and the shadows of war cannot be lifted from the world. Rather, now that Soviet Union and America have reached peace, smaller dangers will rise with greater force and just as the volcanos do, no one in the world will be able to stop them from raining fire. This is because the interests of certain Super Powers desire that provocation should continue at one place or another. As the Urdu poet **Ghalib** says:

"The provocation of the fair ones should continue, O Asad if there is to be no meeting then let there at least be unfulfilled longing"

These great nations which were not the fair ones have been provoking one another for some time. Now these great nations have become friendly and the small nations have become the fair ones for them. They cannot have a meeting (of minds) with them but their longing to meddle with them continues. This couplet does not entirely fit this situation therefore I shall have to modify it a little to apply to this situation. When this provocation of longings takes place between the lover and his beloved, it is always the lover who suffers because the beloved is stronger and has the authority over the lover. The difference in the words tell us that the beloved is the one who should rule over the lover. The situation here is not that of intense love and the lover, but it is indeed a question of power and subjugation. There is definitely the relationship between power and weakness. So if here there will be provocation of the fair one, then the regret will always be the lot of the weak ones. Regret is never the lot of the beloved. It is always the lot of the lover. So there are many kind of regrets which are in store for the weaker and poorer nations and these powerful countries will never stop their provocation.

DUTIES OF THE AHMADIYYA MUSLIM JAMAAT

Therefore it is the duty of the Ahmadiyya Muslim Community to make the politics of the world aware of the teachings of the Holy Prophet Muhammad[sas]. Wherever the Ahmadis live, they should wage

Sixth Friday Sermon Nov 16, 1990

a holy war, saying, that their final analysis tells them that the basis of all kinds of fears, is in selfishness and injustice. You may enter into which ever agreements you wish between the nations of the world, and draw whatever new maps you want, but as long as you will not turn to the justice of Islam, as long as you will not seek shelter in the morals of the Holy Prophet Muhammad[sas] who was sent to the world as a "Mercy for Humanity", you will not succeed. It is his teaching alone, which can grant peace to mankind. The rest is all delusions, lies, mischief of politics, intrigues of diplomacy and are devoid of reality.

LAUNCH A HOLY-WAR FOR THE ESTABLISHMENT OF PEACE

So for the sake of establishing world peace, today, it is only The Ahmadiyya Muslim Community which has to lay the foundation of a worldwide holy-war on these proper lines. Therefore I want to remind you all that you should begin a holy-war against the prejudices of the world, and start the holy-war to end the tyranny and injustice of the world. You should begin a holy-war to introduce justice to politics. If all of this is done, then a revolutionary change will be brought about in the thinking of the United Nations. Then they will form Committees of the United Nations which will ponder over the kinds of threats I have put before you and will start working to remove those threats. For this purpose they can find such upright retired judges in the world whose impartiality is beyond question. For instance there is **Justice J. Dechene of Canada**, who is well renowned from the point of view of impartiality. In Pakistan there was a Zoroastrian Justice by the name of **Dorab Patel** who had resigned because he felt that certain actions taken there after the military revolution had no just basis. From the point of view of justice, he is on a position of righteousness. Righteousness (*Taqwa*) is a word with vast meanings and it also applies on non-religious values, because in fact, all good moral values in their final form, relate to God alone. So a judge who rises above other interests and influences, we can call him righteous with respect to his sense of justice. So you will find such righteous judges in Pakistan, in India and in Spain as well. When I visited Portugal, I met a retired judge who was not given due respect by the Portuguese government. The United Nations had given him the responsibility to consider certain International matters where injustices had been committed and some of his decisions were against Portugal. When I met him he, jokingly said that I was telling him the tales of atrocities against my Community and urging him to raise a voice against them; but for which ears? He complained that although he was a Judge all his life, yet even his own country was not giving him a fair treatment, and that all nations of the world were based on unjust principles. I talked to him at length in a friendly atmosphere. He is very old now and people respect him for his regard of human values but he has been cast aside as far as politics is concerned. So one can find such just and noble retired judges who are world renowned, or other politicians who become famous for their fairness may be found and who may be selected on the basis of their qualities rather than political affiliations. As such one should select such people from the point of view of fairness and make Committees of them with regard to the various dangers facing the world. These Committees may then decide to resolve the world conflicts after pondering over their root causes and may decide to advise other nations. They should try their best to understand the essence of the conflicts and to reach to their bottom and talk to the quarrelling nations. The whole world should be educated from this point of view. The public should be informed about the kinds of quarrels and about what the Committees have done and about the true picture which would emerge. One cannot think of all the solutions immediately at this stage because some of the conflicts are deeply complicated, but it is necessary to try to find solutions.

Therefore, the nations which see a danger in Iraq today, I can show them thousands of dangers spread throughout the world. If they are truly desirous of world peace then in accordance with my advice, they should become established on fairness; on the fairness of Islam which differentiates neither between East and West nor between North and South. Rather, keeping God in view it puts forward a concept of justice and fairness. If they will try to resolve their conflicts and the conflicts of the world according to this fairness then I assure you that the world can achieve peace. But this peace can be achieved through the affectionate hand of the Holy Prophet Muhammad[sas] because he is the only Prophet who has been declared "a mercy"

forall creation and who has been sent by God for the whole universe. So long as you do not extend your hand toward him; so long as you do not benefit from him, you cannot grant peace to the world. The Ahmadiyya Muslim Community should start a world-wide "holy-war" in this connection.

May God be with us.

Amen.

In the name of Allah, the Gracious, the Merciful

SEVENTH FRIDAY SERMON

NOVEMBER 23, 1990

THE QURANIC COMMAND OF HOLDING FAST TO THE "ROPE OF ALLAH"

After the opening chapter, Al-Fatiha, Hazoor recited the following verses of the Holy Quran:

يَاۤاَيُّهَا الَّذِيْنَ اٰمَنُوا اتَّقُوا اللّٰهَ حَقَّ تُقٰتِهٖ وَلَا تَمُوْتُنَّ اِلَّا وَاَنْتُمْ مُّسْلِمُوْنَ ۝

وَاعْتَصِمُوْا بِحَبْلِ اللّٰهِ جَمِيْعًا وَّلَا تَفَرَّقُوْا ۪ وَاذْكُرُوْا نِعْمَتَ اللّٰهِ عَلَيْكُمْ اِذْ كُنْتُمْ اَعْدَآءً

فَاَلَّفَ بَيْنَ قُلُوْبِكُمْ فَاَصْبَحْتُمْ بِنِعْمَتِهٖۤ اِخْوَانًا ۚ وَكُنْتُمْ عَلٰى شَفَا حُفْرَةٍ مِّنَ النَّارِ فَاَنْقَذَكُمْ

مِّنْهَا ؕ كَذٰلِكَ يُبَيِّنُ اللّٰهُ لَكُمْ اٰيٰتِهٖ لَعَلَّكُمْ تَهْتَدُوْنَ

(Sura Al-Imran 3: 103-104)
Following the recitation of the verses Hazoor said:

TWO QURANIC COMMANDS

In the first verse Allah says: O ye who believe adopt *Taqwa* (fear of Allah and righteousness) as *Taqwa* merits to be adopted; and let not death overtake you except when you are in a state of Islam or in a state of complete submission.

This verse contains two commands and each, in turn, raises a question. It says: Adopt *Taqwa* (righteousness) as *Taqwa* truly merits to be adopted. The question is: How should *Taqwa* be truly embraced? How can we fulfil the requirements of properly adopting *Taqwa*? The second command is: On no account should you die until you become Muslims. But dying is not under one's own control. So the question arises: How shall we gain control over our death? How can we fulfil this command, being unaware as to when death would overtake us?

In fact, each one of the parts of this verse raises a question and each contains an answer to the other.

Seventh Friday Sermon Nov 23, 1990

THE IMPORTANCE OF A BALANCED REACTION UNDER ALL SITUATIONS

If you embrace *Taqwa* in a most befitting manner, then you will keep a watchful eye on your actions and it will help keep you in a state of being a Muslim (submission). Here, the word "Muslim" does not imply that you adopt Islam because the address is already directed to the believers. It is stated: "O ye who believe"! We command that you should die only in a state of Islam (complete submission to the will of Allah) and you should not die in any other state. So, the word Islam, in this context, means being obedient to Allah, and always remaining in a state of total submission to Him. This is how *Taqwa* deserves to be embraced. Now, the believers have been asked to embrace *Taqwa* but a question might crop up in some minds: We do not know how to adopt *Taqwa*? This verse furnishes an appropriate answer to such a question.

Taqwa entails constant vigilance; keeping such critical watch over one's actions that the possibility of any rebellious action is so completely ruled out that you are not likely to die in a state which contravenes the subject of this verse. To be critical of one's own actions is extremely difficult because many a time our reactions may be motivated by influences of our environment and such reactions may be far removed from the requirements of *Taqwa* and may not be called the actions of one who has surrendered himself to Allah.

If you analyze the factors which impinge on the human disposition, you will see that our reactions usually lack balance - and whenever human beings lose their sense of proportion, the path of *Taqwa* is lost and a condition of disobedience and transgression appears. So, if we explore this subject more deeply and minutely we discover that not only does it govern every moment of our lives but it also guides us as to how we can be watchful of every instant of our lives. For example, a man who is sitting peacefully, without any kind of agitation, is susceptible to various potential stimuli that may elicit an unusual response from him. Suppose a person comes to him and without any reason says something repulsive and annoying. Or, let us say, someone conveys a bad news to him or addresses him harshly, thus hurting his feelings. In such cases his reaction would be far more intense than his normal response. Most people are unable to keep their reactions within limits under such circumstances. If a person causes another person some pain and anger - for example by slapping him-then his immediate reaction would be to slap him back ten times as much. if one abuse is hurled at a person, then in reply, he does not stop after reciprocating with just one abuse. Indeed, there are some who may not feel satisfied even after flinging ten, fifty or a hundred abuses back. Peck someone on the head, he might feel so much insulted and annoyed that his anger might not cool down till he beats the assailant to a pulp.

Reacting aggressively and disproportionately is an act of transgression and rebellion and not submission and surrender. If someone dies in this state, then such a person will not have given up his life in a state of Islam.

In this context, **Hazrat Musleh Maood** (The Second Successor to the founder of the Ahmadiyya Muslim Jamaat) used to recount **an amusing anecdote** that once a well built wrestler was returning from the ring - his body well oiled, head shaven, and gleaming in the sun. Following closely behind was a very weak man, who could not have survived even one feeble blow of the wrestler. Seeing his gleaming shaven, head an irresistible urge to do mischief welled up in him, and in full view of all people in the marketplace, he jumped up and gave the wrestler a peck on his head. The wrestler turned back in surprise to see his puny assailant. People in the marketplace burst into a fit of laughter. In anger, the wrestler pummelled this man out of his senses. When he was done, this man said to him: "You can beat me as much as you like but you will never have as much fun as I did when I gave you that peck on your shiny head."

This is only an anecdote, but it illustrates a deep secret of human nature. Apparently, a man was given only one peck on his head but, as a result, he felt so humiliated and annoyed, and thought that he had been so greatly disgraced in front of the public that his reaction was totally out of proportion. And usually such is the reaction in these cases; with the exception of those who fulfil the demands of *Taqwa*.

When you hear some good news, your reaction may also take different forms. Some people begin to jump up and down in joy doing silly things, become boastful and go crazy. Hearing a good news, or when celebrating a happy occasion or gaining victory over someone or getting a windfall profit, in every such situation a person's reaction may be excessive. Such a condition cannot be termed "Islamic" and is not what Islam demands from a Muslim.

Seventh Friday Sermon Nov 23, 1990

Hearing a sad news, some may become completely overwhelmed and get buried under the weight of their grief. People are usually gripped by fear at hearing some upsetting or frightful news. Referring to this condition of the disbelievers, the Holy Quran says: فَرِحٌ فَخُورٌ They are those who become exceedingly happy at small things and become exceedingly boastful at attaining a minor success. In excitement they jump up and down and proclaim their superiority.

In fact, in our everyday life, at any moment when external factors affect us, that is the time to measure up to the demands of *Taqwa*. At such times one is usually off guard and never critically scrutinises his actions. One seldom ponders as to what should be one's correct and measured reaction as a God-fearing person, in response to one's experience of a treatment or a sudden change in one's circumstances.

But a person who lives in the sight of God is always moderate. His reaction never exceeds the prescribed limits. If you are in the presence of an awe-inspiring person and if someone insults you in front of this person, you would never start abusing the offender as you would in the absence of this personage. At such a time, if someone offends you then your reaction would be subdued and minimal, for you would feel that if you over-reacted, this dignified person would be embarrassed.

Children react entirely differently in the presence of their parents than otherwise. The reaction of the courtiers, if mistreated in the presence of their King, is completely different from their reaction to a similar event in the streets.

WHAT IS MEANT BY FULFILLING THE DEMANDS OF *TAQWA*

Thus *Taqwa*, and fulfilling the demands of *Taqwa* means that at any time in your life, when external forces which are likely to disturb your state of equilibrium are operative then, while reacting to those, you must not forget that God is watching you. If you stay in the sight of God in this way then this is *Taqwa* - another name for which is Islam - that is to say, to be in a state of submission before God at all times, remaining within the bounds of His authority and remaining ever so obedient to Him and completely surrendering to Him. Thus this short verse raises two questions and itself provides the answer to both of them. But a more detailed exposition is given by the next verse, which presents a new picture of Islam to which the verse under discussion does not explicitly draw attention until this subject is fully expounded for everyone's benefit. God says: وَاعْتَصِمُوا بِحَبْلِ اللهِ جَمِيعًا

The context of this verse is that, if you claim to be among those who fulfil the obligations of *Taqwa* and if, as a consequence, you become content that you will give-up your life in a state of "complete submission to God" then examine yourself on the basis of this touchstone to be sure that you do not deviate from its true spirit. God says:

$$وَاعْتَصِمُوا بِحَبْلِ اللهِ جَمِيعًا$$

true Islam is such that you **collectively** hold fast to the rope of Allah. This state of obedience must be demonstrated collectively and not individually. Thus a new topic is unfolded here which is a logical extension of the earlier subject.

What is meant by the rope of Allah? **(Hablellah)** First I wish to say something about this and then I will shed some more light on the main topic. When translating the word *"Hablellah"*, according to the idiom of the Holy Quran, two other verses come to mind where the word **"habl"** has been used. In one such verse God says:

$$ضُرِبَتْ عَلَيْهِمُ الذِّلَّةُ اَيْنَ مَا ثُقِفُوا إِلَّا بِحَبْلٍ مِنَ اللهِ وَحَبْلٍ مِنَ النَّاسِ$$

(Al-Imran: Verse 113) that these are the people who have been smitten with abasement, wherever they be found, unless they are protected by a "covenant with Allah" and by a "covenant with men" i.e. unless the rope of Allah should grant them a measure of protection in this respect. Here by *"hablellah" and "hablennas"* one and the same thing is meant because the same word *"habl"* has been used both for Allah and for men. All commentators agree that *"habl"*, in this context, means the covenant. So that the word *"hablellah"* means a covenant of God which protects men. As a consequence of this covenant nations are sometimes granted respite from abasement and disgrace because they have a covenant with Allah, the Exalted, who in accordance with the nature of the covenant, whenever the need arises, shelters them from affliction and dishonour. So at such times, the covenant of God reaches out to them and protects them. Similarly, nations too make covenants with one another. One nation enters into

Seventh Friday Sermon Nov 23, 1990

an agreement with another that if any enemy attacks us then you will come to our defence. Such covenants sometimes save nations from a great deal of harm. On this basis, *"hablen minallah"* (covenant with Allah) and *"hablen minannas"* (covenant with men) signify that the basic meaning of *"habl"* is, a covenant. The second occupance of the word *"habl"* in the Holy Quran is in the expression: *"hablel wareed"* (50:16). The jugular vein is referred to as *"hablel wareed"*. This is the "rope" which connects the heart and brain to the rest of the body. If this rope is cut then the connection of the body with both the heart and the brain is severed - another name for which is death.

In the verse the word *"habl"* is in fact used in both these meanings. That is to say, that you must maintain a strong relationship with Allah, which is the guarantee for your survival. If this relationship is harmed then, to that extent, you will become deprived of life. The second meaning of *"habl"* also fits the context and further expounds the first meaning that the Holy Quran has bonded all believers on the basis of a covenant with His Prophets and *Shariah* (Divine law). And this covenant, or commitment, of Allah the Exalted has been taken with all the nations since the beginning of mankind to this day. Thus every law-bearing Prophet and his law becomes practically the rope of Allah because the believers become bound to both of these by means of the covenant with Allah. Thus obedience to the law and to the bearer of this law (the Prophet) becomes essential. If this is the real meaning of *"hablellah"* (rope of Allah), then if a law-bearing Prophet presents a law (*Shariah*) and then dies, could it be claimed by all the believers that as a result of the "rope of Allah" we have established a link with the law-bearing Prophet and since we are sincere in our covenant of allegiance with the Prophet and his law, therefore we do not require anything else? That is to say that their "submission to His will" (religion of Islam) is perfected because they have accepted a law-bearing Prophet and have established a relationship of obedience with his law? This question does arise but this very verse gives the answer to this question that Islam does not mean that one may individually establish a link with the law and the law-bearing Prophet. Rather *"hablellah"* means that a **collective** link should be developed.

Your apparent link with the law-bearing Prophet may remain intact but as soon as you become fragmented and disunited, you will toss yourself out of the state of submission(Islam). Thus, just holding on to the "rope of Allah" individually is not enough, it is essential to cling **collectively** to the "rope of Allah."

THE IMPORTANCE OF ALLEGIANCE TO *KHILAFAT*

This is a very important topic which draws our attention to the fact that the *Ummah* (brethren in faith) must never be allowed to become disunited, otherwise, their linkage with the *Shariah* (Divine law) or the law-bearing Prophet will be of no avail! Apparently it might seem that you have an affiliation with the Prophet and his Law but as a result of your hollow words and deeds the unity among the "brethren in faith" would start to crumble and they will no longer be counted among those holding fast to the "covenant of Allah". Such people merit punishment in the sight of Allah.

So, this was a further exposition of the real meaning of the term Islam (surrender to the will of Allah), which did not come to mind while reading the first verse. But the second verse fully explained its meaning.

Therefore, entering a covenant of **allegiance to the Khilafat** becomes imperative, not because some law-bearing person is raised as a Khalifa but because, after the demise of the law-bearing prophet, it is not enough to simply have a link with the Holy Quran or a revealed Book. The pertinent question is: How can the unity of the *Ummah* be attained? Unity is attained through centralization. The institution of *Khilafat* is what makes unity attainable. Once there is a breach of the linkage to *Khilafat*, nations split up. The fact is that whenever the "brethren in faith" split into several sects such that none has a link with the unifying institution of *Khilafat* then, in accordance to the teachings of Islam, their link with *"hablellah"* (the covenant with Allah) is nullified. It is a fact that apart from the institution of *Khilafat* there is no other system in the world that can guarantee unity. You can observe many sects but no sect shows the unity which is the hallmark of the system of *Khilafat*. Notice how the *Ummah* began to splinter after the Muslims lost the institution of the **"Rightly guided Khilafat"** that commenced after the demise of the Holy Prophet of Islam. The unity which was observed among the Muslims when they were attached to the institution of *Khilafat* never existed in any subsequent era. Once they lost *Khilafat*, they continued to break-up into pieces and got scattered. Establishing a viable link with the law-

Seventh Friday Sermon Nov 23, 1990

bearing prophet is a very important subject of True Islam. That is to say, establish a link with his person as well as with his law, because the covenant with God that is established through a law bearing Prophet, does not involve the mere acceptance of the Prophet. Rather, it involves loyalty to his person as well as sticking to the law revealed to him. Thus, after the demise of the law-bearing Prophet, the concept of unity cannot persist if *Khilafat* is not established. Otherwise one must conclude that, after the demise of the Prophet, every person can hold on to *"hablellah"* (the rope of Allah) individually, and this would be enough for him. On the contrary, the Holy Quran says that this is not enough. You must hold on to the rope of Allah, collectively. Logically, there appears to be no other way except that *Khilafat* should be established immediately after prophet-hood and that once the institution of *Khilafat* fades away it is bound to be re-established through prophet-hood, even though it be a repetition or revival of the earlier *"Sharia"* (law). Thus a new *"hablellah"* descends from the heaven, granting a fresh taste of unanimity to the followers. Without *Khilafat*, unity can never be attained.

Then God says:

وَاذْكُرُوا نِعْمَتَ اللهِ عَلَيْكُمْ اِذْ كُنْتُمْ اَعْدَآءً فَاَلَّفَ بَيْنَ قُلُوْبِكُمْ فَاَصْبَحْتُمْ بِنِعْمَتِهٖ اِخْوَانًا وَّكُنْتُمْ عَلٰى شَفَا حُفْرَةٍ مِّنَ النَّارِ فَاَنْقَذَكُمْ مِّنْهَا كَذٰلِكَ يُبَيِّنُ اللهُ لَكُمْ اٰيٰتِهٖ لَعَلَّكُمْ تَهْتَدُوْنَ ۞

"Remember the time when you were enemies of one another, It was Allah who bonded your hearts together with the relationship of love. What an unusual and distinctive miracle - you, who were enemies of one another, were transformed into the bond of brotherhood with one another, while you were standing at the brink of a pit of fire: It was indeed Allah who saved you from this pit. He took you away from the ledge of this pit. Thus does Allah unravels His revelations to you that you may be guided."
(Al-Imran: Verse 104)

THE FLAMES OF WAR ARE FLARED BY DISCORD

Now in this second part of the verse, just quoted above, it is mentioned that mutual discord necessarily leads to the fire. People generally think that by the word "fire" is meant the fire of hell. In the Quranic idiom the word "fire" does not only mean the fire of the Hereafter but also means horrifying wars. The fundamental cause of wars among the nations of the world is division and discord. When the intensity of discord and division exceeds all limits then such nations are plunged into the "fire" of war. This is another touchstone given to us to identify our malady. God says, if you are really Muslims, i.e., if you are truly obedient to Allah the Exalted, and continue to cling to the *"hablellah"* (rope of Allah) then it is inconceivable that you will fight among yourselves, and it is impossible that you will be thrust into the blaze of war. Allah has taken you far away from this fire. That is, as a consequence of holding on to the *"hablellah"*, you have been distanced from the ledge of this fire-pit. If you had been standing at the brink of this pit of fire, a strong gust of wind or a push given by an enemy could have thrown you into the pit of fire. Those who are taken farther away from the brink are saved from the fire and they are not vulnerable to a few gusts of wind or a little shoving by the enemy. Indeed, whoever clings to the *"hablellah"* (rope of Allah), he is taken so far away from the brink of fire that no worldly power can thrust him into it.

Having explored this subject at length, let us now revert to the unfortunate condition of the Muslims of this age. During the **Iran - Iraq war**, Muslims continued to shed the blood of their brethren-in-faith for 8 long years. Can we, in the light of this injunction of the Holy Quran, have any doubt that they were standing at the brink of fire? Considering this verse, can anyone claim that they were holding fast to the "rope of Allah"? And were they collectively clinging to this "rope"? This verse is not just presenting a philosophical ideal; it is making us aware of the profound realities of the world. These are hard, cold, realities that mankind cannot evade. These realities encompass nations in their entirety. You may choose to ignore them, but you cannot escape from their inevitable repercussions.

THE CONSEQUENCES OF DISOBEYING QURANIC COMMANDS

Thus the command of the Holy Quran to adopt *Taqwa* in relation to Allah, in the way that *Taqwa* merits to be adopted, and not die until you became Muslims, makes it incumbent upon the Muslims to stand united in the obedience of Allah the Exalted, and collectively hold fast to the rope of Allah and cling to it so strongly that their grip on the "rope of Allah" should never slacken even for a moment. That is to say, on the one hand they should be collectively holding fast to the "rope of Allah" while remaining absolutely united in their common goal. **This is the true picture of the unity of the Muslim brethren presented by these verses of the Holy Quran.** It is unfortunate that the Muslims who read the Holy Quran do not ponder over its meaning. Their majority is neither able to read the Quran nor ponder over its subjects. It is ironical that their leaders, after reading the verses of the Holy Quran, are bent upon distancing the Muslims from each other, instead of uniting them. **The Holy Quran promises the Muslims, that if they collectively hold on to the "rope of Allah" they would be sheltered from all kinds of fire.** Even if you were at each other's throats, by virtue of the blessing of the "rope of Allah", Allah the Exalted will pacify you. Through His blessings, the condition of enmity will give way to a state of closeness and it will forge ties of fraternity. What a splendid outcome is shown in consequence of adopting *Taqwa*. But, on the contrary, the Muslim Clergy is engaged in inciting hatred against one group or another, their mouths frothing in their frenzy, quoting 'references from the Quran' in the same breath. For eight years the world witnessed this farce that Iran advocated the killing of Iraqis by giving 'references from the Quran', saying that they were infidels, and killing them would make the Iranians religious heroes. And if the Iranians were slain at the hands of the Iraqis they would become martyrs. On the other hand, the Iraqi Muslim divines were giving this glad tiding to the people of Iraq, with the same intensity, that if they were killed at the hands of the Iranian infidels, they would certainly enter Paradise and in the sight of Allah, their status will be that of martyrs. But if they succeeded in killing the Iranians, they would accomplish the noble task of dispatching the disbelievers to their well deserved hell.

Such inflammatory speeches and sermons were not a temporary outburst meant for the consumption of their peoples; these were news items carried by the newspapers, radio and television throughout the world, on a daily basis, for eight long years. Now you can judge if this is the teachings of the Holy Quran about grasping the *"hablellah"* **(rope of Allah)**. At first the Iran - Iraq war was labelled as a war between the Islamic and anti-Islamic forces. Later, it acquired different colours. Sometimes it was referred to as a war between the Sunni-Islam and Shiite-Islam. Sometimes it is dubbed as a war between the wicked apostates from Islam on the one side and the righteous people on the other. At other times, it was described as a war between Arabs and non-Arabs. The fact of the matter is that all the countries who supported Iraq in the war did not do so in the name of Islam, since there were a number of countries with a Shiite majority who sided with Iraq because of their common Arab origin. So the war was cast in terms of an Arab and non-Arab conflict. They helped Iraq on this basis but used the name of Islam. Their contention was that here was a tyrannical regime (Iran) that had strayed away from the path of Islam and was now committing yet another felony by attacking the Arabs and Muslims. You can see how Islam, (whether it be the Sunni Islam or the Shiite Islam) has been split asunder, and many Arab Muslim countries have allied themselves against another prominent Muslim country, Iraq. The threat of an all out conflagration has reached the flash point. This is similar to the inferno about which the Holy Quran has stated that you had reached the very fringe of the holocaust, but Allah saved you.

They have not yet fallen into the pit of fire. If they have firm faith in the truth of the Holy Quran, then I beseech them most humbly that they should ponder over this verse. This verse should be the focus of the sermons from their pulpits. It should be aired on the radio and television and published in the newspapers so as to educate their people about what Islam expects from the Muslims. **It should be made clear to them that if a war eventually erupts and results in the annihilation of any country, it would on no account be interpreted as the demise of Islam.** The Holy Quran is infallible. Your claim of being true Muslims can be false but it is not possible for the Holy Quran to be in error. The Holy Quran says: "never be divided", continue to hold fast, collectively, to the "rope of Allah" - this alone is the prescription which can save you from the affliction and tortures of war.

Seventh Friday Sermon Nov 23, 1990

Thus, all the Ahmadi Muslims of the world must draw the attention of the Muslims to the fact that these verses which I recited at the beginning of this discourse contain the prescription of saving them from certain death. I beseech you to fear God and ponder over these verses. A Muslim must immediately stop beheading a Muslim brother. Otherwise neither the victim thus slain will die in a state of being a Muslim nor the assassin be considered a champion in the sight of Allah - rather he will be deemed a murderer of a Muslim. It becomes all the more abhorrent if, in addition to this injustice, you start inviting other non-Muslim nations to come and help you in this slaughter of your own brothers. This is a time for concerted prayers because without prayers the sealed hearts cannot be unlocked. Mere advice is not the key that unlocks the sealed hearts unless Allah so ordains. Thus you should offer sincere prayers and try your utmost to draw the attention of the Muslims, repeatedly, to the lessons contained in these verses, cautioning them that their very survival is embodied in these verses - abandoning them would spell their certain death. A death so awful, about which this verse of the Holy Quran stands as a testimony that this death was neither in a state of righteousness nor in a state of Islam. Thus, how unfortunate it would be if you spent all your life calling yourself a Muslim and trying to follow the teachings of Islam, and apparently dying in defence of Islam, yet to have such ignoble end that the Word of the Holy Quran should stand as a witness against you as if saying: O ye who prattled about faith! O ye who babbled about *Taqwa*! O ye who spoke of Islam! Listen, the Word of Allah bears witness that you tasted nothing of faith nor were you aware of the fundamentals of *Taqwa* nor do you have any right to brag about Islam.

Thus we are seeing the signs of very ominous times for the future. There is indeed only one Jamaat (Community) in the world which is affiliated with the "rope" of the *Khilafat* instituted by God the Exalted, and which is attached to that rope of Allah. This is the only Community which has fulfilled the demands of this verse by uniting on one hand and entering into a covenant of loyalty with Muhammad[sas] and his *Shariah* and grasped the "rope of Allah" collectively.

Therefore, not only should you continue to hold fast to *Khilafat* but should also invite others to this road to salvation which alone holds the guarantee of survival. May Allah the exalted, grant us the ability to do this and grant this opportunity to all those who would hear this message. May Allah help them to understand this subject and act upon it and extract from it the life-giving elixir, but for which there exists no other means for survival.

In the name of Allah, the Gracious, the Merciful

EIGHTH FRIDAY SERMON

JANUARY 11, 1991

CONTRADICTORY ATTITUDE OF THE WESTERN POWERS

After reciting the Opening Chapter of the Holy Quran, Al-Fatiha, Hazoor said:

AN ESSENTIAL EXPLANATION - ISLAM ALLOWS NO PREJUDICE

When the fortress of Khyber fell to the Muslims and thereafter the Holy Prophet of Islam married **Hazrat Safia**, he spoke to her on a particular topic, on their return journey from the expedition, while she was seated behind him on the same camel. That conversation is recorded in the (Hadith) "Traditions" of the Holy Prophet of Islam.

Concerning the expedition of **Khyber** and the hard-times the Jews had to face when the fortress was being conquered, the Holy Prophet said to her: Safia, I must apologize to you from the bottom of my heart about what I did to your people. But I must also tell you how they treated me earlier, so that you may not remain under the misunderstanding that it was any prejudice or wanton cruelty that prompted me to attack the fortress of Khyber. So the Holy Prophet chronicled the whole gamut of cruelties that the Jewish tribes had committed towards the Muslims from the very beginning. In particular he dwelt upon the saga of Jewish attempts at his own character assassination, personal innuendo he had to face, and the invective hurled at him. The purpose of this conversation with Hazrat Safia was to clear any misunderstanding or doubts about this aspect of the Holy Prophet's personality, before the new bride entered his home.

I have delivered several sermons recently, in the context of the Kuwait - Iraq dispute, regarding the treatment being meted out by the Western nations to the Muslims. It has occurred to me on several occasions that the Ahmadi Muslims with origins in these nations may, in consequence, have a misgiving that our tirade against these Western nations in this respect is prompted by any latent racial prejudice on our part. Therefore, I would like to clarify at the outset that an important dimension of the holy Prophet's message - the truth of which he demonstrated by his practice, in addition to his profession - was that **religion is impervious to racial discord. And religion brooks no dispute with any one that is motivated by racial-prejudice or intolerance.**

The Ahmadiyya Muslim Jamaat is a true follower of the moral precept of the Holy Prophet of Islam; and, in fact we even revive the defunct portions of his moral precept. The Jamaat is firm in its resolve to revivify the 'Practice' of the Holy Prophet of Islam in the conduct of its members, and to resurrect the beautiful aspects of it that have been forgotten by the generality of the Muslims. **So, let no one in the world labour under the misconception that, God forbid, the Ahmadiyya Muslim Jamaat too has a position of racial prejudice along the lines of the East versus the West or Black versus White. That is so because racial prejudice and Islam cannot co-exist!**

<u>NATURE OF MY CRITICISM</u>
So, whatever criticism has originated from me or will emanate from me, would be predicated on the noble moral principles of Islam. And it will be directed towards whoever is deserving of it - not with a view to hurting anybody's feeing but in order to bring out the fact and illuminate the issues involved.

In view of the aforesaid, whenever I deliver a critical commentary, I check out my innermost feelings and make it a point to never level criticism rooted in any prejudice. Rather I cleanse my heart, feeling the presence of God, and try to present the facts and state the truth. Such a dose of truth tastes bitter, to one group of people or another, at times, but it is involuntary on our part. We cannot give perpetually biased support to anyone. We shall always side with the truth and constantly lean towards the Word of God and the 'Practice' of the Holy Prophet of Islam.

Whoever seeks our eternal friendship must befriend the Word of God, the Sunnah of The Holy Prophet, righteousness and the truth. In so doing, he will always find us by his side.

THE CURRENT INTERNATIONAL SITUATION

After this brief clarification, I revert to the world situation in the perspective of the Kuwait - Iraq issue, about which I have spoken in many sermons, with the exception of the last two. There are but a few days remaining now, as evidenced by the flurry of peace-making activity that is being observed. My eventual word of advice would follow the same course as my initial exhortation did, i.e. calling attention to the teaching of Islam.

I had called upon the nations of the world to let this issue remain an "Islamic issue": to be resolved by the mutual efforts of the Muslim world. The Arab-world may try to resolve it but it would be inherently wrong to approach it as an "Arab issue". But unfortunately, the efforts directed towards this end are woefully belated. Now the major powers have started to view it as more of an Arab-issue than a global-issue, but as for its being an Islamic-issue, the matter was given a thought in a foreign-ministers conference in Pakistan. Pakistan took the position that Muslim countries should direct their collective energy to resolve this matter. But this initiative has apparently come so late that it is likely to remain ineffectual.

The present situation is that the U.S. and Britain are the leaders of that group of nations which is bent upon crushing Iraq with full might. It is under their leadership and supervision that the trumpets of war are sounding. It is being repeatedly asserted that Iraq's destruction is essential if the rest of the world is to be saved. That is to say, if Iraq stays unharmed as it is, then not only the peace of the rest of the world will be jeopardized, but the very existence of the world will be threatened. This view is being vociferously touted before the world. The summary of this standpoint, which is voiced in various interviews as well as reported by the print-media, is that look, how heinous are the crimes perpetrated by Iraq against Kuwait; how can the world opinion ignore these crimes? What right of existence do these perpetrators have, who killed, plundered and torched the houses? If the comity of nations does not march in unison against such atrocities today, and punish the culprit, then a Pandora's box of future atrocities will be opened, and no one will be able to stem the tide of potential transgressions.

The Iraqi viewpoint, as opposed to this, is that the West is talking of lofty principles and high morals, and is conveniently forgetting the

Eighth Friday Sermon Jan 11, 1991

fact that it is the author of whatever restlessness and disquietude prevails in the Middle East today, that frequently jeopardizes peace. And whenever any opportunity for resolving Middle Eastern problems arose, it was the West that threw hurdles in the way.

Now, Iraq's occupation of Kuwait that is termed unlawful by the West, Iraq argues, is very similar to Israel's occupation of Jordan's West Bank in not too distant past. Further, you invoke the recent U.N. resolutions on Kuwait, whereas the same U.N. passed several resolutions designed to force Israel to relinquish its occupied territories, but it was U.S. that distinguished itself by creating impediments in the way of their enforcement - or simply vetoed them if it came to that.

So Iraq addresses the U.S. and the U.K. and says that this talk of high morality is not becoming of you. And if these ideals really mean anything to you then you must try to use the **same yardstick for measuring all the problems** found in the region, collectively and adopt a consistent and uniform policy with regard to the already existing issues that are very similar to the Kuwait-Iraq issue. If you agree to that then, on the same principles of justice, we will show our compliance.

HISTORY STANDS AS AN INCRIMINATING WITNESS AGAINST WESTERN POWERS

The Western viewpoint on occupation of a country by a more powerful country and their viewpoint on tyranny are presented separately - as if there is a dichotomy in these views. It is surprising that the nations who are talking of **high moral standards** have their own history as the most incriminating witness against them. Seldom has any nation's own history belied its posture so convincingly as does the history of some Western nations. The present rulers of U.S. have European origins. Their forefathers migrated from Europe to America when it was discovered in the beginning of the 17th Century. Thereafter they forcibly occupied North America as well as South America. And the atrocities they have committed and the policy of genocide they practised in these lands are unparalleled in human history. The assortment of various peoples who inhabited this great continent - collectively referred to as the **Red Indians** - were subjected to a coldly calculated genocide, until they were reduced to the level of historical remnants. These Western nations are the same who present themselves as great **animal-lovers**, and use their news-media to raise concern about certain endangered species of animals, and make appeals to save them from extinction. But they themselves killed the Red Indian nations that spread throughout the continent, with such savagery that many of these nations are now completely annihilated. There is but a handful of these nations whose mention we now find in the Western history or in their literature. Now they are confined to the realm of their movies or their literature; otherwise most of the tribes are no longer in existence. The atrocities committed against them would need a long narrative.

Then the plunder and pillage and **colonization of the African Continent** by the European nations is a case in point. How heinous were the atrocities committed against the African nations; how the hundreds of thousands of them were enslaved and sold as chattel! How forcibly slave labour was extracted from them. The U.S. had the greatest demand for these enslaved Africans who were sold as **slaves** to the American customers. The population profile of the U.S. today presents a grim reminder of this history of the U.S. in the form of existing generations of Black Americans.

They remind us of an American historical era when human beings were subjected to such cruelties that imagining it is enough to give one a jittery feeling. I have seen one of the forts where these black slaves were held. So many slaves were packed into such a small place - a virtual black hole - that many inmates would die of asphyxiation. Those who survived were herded like animals to board ships. Those ships were in such deplorable condition that, according to American historians themselves - a substantial number of these slave-passengers would die of the hardships they faced on board. Those who still survived, would reach their destination in an undescribable state, and then they were herded like animals again, slave labour was forced upon them, and they were flogged with whips. They were either forced to substitute for animals in pulling the carts of their masters or their ploughs. Whatever tasks were normally assigned to beasts of burden, were forced upon these human beings!

So, imagine a nation with such historical record to be clamouring today that it is motivated by its humanity and high

Eighth Friday Sermon Jan 11, 1991

morals to come to the help of the weak and restore the land of Kuwait to its people! It is claiming that it is forced to react against cruelty to humans because of its deep sense of "humanity and high moral values". And if it did not intervene - it claims - then humanity would disappear from the face of the earth, and there would not remain any guarantee of peace for any poor and weak country in the world.

If such sentiments are genuine, and if America has awakened to a new sense of sublime values - even though much too late - then why not apply these same values at home and relinquish the Red Indian land in their favour and return to your old country which was your ancestral land? If you say that to them, they will reply: What are you talking about? It was "another matter altogether". Have you lost your mind? Obviously, one cannot argue with this 'it-was-another-matter' attitude.

Britain which has a passionately anti-Iraq stance, in cooperation with the U.S. and repeating the latter's arguments in this context, has a great resemblance with the U.S. in that Britain also colonized a continent i.e. **Australia**. The British cruelty against the inhabitants of Australia was so horrifying that the fore-mentioned American atrocities are nothing in comparison.

A basic difference between the **Australian Aborigines** - who were the original inhabitants of Australia - and the original inhabitants of the American continent was that the latter were martial- races who knew how to fight valiantly to defend their land, and they gave tremendous sacrifices in their struggle. But in contrast, the Australian Aborigines were peaceful people who had no knack for fighting. The British hunted them down in the forests in a manner that resembles a deer-hunt. Those who survived this hunt, were captured and castrated. This horrible campaign of genocide was all-encompassing. As a result, now there is only a few dialects spoken by these people that now remain on record; the rest of the 600 dialects that once existed have vanished. **And only a small portion of the surviving tribes are now being guarded in settlements - like animals in a zoo - to put on a show for future generations that these are the vanquished people from whom we snatched this country. A policy of non-proliferation with regard to these races is being practised. Now, this is Britain's history, in this context.**

DOUBLE STANDARDS OF WESTERN POWERS

In addition to this what Britain did to India and Africa is too long a story to permit me to even outline it here. But let me stress that when you make something a matter of principle or invoke high standards of morality then you must know that higher principles and standards of morality are timeless entities. They do not change with the passage of time. For instance, now there is much talk of U.N. sanctions against Iraq. In the recent past there have been U.N. sanctions against **South African government**, which took years and years to table. Now, they have not been effectively enforced and they have not made much difference yet. But as a result, we have not heard a single voice of concern that the sanctions against South Africa are not working and the time is running out; so there is need for the whole world to invade South Africa. And the Western countries, including Britain, did not support those sanctions on many occasions. Even when the British public opinion criticised their own government in this matter, the public opinion was disregarded by the British government. These are not the forgotten tales from an ancient history; these are matters of contemporary history.

No country suggested that those countries who are not actively supporting the anti-South African sanctions must be militarily forced to comply with these sanctions. There was not even a hint that since South African sanctions are not proving effective, let us do something else about it. Yet, in the case of Iraq, both these views were strongly propagated. First, the economic-boycott must be so comprehensive that even food and medicine are not to be allowed into Iraq. And secondly, these sanctions were so strictly and forcibly enforced that Iraq was in a state of siege from all directions - even Jordan had to share in this misery, for it was feared that the sanctions may be violated through this route.

Notice the persistence of the Israeli occupation of Jordan's West Bank - in the same neighbourhood - but there are no sanctions against it. No protest was made against the atrocities committed by Israel against the Palestinians. The argument that is being used against Iraq now, if it had also applied to Israel, then the current problems would have been resolved long ago.

An analysis of American history - even that which is compiled by American historians themselves - and some reference books containing

Eighth Friday Sermon Jan 11, 1991

statistical record, reveal that the U.S. has used C.I.A. to infiltrate numerous countries in the world - as dictated by American interests - and have not abstained from terrorist activities of any description. They have indulged in it as a matter of their right! Recently a book has been published by John Brados with the title "Secret wars of the President"; it reveals that all kinds of criminal activity was sanctioned under the guise of covert operations i.e., it was allowed to do whatever you want, kill whoever you fancy, poison the water-storage if necessary, contaminate the food-stuff if it serves your purpose; you can even indulge in genocide provided you do it covertly and maintain the element of potential deniability. This new term "deniability" is quite interesting. It simply means that even though the U.S. President may sanction practically everything, but a margin of face-saving must be maintained for him. So that if something is publicly exposed and the President is questioned as to whether he ordered a particular action, he should be in a position to flatly deny his involvement and promise an investigation of it. This is called "deniability"!

Not to speak of Israel, the U.S. herself has committed thousands of times greater acts of terrorism than she attributes to various Muslim countries. And it is an ongoing process. The CIA is as busy today as ever. Somewhere a *coup d'etat* is being staged; in some other countries such as Vietnam, Korea, Laos, Guatemala or Iran, some other conspiracies are being put into practice. All these shocking details are contained in this book written by none other than an American author who is well-known and has authored several authentic books on related topics.

Now, tell me: Where are those principles and moral ideals in all this? The only difference in these activities and those of some Muslim countries is that the Muslims, unfortunately for them, conduct themselves with such simplicity that is bordering on folly. They do not practice the language of Western diplomacy. Instead of resorting to a covert operation they openly declare: "Rushdie, we will kill you!" Or challenge someone else saying that : "Islam does not allow us to treat you kindly, so we will take revenge from you, the way we want to." They are ill-equipped; they beg for arms from the same countries that they speak against. They are engaged in undermining the very foundation on which they have raised the edifice of their own existence. How unwise! It is not even unwise, it is cruel: it is cruel towards Islam because they ascribe all their foolhardy ventures to Islam, and thereby cause great difficulties, in the whole world, for those who are inspired by the true love of Islam.

On the other hand the Western nations are continuing in their transgression : they can treat the rest of the world the way they want; they can exercise their dominion wherever they please; they can eliminate any people they want and obliterate the citizens of whichever country they want. But all this is carried out under the cover of diplomatic language and euphemisms. And on the other hand, those who are virtually powerless to act out their wishes, they resort to absurd boasts and not only earn humiliation for themselves but, in so doing, attempt to besmirch the pretty face of Islam!

So a corollary of my advice to the Muslim world is that you should come to your senses, and act wisely. First learn the art of combat from the nations you wish to antagonize. Learn to speak the language that these nations employ against you or others. Anyway, this was just a tangential remark.

STRANGE AND SHAKY STANDPOINT OF MUSLIM COUNTRIES

Now I come to a third issue. I have so far re-iterated the positions taken by Iraq and the Western nations respectively. Other Muslim countries too have adopted a standpoint. Their majority has supported this view of Saudi Arabia that it is essential for a large number of Muslim countries to join hands in the collective attempt to demolish Iraq. Furthermore, it is being propagated that, today the Muslims are not faced by the issue of Kuwait alone; the issue extends to the need to provide a blanket of security to the Holy cities of Mecca and Medina and the Holy land of Hijaz. It is the sanctity of these cities where the Holy Prophet of Islam once breathed and the soil that he walked upon - these are in need of protection. Muslim sentiments are wilfully aroused by giving this matter a sanctimonious colouring. Pakistan has repeatedly made announcements of this sort that it is sending two thousand soldiers to protect the Holy Land; or that three thousand or five thousand troops have been despatched to this effect - as if they are undertaking a great sacrifice for the sake of the Holy Land.

But let us see what is, in fact, the history of this Holy Land itself? and let us see what has been the true character of those who are now

Eighth Friday Sermon Jan 11, 1991

busy garnering the Muslim public opinion in their favour, by appealing to the sanctity of this land and the Holy Prophet of Islam?

As a matter of fact the Saudi Dynasty forcibly occupied the land of Hijaz. The military expedition to this effect was started in 1801 A.D. under the command of Saud - son of Abdul Aziz who was the patriarch of this dynasty. Saud had become famous as a result of his expertise in major military manoeuvres. He started his advance in Iraq and captured *Kerbala-e-Mo'alla*. He razed all the holy shrines in this area to the ground, on the pretext that they symbolize idolatry and are devoid of any sanctity. These edifices of bricks and stone deserve to be demolished. Then he conducted a massacre of the Muslim residents of Kerbala - the majority of who were Shiite - and marched towards Basra. Almost all the area between Kerbala and Basra was ravaged; the towns were set ablaze, large scale massacres took place and the atrocities which the Saudis committed in Iraq were much more severe, and affected a much larger area, than the alleged crimes that are being attributed to Iraq today.

Having mustered strength in Iraq, Saud turned towards what is known as the Holy Land, and captured Taif. In 1803 A.D. he entered Mecca and Medina and ravaged them. A massacre was let loose and many mausoleums were demolished. Many holy relics and remains e.g. the birthplace of the Holy Prophet of Islam and that of Hazrat Abu Bakr, and similar other enclosures were either obliterated or unabashedly desecrated on the flimsy pretext that Islam put no value on these symbols, and they personify the act of idolatry. There is no definitive record of this gory drama, but historians have noted that even unarmed, harmless and non-combatant civilians were savagely massacred.

In 1813 A.D. Muhammad Ali Pasha - the ruler of Egypt purged this area of the Saudis. But in the beginning of the twentieth century the Saudis once again raided the land of Hijaz - this time with the full military force of the British in tow.

The British generals would plan the strategy of military advance, and the arms and ammunition as well as financial support was all provided by the British, under treaties with the Saudi dynasty.

In 1924 A.D. the Saudi dynasty captured the land of Hijaz twice. And much desecration of the holy shrines and unbridled massacre took place during this occupation by Saudis too. Recently, in a documentary that was aired by the BBC, the compere recalled the British support that was given to the Saudi dynasty even before 1924, and adopted the stance that since the Saudis captured their country with the British help and the British force, so today they are naturally dependant upon British support to defend their country.

Viewed in this light, the current situation takes on a wholly different shape. Whatever government of occupation is ruling over these holy cities, was empowered by the British force or by the Western powers. Now this government is not even capable of self-defence and has no option but to call the Western nations for help. Of course the British Empire is no more now, and the image of Britain has undergone a change in the world. Now Britain has entrusted its historical heritage to the U.S., and the two have become completely attuned to each other in their world-view; so much so that the two powers are almost indistinguishable from each other. That is why their decisions, in the contemporary times, have been unanimous. Europe has some distinguishing features but one need not get into that at the moment.

To sum up: the entire effort to collectivize the Muslim countries to defend the Holy-Land is nothing but a humbug.

The military participation of other Muslim countries is uncalled for in this supposed need of defending the Holy land. They are irrelevant to this context. Nor is there any real danger. If these areas are under any threat, it may be from non-Muslims. From among Muslims, such danger has already manifested itself through the Saudi dynasty, which could not capture these holy places without the help of non-Muslims. So the truth of the matter is that the security of these holy places has again fallen into the hands of the non-Muslim forces, irrespective of the participation by any Muslim country. I mean, the participation by any Muslim states in this imagined 'defence' is largely irrelevant. If you view the situation dispassionately, there is no likelihood of an Iraqi invasion of Saudi Arabia. Iraq is faced with a collective invasion of Super Powers, and is unable to even defend itself. The whole world is in stupor at the precarious imbalance that Saddam Hussein is facing and his audacity to continue rejecting one peace-effort after another. He knows that he will be crushed under this great pressure like grain is ground under a millstone. Defence of Iraq or Kuwait against the collective might of Super Powers is an impossibility. This opinion is

Eighth Friday Sermon Jan 11, 1991

held by world-renowned military experts. They are stunned at what is happening : What does President Saddam Hussein has that is allowing him to nullify every attempt at bringing about a truce.

So, as a matter of fact, it is only the Western powers who are poised in this region to undertake any effective military operation, for they alone have the capability. The participation of Muslim countries has been procured for another reason that has nothing to do with the holy places altogether. Muslim countries are not alone in this token participation; certain European countries have similarly been included as mere tokens. Japan's participation has been secured under duress, and many other nations from both East and West have been sought out to participate in this effort. This was not because they were needed, rather what was needed was to present this issue as the entire world-opinion squaring off against one tyrant. So that whatever drastic measures the Super Powers may take, to honour the world opinion so mustered, may be considered irreproachable. If Iraq is subjected to extreme degree of cruelty, and Pakistan has already become a willing partner in this, now when Egypt, Turkey and other Muslim countries have also become participants, then how can they later turn around and say to the Western powers that you have committed a great injustice?

So the Western powers have preempted the defence of their preplanned high-handedness, by garnering the world opinion at such a cost and by coercing other countries to contribute to these transgressions in nominal terms; then they can watch the show from the sidelines. It is born out by the fact that some Muslim countries who have sent their troops are openly making statements that we will not be a party to the actual invasion, we will be simply stationed in Mecca and Medina to protect the holy places. The government of Pakistan has made a similar unenlightened statement. This implies that the (Iraqi) army that would reach Mecca and Medina - after routing the armies of Super Powers - it would be left for the Pakistani army to take it on! What a preposterous thought!

In fact these countries have been given to understand that you need not worry; come sit in our lap, in peace, and enjoy our protection. We just want your nominal participation; that is sufficient for our purposes.

This is an awesome international plan, and all this paraphernalia that is being used these days is directed towards beautifying this plan deceptively before it is unfolded to the world.

SADDAM HUSSEIN HAS ONLY ONE OPTION OPEN TO HIM

The question that arises again is that why can President Saddam Hussein not discern this plain reality.? Why can he not perceive it, and why is he insisting that he is not prepared to withdraw from Kuwait on the prescribed conditions? Among other things, I think, the evacuation of Kuwait by Iraq is not the ultimate objective. It has been decided that Iraq would be completely disarmed and rendered powerless. Iraq's withdrawal from Kuwait is the first step. That is why they do not promise that if this withdrawal is achieved then we will not invade Iraq. Nor do they say that then we will end the world's boycott and lift economic sanctions. They do not say that we will not destroy or interfere with your factories producing materials for chemical warfare. They do not say that we will not make further demands or add further pressure to put an end to your nuclear power facilities.

But in spite of not saying all this, it is implied in every context that there is something that would be done to Iraq once it withdraws from Kuwait. And Iraq knows it very well that it is no more a question of withdrawal from Kuwait: even if Iraq withdraws from Kuwait, this act would not fulfil those wishes which have prompted these countries to support Kuwait, until Iraq is completely de-clawed. So practically, President Saddam Hussein does not have two courses of action: he has only ONE course left open to him. And that course of action is that of desperation - that if the enemy has come to do the worst to Iraq that Iraq must deliver a finishing blow to them, before its own debacle, that is designed to wreak as much havoc on the enemy as possible, to blunt its pride and prowess. So, as far as I can see, that is the reason why President Saddam Hussein is insisting that he will not withdraw from Kuwait on the conditions laid down by the Western countries.

It is possible that the U.N. Secretary General Mr Perez De Cuellar's visit to Iraq may bring out certain facts. I do hope that his parleys may result in a U.N. guarantee to Iraq that if it leaves Kuwait then (i) the U.N. will look upon the whole Arab issue in a united

Eighth Friday Sermon Jan 11, 1991

perspective and, (ii) after Iraq's withdrawal from Kuwait, no reprisals will be sought against it, and after lifting the international boycott, Iraq would be left to itself.

If these two proposals are placed before Iraq in unequivocal terms, then I do hope that Iraq would be willing to have a peaceful settlement based on these terms. But my concern is that these are the very terms which are inimical to the interests of those countries who have blown this issue out of all proportion in the whole world. These two terms are the very conditions that are not acceptable to these countries in any case. If breaking Iraq's military prowess and building up Israel's defence was not the motivating force behind their moves, they would not have raised a single voice in consequence of the occupation of Kuwait. Kuwait has no significance in this whole scheme of things. These are the two objectives for the sake of which they have caused this storm. So how can they thwart the achievement of these objectives?

This is the final analysis of the situation. I would like to point out to the Ahmadiyya Muslim Jamaat, as I have plainly stated at the very outset today, that we cannot harbour prejudice against anyone, or base our decisions on prejudice, due to national differences or religious contentions. This is so because we really strongly believe that anyone among us who is motivated by a prejudice and takes biased decisions ceases to be entitled to being called a true believer and a Muslim. Prejudice and Islam are poles apart, just as the East is apart from the West. True Islam demands that every decision should be taken by invoking the presence of God at the moment of that decision. That is what is known as *Taqwa* (Fear of incurring the displeasure of God). Fear of God is the basis of everything and every Islamic-value is predicated on God-fearing.

The beauty of the concept of God-fearing is that it cannot be monopolized by any religion. Rather, God-fearing by its nature, must be the pivotal point of every religion, around which the teachings of that religion must revolve. God-fearing means subjecting each thought to the Will of God, and before you take any decision in a situation, find out what is it that God demands of you.

PRAYERFUL OBLIGATIONS OF AHMADIS

So my expectations from the members of the Ahmadiyya Muslim Community is that, keeping this spirit of God-fearing in view, you will pray for the whole human-race, that may God not punish mankind on account of their decisions taken without the element of God-fearing. Such decisions generally invite Divine Punishment, so pray that God may transform the thinking of these people to an unusual extent and may enable them to reform the situation and revert to the truth. You should pray for the whole world to become the recipient of peace from God. This peace does not signify apparent peace; rather this peace is of the kind that encompasses the hearts and minds of the people. Because I am seeing it as a solid and firm reality that world peace depends on peace in the hearts and minds of the inhabitants of earth. If their hearts and minds are not at peace then the international environment cannot remain peaceful: either the world will be threatened by them or they will be threatened by the world. So external maladies are just a reflection of internal maladies that exist in the heart and minds. Therefore pray that God may reform their thinking and the way they feel. May God reform their society and set their minds and heart at peace so that mankind as a collective entity may experience peace and tranquillity.

In this context, you must especially pray for the Muslim countries that God may still grant them some wisdom so that they may not become collaborators of non-Muslim nations in this tyrannical venture that is designed to annihilate a great Muslim power for the achievement of the ulterior objectives of these countries that they regard supreme. May the Muslim countries not affix their stamp of approval in this venture and be not remembered in the annals of mankind as a nation that made the most sinister decision of their history that could only have been written with the most sinister ink! These decisions forebode such gruesome transformations of the world that the future historian will write that it was after these decisions that world-peace became a rarity for all times to come: the war that was fought in the name of peace, begot further wars and disquietude spread throughout the world.

If the Muslim countries did not come to their senses and set their thinking straight and withdraw from their commitments while there is still time, then the future historian would write this tomorrow, but we can discern it today. Anyway, if the Muslim countries remained committed as they are now, then regardless of whether Iraq's existence remains intact or it goes under, the peace of this entire region would remain elusive forever. The Arabs will never regain their present position; Israel will emerge as an even greater power, and no Arab power would ever be able to even imagine that it can take any action against Israel. This situation would persist, at least, for a very long time if not in perpetuity. It would cause severe financial crises in the world, and since the developed countries of the world, are themselves beset with financial crunch, therefore the financial fiasco in the Third world countries would spawn such political fall-out and touch off such a chain of wars that the world-peace would diminish day by day. This is a summary of what tomorrow holds in store, if the Muslim countries did not set their own house in order now.

The Western ideologists are repeatedly saying that the ball is now in Iraq's court, and it is up to President Saddam Hussein whether he hit the ball towards peace or war. But this is quite untrue. You have tied Saddam's hands and raised this issue in such a manner that it is no longer a case of Saddam Hussein being at crossroads: he, in fact, faces a *cul-de-sac*. A forward move spells doom and a retreat would be catastrophic. If he marches forward then his end would be speedy but the enemy would suffer heavy losses too. If he retreats he will be strangled to death. So, you have not left President Saddam Hussein at a cross-road; rather you have severed the second route from him. If you had left an honourable way open to him for settlement then he could have decided whether to opt for peace or war. As it stands now, the decision involves choosing a speedy but honourable death or the humiliation of being strangled to death.

THE DUTY OF THE MUSLIM COUNTRIES IN THE PRESENT SITUATION

But this proverbial ball, though not in President Saddam Hussein's court, is certainly in the court of Muslim countries. If they can correctly gauge the current situation with accuracy and think of tomorrow's historian, if not today's historiographer, and if they want to escape the reproachful verdict of history - then they would revise their current position and announce that we alone will deal with Iraq and the Western forces should withdraw from our countries. If you want to help, then you may supply arms - as you had supplied Iraq with arms, in the past - but otherwise leave this matter to us, we will deal with it. If they make such an announcement today then the Western powers are not left with any excuse to invade Iraq, and even if they decide to go ahead with it, it will no longer be such an easy target. All Muslim countries would rise up in revolt against the Western powers. So, this is the crux of the matter and the essence of this situation. Pray that God may grant a measure of insight and wisdom to the Muslim countries. May they adopt the right thinking pattern and have the courage to take such an initiative that would deprive the alien powers of the excuse to continue their intervention in the Muslim world.

SELFISHNESS OF SAUDI GOVERNMENT

But I do not see this happening. The extent to which the Muslim countries have got involved with the West can only be dictated by acutely selfish considerations. Not to speak of Islamic relations, they have disregarded both Arab- relations and their neighbourly relations. They do not seem to be concerned at all about what might befall the Arab world. All these are secondary matters to them. They are principally guided by their petty self-interests which have overshadowed all else. If you have given this matter some thought, you must have wondered why so much stress is being laid on the date of January 15. Has God ordained January 15th as the deadline? Just a few months ago you were saying that we have imposed sanctions on Iraq and they are bound to produce results within a year, if not within six months. The U.S. and other Western countries used to present such estimates. So what has suddenly happened now? If those sanctions have gone into effect and are hurting Iraq then one would expect you to wait and let Iraq get weakened further and provide you with a more appropriate opportunity to attack. What is this hurry all of a sudden, and why January 15th ?

I have thought about it and I think it is related to the selfishness of Saudi Arabia and its partners. The Saudi government is supposed to foot the bill of this entire war, and despite being filthy-rich they are extremely miserly at heart.

At the rate of billions of dollars that the Saudis are called upon to spend, they estimate that by the time Iraq is undermined we ourselves will be rendered paupers, and our bank-balances would have been frittered away by then. So they are in a state of great consternation. The prospect of being impoverished during wartime is gnawing at them. So they are pressing the U.S. for preemptive action, and the U.S. cannot let the world know about who is putting the pressure from behind the scene.

President Bush is taken to task in his own country. Congress is asking him about his sudden change of mood, whereas he had laid out a one-year plan for the sanctions to work against Iraq and bring it down on its knees; how is it that now there seems to be nothing on your mind but imminent war? How can President Bush say that he is acting as a mercenary, and the one who has hired his services, and is the financier of this war, is pressurizing him to hurry up because he cannot pay up beyond a certain amount. So this is the reality of the current situation.

When I say that the ball is in the court of Muslim countries, it was general speaking. The fact of the matter is that this decision rests with Saudi Arabia whose mounting bills in the financing of this war are forcing it to ask for a speedy end of this conflagration so that it can go back to square-one. **But this is a great folly on its part to think that it can go back to square-one, for no such starting point would remain. If Iraq is undermined then along with it the entire heritage of the past would be annihilated.** The Arab psyche would have undergone a change; their ways of thinking would have become quite different. New set of circumstances would spawn new era. Those who are indulging in their silly dreams that once the issue is quickly put an end to, they would be able to go back to where they were - they must know that they will never be able to take a leap backward to their original state. Rather historical forces would coercively drag them into future where there are gruesome circumstances that the futurity has in store for them, and they will not be able to escape their lot. They are riding the deep-running waves of rapids that are spewing foam in their fury of motion and even a strong and big vessel is no more than an ordinary straw on their turbulent surface. When such rapids assume the form of a waterfall and come down from mountains they can smash even the strongest resistance into smithereens. So, they are riding the strong tidal waves of time and are irrevocably involved in a situation from which they cannot retreat.

A FORCEFUL APPEAL FOR PRAYERS

There is only one way left open for them: adoption of *Taqwa* (God-fearing) and basing their decisions on an invocation of God's presence. They must keep the collective interest of the Muslim world supreme, and sacrifice their own self-interest for its sake. If they do that, then Insha Allah (God willing), a new era will begin for Islam. It will be a new era because we cannot go back in time. But this new era would be thousands of times better than the earlier epochs, and it will continue to get better still. So I hope that God will grant them insight, and if there is no hope then I pray that God may unusually enlighten their minds. I draw the attention of Ahmadi Muslims to the fact that although we are very weak but we still have the power to pray and we know how to pray. We have reaped the fruits of prayer in the past and we continue to do so at present.

So when you reach the prayer:

$$اِیَّاکَ نَعْبُدُ وَاِیَّاکَ نَسْتَعِیْنُ$$

"Thee alone do we worship and Thee alone do we implore for help", as part of your daily prayers, then keep the current situation in a special perspective. And beseech God that the sanctity of Mecca and Medina is attached to the acts of worship, and it will forever be so; these towns are holy because the Prophet Abraham[as] and the Holy Prophet of Islam, peace be on both, worshipped in these localities. And today we, as Thy humble servants, are the ones to revivify the spirit of those worships - perhaps not to that sublime degree, but we try with whatever capabilities we are endowed with, to revive the spirit of that worship. So, O Lord! grant acceptance to our acts of worship and send us Thy Help, for if Thou did not come to the help of those who truly worship Thee then there would be no more worship left in the world, and the taste of worship will be forgotten in the world. So do Thou accept our supplications.

$$اِیَّاکَ نَعْبُدُ$$

"Thee alone do we worship": We are not looking up to any worldly power, we are only looking up to Thee. So do Thou help us.

If this prayer wells up from the innermost recesses of our hearts, and is granted Divine acceptance, - and if all Ahmadi Muslims everywhere in the world are praying like this then it may well be

Eighth Friday Sermon Jan 11, 1991

accepted - then you will see that, God willing, this "ball" will not remain in anyone's court, but will go towards the Court of God's Will. And it is your prayers that grasp at this Will of God or fall prostrate before it, beseechingly, so that the Will of God changes colour along with your supplications. It is time now for you to show this spectacle of changing colours to the whole world and demonstrate to the world that God is with you and that God will be with, whoever you are with!

In the name of Allah, the Gracious, the Merciful

NINTH FRIDAY SERMON

January 18, 1991

A WAR SOWING SINISTER SEEDS OF EXTREME UNREST

After reciting the Opening Chapter of the Holy Quran, Al-Fatiha, Hazoor said:

EXTREMELY PAINFUL REALITY

Pir of Pagara, a senior among Pakistani politicians, has a unique gift of subtle humour which sets him apart from all other Pakistani politicians that I have observed. Some times he utters such basic truths, wrapped up in subtle political humour, that their effectiveness could not have been achieved if those were plainly stated. He can say things this way which he otherwise may not deem fit to be a part of his normal discourse. But in the language of insinuations embedded in humour, he has a knack of expressing himself very well. Some time ago, he was asked about his opinion on the issues that beset the former East Pakistan. He replied:

"Why do you talk to me about East when you know that our *Qibla* is towards the West, and we face the West when we fall prostrate. So ask me about the West".

This is such a subtle and profound observation. Though cast in terms of humour but it is a painful reality which is becoming manifestly clear with the passage of time. The countries situated towards the East of Mecca, would necessarily have their *Qibla* towards the West. But this is not what Pir sahib meant. He meant that the apparent *Qibla* is towards the West and the *Qibla* of their hidden desires is towards the Western nations. But one is surprised to find the so called "defenders of Ka'ba", placed squarely at the House of Allah, to be still facing the West (Western nations) when they fall prostrate.

Ninth Friday Sermon Jan 18, 1991

The best way of shielding Muslims from International intrigues is that they straighten their *Qibla*. Until such time as our *Qibla* is set right, none of our problems can be solved. There was a time when the Muslim nation was split into two camps: those countries which had their *Qibla* towards the East (i.e. they looked up to the Eastern powers for the solution of their own problems) and the other countries whose *Qibla* was towards the West (i.e. they looked up to the Western countries for help in their problems) and none of these Muslim countries had the house of Allah as its *Qibla*. The recent political changes that have taken place within the former Soviet Union and those that have occurred in the mutual relations between the former Soviet Union, and the United States, have led to the demise of one *Qibla* and the second *Qibla* remains for now. **But the genuine and true *Qibla* stands rock-firm. It is eternal and indestructible. It is designed to be the instrument of eternal deliverance of the Muslims, yet they do not make a recourse of this *Qibla*. The need of the hour is to set the *Qibla* straight.**

THE STANCE OF THE AHMADIYYA MUSLIM JAMAAT ON IRAQ

The painful situation that the Muslim world is currently locked into, and various reactions spawning from it, call for an explanation that I will briefly provide to the Jamaat and then advise the Jamaat as to what its reaction ought to be, in the light of Islamic teachings.

A sizeable number of Muslim countries, led by the Kingdom of Saudi Arabia, has placed its total reliance on the Western powers, and does not seem to care that the fragmentation of the Muslim-world continues and its mutual rifts are widening day by day. As I have dwelt upon the subject in previous sermons, you know that the Ahmadiyya Muslim Community has never supported the act of Iraqi invasion of Kuwait. Our stand has always been in accord with the teachings of the Holy Prophet of Islam[sas], that you can help even your cruel brother by preventing him from committing acts of cruelty. So, in this sense, we repeatedly tried to help Iraq: messages were sent, sermons were devoted to elucidate these points that two things make Iraq a party to tyrannical transgression; and if Iraq seeks Divine Help then she must desist from these. **Firstly, Iraq must withdraw its forces from Kuwait,** and present her case in front of the comity of Muslim nations- not the whole world- for the peaceful resolution of its conflict with Kuwait. This is the teaching of Holy Quran, and we advised Baghdad accordingly.

Secondly, they were advised that foreign diplomats that are assigned to various tasks in Iraq, and others representing their respective countries, are a trust from God. Iraq must not betray this trust. Whether or not, this piece of advice reached Iraq is not known, but Iraq took an initiative based on reason and fairness that it does not need any "Human shield" and allowed the foreigners to have freedom of movement and freedom to leave, if they so desired. The foreign News - correspondents have been extended such unusual facilities that it is inconceivable that the West would do likewise while engaged in the battle for its own survival. Iraq has abandoned this aspect of cruelty, but it is not known what strategical interests or other factors caused Iraq's inability to respond to the necessity of its withdrawal from Kuwait and adopt such adamant stand. The horrible war that is now being waged in that land as a result of this obduracy, is obviously quite unilateral. The anti-Iraq powers have included a Muslim contingent among the ranks to make the world believe that this war is not between Islam and non-Islamic forces; rather non-Muslim countries are undertaking a great sacrifice by helping Muslim countries against a tyrant among themselves. The reality of this "sacrifice" is plainly obvious to the world. This sacrifice is of such nature that the West is reaping such benefits from it that are unimaginable for an ordinary mind. The propaganda carried on the radio and T.V. is making many facts and realities. Without understanding these, you cannot guess which power will reap all the benefits and which side will be damaged.

<u>A JUDICIOUS ADVICE TO IRAQ</u>

As far as Iraq is concerned, you can foresee nothing but a continuum of loses that spell a very painful state of affairs. I had advised in clear terms that it behooves Iraq to practice restraint. If God had made it a power, it had ample time to develop it further. **Whatever decisions Iraq has taken, are immature, untimely and inappropriate. So Iraq must disengage itself from this tyranny and set itself on the course of progress.** On the occasion of the last Annual congregation, I had called upon the Muslim world to pray to God to grant us a *Salahuddin (saladin)*. Some days earlier, I turned

Ninth Friday Sermon Jan 18, 1991

on the T.V. for the latest situation in Iraq. In this programme several Muslim scholars (ulema) were proclaiming President Saddam as the reincarnation of Saladin in their passion-driven rhetoric. But Saladins are not the product of emotionalism and blind faith. When I had called for a Saladin, I had not hoped for a icon erected in the realm of emotions that would be named Saladin. Becoming Saladin requires a lot of qualities, and it takes a long interlude of patience to nurse them. The first goal that Sultan Salahuddin had set for himself was to unify the world of Islam. He spent the better part of his life in consolidating the fragmented Arab states and bringing them under the sway of a central government. It was only when he had put his own house in order, to his complete satisfaction, that he challenged all the world powers in his defense of Palestine. It is a widely known historical fact that all the Western powers got united with the vengeance, to make repeated attempts to break Saladin's power. The united front they had put up against Saladin was no less, perhaps more, than the present united Western opposition to Baghdad, and they rallied together with such zeal as if they were going to engage in a religious war. In fact their zeal had reached maniacal proportions in this respect. But in spite of the fact that Saladin was comparatively less strong and had no claim to being an accomplished military strategist, he achieved victory after victory by the grace of God Almighty. He had several outstanding qualities. For instance, he was a pious and righteous man who placed his trust in God. He is unique in respect of his character being found above reproach by even the most prejudicial among his European critics. They could not point an accusing finger towards him, charging him with any act of tyranny or immorality. Some have admittedly, looked for at least one instance in which Saladin may have run counter to a sense of humanity, outraged human values, acted tyrannically or been guilty of immorality. They acknowledge that no such instance could be found in his life.

But there is one episode which, according to the same writer, the West did its best to orchestrate, although it has no substance. This episode is set against the backdrop of an expedition in which a European prince had set out for Medina with the evil intent of extirpating the burial place of the Holy Prophet of Islam[sas]. Saladin caught up with him when he had reached very close to Medina, and thwarted his evil designs. When this prince was brought in captivity before Saladin, he saw a glass of beverage lying there and proceeded to help himself with it, to quench his thirst. Just before he could do that, a swipe of Saladin's sword flashed and smashed the tumbler of beverage to smithereens! Actually Saladin's strategy had caused the much superior force led by the prince to wander about in the desert in such a way that they lost contact with their water supply. So they surrendered because of the clever strategy employed by Saladin, and not because of his military strength. The commander-prince, therefore, reached Saladin's court, enervated by thirst, and the swift strike of Saladin's sword denied him the glass of beverage. This was the only blot on Saladin's character that the historians discovered. This historian whom I read a long time ago and whose name I cannot recall now, writes that Saladin's deprecators don't understand the Arab psych, nor are they conversant with the high moral traditions of the Arabs. The noble moral traditions of the Arabs prevent them from taking the life of a person who has shared water or broken bread in their home, no matter how serious an offence he may be charged with. But the prince's bid to desecrate the grave of the Holy Prophet was such a heinous crime which could not possibly have gone without capital punishment being awarded for it by Saladin who was infused with true love for the Holy Prophet[sas]. It was not an act of immorality to let the prince suffer from the thirst, seconds before his death. Rather, in Saladin's judgement, it would have been an act of great immorality to have let the prince drink water from the Saladin's table and then as a result, render himself incapable of putting the prince to the sword. This incident demonstrates how great a personality Saladin was, and it also sheds remarkable light on the practice of Islamic morals. Such traits of Saladin's character caused the historians to describe him as **Umar bin Abdul Aziz** - reincarnate. That is to say, the capabilities, spirituality and high moral standards of Umar bin Abdul Aziz resurfaced, several centuries after him, in the person of Saladin. So, it is not emotionalism that gives birth to Saladins. The name Saladin requires many capabilities. So, one wonders if some Ahmadi viewers of this T.V show, too, got carried away and thought the answer to their prayer materialised so soon. This line of thought is childish. You must be mature in your thinking, for you have been created to lead the world. I remind you of your elevated rank: you derive your right to leadership by virtue of being the humble servants of the Holy Prophet of Islam, who was created to lead the whole world and to administer correct and sane counsel to the world. Never did human wisdom attain such maturity as it did in the person of the Holy Prophet of Islam. His heart and mind were equally perfect in their maturity, and the emotions of his heart were not allowed by him to cloud his faculty of reason.

AN EXTREMELY PAINFUL SITUATION FOR THE MUSLIM WORLD

The extremely painful events that are unfolding these days, hold the same fascination for some people as if they are watching a cricket match glued to their T.V. sets for the better part of the day. But this is no cricket match. This is a horrifying and torturous war. You must have heard the phrase **'carpet bombing'** being mentioned frequently, these days. This refers to a complete destruction of an area brought about by such heavy bombing that craters formed by the bombs are laid out as a continuum. One can get some idea of the bombardment let loose on Iraq, by the fact that the total strength of the bombs dropped on Iraq on the very first night exceeded the strength of the atomic bombs dropped on **Hiroshima**. And this situation continues unabated.

This state of affairs has caused tremendous heartache in the Islamic world. I am referring to only that cross section of the Islamic world which truly loves Islam and humanity, and which is desirous of world peace and would like to see human values being upheld - and cannot be happy to see any nation's prejudice emerge victorious. That segment of the Islamic world is going through an excruciatingly painful experience. They have agonizing days that are only followed by agonizing nights. **It most certainly does not mean that they are supportive of every action taken by President Saddam. Not at all.** For instance, President Saddam's decision to target Israel with scud missiles has caused even less damage than what you can expect in a traffic accident involving a passenger bus, but the whole world is appalled at this attack on Israel. Even a minor tremor of an earthquake proves more damaging than these scuds have been for Israel; even **Irish terrorists** wreak more havoc here due to their bomb blasts. But, in the words of the British Prime Minister, the world is appalled at this scud attack, and has no appropriate words to express its shock and horror. The real reason, it seems, for being appalled is because it is known how much havoc an Israeli retaliation would wreak upon the citizens of Iraq: it would exceed the damage done to them by the allied forces so far. Also, a selfish-interest seems to be at work, behind this reaction: if Israeli reaction to these attacks causes a rift among the Muslim countries currently siding with the allies, and some of them started supporting Iraq's action, in consequence, then it would add complications to the allied plan regarding Iraq.

Now, if the people of Iraq are going to be brutalized and punished for the wrong steps taken by President Saddam, then which decent citizen of this world, whether Muslim or not can be happy over this misery? Nobody who loves humanity and Islam can, in any case, be happy over this. But one is shocked to watch on the T.V., the lazy-rich Kuwaitis and Saudis, with their vaults full of money, listening to the radio bulletins of Iraq's destruction, and gloating over it and laughing at it aloud.

Such scenes cause indescribable horror in one's mind. It amazes one to observe that there is a bunch of Muslims who have been orchestrating their piety in front of the world and posing as the front-line soldiers of Islam - those who called themselves the caretakers of the holiest places of Islam, and the key-holders of Kaaba, and never tired of reminding us of the great honour and responsibility bestowed upon them by God - the true face of their values can be seen in the fact that they are the silent spectators of the terrible atrocities being committed against their neighbourly Muslim country. When the misery of their condition would be documented and assessed in the post-war period, humanity would mourn this tragedy for a long time to come. Halaku Khan's tyranny is passe now: the havoc of World War II reduced his legend to an anachronism. Even the allies are admitting that their bombardment of Iraq has now far exceeded what they did in World War II or Vietnam. To laugh and express delight at the destruction wrought by such dreadful means, is a very cheap display of meanness. I have seen this kind of display for the first time. It shocked me to think that these are the people who have been made the custodians of such enormous piles of wealth. Is this their dignity, their wisdom and their understanding of life. None of them thought of

Ninth Friday Sermon Jan 18, 1991

seeking forgiveness from God. It occurred to none of them to pray to God fervently that: O, God ! we have landed ourselves in a big mess. Deliver us from this situation.

And if they have been forced into participating in this genocide of their own brothers and sisters, then they must give charity for the expiation of their sins, and take measures to alleviate human misery, and make sensible use of the enormous wealth that is at their disposal. But instead of mending their ways, they are just languidly waiting for the day when Iraqi power would be totally annihilated, and they would return to their tiny state, swaggering. Then their country would be rebuilt by the Western powers, whereas Iraq would have been obliterated from the face of the earth.

Now, the question is : who is the primary beneficiary of this turmoil - this dangerous turn taken by international events? This morning, an interview of the deputy Defence Minister of Israel was aired. When it was pointed out to him by the interviewer that a possible Israeli retaliation for Iraqi scud attacks is likely to seriously damage the accord between Muslim countries and the West, he said: What are you talking about? Your statement is pointless. Do you think that the U.S., U.K and European countries should be grateful to Saudi Arabia, Kuwait and Egypt for siding with the allies? These countries are deeply indebted to you and are bearing your yoke. They totally rely on the West. These countries will not care a hoot if Israel, or for that matter, any country destroys Iraq. These countries have been rendered incapable of voicing their angry dissent with the West.

This observation is profoundly true and it accurately portrays the contemporary situation. But I completely disagree with that aspect of his observation which says that the West has done these Muslims countries a great favour by stepping into this war. This is completely untrue! The West has neither done the Islamic world, as a whole, any favour, nor has it done any favour to those countries in whose name the West is continuing this war. As always, the West is in it for serving its own selfish interests. And this horrifying instance of pursuing self-interests is just one in a chain of similar instances which characterize recent history. The advanced nations of the world have always tried to extract the maximum benefit out of a situation of turmoil anywhere else in the world. So, if you pursue this line of thought a little further, you will begin to understand what I am talking about, and who the beneficiaries are. The continuous supply of sophisticated armament to the battle areas is costing billions of dollars - literally, mountains of money - and you must have heard of the agreement that the kingdom of Saudi Arabia will foot the bill for fifty percent of the war-expenses. The remaining fifty percent has been left unspecified, and has not been allocated to any country. But I can assure you that it will be wrested from Kuwait or Bahrain, or other states in the Sheikhdom. At least the better part of it will be collected from them. In the ultimate analysis, then, this war is benefitting a party that is not among the active combatants - and that is Israel. In an interview that was aired today, a Western politician has openly admitted that our call to destroy Iraq has always been due to our concern for a potential threat to Israel. These scud missile attacks have validated our concerns; for these abortive attempts by Iraq to hit Israel - due to the primitive delivery system and rudimentary power of destruction - would have proven far more destructive. If this war had not interrupted the weapons-development programme of Iraq, these missiles would have been fitted with far more lethal war heads and would have targeted Israel much more affectively.

A WAR GIVING BIRTH TO A DREADFUL AFTERMATH

Thus, as far as the objectives of this war are concerned, Israel is the primary beneficiary. As for the economic benefits of this war, all Western countries are the beneficiaries. The reason for this has to do with the truce reached with the Soviet Union which has rendered the bulk of these armaments (now diverted to the war in the Mid-East) useless and without any intended target. Most of the war expenses are on account of the price of these armaments. The transportation expenses of these is mainly borne by the freely flowing Arab oil. At any rate, the margin of saving that goes to the Western powers is great, who are marketing their weapons, new as well as the outdated ones, in a war which is being financed by someone else. The economic gain from this war is, therefore, entirely that of the Western nations. A lot of Western manpower is being used to wage this war; some Western lives will be lost but a lot of economic pay-off would also be funnelled to the West. The Islamic world has nothing to gain but great losses to sustain.

Ninth Friday Sermon Jan 18, 1991

If Iraq is completely wiped out then this in itself would be a great loss which the Muslims will mourn for decades to come. But even if you ignore it for a moment, the post war balance of power in the region will be very precarious.

An immediate danger stems from the likelihood of another irresponsible attempt by President Saddam to drag Israel into this war merely to cause some Muslim countries, currently siding with the allies, to break ranks with them. In that case, no Western power would stem the tide of Israel's eventual brutal retaliation against Iraq. Nor would the Western powers feel for the wounded sentiments of that cross section of the Muslim world which is helpless in the matter of war, but which truly loves God and the Holy Prophet Muhammad[sas] which is justice loving and is desirous of world peace. The aftermath would be a tremendous upheaval in the Muslim world.

An apparent victory of the West would sow the sinister seeds of discontent that would sprout right and left, causing breach of peace here and there. **Muslim soil will be the playground of these disruptive ventures. As a reaction to this, attempts would be made in some cases to overthrow Muslim governments.** In some cases the horrible fundamentalist **"Mullahism"**, will raise its ugly head which bears no connection with the Holy Quran , but is the progeny of the middle ages. A leadership that is rooted in religious bigotry, and therefore devoid of the love for God and the Holy Prophet and the Holy Quran, - a leadership that is essentially the product of political fallout - is always more destructive than its predecessor, and leads the nation into an even worse predicament. So, the aftermath of this war will bring a host of problems and these will, in turn, give rise to further problems. Every one of these would threaten world peace and the derivatives of these problems would themselves threaten world peace. This is so because the explosions caused by religious hysteria or a sense of political deprivation, have far-reaching consequences. The resonance of these blasts is transformed into the agitation of the hearts which inflames the minds, and result in destruction schemes. Whether these explosions take place in Egypt, or Kuwait, or Sudan, or elsewhere in the world; each explosion would give a jolt to the Muslims everywhere and give rise to many upheavals and uprisings. If these explosions have nationalistic connotations then they cause national upheavals, and they will! This is an involved matter and I do not wish to spend more time on it. You all understand that when this contemporary conflict comes to an end, it will not spell an end to the conflict itself. Rather, it will assume larger proportions, and threaten to involve the whole world which may erupt in a worldwide conflagration which gives one goose flesh even to contemplate. Then, those countries which are destroying one country and watching the spectacle from a distance, will themselves go through circumstances that will make them a part of the same spectacle. These circumstances, therefore, contain very deep-seated horrors and dangers.

COMPREHENSIVE PRAYERS FOR THE VICTORY OF TRUTH

I do not exhort the members of the Ahmadiyya Muslim Community to pray for the victory of any particular side in the war. Instead I advise you to pray for world peace. Pray to God:

> O, God! we love the name as well as the message of the Holy Prophet Muhammad[sas]. We love him because nobody in the world ever loved Thee as much as he did. So we adore his name, his work, his personality and character, his religious dispensation. The Holy Prophet was created as a "Mercy for both worlds", and his heart was deeply imbued with the love of humanity. So our love for the Holy Prophet demands that we must feel for the suffering of all humanity and do our best to ameliorate its miserable existence. But O, God! we have nothing except the capability of praying to Thee. We are weak, unarmed and an oppressed Community. But we fall prostrate in front of Thee, O, God! in the name of Muhammad[sas], and we supplicate before Thee to have mercy on his progeny and the rest of mankind, and to protect them from a worldwide tribulation-whether it be a man-made disaster or one that is pre-destined for mankind, unknown to us. whatever may transpire, O God! let victory be the destiny of Islam and of humanity. Those moral values that have been long lost in the East as well as in the West, let them take root in this world once again and let them

Ninth Friday Sermon Jan 18, 1991

be the order of the day. O God! fulfil the promise that Thou made in the Holy Quran that:

$$لِيُظْهِرَهُ عَلَى الدِّيْنِ كُلِّهِ$$

(Chapter Al-Saff: Verse 10)
Thou sent the Holy Prophet Muhammad[sas] into this world so that Thou may cause him and his religion to reign supreme over all ideologies in the world. So we are not praying for the victory of any particular nation. Rather we pray for the victory of the truth; we pray for the victory of Islam and human values. O God! if thou did not accept our prayers today then there would be no hope for the deliverance of this world. We are lying prostrate in front of Thee, in complete sincerity and total humility and we are crying in front of Thee, O God! Accept the supplication of the humble servants of Muhammad[sas] and cause that blessed revolution to come about in the world for the sake of which Thou hast created us. Let us see the fulfilment of all Thy promises related in this grand spiritual revolution that, Thou foretold, would be brought about through the agency of those who will come in the **latter days**. We are the ones who are commissioned by Thee, O God! in these latter days. So fulfil Thy promise and make us the instruments of prayers which will cause that revolution wherein lies the salvation of this planet. May God grant acceptance to these humble entreaties of ours and grant us the requisite capabilities.

AN IMPORTANT ADVICE

A further advice in this regard is called for : God has instructed us that in times of trial and tribulation, we must give expiatory charity along with prayers. **As I pondered over the contemporary difficulties of the world of Islam, my attention was diverted to the hungry millions of the African continent who span vast areas and several countries. Humanity is dying of hunger in Ethiopia, Somalia, Sudan, Chad and many other countries; and mankind is not mindful of this problem as a very human problem.** Whatever little has been done to address the problem, the credit for that goes to the Western countries. These countries have such charitable programmes in which pictures of these ailing, hungry and emaciated human beings are displayed who are reduced to mere skeletons. These displays arouse the sympathy of the people who offer sacrifices in this respect. But those oil-rich Arab states who have amassed literally, mountains of wealth and who have forsaken the spirit of the Holy Prophet Muhammad's[sas] message though, ironically, they associate themselves with his name -it never occurs to them, how some African states in their neighbourhood are suffering from the rigours of the famine. Sudan, for instance, is right next door with a Muslim neighbour, but countries like Saudi Arabia, Iraq, Kuwait, Bahrain and other states of Sheikhdom remained quite unmoved, God has made these countries custodians of enormous riches for a considerable length of time, but their conduct in this regard has been disappointing. They have forgotten that the sympathy and love for the downtrodden was the hallmark of the Holy Prophet's message. It is quite inconceivable that one may think about the blessed life of the Holy Prophet of Islam and not conjure up the clear image of his love for the disadvantaged, the poor, and his lifelong treatment of affection and kindness that he devoted to the needy. The love and the sympathy for the poor shines forth along with the light of the Holy Prophet Muhammad[sas]. **The Holy Prophet once remarked: If you want to look for me on the day of judgement, try to find me among the poor.** He further instructed his followers: Take good care of the poor and the needy among you; all your cheer and your wealth is because of them and their toil. The least you can do is to be kind and sympathetic towards them. The Holy Prophet was the greatest sympathiser of the poor in the world. Some countries who got extremely rich, because God endowed the descendants of the Holy Prophet with it, now look at the profound poverty that besets their neighbouring countries and it brings no feelings of mercy in their hearts. What a lack of humanity! If these Muslim countries had remained devoted to prayers and philanthropic pursuits them, I firmly believe, they would not have found themselves engulfed in such a horrible trial as they are today.

Since our Community, despite its meagre financial resources, sets examples in every field of virtue, for the world to emulate, so we must take initiative in this respect as well. You must not only pray, but remind them to pray; you must not only give expiatory charity but

Ninth Friday Sermon Jan 18, 1991

remind others to do the same; and you must practice patience and advise others to do likewise. The Holy Quran informs us that only that group of people will be victorious in the latter days which will practice patience and exhort others to do likewise.

$$وَتَوَاصَوْا بِالصَّبْرِ وَتَوَاصَوْا بِالْمَرْحَمَةِ$$

"They exhorted one another to perseverance and exhort one another to mercy"
(Chapter Al-Balad Verse 18)

So I have decided to present on the behalf of the Jamaat, a charitable donation of **ten thousand pounds**, although it seems to be a modest drop for the famine relief efforts for the needy African countries. I will make a personal contribution as well; and the Communities in each location can allocate its funds towards this noble cause. The Holy Quran says:

$$يَسْأَلُونَكَ مَاذَا يُنْفِقُونَ ۖ قُلِ الْعَفْوَ$$

(Chapter Al-Baqara: Verse 220)
"And they ask thee what they should spend. Say: What you can spare"
The word used in the Holy Quran is *"Afav"* which can also mean that whatever an individual or a community can spare from different expenditure heads be spent on the service of the destitute. Although all the assets of the Jamaat are indeed the assets of God and are spent in the service of God, yet this is an additional worthy cause where money can be spent in the service of God. So, I am not establishing a specific fund for this purpose, but I urge you to contribute towards this charitable cause, with the sincerest motivation that God will grant acceptance to your sacrifices in the cause of world peace. Our prayers will be dedicated towards these objectives. Our benevolent funds, according to our capacity, are, for all worthy causes but this charity will be exclusively for the famine-stricken people of Africa. May He eliminate the troubles of the Muslims, and open the eyes of our Muslim brethren who received the virtuous teachings of the Holy

Quran but turned a blind eye towards what this teaching requires of them in this situation.

Amen.

In the name of Allah, the Gracious, the Merciful

TENTH FRIDAY SERMON

January 25, 1991

FUNDAMENTAL DIFFERENCE BETWEEN POLITICAL WARS AND JIHAD

After reciting the Opening Chapter of the Holy Quran, Al-Fatiha, Hazoor said:

A BASIC PRINCIPLE : ISLAM HAS NO TERRITORIAL BOUNDARIES

Islam has no territorial boundaries. Islam embraces all nations. During various upheavals and conflicts in the world, Muslims in some countries in forgetfulness of this fundamental principle sometimes commit errors. As a result, not only do they suffer themselves but also earn Islam a bad name. Muslims have been asked to specify their allegiance. In many countries, a large mass of the population is non Muslim. They require the Muslim minority to clearly state whether it owes allegiance to Islam or to the country.

The fact is that Islam is not confined to any nationality. Islam embraces all nationalities. In this, are concealed secrets of profound wisdom. It becomes obvious that nowhere in the world can there be a conflict between Islam and a national state, in other words there can be no possibility of a clash between the true universal principle of Islam with any segment of the world because, rationally, it is incomprehensible for the whole number to clash with any of its parts.

Had this not been the case it would have been impossible for Islam to be the religion of people living in various parts of the world. Islam would not have been a message of mercy for them. Islam could not have claimed that its message was of universal peace for all peoples. Subjects of a non-Muslim country could assert that for the Arabs, Indonesians, Malaysians or Pakistanis, Islam may carry a message of peace but Islam has no promise of peace for them because the Muslims are opposed to their national identity. This is a basic truth which at times is, unfortunately, forgotten by Muslims. They foment the concept of some form of Islamic nationalism and thus bring the Muslims in conflict with non-Muslims.

The fact is that we have to win the heart of the world. Hearts cannot be won by wars but are won in a different way. The struggle for the deliverance of a spiritual message entails procedures which have no resemblance to worldly fights. God taught various prophets different principles and strategies to wage this "spiritual battle" which cannot be applied to political wars. **For instance, the weapon that Jesus Christ[as], gave to the Christian was that if he is slapped on one cheek then he should offer the other. This is the approach that was prescribed to wage spiritual battles.** In practice, however, the Christians failed to grasp the meaning of this precept. As it was impracticable in every day life, they discarded it altogether. Therefore, not a single country in the world today acts on this wonderful spiritual teaching of Jesus[as]. If one misreads an injunction for a spiritual battle and tries to superimpose it on to a purely military affair, one is bound to find such an injunction impossible of performance. This can result in the total rejection of the spiritual injunction, even for appropriate occasions. The same is the situation today.

Religion is concerned with the spiritual world and its battle is fought in spiritual terms. **When it is said that Islam was created to triumph over all other religions in the world, this does not imply that one should pick up the sword and behead those who reject Islam. It does not mean that the promise of peace is only in favour of those who bow their heads and accept Islam, and for the rest, the Muslims become a message of war and disorder. This principle does not appeal to wisdom, neither is it practicable in the world nor will it ever succeed.** The Ahmadiyya Muslim Community should always have sight of this important principle. When we talk of striving for and aiming to establish the supremacy of Islam over all mankind, we talk in the terminology taught to us by the Holy Quran and by Muhammad[sas]. It is unrelated to the military terminology of the world.

This is the reason that today, Muslims who have failed to understand or who cannot understand these principles because their leaders have led them astray, find themselves in difficulties everywhere. Day by day this situation is worsening. There are weak

Muslim minorities in different countries. As a result of the misrepresentation of the teachings of Islam, they are unable to follow the right path. They are on the wrong path and, therefore, they suffer extreme harm. They misrepresent and thereby defame Islam.

A QUESTION OF LOYALTY TO ONES'S FAITH OR TO ONE'S COUNTRY

The question of loyalty to one's faith or to one's country is being raised everywhere in the world and now it is also being raised in Britain. Because of the lack of a convincing answer by the Muslims and because of their reaction based on ignorance, Muslims in Britain now face increased dangers. Their places of worship are being set on fire, they are being threatened; and they face dangers in every day life. There was news today that two taxi drivers were held up and badly beaten because they were alleged to be supporting Saddam Hussain.

All these violent reactions result from ignorance and misapprehension and have no link with Islam. The teachings of Islam have a universal appeal. Because of its inherent strength, it is invincible. No one can successfully oppose it because it is based on truth. Therefore, the Ahmadiyya Muslim Community must always and particularly in these times keep in mind the reasons for these reactions and respond with wisdom. Whenever, there is emotional excitement in the air, it is also reflected in the heart. The heart feels the tremor. That is the time of self analysis to examine whether one is following the true path of Islam or otherwise. One must also monitor his feelings, keeping in view, personal, national prejudices and differences. It is in times of extreme excitement that a God fearing man can make an appraisal of the depth of his faith. He can see his relationship with God reflected in the mirror of his heart. The members of the Ahmadiyya Muslim Community, all over the world, must comport in such a manner that an English Ahmadi, without hesitation can say with confidence that Islam teaches the truth, and that to a Muslim there is no conflict between his allegiance to his country and his faith. An Ahmadi from Africa can also proclaim that Islamic teachings are universal and based on truth and there is no question of any conflict with his national identity. The fact is that if the world was ever to consent to a universal teachings, then it is only Islam which presents such a teaching because it is above and beyond narrow nationalism. It is never opposed to nationalism because truth can never be in conflict with rational nationalism. If the concept of nationhood in any country is wrong, then it can be proved to be wrong by examining it in the mirror of **absolute truth.**

Therefore, when I say that Islamic teachings do not clash with nationalism I do not claim that the concept of nationalism of ALL countries is in agreement with the teachings of Islam. It is quite possible that the very concept and definition of nationalism in some countries might be distorted, as is the case in the **conception of JUSTICE.** The definition of loyalty has thus altered.

Sometimes, **"nationalism"** is understood to mean that one should remain loyal to one's country, whether it is on the right or wrong, irrespective of whether one is disloyal to the God-given higher human values!

If this be the definition of nationalism then Islam is certainly in conflict with it, but only in the sense that Islam will attempt to rectify this definition, irrespective of the sacrifices which such an action will entail, and so long as mankind does not follow the path of God and His teachings, Islam will resolutely oppose any distorted or erroneous nationalistic leanings and philosophy. The conflict arising from such opposition will result in many supporting voices being raised from all parts of the world.

The stand taken by The Ahmadiyya Muslim Community in the present world situation has found favour and many voices of approval are heard rising from many countries. Just two days ago, an Ahmadi from a Western country informed me that a well known and influential commentator had expressed identical views on the present crisis as though he had read my sermons. He enquired if I, or some other Ahmadi was in communication with him. This was not an isolated letter. I have received similar letters from many places. Apparently it is a tribute to my sermons but I am not so naive as to accept this as personal praise. *Praise is not due to me but to Islam.* All praise belongs to God and to God's revealed religion and this is the proof of the truth and excellence of that teaching.

However, that was a clear indication that people are beginning to recognise truth; this gave me satisfaction in the sense that my confidence was strengthened. That made me believe that whatever comments I have made on this situation are in accordance with the teachings of Allah. Otherwise such comments would not have found support both verbally and in writing in various countries.

The present crisis is a difficult time for the Muslims. At this difficult time you should be in control of your sentiments, emotion and thoughts, and keep them within the peaceful confines of Islam. The moment you step outside this circle of Islam, you will face danger.

DEFINITION OF JIHAD

The second question which is being frequently raised at the present time is about **Jihad**. Ahmadis from various countries ask me what reply should they give. Is this war a Jihad i.e Holy-War according to the teachings of Islam? I will respond to this question through this sermon because one cannot explain all the details in letters. As far as the definition of the concept of Jihad in Islam is concerned, the most comprehensive definition has been given in the Chapter Al-Haj of the Holy Quran in the verse which I have mentioned a number of times.

اُذِنَ لِلَّذِيْنَ يُقَاتَلُوْنَ بِاَنَّهُمْ ظُلِمُوْا

"Permission to fight is granted to those against whom war is made because they have been wronged." (Al-Haj:40)

That is, those people are granted permission to raise their sword against those who are engaged in fighting against them. They can raise their swords **only** against those who first commenced hostilities against them, not because of any justifiable cause but because they are oppressed and have been wronged. This verse develops this subject further and it is not possible to give a finer or more perfect definition of Jihad than this. **If we apply this definition to the present situation then it is definitely not Jihad in the Islamic sense. It is a political war.** A political war, whether it be between Muslims and non-Muslims or between one Muslim nation and another Muslim nation, does not become a Jihad. In fact some people misconstrue a **just war** to be Jihad and since each party believes that it is in the right, it declares that such a war is in the name of God for the sake of truth and therefore, it is Jihad. This may be a secondary definition of Jihad but however, as Jihad is defined in Islamic terminology, its definition does not apply in the present situation. Such a definition is against logic because whichever of the two fighting parties believe its struggle based on truth, it will consider its war as Jihad. Idolaters fight other idolaters. Followers of one religion fight the followers of another religion. Nations fight other nations, blacks fight whites. All kinds of wars are being fought, have been fought and will continue to be fought in the world. Whenever, two parties are fighting, it is obvious that if one party is not fully right, it will at least be partly right. It is not possible save perhaps, very rarely, that both parties are equally right or equally wrong. Generally, one party is oppressed and the other is the oppressor; the war of every oppressed people cannot be called Jihad. **Only the war of an oppressed group which is being prevented from declaring its faith in God or which is fighting against religious persecution on itself can be called Jihad.**

The Holy Quran says:

$$اِلَّا اَنْ يَقُوْلُوْا رَبُّنَا اللهُ$$

"They have committed no wrong except that they say: Allah is our Lord" (Al-haj 41)

If a war has been imposed on the Muslims only for declaring their faith in God, if it was the enemy that initiated the war, not the Muslims. If the Muslims have committed no wrong except that they declare God as their Lord and deny any associate with God. If the Muslims fight to defend their FAITH, in such circumstances, such a war is called Jihad. Jihad is not a war based on truth perse, but is the name of a war based on truth, in the sense that I have explained. **This situation does not apply to the war of Iraq with other nations.** Kuwait had upset Iraq for some reason. As a result, Iraq was displeased. Iraq believed that this tiny country was once part of Iraq but the British carved Kuwait out of Iraq and created a separate state. Iraq believed Kuwait is a part of its territory. To Iraq, Kuwait was just a puny country. After all, Iraq had fought for 8 long years with Iran and at one stage was poised to overpower this huge Muslim country. The Iraqi army had penetrated deep into Iranian territory. Later the Iraqis were pushed back. The see-saw in the battle fortunes went on during the war. Compared to Iran, Kuwait was of no consequence. Iraq may have thought that it could occupy the tiny country of Kuwait in no time and that is why it seized it. Whatever the reasons for Iraq's occupation of Kuwait could be, the world, particularly the world of Islam, should have collectively pondered over the rights and wrongs of the conflict and considered the whole episode against the general background of events.

THE REASONS BEHIND THE LABELLING OF POLITICAL WARS AS JIHAD

Therefore, we can neither call this war which was an aggression against Kuwait, a Jihad, nor can we call the war in reprisal against Iraq, as a Jihad. Many Muslims misuse Islamic terminology and therefore, become a source of defaming Islam. Islam is ridiculed throughout the world. The world mocks at Islam. Many Muslims do not realise their folly when they make such irresponsible utterances.

Nevertheless, we should consider why ordinary people are repeatedly deceived by their leaders and suffer exceptional sacrifices in these wars which are not in fact, Jihad but are misnamed as Jihad. There is certainly some deep rooted cause for this. We must discover what it is. If we understand the secret we shall also discover that the Western nations are themselves largely responsible for the incorrect interpretation of Jihad. If we analyze this situation correctly we find that those who pour scorn on Islam are themselves responsible for this misinterpretation of Jihad. For many centuries, this wrong notion of Jihad has been imported into Islam and it has created a sense of unease in the world. This undercurrent of fear about a holy-war cannot be traced to any particular source, but is quite generalised. **It could be due to fear of the unknown.** Islam came into the world as a new and powerful influence. One tries to locate the source of such fear but one fails to do so. In human relations, any fear or phobia once aroused generally remains, and tends to spread over time to different parts of the world.

ANTAGONISM BETWEEN THE EAST AND WEST

The manner in which the West has treated Muslims for centuries has convinced Muslims that its hatred for Muslims is based on religious differences. Whether the name of Islam is used or not, the West cannot tolerate the progress of Muslim Nations. Due to the fear of Muslim advancement, Western nations always adopt measures which aim to destroy Muslim power. This Western antagonism has been impressed on the minds of ordinary Muslims, whether or not they have studied any history. Certain trends and events have become fixtures in man's perception of history and merge in man's mind-set in the same way as some solubles mixed with water become part of the liquid element. One would know of the additives to the water for its taste, even if one does not witness the mixing. The Muslims in view of their long experience in history of Western antagonism and enmity are convinced that, in any crisis, the West is out to destroy and do harm to Islam.

During the present conflict and even before it, this impression has become stronger particularly in view of the attitude of U.S. Take for example, the establishment of Israel in the Muslim region. Although America was also involved in a major way, yet this mischief was initiated by British. It is the product of British minds.

Whenever there are wars, some secret pacts are made between nations and peoples. At that time, Britain entered into a pact with the Jews. Britain would grant the Jews land in the heart of Arabia to establish a Jewish independent state. The Jews would rule in the name of the **Kingdom of David** and exert its influence over the whole of Arabia and the world. This pact may not have been written in these words, but at the time of the drawing up of this pact, this was the message being conveyed to the Jews, because this was their dream which was being fulfilled.

HAS THE U.N. THE RIGHT TO CREATE NEW COUNTRIES?

Israel was created in the name of the United Nations and the greatest role played in its establishment was by the U.S. One matter that still amazes me is why was no question raised as to whether the U.N. has the right to create a new country in the world? The establishment of countries is a historical heritage which has continued on its own.

The authority of the U.N. only applied to those countries which then existed and had voluntarily joined it. There was no world mandate which stipulated that anyone whether it had joined the U.N. or not, would submit itself to United Nation's authority. Nor was the U.N. granted authority in the exercise of its jurisdiction to create a new nation state, or destroy a nation state, at its own discretion.

Therefore the U.N. acted ultra vires in creating Israel. There is no basis for the creation of that country. In creating this country the most dreadful and oppressive role has been played by U.S. This is a fact implanted permanently in Muslims memory. Although, for a long time, the Arabs have called it an Arab issue, yet the rest of the Muslims have automatically been involved in this issue because this has remained firmly established and engraved in their heart.

ISRAELI EXCESSES AND THE AMERICAN VETO

In fact the creation of Israel is not an act of enmity against the Arabs but against Islam. Time and again, this has manifested itself in various forms. For instance, at times, Israel has committed such dreadful atrocities on the Palestinians that even the mere thought of it makes one's hair stand on end and hearts bleed. The Israeli's have butchered men, women, children and elderly in such a way that in one camp they did not leave a single soul alive. They even butchered suckling babies yet the whole world did not pay any heed to it nor did America feel any shame. Rather, whenever the U.N. tried to pass any strongly worded resolution against Israel, U.S. always vetoed it. This has been going on for a long time.

THE UNITED NATIONS - DOES IT MERIT THIS NAME?

Now the question arises, does the U.N. deserve such a name when **only five nations** i.e. those permanent members who have the **VETO** power, possess the right to determine the destiny of the world? Even if world opinion is united, one of these five countries has the right to reject that opinion. For all intents and purposes that one country will then become the whole world. In fact, the same principle operated in the background to the present U.N. decision. **When President Bush haughtily asks the question "how dare Iraq stand up against world opinion" everyone knows that by world opinion, it is the American opinion that is meant or the opinion of President Bush. In that threat, there is such conceited arrogance that human nature abhors it.**

From the Muslim view point, Western military action is usually biased against Muslims and so the attack on Iraq is viewed in that light irrespective of the fact that Iraq was the first to commit aggression.

Tenth Friday Sermon Jan 25, 1991

The unspoken feelings of a Muslim is that Iraq was attacked in the interest of Israel. The accumulated experience of Western antagonism will affect Muslims thinking. An ordinary Muslim cannot but feel that the West is only active as usual in enmity to the Muslim world.

ISRAELI ATTACK ON IRAQ'S NUCLEAR PLANT

Israel has the right to send its jets to attack Iraq's nuclear plant and destroy it. Who determines that the nuclear plant is being built for the production of atomic bombs and not for peaceful purposes? Did the U.N. grant Israel this authority to raid and attack or did Israel, of its own, come to that decision? No one has ever claimed that Iraq has the right to take retaliatory action against Israel whenever it likes. Is it up to Iraq to decide whether it retaliates against Israel today, tomorrow or next day? After this naked Israeli aggression does the U.N. confer the right or to avenge itself? I have not heard of it, nor have my eyes read such news.

MUSLIM IMPRESSION IS BASED ON FACTS

The impression of the world of Islam that the present stance by the West is anti-Muslim is founded on fact. The world at large has seen the injustices and inequities perpetrated on the Muslims, and even if the world remains silent, it cannot erase such memories from its collective consciousness. It is strange that when Iraq attacks and fires its scud missiles at Israel and some parts of Israeli cities are damaged, the whole world raises a hue and cry against it and does not remember Palestine. It does not remember the air raid by Israel on the nuclear plant. Despite these attacks, Israel is laying the foundation for future atrocities against Muslims. These are facts which continually bruise and exacerbate the feelings of Muslims. **When they express their frustrations and injured feelings, the nations in which they live ask them if they owe allegiance to Islam or to the nation or states where they reside. What sort of justice is this? It is gross injustice to raise the spectre of nationalism or national loyalty, when citizens are expressing their opinions on factual issues and world events. Is the issue of nationalism raised to suppress true expression? This analysis is based on facts and truth and Muslims have every right to discuss and propagate it.**

The Gulf Crisis & The New World Order

Some of the dreadful things have manifested themselves. Far more are yet to come.

ISRAEL PERSUADED TO WAIT UNTIL U.S. HAS LIQUIDATED IRAQ

U.S. has had some secret talks with Israel when it sent an important government representative there. They decided amongst other things, certain secret matters which will remain secret for sometime. One of the matters discussed concerned about more than $6 billion given to Israel. It was not given to dissuade Israel from attacking Iraq during the Gulf war, it was to persuade Israel; to wait until U.S. has punished Iraq properly, and then Israel could go in to attack Iraq and avenge itself on Iraq as it thinks fit.

In the past, there used to be a custom that when a tyrant or someone considered to be a tyrant died, people who wanted to take their revenge used to dig up and hang his remains. The agreement between U.S. and Israel allows U.S. the opportunity to make a corpse of Iraq. The United States is rendering this service for Israel and will continue to undertake this service for Israel. **Once the U.S. has killed Iraq then it will hand it over to Israel so that Israel may hang that corpse whenever it wishes.** Now the question is, can all these things be called justice? Is such an arrangement human? Another fact the world has failed to notice is that the most lethal bombs dropped on the innocent civilian population of Iraq have been dropped subsequent to this agreement, mostly on the population of Western Iraq. If Iraq had committed injustice, injustice a thousand fold has been done to Iraq. If one Israeli home was destroyed then hundreds of Iraqi homes have been destroyed. If one Israeli was injured then thousands of Iraqis have been killed. Those who have returned from Iraq say that there is such a stench of dead bodies that some areas have become impassable. There is a smell of burning and rotting flesh, and the whole area is desolate. This is what U.S. has done on behalf of the Jews. This is the evidence of the secret protocols the details of which have not been revealed, but which in fact are open secrets.

U.S. PREACHING HUMANITY AND MORALITY TO THE WORLD

Yet U.S. claims to be the standard bearer of humanity. It talks from a high moral ground preaching humanity and morality to the world! U.S. often denounces other nations for alleged disgraceful conduct. It censures the world for its ignorance of humanistic values. U.S. blames Iraq for bombarding unarmed innocent Israelis. Iraq's bombardment is no doubt utterly wrong.

Islam does not permit the harming of unarmed innocent citizens in any way whatsoever. The religion of Muhammad[sas] does not allow it. Whenever Jihad of the sword was invoked the detailed instructions Hazrat Muhammad[sas] used to give to the armies, before they departed, was that they must not kill civilians, the elderly, women and children. Muslims must not harm such people. This correct Islamic teaching derives from Hazrat Muhammad[sas] instructions and from his practice.

Therefore, I don't say that what Iraq did was right. However I do say that even if Iraq had committed a wrong then according to the rules and regulations of the world of which U.S. claims to be the "standard bearer", U.S. should have viewed this action of Iraq as retaliatory in nature. The Muslims who reside in Israel are shot at day in and day out; they are unarmed and are murdered and have become targets for bullets. If some retaliatory action is taken on their behalf, the U.S. does not accept that it is justified and lawful. U.S. considers this is blatant injustice, beastly oppression and an aggression for which Israel has the right to strike back. Then U.S. makes secret pacts with Israel and gives money to Israel to enable it to commit dreadful atrocities on Muslims, to satisfy Israel's full sense of revenge. U.S. in effect is handing over all the innocent survivors who lived through its attacks to Israel to deal with, in accordance to its whims. Israel can hang Iraqi corpses to satisfy its lust for revenge in full measure.

ARE THESE ATTACKS INTENDED TO PUNISH SADDAM OR THE INNOCENT PEOPLE OF IRAQ?

These matters are totally opposed to the moral values the U.S. and the West widely proclaim. Their actions speak louder than their words. The propaganda they have initiated is that President Saddam Hussein is a dangerous dictator and is being punished because he has enslaved his citizens. They are punishing him because he is persecuting the citizens of his country and has tyrannised over them. They say they are against President Saddam, and not against the people of Iraq. They are liberating the people of Iraq from the despotism and tyranny of a vicious and ruthless dictator. But U.S. and the West are punishing the innocent people who according to their statements, President Saddam has been killing, maiming and oppressing for years. Then what is the crime of these innocent women and children? According to U.S. and Western claims these Iraqi women and children have been oppressed. This war was started to liberate them. Therefore, why should U.S. and the West punish them for the crimes which President Saddam has committed against Israel?

The punishment inflicted on these innocent women and children is so fierce that no example of such punishment can be found even in the history of the Jews. What right has U.S. to debase and sally the pure teaching of Christianity and stain the history of Christianity with blood in the same way as the history of the Jews has been stained with gory blood. These are inequities. They are against justice. They are against Righteousness. These create a negative reaction in the heart of Muslims. In spite of this, Muslims are peaceful citizens of the countries in which they reside. They raise their voice in protest against this injustice without infringing the law of the land yet they are declared to be traitors, and the West takes action against them. What kind of justice is this? An Ahmadi Muslim telephoned and told me that he was being asked to give an interview on a T.V channel or the BBC. He asked me what our stand was. He wanted my advice as to what comments or views he was to give on the present situation. I told him to say that his view is exactly the same as that expressed by **Tony Benn the British M.P.** I further advised him to give the following answer.**'If a fair-minded person is raising the true voice of my heart then what need have I to raise that voice myself, because if I raise it you will denounce me as a traitor, but if Tony Benn raises that voice, you will not dare to call him a traitor'**

NO MUSLIM RULER IS JUSTIFIED TO TERM THIS WAR AS AN ISLAMIC JIHAD

Whatever is happening is against justice. It is against righteousness. There is no law, there is no principle, there is no high moral ground. The U.S. and West have descended to the lowest levels of moral degradation. In the light of righteousness what I have said, is the correct situation at present.

Tenth Friday Sermon Jan 25, 1991

In spite of this, no Muslim scholar or Muslim ruler has the right to call these wars Islamic Jihad. However, when the Muslims masses are summoned to arms in the name of Jihad, they will enthusiastically answer the call because deep in their hearts and from their sad experiences they had undergone again and again, are aware that there is a strong undercurrent of enmity and animosity against Islam. This animosity underlies and fuels these wars against Muslims.

When such people so aroused fight and are killed, I have firm faith in Allah's mercy that He will treat them mercifully even though they cannot be declared to be martyrs in the context of perfect teachings of Islam. These people fight in good faith and firmly believe to right the wrongs and injustices done to Islam, therefore, Allah will treat them with mercy and forgiveness. However, **I repeat that neither the Muslim clergy nor the Muslim rulers have the right to declare their political wars as Jihad even if they are at wars against oppression.**

HATE BEGETS HATE

In fact, the animosity against Islam that I have described is becoming more evident and manifest day by day, and it is a continuing hatred. Vague utterances for peace may be made in public, but an underlying current of hate is detected when the utterances are closely analyzed. U.S. and the West continue to depict Muslims as evil, painting them in very dark colours. These wicked images of Muslims are publicised by the media to the world to subvert Islam. In such an atmosphere, one thing is certain; there can be no peace. The atmosphere is too poisonous for the launching of any peace process, as hate can only beget hate, not peace.

All the so called efforts now being hatched to establish peace in the Middle East will come to nought. When so much hate has been sown it is not possible to bring in a harvest of peace, only a harvest of hate. These are seeds of war, not peace. So in effect what the U.S. and the West are now doing will certainly produce turmoil and commotion in that region and destroy all chances of peace in the world. God will, in due course, punish those responsible for this tragedy, because man is helpless.

UNPREJUDICED COMMENTS

The Ahmadiyya Muslim Jamaat expresses it views frankly, openly, honestly and impartially, not out of spite, prejudice, bigotry or with ulterior motives. The Jamaat believes in the Oneness and Unity of God, and acts and speaks in that belief. In the circumstances, the Jamaat cannot harbour prejudices, bigotry or ill-feelings, because such feelings cannot co-exist in the minds of those who believe in the Oneness and Unity of God. Once a person believes implicitly in the Oneness and Unity of God, that person cannot possibly entertain feelings of prejudice or bigotry in expressing his views. This is a fundamental and unchangeable law.

I declare on behalf of the Ahmadiyya Muslim Jamaat that the comments I make are based on truth and I do so honestly and impartially. They may appear bitter to some. But no matter how bitter they may appear to be, the world, if not today then in the near future, will accept the truth of what I say and will agree to this truth that I made these comments without any trace of prejudice, bigotry or ulterior motives.

However, there are other matters which need to be addressed, matters which cause us deep and painful distress. Take for instance the haughty and arrogant posture of the U.S. President, when he talks of Iraq or those countries which have not submitted to his will. He talks and acts as if he were "God Almighty" descended on earth. A true believer in the Oneness and Unity of God cannot and will not bow his head to such arrant arrogance.

There are various kinds of idolatry and false objects of worship but the most detestable and abhorrent form is that associated with arrogance. Therefore, it is the foremost duty of a believer in the Unity of God to raise his voice to protest against the manifestation of overweening arrogance. The Ahmadiyya Muslim Jamaat is the foremost among those who believe in the Oneness and Unity of God, it is the standard-bearer of that belief, and in fact the duty of preserving that concept and belief has devolved on it. Therefore, The Ahmadiyya Muslim Community raises its voice of protest against all forms of idolatry and the setting up of false idols and all kinds of arrogance. No fear of the world can stifle this voice. We will do so without fear or trepidation because we must condemn false idols or entities masquerading as "God". We will never submit to such false

Tenth Friday Sermon Jan 25, 1991

entities who may believe they control this world, as such false entities are in direct opposition to the pure concept of the Oneness and Unity of God, the sole creator and master of the worlds.

Some Ahmadis write and ask me why do I publicise my views and comments, and they express serious concern for my safety and physical well being. I tell them that I am following in the footsteps of my lord and master Hazrat Muhammad[sas]. When he raised his voice in support of the concept of the Oneness and Unity of God, then not only Mecca but the whole world opposed him. His followers begged him to refrain from his preaching as his own life was in serious danger. But Hazrat Muhammad[sas] told them then and repeatedly on later occasions that he was ready to undergo any sacrifice in the cause of proclaiming the Oneness and the Unity of God. He said, "This is the purpose of my life. This is the essence of my message and this is the spirit of my faith. Therefore, you isolate me from everything else but you cannot prevent me form proclaiming the Unity of God and from conveying the message of His Oneness. What is it that you say? By God, if you put the sun on my right hand and the moon on my left, I will reject them but I will never abandon the concept of the Unity of God."

And those of you who worry about my safety I say "What do you think I am scared of? I am not in the least concerned about the power of the U.S. or that of the Jews or that of Britain or for that matter the combined strength of the powers of the whole world. If in proclaiming again and again the Oneness and Unity of God I become shattered into bits and pieces, by so doing, even then every bit and piece of my shattered body will rise to proclaim:-

فزت برب الكعبة   فزت برب الكعبة

"I swear by the God of the Holy Kaaba, that I have succeeded"
"I swear by the God of the Holy Kaaba, that I have succeeded"

This is the voice which should rise today from the hearts and souls of all Ahmadis throughout the world. It should rise from each and every particle of their body.

VERDICT OF DESTINY

What programmes are the U.S. and the West preparing? On what powers do they rely? They talk of *desert storm*! Little do they know that the real and dreadful storms are in the hands of God. I do not know what the decree of Allah will be but I do know for certain that the decree of Allah will eventually cause the destruction of the arrogant and the boastful.

If not today, then tomorrow, this over bearing arrogance will be utterly destroyed. This is so, because to God belong the Kingdom of heaven and God's Kingdom will certainly be established on earth also. So if not today, tomorrow, if not tomorrow then the day after, you will see that this arrogance will be destroyed and erased from the world. The storms they started will turn on them, and in fulfilment of God's decree, those storms will be so violent and ferocious that their combined collective forces will be annihilated and crushed into oblivion. Existing unjust system will be destroyed. You must remember this and remain steadfast. Remember and do not ever forget that these obsolete powers which in effect constitute what is known as the United Nations today use means and pursue policies which cannot last. These nations will disappear and become national relics of bitter memories from which lessons can be drawn. It is from their ruins, that YOU O' worshipper of the Unity of Allah, Yes, it is YOU who will build a new structure; YOU will erect a magnificent and lofty building for a new United Nations which will reach up to the heavens. O servants of Messiah of Muhammad[sas] it is YOU to whom has been granted this task. You will see it, if not today, then tomorrow; if you see it not, your future generations will certainly see it. **These are the words spoken by Allah and His decree cannot be altered in the world. You are the workers who have to build these new structures. The foundation of the new United Nations have already been laid in heaven. It is YOU - who have to build from the foundation and raise the building to a great height.** You must not ever erase names of those workers i.e Hazrat Abraham[as] and Hazrat Ishmael[as] from your hearts. Always remember

Tenth Friday Sermon Jan 25, 1991

them and continue to exhort your future generations as follows: O' workers in the cause of Allah remain firm in the path of righteousness, honesty, sincerity and the Unity of Allah. Let that Unity enter into every vein and fibre of your being and continue this glorious work of construction; if necessary continue it into the next century, and into the century after that, until this building reaches its completion.

The foundation of this building was laid by Hazrat Abraham[as] assisted by his son Ishmael[as]. Allah has decreed, and His decree is immutable that when the erection is finished, the honour of its completion will be awarded to our lord and master the Holy Prophet of Islam[sas]. We are mere labourers; we are menial servants of Hazrat Muhammad[sas]. We are his humble servants. You should continue to work faithfully, you must remind your children, generation after generation, that they must continue to work as labourers in the cause of Allah; even if such work may entail the shedding of the blood and sweat; they should never tire nor desist but continue working until God's will or decree is fulfilled. لِيُظْهِرَهُ عَلَى الدِّيْنِ كُلِّهِ

God's decree is that the religion of Muhammad[sas] was sent to the world for the purpose that it will eventually embrace and incorporate all other religions and there will be only one flag which be the flag of Hazrat Muhammad[sas] the Messenger of Allah and there will be one religion that of God and Muhammad[sas]. There would be only one kingdom ruling the world, the kingdom of God. May Allah so destine that we may see this happening with our own eyes; if not then our children should see it, and seeing it they shall remember us; and if our children cannot see it, then their children will see it with their own eyes.

I assure you that, whether you can see it with your worldly eyes or not, the eyes of my soul see these events today. My eyes see these great changes as if they are happening before me. After our deaths our souls will be made aware of them. They will be told O' slaves of Allah O' those who passionately love Allah, find ever lasting bliss and tranquillity, because the paths on which you had made sacrifices have become highways. The buildings on which you had placed brick, stone and pebbles have reached completion and attained heights of a magnificent

and glorious edifice to the UNITY OF ALLAH. It shall happen, it shall so happen. May Allah enable us to serve our utmost to achieve this goal.
Amen.

In the name of Allah, the Gracious, the Merciful

ELEVENTH FRIDAY SERMON

FEBRUARY 01, 1991

THE ATTITUDE OF THE MUSLIM COUNTRIES IN THE GULF WAR

PRESENT WAR HAS ITS ROOTS IN THE CONSPIRACIES HATCHED A CENTURY AGO

REAL SOLUTION TO THE CRISIS LIES IN TRUE TEACHINGS OF ISLAM

After reciting the Opening Chapter of the Holy Quran, Al-Fatiha, Hazoor said:

HIGH TREASON AGAINST ISLAMIC INTERESTS

Islamic history is sullied with horrifying instances of treacherous betrayals. With the exception of the era of the Holy Prophet Muhammad[sas] and the time stretching until a little after the four Caliphs, if you take a slice of the remaining history, its study reveals that some traitors from among the Muslims had always been procured to inflict damage on the Muslims; without their assistance the Muslim nation could never be damaged. Against the backdrop of such history, the current war adds the saddest chapter, for never before did so many Islamic governments join in hatching such a horrifying conspiracy against the interests of the Muslim nation. Regardless of what the contemporary observers might say, to bamboozle the collaborating Muslim countries, the researchers and historians of tomorrow in the Western world, would say the same thing that I am saying today: that some Muslim countries joined hands with anti-Islamic powers, thus committing high treason against the Islamic interests, and tried to annihilate an up-and-coming Islamic country. Up to this moment we can only say that the future historian would record the fact that these

Muslim countries fully collaborated with the enemies of Islam to destroy a great Islamic nation, and that they did not display an iota of justice, compassion or even national pride.

EGYPT AND SAUDI ARABIA

I expected such behaviour from a few countries such as Saudi Arabia and Egypt. **Egypt:** because it has yielded to international pressure and, in order to regain some of its lost territory, is shackled by its treaties with Israel and Western powers now regard Egypt as its satellite. **Saudi Arabia:** because its treacheries against the Islamic world are of historic proportions. **Saudi Arabia was born of treachery and established through treachery.** It has consistently served the purposes of Britain and the United States. Occupation of two most holy cities of Islam was reason enough for it to don the sham mantle of religious ostentation which awed many Islamic governments and they forged a loving relationship with Saudi Arabia out of the simple reason that they thought that it represented Mecca and Medina or, in other words, it was a representative of the Holy Prophet Muhammad[sas], and God.

THE RELATIONSHIP BETWEEN THE U.S. AND SAUDI ARABIA

In this regard, I have repeatedly tried to convince the representatives of some Muslim countries that you have fallen prey to a great deception. I am well aware of the history of Saudi Arabia, and fully conversant with the history of **"Wahabi"** sect of Islam.

Do you think that the sounds emanating from the minarets of Mecca and Medina are those of Allah and His Prophet? The truth is that these minarets simply project the loudspeakers which are connected to the microphones located in Washington where Israel is the speaker using these microphones. This is such an obvious fact that no intricate debate is needed for it. Anyone who is even mildly aware of the contemporary situation knows this fact very well that Saudi Arabia is completely in the clutches of the U.S. and that the U.S. has completely capitulated to Israeli ascendancy and has practically incorporated Israeli primacy as part of its policy.

WHO ARE THE "BRITISH AGENTS" AND THE "JEWISH AGENTS"?

This situation is so transparent, but Muslim countries remained blind to it all along. One reason for this is the false and malicious propaganda that the Ahmadiyya Muslim Jamaat has been subjected to, in accusing us of being "British agents." So whenever we cautioned the representatives of Muslim countries regarding Saudi Arabia, they would interpret it as our attempt to take revenge from Saudi Arabia and thought that there was no truth to what we said. But now the truth has been laid bare for the whole world to see. Even the Muslim Clergy who were on the Saudi payroll and would brand Ahmadis as "British agents" or sometimes "Jewish agents", now are declaring using such filthy language in their statements as is the common street language in Pakistan and is unbecoming for us to even quote; they used similar language here in the United Kingdom as well that the Saudis are "Jewish agents" or "Western agents", and that the Islamic world has only now found out the truth.

ECONOMIC MISERY MAY HAVE FORCED CERTAIN NATIONS TO BARTER THEIR FAITH

In a word, the treachery of Saudi Arabia warranted no surprise on our part, we were sure that they will act the way they did, this has been their policy which they have always adhered to. But it is very unfortunate that some countries, more recently, have betrayed the interest of Islam in such a way which was not even remotely expected of them. I think, this too has been due to the U.S. and Saudi pressure and influence over these countries who, on account of their economic misery, decided to barter their faith away. Those, from whom one would not have ever expected to behave this way, include Pakistan, Turkey and Syria.

I did not expect this from **Pakistan** because, no matter how pro-U.S. the government of Pakistan may be, I know, being a Pakistani myself, that the people and armed forces of Pakistan have a spirit that cannot allow them to attack another Muslim country in collaboration with Western powers, or to join their ranks to justify their belligerence. It was impossible for Pakistani psyche to accept this state of affairs. But in spite of all this, when the present government of Pakistan fully sided with the allies in their atrocious venture, I was shocked beyond belief as to how can this happen! But thank God that

Eleventh Friday Sermon Feb 01, 1991

a couple of days ago the Chief of Pakistan Army Staff, **General Aslam Beg** has shredded the myth that the stance of Pakistan government found any favour in the army. He outspokenly absolved himself of this act and voiced his strong disapproval of the government's decision which he described as a wrong decision which is inimical to the interest of the Muslim nation.

As for **Turkey**, it has, for centuries, earned such a good name as the protector of Muslim interests all over the world that Europe knew Turkey principally on account of this role; and the Osmani government of Turkey used to send shock waves through them. Europe knew that as long as Osmani government of Turkey is intact, there is no chance of European diffusion in the Islamic world; none whatsoever. **So, by a single decision, now Turkey has tarnished its long and great history**; it has besmirched the Turkish nation in a way that would not be undone except, maybe, with their blood that may wash this ugly scar, perhaps in the wake of a great revolution. As for **Syria**, I did not expect them to act the way they did, on account of several reasons. For one thing, Hafiz-al-Asad has been fighting against Israel because the Syrian territory of **Golan Heights** was annexed by Israel. Also Syria has given many sacrifices ever since the historical era of Israel's establishment began. Syria has lost its territories but did not change its standpoint. **Moreover the frightening image of Saddam that the Western nations are projecting these days, is nothing compared to the horrifying and ugly picture of President Hafiz-al-Asad that was once painted by these very nations, and that still stands.** So, I could not imagine, in an atmosphere of invective being hurled against President Saddam by the Western nations who are indulging in his character assassination, how President Hafiz Asad would ever feel comfortable embracing these Western powers. But I saw President Bush and President Hafiz Asad on T.V., seated on the same sofa, engaged in a friendly chat, thus enacting a stunning change in their policies.

<u>COMMENDABLE BEHAVIOUR OF IRAN</u>

I did not expect any treacherous behaviour from Iran, nor do I at the moment. That is because, as I have openly admitted a number of times that their religious differences notwithstanding, the Iranian nation does not behave hypocritically when it comes to Islam; they are the true lovers of Islam. It may be that their perception of Islam is distorted; it may be that we differ from some tenets of the Shiite dogma. It may be that their temporal perspective on Islam or their political conceptualization of Islam may be erroneous, and I think that it is, but it is inconceivable for the Iranian nation to deliberately betray Islam. Their history is also illuminated with great deeds in the service of Islam. In fact, the academic and scholarly service of Islam conducted by the Greater Iran, some of which is now under Russian occupation, if that service is juxtaposed with the services performed by the rest of the Islamic world, there would hardly be any comparison. Iran's services to Islam are second to none.

Thank God, that Iran has fulfilled what was expected of it. Iran has had a deep resentment and dispute with the government of President Saddam with which they have fought an eight-year bloody war. If Iran had stood up now against Iraq, the world would have found it understandable; the historian too would have forgiven Iran for taking advantage of this situation after such a horrible war. After all, at times, human emotions get inflamed out of control. At such times one cannot be given to profound analysis of the interests of Islam and the Islamic nation; one is given to sentimentalism. So to that extent the historian would have forgiven Iran.

Iran, though it has not thrown its weight behind Iraq, has struck a completely neutral stance, and reminded Iraq of Iraqi inequities and pointed out to the Western powers their injustice. In other words, **Iran stood firm on the principle of justice.** From this viewpoint, Iran would always be remembered most honourably in the annals of Islam. *Insha Allah.*

AN UNPARDONABLE CRIME OF SAUDI ARABIA AND EGYPT

This was a brief commentary on the political faithfulness or unfaithfulness to Islam. When I refer to Islam, in political parlance I am referring to the Islamic Nation or *'Millat'*. In this context I would further like to say that two Muslim countries stood out from the religious perspective; Saudi Arabia has been lucky to be the custodian and caretaker of the holiest places of Islam which undeniably confers a unique distinction on it within the entire Islamic world; then Egypt, as the embodiment and cultivator of Islamic learning - the scholarly achievements of **Jamia Al-Azhar** in the latter part of Islamic glory are

Eleventh Friday Sermon Feb 01, 1991

unparalleled in the whole world. So it was not even remotely expected from these two counties, given these facts, that they would betray the Islamic nation. They remind me of a couplet I had heard when I was young and liked it much, but now, only so-so, namely;

آگ دی صیاد نے جب آشیانے کو میرے
جن پہ تکیہ تھا دی پتے ہوا دینے لگے

"When the hunter torches my nest, to set it ablaze; the very foliage that the nest rested upon, whipped up the fire."

The two countries on which the "nest of the Islamic world" was resting, as far as sanctimonious regard and scholarship is concerned, when the enemy set the nest of the Islamic world on fire, these two countries were among those who fanned this fire. It is a crime which history would never adjudge as pardonable.

Allah alone knows what is destined for today or tomorrow, whether His Reward or Punishment is going to be manifest in this world or in the Hereafter; God alone is the Master Who can bring the best judgement. But as far as worldly perception goes, the ill effects are partly unfolding now and the remaining ones would stretch well into the times to come, and these would not remain confined to this part of the world, rather these would be much broader and would spread much farther.

THE WAR AS EVALUATED BY WESTERN COMMENTATORS

Another aspect of this war that I wish to put before you, concerns the purpose of this war; why is it being waged? What is its motivation and significance? Unless we understand it well, we cannot say what should be the correct stand of the Islamic nations or what should be the world view, or what action should the United Nations take in this regard. Appropriate remedy cannot be prescribed in the absence of a proper analysis of the disease and its diagnosis.

So, in the remaining part of this sermon, I will present a brief analysis of the causes, real motives and objectives of this war, so that in light of this, I may present some suggestions for the benefit of the United Nations as well as for other nations of the world including the Muslim world, as to what is the solution to these problems from the Ahmadiyya Muslim viewpoint. And if serious consideration is to be given to establishment of peace in the world in future, how should one approach it.

Right now we are hearing the Western claims, and President Bush is most vociferously projecting these claims, that this is not a religious war; this war is not intended to serve any selfish interests; it is not an oil-war; it is not a war to further Western interests; it is not an Islamic war or a Jewish war or a Christian war.

What kind of war is it then? They claim that this is a war for truth and justice; this war is between truth and falsehood; between virtue and vice; this war is being waged by the whole world against a ruthless barbarian Saddam. This is the American view which is being so forcefully propagated through radio, T.V. and newspapers that the majority of the Western world has accepted it as the truth.

But there are many just-minded and perceptive observers - I am speaking of the Western observers - which include politicians, intellectuals, journalists and people from many other walks of life, who are raising their voices that this is all false and mere propaganda; our leaders are openly deceiving us. This war is for something else. **Mr. Edward Heath**, the former Prime Minister of U.K. is among the greatest living personalities in Britain who are endowed with foresight and political acumen as well as extensive political experience. He has consistently held that our present political leadership is practising deception upon us, and that this war is extremely selfish, brutal and foolish for, according to him, it will produce horrifying evil consequences in the post-war era.

Anyway, I do not wish to go into any further details as to what is being said by the Western thinkers in general. Summarily, this is the second voice that is being heard that this war is for oil; it has selfish motives; it is in defence of Israel and it is a war to achieve the Israeli objectives. Some say it is a war between President Bush and President Saddam and, according to this view, it has become a matter of personal ego for President Bush and his decision-power as his emotions are no longer in his control. When he speaks, he loses self-control and uses such childish prattle that it does not seem as if a great national leader is speaking. Those who hold this view stress their point that this war is really President Bush's war because President Bush has extreme hatred against President Saddam due to the latter's

Eleventh Friday Sermon Feb 01, 1991

refusal to accept American hegemony and control; this has given rise to the American wrath which is getting out of hand.

THE LONG DRAWN PLAN OF JEWISH DOMINATION

Now, let us see what the reality and truth is, because the Ahmadiyya Muslim Jamaat should not reach sentimental decisions because we do not have just ourselves to worry about, but the entire world to care for. Even though we are weak, small and powerless, everyone of us believes that God has entrusted to us the leadership in service to mankind, in this world.

We have been made leaders in the world, whereas "leader" has the same meaning as explained by the Holy Prophet[sas],

$$\text{سَيِّدُ الْقَوْمِ خَادِمُهُمْ}$$

i.e., *"A nation's leader is its servant."* That is to say, a leader and a servant are synonymous. If someone does not know how to serve, then he has no right to lead and if someone gets to be a leader then it is his duty to devote himself to service. So it is only in this sense, and in no other sense of the word that I speak of us as being leaders. Therefore, we have to serve mankind, we have to teach them how to recognise the right from the wrong and to convince them as to where the interest of all humanity lies; what is in their own benefit and what is not beneficial for them. From this point of view I wish to describe this matter in full detail, so that Ahmadi Muslims, wherever they may be, they must raise their voice accordingly and try to alter the opinion and thinking in their environment.

This issue actually was born near the end of the last century. **The war of today has very deep roots.** In 1897, a council was established to achieve Zionist objective. It consisted of that part of the Jews who believe in the Kingdom of David[as] which, according to their beliefs, will definitely be established one day. They are known as Israelis or the Zionists. So, a Zionist Council was established which proclaimed its declaration, the details of which, we need not go at the moment.

At about the same time another Jewish document or manuscript came before the world for the first time, namely: *Protocols of the Elders of Zion*. This is the same Zion that I have referred to earlier, which stands for Israel. Zion is the name of the mountain on which, it is related, David[as] was promised the Kingdom. This was a scheme of the top leaders of Israel, who believe in Zionism, as to how they shall dominate the world, what mode of action shall be adopted for this purpose, what will be the work principles and objectives, what means will be adopted, etc., etc.

It is a small booklet, the date of its publication, I do not remember but I can recall with certainty that towards the end of the 19th century, around 1897, this document, was for the first time, discovered by a Russian woman who was in fact working as a secretary for these Elders of Zion in Germany, and one of them was her friend. In Germany, one night, as she waited for the arrival of her friend in his house, she casually picked up a manuscript from his table, just to kill time. This happened to be the manuscript known as The Protocols of the Elders of Zion. She became so flabbergasted upon reading through an awe-inspiring scheme to conquer the world that she ran away with that manuscript and smuggled it to Russia where it was published for the first time and its first English translation appeared in 1905.

So, it is around the same time when they hatched a secret plan and on the other hand revealed a more apparent programme, the latter being the subject of no controversy or dispute. The Jews assert that it is true that they had a programme of action which was made public, and it consisted of promoting their influence impinging on the relations between various governments with the objective of achieving Israel as their separate and independent homeland.

The second plan envisaged a "United Nations" (although the U.N. did not exist at that time, not did the League of Nations, for that matter; but this plan contains all these ingredients) and after its description the plan expresses the hope that following these achievements and realizing the goal of establishing the United Nations, the Jews would then acquire control of the United Nations and exercise, through it, their dominion over the whole world. This plan of capturing the United Nations and using it as an instrument to rule the whole world was bound to take a considerable amount of time as it did. However, all the intermediate steps envisaged in their plan did come to pass in the manner mentioned in the plan.

When the Jews absolved themselves of this plan and maintained that it was just attributed to them, the learned observers, politicians and intelligentsia, debated that claim all over the world. It led to litigation in several courts. A protestant from Britain has published a well documented book entitled *"Water Flowing Eastward"* which discussed all aspects of the plan. I had an opportunity to read the book about 20 years ago. Someone borrowed it from me and then it changed many hands until it no longer remained possible for me to locate it. I have looked for it in the United Kingdom but it is not available. This book also mentioned that the Jews lifted this book off the market immediately. Regardless of whether the Jews do it or someone else does, but it is a fact, and I have witnessed it, that it did disappear from the market. Therefore, I will not be able to quote the precise words but my statement of its subject matter is primarily correct.

The author of this book mentions that when a Western politician was asked if the manuscript attributed to the Jews is in fact authored by Jewish leaders or is it just a conspiracy against the Jews and an attempt to malign them. The politician responded that in his opinion there are only two possibilities: either this plan is in fact drawn up by those to whom it is attributed - for all the subsequent events that have transpired are precisely in accord with this plan and could not have occurred in the same order and detail as foretold in the plan - or perhaps this is a revealed book of a prophet of God who gained this prior knowledge from the Divine and thus prophesied!

So the Western statesman could find only two possibilities: either the plan was conceived by those who are flagrantly belying its authorship now or it may have come from a true saint who was informed by God that such events would transpire in the future.

THE JEWISH PLAN WILL NEVER SUCCEED

The era we are passing through now is the last phase of the completion of this plan. When the rapprochement between the USSR and the Unite States started and the Berlin Wall started to come down, I recalled this plan. I did not have it with me at that time to refresh my memory of it but I did recall what it stated in its epilogue i.e., we will first divide the whole world and them unify it; and this will happen when our occupation of the 'United Nation' would have become complete.

I was, therefore, apprehensive that perhaps that dangerous era is close at hand. But in spite of this fear, which is a natural reaction to my being a witness to several major indications of the time, I do have the perfect faith in the ultimate failure of this plan. My assertion is based on a 1901 revelation of the Promised Messiah[as], that:

"فری میسن مسلط نہیں کئے جائیں گے کہ اس کو ہلاک کریں"

"Freemasons will never be imposed, lest they destroy you."

The grandeur of this revelation of the Promised Messiah[as] is further established when we consider that this revelation was made in 1901, while the manuscripts were translated into the Russian language in 1905. The English rendering was not even published by then. At that time, the world did not have the slightest idea of a Jewish plan to dominate the world. One is astonished to learn that at a time when no one knew about the "Freemasons", God revealed to the Promised Messiah[as] in the tiny and unknown village in **Qadian** - India, that a plan would be hatched for the Jewish domination, in which the "Freemasons" would play a significant role. In other words, "Freemasons" will gain dominance. But God promised that the "Freemasons" would never gain domination over you or upon your Community.

So, I am definite in my belief that this plan would ultimately fail but before meeting its destiny it would have caused its extremely dangerous venom to spread throughout the world, resulting in many quakes and several disasters would have engulfed many nations.

A very dangerous era awaits us because a huge plan of such dimensions is unlikely to suddenly flop under its own weight. This plan will push through with full force and become fully fledged, then the Will of God will square off against it to demolish and definitely neutralize it. But in the meantime, we must get mentally prepared for the fact that mankind will go through many severely trying times and face great hardships. And some part of it is bound to rub off on the Ahmadi Muslims, for it is impossible for the Community of the Truthful to remain totally unscathed during tribulations and chastisement of international proportions; it would share hardship to some extent.

But when all this is over, the day of Islam's propagation and victory and the dominance of Ahmadiyyat will come. This is indeed that final destiny which will definitely take over and that

Eleventh Friday Sermon Feb 01, 1991

indeed will be the New World Order, and not the new world structure which is in President Bush's mind and which he wants to sell to the world as the New World Order.

But I now leave this subject and would like to revert to the earlier topic and say that contemporary world situation is rooted in the plan that was founded around the year 1897, at least apparently, because it was then that the efforts directed towards the establishment of the state of Israel were started. After that, the second big step seems to have been taken in 1917 when the then British Foreign Secretary Mr. Balfour wrote to Rothschild who was a rich and influential member of the Jewish community.

A FRIGHTFUL ERA OF DREADFUL CONSPIRACIES AGAINST ISLAM

The First world Zionist Congress, whose then president was Dr. Theodor Herzl, was held in the year 1897 and their plan was formally published in August 1897. In 1916, Mr. McMahon who represented the British government wrote a letter to Sheriff Hussein of Mecca and Medina who was then the Governor of Hijaz, (he hailed from an East Jordanian dynasty and was representing the Turkish government in the land of Hijaz). This letter can be summarized as proposing that if you agree upon showing us some favours, then, as a reward for those services, we will help you to get rid of the tyrannical government of Turkey and set up an independent Arab State. Some areas, on a map, were marked as **A** while others as **B**, in other words, designating some of them as areas of English-dominion and others as those of French-dominion.

Briefly, those conditions meant that, if accepted, the agreement would empower the British and the French, in their respective spheres of influence thus carved out, to be solely responsible for formulating foreign policy. Hijaz will be bound to conduct its external affairs only with the approval and permission of the respective governments of Britain and France, depending under whose territorial influence the affair belonged. So much so, that they would not be allowed to invite any European observer or advisor unless permitted by the British in their sphere of influence or by the French in their sphere of domination.

While these parleys with the **Sheriff of Mecca** were in progress there was a conspiracy simultaneously brewing with the Saudi dynasty, i.e. the leader of the *Wahabi Sect*, that if they agree to accept British hegemony in the area permanently and agree to the formation of their foreign policy with the consent of the British government - and several other conditions - then the British government would help this dynasty and install it in power in the land of Hijaz and would permanently protect them against any possible aggression. With this agreement in place, a pre-planned attack was launched within a few years and the Sheriff of Mecca was ousted.

So, in the period of 1915-1917, on the one hand Sheriff of Mecca was getting one kind of signal and so also were the opponents of the Sheriff of Mecca, and on the other hand Russia, Britain and France had entered into a tripartite agreement to divide up the Ottoman Empire and designated the areas so divided which were to be occupied by the Russians, the British and the French, respectively. In addition to that, there was another Anglo-French, agreement to divide and gobble up the Arab lands. Therefore, under this plan, that part of the world was to come under the domination of three Super Powers. Russian influence in the Arab lands was not provided for in these plans. Arab lands were agreed to be subjected to Anglo-French monopoly. The subsequent wars and the role played by these two nations in this area is easy to understand now in retrospect.

THE MYSTERY: THE RICHEST LAND BUT THE MOST POORLY DEFENDED

Now, when we analyze the current situation from this perspective, various motives and objectives are quite easy to see through. Before advancing it any further, I would like to touch upon a mystery which is deeply connected to these issues. One would not expect two things to happen but they did happen. For one thing, the Middle East is the richest part of the globe and 60% of the world oil production comes from here, but in spite of that it is the weakest part of the globe as far as self-defence is concerned. It is also the weakest in regard to the industrial growth as well. So what is this puzzle, what is this mystery? Why is there no guard standing over these mountains of riches.

In a bank where there are just a few bricks of gold, strict security arrangements are made. But in this part of the world there are literally mountains of gold that are accumulating and despite that, from the military point of view, there is a vacuum in this area. Whatever

Eleventh Friday Sermon Feb 01, 1991

defense capability you are seeing now, it bears no relation to the wealth that is located there. Why is that so? Why has this part been as a weakling whereas Israel which is a minor part of that area and is not endowed with oil, has been bolstered up to an unusually strong position? **So to say, the enclosure of wealth is defenceless and the quarter from where burglary is expected has been beefed up! This is a puzzle which needs to be resolved.**

The second mystery is that when President Saddam proposed a linkage of the issues involved, why was this proposal of linkage rejected out of hand? An analysis of this rejection causes wonder, but once you understand it then you will have no difficulty in reaching the final conclusion as to what is the solution.

The U.S. and its allies have been persistent in their denial of any linkage between the occupation of Kuwait and any other issue. President Saddam maintained that there is a linkage and a simultaneous solution is called for. If this linkage had been accepted then the solution of the current problem would have been like this: President Saddam would withdraw from Kuwait and reverse his aggressive advance, while the Jews or Zionists who have usurped the West Bank of Eastern Jordan would withdraw from that area. Undoing of one aggression could have been procured at the price of nullifying another aggression. Both sides would have been restored equitably. Justice would have been served and this issue would have not advanced any further.

This was the purpose for which President Saddam was constantly stressing the linkage of issues. The Super Powers of the world who had an axe to grind in this conflict presented a deliberately distorted version of President Saddam's viewpoint, although it was as simple as I have stated before you.

THE WEST DISTORTS A JUST STAND

The Western world was given to understand that President Saddam's position is that since Israel has occupied some territory of a brotherly Muslim state, therefore, in his anger he too has occupied a brotherly Muslim state, and they were derisive of the theory of linkage as an irrational, illogical and senseless idea. They held that it is plain to the whole world that Iraq had some disputes with the Kuwaiti government about oil production. So on this pretext,

Iraq had decided to occupy Kuwait to capture its oil-wealth. So where does "linkage" enter into this picture? The issues are unrelated....

But as I have pointed out, there is a deep-seated link. He said that if you are against aggression then you should undo the aggression that has already occurred in this area, then I would undo my aggression in response. This would have put an end to this matter. But the Western powers would have none of it. But why didn't they? What is the reason behind it, what are the relationships with Israel and why are they so sensitive? Why is it so imperative to serve its interests that such high price is readily being entertained for this? Such high cost is hard to encompass by common people of modest means like us, for instance the amount of a billion dollars. For us even a billion rupees is a huge sum but of course a billion dollars is bigger still. The facts and figures of this war that have so far been made public indicate that the war is costing one billion U.S. dollars a day! This expense will stretch along with this war. In addition to the U.S., the British and the French are spending too, and it has reached a state where they are making rounds with a beggar's hat in their hand, before the international community.

The British are much more sophisticated in the art of diplomacy compared to the Americans and that is on account of the former being possessed of the diplomatic finesse which comes from centuries of training. So when our Foreign Secretary visited Germany and received six or seven hundred million dollar aid, the remark he made concerning this aid was 'look, I did not come here with a beggar's hat in my hand, see for yourself I have none; I did not even have any sum of money in my mind that I could have thought of asking for. Germans are our kind brothers, they are a great nation, they sensed that it was their duty to help their brothers in their difficult hour by taking part in the war-effort. So we accept this aid gratefully...'

Last night, **Edward Heath** who took part in this debate said that your lies and duplicity have reached their limits now; you have disgraced the nation before the entire world by running around with a beggar's bowl in your hand. Why did you get involved in a problem that you could not handle and for which you have besmirched the honour and dignity of Britain by acting like a beggar.

Eleventh Friday Sermon Feb 01, 1991

The Americans, on the other hand are coarse politicians. The U.S. Vice President **Mr. Quayle** is visiting here (his mental and political capabilities are constantly the butt of jokes in the American press, but this is their internal matter and does not concern me). He does not have the knack of diplomatic language and can hardly conceal certain matters. He tried to project U.S beggary in such terms that it reminded me of a proverbial **"Beggar with a Rod"** in Punjab who would not beg for alms by beseeching in the name of God that please help me I am dying of hunger, please have some mercy on me.... Rather he would brandish his rod saying, "Give me the money or I will break open your head!.." Dan Quayle's plan of action is the same as that of the "Beggar with a rod". When asked by a correspondent as to what financial help the U.S. expects from the world, he replied by saying something like, 'What expectations? We have decided to levy so much from such and such country. We are not going to beg this of them. We are just going to ask them to pay so and so' The news correspondent interjected and asked what would he do if those countries refused to pay? Mr. Quayle delivered a veiled threat by saying that in that case those countries should never count on U.S. support. In other words, they are prepared to pay such a big price for this war. **They have squandered whatever goodwill they had built in the Islamic world.** Not long ago, there was a time when Pakistan had practically become an American satellite and the people of Pakistan had resigned themselves to this fact. Every politician would make a run to the U.S. to gain some measure of credibility and worth, and the people had ceased to resent this attitude. Now, within the past few days such a fire of hatred has sprung up that the word "American" has become a term of abuse there. Similarly, Britain has torn up the rapport it had established with the Muslim countries and whatever goodwill they had built up has been totally lost.

THE NEED FOR A DETAILED ASSESSMENT OF THE SITUATION
Why are they paying such a heavy price? Why did they not accept the principle of linkage and ask Israel to vacate the territories in question and secured the Iraqi withdrawal of the territory in question, and thus put a quick end to this matter? We need to have a more detailed perspective in our analysis of the motives at work in the current war. We would have to investigate the charge that the alleged

restoration of Kuwait is a mere excuse, in fact it is their joint interests which have motivated these countries to eliminate Iraq.

Secondly, the other charge will have to be scrutinized whether or not the whole drama is being played for the sake of the Jews. Rather one should not say the "Jews" but say "Israel" (for some sects among the Jews are against Israeli policies. Many gentle Jews openly criticize the aggression of Israel and do not support its actions in any way). Whenever Israel was in clash with the Arabs, what has been the role played by these nations. Why have they supported Israel on every occasion? Is there an element of religious prejudice at work here or is it simply a case of joint self-interest. What is the real motive behind the establishment of Israel and why efforts are being made to keep it intact at all costs?

PROMISE TO PRESENT THE ISLAMIC SOLUTION

I shall try to present answers to all these questions in the next sermon. *Insha Allah*. And I shall pick up the historical context of this debate right from where I am leaving it today, and I will present major events up to the present time that have occurred since, so as to refresh your memory.

At the conclusion of this analysis, time permitting, maybe in the next sermon or in the one following the next, I will try to present the solution to these problems from the Islamic viewpoint. Since I have taken up enough time today, therefore, I stop this discourse now. May Allah enable us, as the servants of the Holy Prophet Muhammad[sas], to present such a solution to the problems of the world that its innate strength and power may cause its acceptance to become the guarantee of peace for the human race. If they reject these proposals, then they may do whatever they can, world-peace will remain evasive. An ultimate and correct solution is such that it is fortified with this power of truth. Its acceptance is beneficial, while its rejection spells harm.

Since I will represent Islam, therefore, I firmly believe that the solution put forth by Ahmadiyya Muslim Jamaat is inherently undeserving of contempt. If you will accept it, it will be to your own benefit and the benefit of mankind at large. But if you turn it down then remember that you remain unable to eliminate transgression from the world, and one effort after another on your

Eleventh Friday Sermon Feb 01, 1991

part will fail. And one war would follow another war, and one instability after another will cause the human society to become awash with blood, and rob the peace and tranquillity of mankind. This is my faith that since I will present the Islamic Solution, by the Grace of Allah, therefore, what I have stated above will come to pass. Either you will accept it and benefit from it or you will reject it and then you will have to suffer the damaging consequences.

I request the members of the Ahmadiyya Muslim Community to pray to God that He may keep my mental and emotional state aligned to the spirit of righteousness (*Taqwa*) so that I may discern, through the light of *Taqwa*, a solution that may guarantee peace for mankind.

In the name of Allah, the Gracious, the Merciful

TWELFTH FRIDAY SERMON

FEBRUARY 08, 1991

THE REALITY OF THE NEW WORLD ORDER OF PRESIDENT GEORGE BUSH

After reciting the Opening Chapter of the Holy Quran, Al-Fatiha, Hazoor said:

It is almost six months since I referred to the invasion of Baghdad by **Halaku Khan** far back in history in the context of the current situation in Baghdad. I had warned that the preparations were afoot to inflict an even greater destruction on Iraq. Such plans have, in fact, been finalized and I am apprehensive, if President Saddam Hussein does not take stock of the situation in its right perspective, a dreadful war of such destructive proportions would be unleashed on Iraq that the holocaust of Baghdad by Halaku Khan would dwindle before it into insignificance.

THE SIGNIFICANCE OF THE GULF WAR
What has happened so far, and whatever has filtered down to us by now, is so dreadful and distressing that it has bled the hearts of the entire Islamic world. We must be under no illusion that the information that has trickled down so far is not even a fraction of the actual devastation and more facts would come to light in the aftermath of this war. To my reckoning hundreds of thousands of civilians and soldiers have been killed and wounded. The massive destruction of civilian population and property has not yet been documented. But the nature and extent of the carnage of the Iraqi defence forces bears no relation to the outcome of a traditional war. Instead it seems as if someone has his hands and feet tied down, and then he is being dismembered limb by limb. In the first place his nails are pulled out, his fingers are chopped, his teeth are extracted, and his hands and feet

are axed. Thereafter, the 'lion-hearted' soldiers are let loose on him to do the rest. These courageous soldiers were not allowed to advance towards him until it was ensured that he was incapacitated to the extent of being unable to even use his mutilated stumps to slap back. This, in a nut shell, is my assessment of the happenings in this war.

The American commanders supervising this war have rightly ridiculed the Iraqi scud missiles in comparison with their own weapons as a **mosquito** compared to an **elephant**. It is true that these powers represent a mighty elephant confronting a tiny and weak creature but, on the other hand, they continue to hoodwink the world by projecting Saddam Hussein as the **Hitler** of this age. So, if this fight between the "elephant and the mosquito" continues, then I think that by the end of the present century they will accomplish the most sinister design of this century against the Muslim nations. Their new plots for the next century would then be placed on the drawing board.

It is not my intention to give a running commentary on the progress of this war, or to simply present to the Ahmadiyya Muslim Community with a diary of this war, or to a guess as to what might come to pass tomorrow. Rather, my purpose is to unravel the factors that constitute the background of this war so that the Ahmadi Muslims all over the world, in light of this historical background, may be able to convey this message to the Muslim fraternity across the world. And so that they may make them fully understand the plots that have been hatched to destroy the Muslims, and to tell them what role the Western nations have played so far in this regard and what they are likely to do in the future. Likewise, I intend to apprise them of the role played by the United Nations and its predecessor, the League of Nations. How they are related to each other and what sort of relations do they have with the Jews, and why. I would also like to point out the mistakes committed by the Muslim nations involved. This appraisal also provides me with an opportunity to put forward some specific suggestions, to whatever extent Allah enables me, for the consideration and benefit of these nations. In my opinion once this subject is fully understood, the solution to all these problems becomes obvious. **Proper diagnosis of a disease is so vital and must precede the appropriate prescription for its cure. If the diagnosis is correct it is not difficult to find the right treatment.** I would extend my advice to the Jews as well as the Christian nations as to what judicious actions based on justice they should take in the future to arrive at a lasting peace. Now I shall briefly discuss the historical background of this issue which is called the **"Palestinian Problem"**, and which now is being reflected in the context of the "Gulf War".

THE BACKGROUND TO THE PALESTINIAN ISSUE

I have mentioned in a previous sermon that in 1917 **Lord Balfour** made some commitments with the Jews. Later, in 1920 a surprising incident occurred on the political scene. The League of Nations gave a mandate to the British government to assume the role of the caretaker of the Palestinian territory. This mandate included a specific provision that whatever promise Balfour had made with the Jews for the creation of a Zionist state shall be honoured by the British government. Paul Harper writes:[1]

> "In 1920, at the League of Nations Supreme Council meeting in San Remo, Britain was assigned the mandate for Palestine, which carried with it the obligation to implement the Balfour Declaration." (Pages 32-33)

This was a display of highhandedness and injustice by this organization that is unprecedented in the history of the world. It was clearly the result of a conspiracy of the big powers. The League of Nations was designed to be a representative body of all the nations of the world, watching their interests with impartiality. It had no jurisdictions to delegate such mandatory powers to anybody. A British Minister wrote a letter to Lord Rothschild, a distinguished banker belonging to a Jewish family of France, that the British Cabinet was contemplating the enforcement of a decision in compliance with the mandate passed by the League of Nations. The question is, who had vested such an authority in the League of Nations to dispose of the fate of a nation in this manner, and then authorize the same country, which had made a promise to the Jews, to go ahead and enforce its

---

[1] Paul Harper, The Arab-Israeli Issue. Wayland Publishers Ltd. England. 1986.

will in whatever manner it liked. During the course of further research on the subject, an interesting fact[2] came to light that:

> "The League of Nations mandate system was devised as a means for non-developed countries to be guided to independence and self-government with the help of the industrialized nations."

This was the philosophy behind the Mandate System. Lord Balfour was fully aware of this but he intentionally contravened its aim. In this regard, he was the man who performed the most sinister role. In order to bypass the spirit of the Mandate System he wrote a secret memorandum to the British Cabinet, which has been included in the book[3] The Arab - Israeli Issue:

> "But Lord Balfour's views on Palestine were contained in a secret memorandum to the British Cabinet in 1919 which said that : ... in Palestine we do not propose even to go through the form of consulting the wishes of the present inhabitants of the country ... Zionism, be it right or wrong, good or bad, is ... of far profounder import than the desires and prejudices of the 700,000 Arabs who now inhabit this ancient land".

As far as the early figures of the migration of the Jews to Palestine, there are conflicting reports. However Paul Harper writes:[4]

> "At the end of the First World War, after 32 years of concentrated efforts 56,000 Jews, according to the British Census of 1918 had been settled in Palestine on some 2 per cent of its land area. British rule was the opportunity for the Zionist movement to turn what was still only a dream into reality."

---

[2] Ibid. Page 33.
[3] Ibid. Page 33.
[4] Ibid. Page 31.

"By 1929 there were 156,000 immigrants owning 4 per cent of the total area of Palestine, but 14 per cent of its cultivable land."(page 35)

After 1929 and until 1948 when the Mandate came to an end there was a rapid increase in the migration of the Jews to Palestine. In 1947 when the U.N. announced the partition of Palestine, thus creating the State of Israel, the population of the Jews had increased from 85,000 in 1919 to a phenomenal 700,000 in 1947.

On May 17, 1939, prior to the beginning of World War II, the British government published a White Paper that spelled a change in its foreign policy. At that time **Mr. Chamberlain** was heading the British government. He expressed the opinion that the world was standing at the brink of the Second World War. At that crucial juncture if the British had to choose whether to decide against the Jews and incur their enmity or to decide against the large Muslim Community and antagonize them, then his advise would be to favour the Muslims. Note, that the earlier British decision in this regard was taken soon after World War I, and the second British stance was expressed, as noted above, just before World War II. It was felt that the earlier decision by Britain was based merely on political expediency, and it was not realistic. In pursuance of this decision the British government formally announced in this White Paper that it does not favour establishing a Jewish state in Palestine and that it did not accept the right of the Jews that they should have a separate state in that area.

Had the British been honest in their intentions they should have surrendered that Mandate to the League of Nations for the simple reason that this Mandate was assigned to Britain under the conditions that prevailed in 1917, but now, in the present circumstances it was an outdated document. In this way their Mandate would have automatically become obsolete and redundant. But again in 1946, as the war ended, they changed their mind on the decision taken before the war and permitted an extended quota of 100,000 Jews to be settled in Palestine. By 1947, i.e., towards the end of the period for which this Mandate was valid, the United Nations announced a plan according to which Palestine was to be partitioned into two separate states for the Jews and the Muslim Arabs. By this time the Jewish population had swollen to 700,000 as against the Arab population of

Twelfth Friday Sermon Feb 08, 1991

2 million depicting a ratio of 1:3. Looking at the original figure of 85,000, mentioned in the mandate one wonders how did it rise to 700,000! Further research reveals that the Jews were secretly smuggled into Palestine, in large numbers. Despite the occasional, genuine, efforts of the British government to stop this influx of the Jews, the process continued unabated. Whenever the British government attempted to interrupt this influx, the Jews rioted and rebelled against the British authorities, threatening retaliatory actions. So the inflow of the Jewish population into Palestine continued unchecked until it reached the ratio of 7:20. Later the United Nations met to decide as to how much territory was to be allocated to the Jews and the Arab Muslims, by partitioning the country. Even in this matter they favoured the Jews by deciding that 56% of the area of Palestine be given to the Zionists and the remaining of 44% to the majority population of the Arab Muslims. They further decided that the City of Jerusalem which was located on the Arab side would continue to remain under international supervision, arguing that it contained the holy places equally sacred to the Jews, the Christians, and the Muslims.

Whatever insignificant area was left behind was supposed to be given to the Arab Muslims but it was not handed over to them. The resolution also had a provision that, prior to the formation of governments of the two groups in their respective areas, the British government would continue to cooperate and coordinate with the United Nations and its nominated committees for implementing this plan. But in effect, the British government refused to cooperate in this matter. Unfortunately, there was no one to organise the Muslims. This led to a complete chaos and disorder among the Arab community for there was no competent Muslim organization to help them form a Muslim government.

When the mandate came to an end in 1948, the hurried manner in which the British government relinquished control and just abandoned the area, is unprecedented. When they left from India, they had ensured that a clear-cut line of demarcation separated the two newly created countries, and legitimate governments took charge of the respective countries. But the British government neither took any such precaution till the final day of their stay in Palestine, nor did it let the United Nations to do it. They packed up everything they had in

Palestine by 11:30 a.m. and their ships left the Palestinian waters at 12:00 p.m. that day. This is how they abandoned that country. It was an act of cruelty towards the Palestinians who suffered the most from this abandonment amid chaos.

As for the Jews, they had two established organizations capable of safeguarding their interests. One of them was working under the command of Menachem Begin which in fact was initially designed to be a strong terrorist group set up well before 1948, to carry out terrorist activities against the Arabs and, when necessary, even against the British. The second organization was operating under the leadership of David Ben Gurion. The Jews were receiving large supplies of arms from U.S. sources, on an ongoing basis. This set up was further divided into three or four sub-organizations whose aim, besides establishing an effective government, was to not only defend their own territory but grab more territory from the Arabs. So, for a period of one and a half years (from 1948 to 1949), skirmishes between the Arabs and the Jews continued in which some neighbouring Arab states also participated. Although these states were assisting the Palestinian Muslims but at that point no formal declaration of war against Israel was made by any Muslim country. Generally they limited their participation to extending a helping hand to the distressed Arabs living in Palestine. With the cessation of hostilities in 1948 when a truce agreement was reached to maintain peace in the region, the Jews had succeeded in occupying 75% of the Palestinian land as against their original allocation of 56%. This provides a fairly clear picture of the conduct of the United Nations and the behaviour of the British government and its ally, U.S., who kept watching these developments as silent spectators much to the disadvantage of the Arabs. This episode is rich in detail, and I have all the pertinent references with me, but I do not wish to encumber my sermons with lengthy debate and complicated details.

The essence of this case is that a conspiracy of the Western powers, in which the defunct League of Nations and subsequently its successor, the United Nations actively participated and the government of Britain and the U.S. played the pivotal role, resulted in the emergence of a Jewish state in Palestine which no standard of Justice, international law, or the Charter of the United Nations would have sanctioned. They could not have moved a step towards the creation of

Israel without the active connivance of these powers. Anyhow, this fateful decision was taken and, ever since, this region has been a scene of armed conflicts and a hot bed of international intrigues.

CONFLICTS OF INTEREST

Two kinds of wars or operations have been undertaken in this region on the pretext of preserving International peace, but were actually calculated to safeguard the vested interests of the West. The first kind of wars were undertaken mostly with the active participation of Britain and France, for serving the Western interests in the region, but the aggressors claimed that they were protecting the interests of the International community. The second kind of wars may be classified as the wars of Jewish expansionism. Britain and France played the most pivotal role in the first kind of wars, and it was done with the U.S. tacit support from behind the scene. The first such operation, conducted to safeguard their selfish interests, was undertaken against Iran. In 1950 the Iranian Parliament proclaimed that since the Iranian oil wealth had become a focal point of international greed and threatened external intervention in Iran, therefore they decided to turn down the offer by the Soviet Union to participate in the exploration of Oil in northern Iran. The Soviet Union argued that just as Iran had permitted the Anglo-Iranian Oil Company to explore and operate the oil fields in southern Iran (which supposedly was done to promote the welfare of Iran, but in fact were deriving lucrative benefits for themselves) the Soviet Union should also be permitted to undertake similar operations to the benefit of both countries. But the Iranian Parliament did not agree to it and remained adamant in their decision that the Soviet Union cannot be granted such permission. Secondly, the Iranian government decided that they would periodically review, their agreement with the Anglo-Iranian Oil Company and that the next such review would take place in 1951. The U.S. administration acclaimed this decision of the Iranian government because they construed it as a pro-U.S. outcome simply because it seemed to be a rebuff to the Soviet Union.

In 1951, when the matter of review of the agreement with the Anglo-Iranian Oil Company came up before the Iranian Parliament, the British or even the Americans, could not imagine that the terms of the agreement could be altered unilaterally by Iran contrary to the

Western interests, in view of the tremendous influence and power-base of the Company. One can imagine the size and stature of the Anglo-Iranian Oil Company from the fact that the amount of royalty from oil proceeds that was paid by the Company to the Iranian government, under the terms of the agreement, was almost half of the total national budget of Iran. The amount paid by the Company to the British government as their share was much more than this, and the profit share they retained for themselves was ten times larger than what they paid the British government. So the Company's profits were about five times the gross national product of Iran. Being so strongly entrenched they could never have imagined that any decision could be taken against their interests. Incidentally, when this matter was about to be put up before the Parliament, the Iranian Prime Minister, who had the reputation of being on the payroll of the Company and was known as their outright supporter, presented a report according to which any decision to nationalize the Anglo-Iranian Oil Company would seriously hurt the interest of Iran. This statement caused an uproar in the Parliament, and the next day or shortly afterwards, the Prime Minister was assassinated. **Dr. Mossadeq** was then elected as the new Prime Minister of Iran. Since Dr. Mossadeq was known to be truly faithful and loyal to the interests of Iran, therefore the British sounded the war bells. The British air-borne division, based in Mauritius was alerted for a possible attack on Iran. Then Britain contacted the United States for consultations. The Americans suggested that an act of open aggression would not be the right approach to adopt and that they should join hands and deal with this matter in a different way. So Britain sought U.S. help in conspiring to overthrow the Iranian government. The details for this plot were worked out between Mr. Sinclair representing the British ISI and Mr. Kim Roosevelt of the CIA. The U.S. government used its international influence to bring about complete boycott of Iran's oil by the rest of the world. Since half of Iran's budget revenue was from the oil proceeds, the boycott of its oil export adversely affected its revenues, and Iran experienced a great financial crises. In the midst of this crisis, Dr. Mossadeq requested the U.S. President in 1952 for short-term financial assistance to overcome this crisis and that, once this crisis was overcome, Iran would readily repay this loan. The U.S. President replied that it was against the interest of the American tax payer for

Twelfth Friday Sermon Feb 08, 1991

them to channelize their tax revenues to Iran. He further advised that Iran can have a simpler solution to this problem if it borrowed the needed funds from the Anglo Iranian Oil Company which was prepared to extend such loans. This response left Dr. Mossadeq in no doubt as to the ill intentions of the U.S. but he could not do much about it. A few days prior to this reply by the U.S. President, he had already given approval to a plan worked out by the CIA and the British ISI for conducting a punitive operation against the government of Iran. It was quite a comprehensive plan but, to be brief, they conspired to win the support of the Iranian police and army, as is the usual *modus-operand* of these powers for staging a *coup d'etat*. This operation was supervised by Kim Roosevelt of the CIA. For this service, he was decorated with a distinguished medal of honour that is reserved only for national heros.

The resulting disturbances caused a rift between the Shah of Iran and the Iranian Prime Minister each vying with the other for gaining greater administrative powers. The Iranian Prime Minister, Dr. Mossadeq, assumed the post of the Commander in Chief of the armed forces and announced the name of the person whom he was going to appoint as Police Chief among his confidants. The newly appointed Police Chief bragged about having a complete list of all the British agents in Iran. The following day he too was assassinated. The Shah later dismissed Dr. Mossadeq as Prime Minister, sparking off large scale demonstrations in support of the deposed Prime Minister. In order to quell these demonstrations the Shah raised a civilian force of 6000 persons. This force was well trained and properly armed to control such demonstrations. But the riots and protests were so severe and wide-spread that the Shah had to bring in 200,000 army soldiers to crush the agitation. According to a well-tailored plan, the Shah of Iran, who was a classic picture of perfect humility and subservience to the U.S. and Britain was again imposed upon Iran as an autocratic ruler. The role played by these external powers in the Iranian affairs must be kept in perspective if we want to understand the current crisis in the Gulf region.

PREMEDITATED ACTION AGAINST EGYPT

An analogous situation was created in 1956 when President Gemal Abdul Nasser of Egypt decided to nationalize the **Suez Canal**.

The background of this decision was that the Americans reneged on their agreement with Egypt to provide promised financial help for the construction of the **Aswan Dam**. Realizing that President Nasser had a tendency of leaning towards the Soviet Union, and because of his disregard of U.S. warnings to moderate and soften his attitude towards Israel, the U.S. government backed out of its commitment to teach him a lesson. At that time the Aswan Dam had become to be recognized as a vital source of the economic well-being of Egypt, and was expected to perform a major role in boosting Egypt's economy and upgrading its agricultural development, without which Egypt could not have become self sufficient in food or experience economic growth. By that time the construction of the Dam had reached a stage where Egypt could not afford to stop the work. Therefore, in order to finance this project, and to meet other expenses, Egypt had no choice but to raise its revenues by nationalizing the Suez Canal. Up until then, the Canal was operated under the joint control of Britain and France because they held the controlling shares in the company that looked after this concern. Britain engineered a plot to punish President Nasser of Egypt for working against their interests. This plot was very crude and immature in character, but still it was recklessly dangerous. In pursuit of this plan, Israel was incited by Britain to attack Egypt and occupy the Suez Canal. This attack was designed to achieve the element of complete surprise, and since Egypt lacked an effective defence force to repel such a sudden thrust, it was hoped that the attack was bound to succeed. It was planned that after having achieved this goal, on the threat of their intervention for the sake of 'peace', Britain and France would order Israel and Egypt to withdraw their forces from the sector of the Suez Canal. It all happened in the same sequence in which the conspirators had it designed. The Israeli forces were mobilized very quickly to the banks of the Suez Canal and the next day an ultimatum was issued by the British and French governments, ordering the two countries to withdraw their forces from the Canal because this war threatened world peace. Israel immediately started to comply with this command as planned, but Egypt took a firm stand that this was illogical for it to withdraw its forces from its own territory because the Suez Canal belonged to Egypt. Israel, the aggressor, should withdraw and that should be enough. Upon receiving this reply, the joint forces of Britain and France attacked

Twelfth Friday Sermon Feb 08, 1991

Egypt. A former Foreign Secretary of Britain, Mr. Nutting has written a book about the British role in this war. The reader of this book can draw surprising parallels between the line of action adopted by the British government against President Nasser of Egypt, at that time, and the one that the U.S. government has now adopted against President Saddam of Iraq. It looks as if the present situation in Iraq were a carbon copy of the events of 1956 in Egypt. The campaign of character assassination, stirred up by the American media, against President Saddam is quite similar to the one conducted by Britain against President Nasser of Egypt, during the Suez crisis. President George Bush has used most obnoxious language against President Saddam, which cannot even be repeated here, for instance he used a slang meaning that Saddam be kicked at his buttocks and thrown out of office. The book by Mr Nutting that I have referred to earlier is not with me at the moment but I have a quote from it which states that the object of the Suez war was **"to knock Nasser off his perch"**. Some commentators believe that the U.S. waged this war against Iraq because President Saddam hurt the ego of President Bush. It is doubtful if this is the primary reason but there does appear some element of personal ego of President Bush involved in the background of the current war. Mr. Nutting's book records the impression that one gathered from the handling of the Suez issue by Sir Anthony Eden, the then Prime Minister of Britain, that he wanted to punish Nasser, being of the rank of a mere colonel, for his audacity to defy the Prime Minister of Great Britain! Some commentators, today, are expressing a similar opinion about the manner and conduct of President Bush. In a way the current events are a repetition of what happened in Egypt in 1956. Today some countries have vital interests in the oil resources of the Gulf; earlier on, their interests were linked to the Suez Canal. Today, Israel still has a vital interest in this area but the United States is keeping Israel in the background and has come forward to do her job. In this war too, the same three powers are prominently active viz Britain, France and Israel, the only difference being that the Israel is represented by the U.S.

WARS OF JEWISH EXPANSIONISM

The second kind of wars fought in the Middle East, can be classified as part of the armed struggle for the expansion of Zionism.

During the hostilities of 1948-1949, the entire blame was put on the Palestinians and their neighbouring Muslims countries for their 'attacks' on Israel. It has been argued that the Jews had to come out in retaliation and, in this process, ended up annexing more territory to their area. But in 1967, Israel's war of aggression was entirely for the purpose of its expansion. There was no element of self-defence involved. It was waged in such a dreadful and destructive manner that the countries of Egypt, Syria and Jordan were decimated within a few days, and it resulted in the further extension of Israeli territory. Therefore Israel succeeded in occupying territory that is many times larger than the territory originally allocated to her under the 1948 Mandate.

Now I will give you a brief account of the continued Zionist expansionism so that you may have some idea of the extent to which the Israelis have enlarged their territory, are still doing so, and would continue to do so in the future.

It was probably in 1937 that for the first time the British government announced, in the context of the Balfour declaration of 1917, how much territory would be allocated for the Jewish state. An area of 5,000 Sq.Km. was earmarked for the Jewish state, but towards the end of 1947, when the matter was reviewed by the United Nations the area was increased to 20,000 Sq.Km. Some additional territory was annexed by Israel during hostilities with Palestinians and Arabs, in the following two years, as stated earlier. In this process an area of 88,000 Sq.Km. came under the control of the Israelis by the end of 1967. Thus one can well imagine that starting from a nominal figure of 5,000 Sq.Km., how rapidly Israeli territory was expanded to 88,000 Sq.Km.

The last war that was fought in this region, before the current war, was in October 1973. That war is often called the **"War of Yom Kippur"** (Passover day, a holy day for the Jews). On that day in 1973, Israel came under attack by the joint forces of Egypt, Syria and Jordan. It is alleged that this war of aggression was initiated by the Arabs and that the Jews were blameless, but this is not entirely correct. The reason is that after the war of 1967, the U.N. Security Council unanimously passed **Resolution No 242** censuring Israel and ordering it to withdraw its forces from the occupied territory which had fallen in its hand during the hostilities. But at the same time a

Twelfth Friday Sermon Feb 08, 1991

mischievous lacuna was left in the resolution (as is normal with the British and Western diplomacies) so that when the time for the implementation of this resolution arrives, new debates can be started on the supplementary issues to confuse the matter. So this provision in the resolution mentioned that it would be the right of all states in this region that their security is safeguarded so that their geographical boundaries are not threatened or endangered. The motive behind this provision was that when the time of vacating the occupied area approaches for the implementation of this resolution, then this provision could be stretched to make the resolution ineffective, in the interest of the Jews, by saying that the security of Israel demands that such and such territorial changes and adjustments be made prior to its implementation. Consequently none of the provisions of the resolution have so far been complied and the matter remains suspended since the end of the 1967 war. Now the question arises that if for the implementation of a U.N. resolution, U.S. and its allies have the right to attack Iraq, using Kuwait as a pretext which is not even their territory, then why cannot the same principle be applied for the restoration of the rights of those countries who have lost their territory to Israel and have been waiting for years for the implementation of the U.N. Resolution No. 242. Why should they not have the equal right to undertake the military action to regain their territories from Israel. The hostilities of 1973 took place because the Arabs had, eventually, decided to try to recover their own land. To call this action an aggression is quite unjust. This was the effort of a weak and oppressed nation. As the great powers were not helpful to have the U.N. resolution implemented, they thought of making an attempt of their own.

This is, briefly, the history of the wars in this region and the conduct and attitude of all these nations in this context which I placed before you. We do not have the time to consider the details of the facts which have come to light in the wake of the present war, but these must be still fresh in your memory. To summarize the case, it is quite apparent now that these powerful Western nations have given Israel the right to resort to the use of force whenever and wherever it desires. It has the right to refuse to vacate the territory forcibly acquired, even if the Security Council of the U.N. decides that it should withdraw from its occupied lands. On the contrary, the aggrieved countries whose territories have been occupied by Israel have no right even to make their own efforts to get a U.N. resolution implemented. But Israel enjoys total immunity and freedom to do whatever it chooses.

One thing I could not mention earlier was that during the period of 1947 to 1949, Israel laid the foundation of modern day terrorist activities, under the command of Menachem Begin. A British Deputy Governor of Palestine was among those killed as a result of these terrorist activities. The king David Hotel in Jerusalem was blown up, resulting in the death of over a 100 people, besides causing a huge loss of property. Palestinians were openly attacked, resulting in the slaughter of over 3,000 Muslim men, women and children in a short period of time. They even clashed with the British, for the reason that in those days the Labour government in Britain, and Mr. Bevin who was its Foreign Secretary, were convinced that the Muslims were the oppressed and the Jews were committing the atrocities. Mr Bevin even made some efforts to stop the illegal immigration of the Jews into Palestine. To quote one such instance, the British forces intercepted a ship carrying over 4,000 Jews intending to enter Israel illegally. Mr. Bevin ordered them back to Germany. The Western journalists launched a strong protest against their action, vilifying and insulting Mr. Bevin to an amazing degree. In fact his government had been assigned the responsibilities as trustees of this region to not allow the entry of any more Jews into Palestine, and he was simply carrying out his duties in sending the ship back to Germany. But the hostile reaction of the British media against the compliance of a provision of the U.N. resolution by their own government was quite astonishing.

A book entitled **"The Making of Israel"** by James Cameron has written about this incident. He states,

> "imagine what terrible injustice it was, that over 4,000 Jews were sent back to the unfortunate and cruel land of Germany..".

But he forgot that this incident happened in 1947, i.e., almost two years after the end of World war II. If Germany was considered such a cruel and unfortunate land, even at a time when the Nazis had been defeated and Germany had been reduced to a rubble and the British, American and French forces had established their occupation - and were indeed the guarantors for the security of the Jews - then what right did they have to migrate to Israel under such circumstances. This is quite obvious that a cross section of the British journalists supported the actions of the Jews. A consensus of Western public opinion was also protective of the actions of the Jews. These events lend support to my contention that modern day terrorism was invented and initiated by the Jews for the purpose of helping Zionist immigrants to enter Israel with safety. This historical background shows that the Western powers accepted the right of the Jews to carry out terrorism and that these activities of the Jews were not to be termed as "Jewish Terrorism". On the other hand, the Muslim countries are not even allowed to retaliate to protect their territorial and political interests, and if they do so then not only are they censured but even Islam is slandered and such efforts are maliciously termed "Islamic Terrorism"[5]. The other rights and privileges which appear to have been accorded to the Jews are that:

1. The Jews have the right to defy the Security Council resolutions and they even have the right to regard these resolutions with contempt, reject them or toss them into the proverbial trash can. Yet no country has the right to condemn this behaviour.
2. Israel has the right to alter the geographical boundaries of its neighbouring countries on the pretext of its security considerations.
3. Israel has the right to produce and stockpile atomic bombs and other nuclear devices. It can even manufacture chemical and biological weapons of mass destruction. No one seems to have the right, particularly the Muslim countries, even to criticize Israel for indulging in such activities.

---

[5] Books for further study on the subject of Terrorism perpetrated by the U.S. & Israel:
Presidents's Secret Wars: By John Prados
The Israeli Connection: By Benjamin Beit-Hallahmi
Israel's Fateful Decisions: By Yehoshafat Harkabi
By Way of Deception: By Ex Director of Mossad

This is the summary of this historical struggle which I have put before you. One thing has clearly emerged from these events that to date, there has been no change in this policy nor would there be any change in future. These privileges of the Jews would always be preserved and kept intact. Depriving the Muslim States of their rights would remain a cornerstone of their permanent policy.

PRESIDENT BUSH'S DREAM OF PEACE

In the light of this background, now let us see what could be the dream of President Bush for a **"New World Order"** for unless we understand that dream it would not be possible to give them an appropriate advice.

Against the backdrop of this aggressive historical legacy, as far as I can see, the dream of President Bush, is in fact not a dream of peace but a long term strategy for causing the death and absolute destruction in the region. **Some people seem to regard death as a form of peace.** I have often narrated **the tale of a sick horse** for illustration. A horse that was much dear to a king, got fatally ill. The king said that he would kill anybody who dared to break the bad news of his horse's death to him. But God's decree had to work and the sick horse died despite all efforts by his men. A person was forcibly deputed to break this bad news to the king. He was threatened with death if he did not comply. The person thought that it was more honourable to die at the hands of the king than otherwise. He was an intelligent person. He went to the king and said, "Congratulations, Your Majesty! Your horse has found perfect peace." The king was very pleased and said, "Tell me more about it. How has it attainted peacefulness?" The fellow replied: "At first one could hear its heaves even from quite a distance, but now I could hear no sound even as I drew close to it. His heartbeats used to shake the earth, but now, when I put my ear to its chest, I could hear nothing. He is lying in complete peace and tranquillity." The king said, "O accursed one! why don't you simply say that the horse is dead". He hastily set the record straight, "Your Majesty, these are *your* words, not mine."

So the fact is that the dream of peace in the Middle East as seen by the President of the U.S., is nothing but a nightmare. The real interpretation of these dreams is that they spell death, even if his dreams be in the name of peace. As far as I have thought, this dream

Twelfth Friday Sermon Feb 08, 1991

means that the oil-rich countries such as Saudi Arabia and other Sheikdoms would be forced to grant a portion of their revenue from the oil reserves as charity to such Arab counties as may be unendowed with oil wealth, or to those who have scanty oil reserves. In much the same way as the U.S. enslaves some of the Third world countries through the trap of economic aid, some less affluent Arab countries would be made slaves of the oil-rich Arab counties through this charity. Just as strings are usually attached to foreign aid, similarly non-economic strings would be attached to this so called economic assistance. The American financial assistance termed as "American Aid" always carries with it political strings that are designed to serve the U.S. interests. In the same way, this aid would also entail some political conditions to serve the Israeli interests, in particular and Western interests, in general. These conditions would dictate that disputes between the countries in the Middle East will not be taken to the United Nations. Any disputes would have to be settled bilaterally with Israel, under American patronage, without the involvement of the U.N. A guarantee will have to be provided that no attempts will be made to get involved in any future war in this region. Further, it must be agreed that whereas Israel shall continue to manufacture nuclear weapons and to stock-pile other devices of mass destruction, the Muslim countries would not entertain any thoughts of making such weapons or devices even for self defense. These are the two fundamental characteristics of the dream of peace which President Bush has visualised. You will see attempts being made to unveil it, in the not too distant future.

There are also some other ramifications of this dream which may or may not materialize. One part is connected with pressurising the Jews to make some conciliatory gestures towards the Arabs. I must clarify, at this point, that all Jews are not alike because there are some gentle-natured and noble-minded Jews who are very much opposed to the creation of Israel as a separate state and reject its policies which they regard as harmful, not only for mankind but also for the Jews themselves. So when I say Jews, it certainly does not imply that I condemn the Jewish community collectively, but by Jews I always mean the state of Israel. Anyway, some Western powers think that they can put pressure on Israel to ameliorate its ways partially. It is just wishful thinking on their part to expect that Israel would ever withdraw completely from the Golan Heights or vacate the West Bank of the Jordan River and that, as a result of this negotiated change of heart by Israel, they would be able to bring peace and reconciliation in this region.

In my opinion, one thing should be taken as a certainty: Israel would never vacate all the occupied areas of the Golan Heights at any cost. I am also sure that Israel would never give up its control over the West Bank of the Jordan River. On the other hand, all pro-U.S. Arab states would consent to the above arrangements and become a party to the agreement in the manner I have mentioned earlier. The reason is quite obvious: the political damage resulting from the permanent Jewish control over the West Bank affects only the poor Palestinian Muslims and the residents of East Jordan and not the oil rich Arabs. It is inconceivable that the U.S. would displease the Jews for the sake of poor Palestinians and East Jordanians. The other reason is that there exists a long-standing plan to bring the Jews from outside and settle them in Israel. In fact, this plan has already been implemented to a considerable extent, and permanent Jewish settlements have been erected. Therefore, even if the U.S. requires so, Israel would never be prepared to give up these occupied areas.

THE NATURE OF U.S. - ISRAEL RELATIONS

The close ties between Israel and the U.S. clearly indicate that President Bush can never afford to displease Israel. When Iraq fired scud missiles at Israel, President Bush repeatedly phoned the Prime Minister of Israel, pleading with him personally as well as sending his top officials to Tel Aviv, to persuade Israel to refrain from taking spontaneous retaliatory action. This behaviour reflects the nature and degree of their close relationship. A few scud attacks have claimed the lives of only two elderly women and no more than two to three hundreds people are said to have been injured, which stands in no comparison to what the U.S. has brought on the Iraqi people. A few scud missile attacks have been widely publicised by the Western media as gruesome and unilateral acts of aggression by Iraq, but the earlier unprovoked and unjustified bombing and destruction of the Iraqi nuclear plant by Israel does not appear to them as aggression, as if it has been accepted that Israel has the right to commit invasions, overfly other countries and bomb them with impunity. When the

Twelfth Friday Sermon Feb 08, 1991

Israeli aggression was committed, neither the United Nations showed any concern nor any Western country objected to this criminal act. Whenever a country is bombed by Israel it seems as if that country even does not have the right to protest, much less take any retaliatory action in self defence. In fact the firing of the scud missiles by Iraq should have been taken as reprisal to Israel's bombing of Iraq's nuclear plant. It has now been established during the events in the Gulf War that it is not necessary to take any retaliatory action immediately. If this matter is given a little more thought the nature of the relations between Israel and the U.S. become quite clear. As I have noted earlier, after the scud attacks on Israel, President Bush repeatedly contacted the Israeli authorities on telephone and pleadingly persuaded them to not take any immediate retaliatory action. Later, he sent his representatives to discuss the matter in greater detail. In the end, Israeli authorities were assured that if they took no immediate military action, the U.S. would take the maximum possible revenge on their behalf. Whatever bombing had been done on the civilian population of Iraq, as a result of this promise, is proof enough that the U.S. kept their part of the bargain. Hundreds of thousands of innocent Iraqis were martyred and their homes destroyed. This was in fact a retaliation on behalf of Israel which the allies had done, in fulfilment of the U.S. commitment to Israel. In addition to this brutal retaliation on behalf of Israel, the U.S. has promised Israel *9 billion dollars* in economic aid. Try to imagine the magnitude of this $9 billion; it is not because Israel has agreed to relinquish its right for a reprisal against Iraq, but merely to postpone their reprisals temporarily. Israel still retains its right to retaliate whenever it deems convenient, wherever it wants to, and in whatever manner! That is why I have said so explicitly that Israel's "right" of aggression has been accepted by the great powers. Whereas no country is allowed to even think of taking defensive measures against Israel's blatant acts of aggression. If any country dared to take any protective measure, then these world powers would come out in Israel's defence and take punitive action against that country. Even after this vicarious revenge by the U.S., Israel is still expected to keep its right of retaliation intact. When and how Israel exercises its "right", is yet to be seen.

So these are the salient features of President Bush's dream of the **"New World Order"** which proposes to guarantee permanent peace in the world. There are other dreadful aspects of this dream, which will be unveiled with the passage of time, as I noted earlier. Israel would not withdraw from the West Bank at any cost, rather I suspect that the foundation has been laid even for the Israeli occupation of Eastern Jordan.

King Hussein of Jordan had no choice but to remain neutral in the present conflict. The only crime he committed, from the point of view of the Western powers, was that in a press conference, held a few days ago, he expressed his great anguish at the grave atrocities of the allied forces against the innocent civilians of Iraq. His comments were based on the claims made by the allies in their own declarations and defence news-bulletins which provided a clear picture of the happenings in Iraq. Imagine the extent of destruction when one bomber is getting airborne every minute for a bombing spree on Iraq. Such extensive bombing has never before been undertaken in the history of the world! **Even the bombardment in the Vietnam war which continued for several years has little or no significance before this carnage.** In such circumstances, a conclusion can be drawn of the extent of death and destruction. There must have been hundreds of thousands of casualties. But President Bush regards such obvious conclusions as an outrage to the U.S. and an affront to Israel. Implicitly, he has warned King Hussein, 'Beware - mind your language. Don't you realize what you are saying, and who has given you the right to level such criticism....'

Dreams sometimes have a few macabre interpretations. His dream of "peace" does carry an overall interpretation of doom for the future of Arab countries. But a macabre aspect of his 'dream' may materialize when a flimsy excuse may be sought to attack Eastern Jordan and thus open the way for the Israeli occupation of the Eastern part of the Jordan river as well. This may only be a conjecture on my part but there are several historical trends, mentioned earlier, which lend support to it. From the very beginning, and to this day, the Jews are continuously extending their territory. Their policy of expansion is not restricted only to multiplying their population numerically, but also includes territorial expansion to accommodate their numerical expansion. The dream of Israel which the Jews had visualised at its inception was to bring in all the Jews from various oppressed areas of the world into a free state to be called Israel.

Twelfth Friday Sermon Feb 08, 1991

I need not go into the statistical details of the Jewish population across the world except mentioning their numerical strength in two or three important countries. In Israel there are 2.5 million Jews, in U.S. 5 million and 2.5 million are said to be settled in Soviet Russia. They are contemplating that the entire Jewish population in Russia be transferred to Israel. By the time this project is completed, 2.5 million more Jews would have been settled in Israel. It is evident that such an influx of population demands a commensurate territorial expansion for their habilitation. It is this urgency which is at work behind their plans. There is an ongoing process of the American Jews who are also migrating to Israel and similar is the case with European Jewry.

ANOTHER SHADY ASPECT OF PRESIDENT BUSH'S DREAM

I shall apprise you of more details on this subject during my next sermon. Now let me remind you, briefly, that the *raison d'etre* of the state of Israel was stated to be the congregation of all the Jews in one place, by encouraging their migrations from Europe and other countries where they felt unsafe and insecure, or had been harassed. Such an ambitious plan could not have been accomplished without the annexation of the areas surrounding Palestine for the purpose of accommodating a huge influx of people. The events of the past have confirmed this contention that they are continuously practising expansionism without which their dream cannot be fulfilled. The dream of President Bush, termed as the **"New World Order"**, seem to have some gruesome dimensions which may call for the forcible Israeli occupation of Eastern Jordan as well. How far this 'dream' will unfold, and how many other nations will get wrapped around its tentacles, is a long saga that the future holds. **But you must realize that a host of Muslim nations are on the moving belt awaiting their turn to become part of the fulfilment of the 'dream'.** Until and unless, all Muslim powers are systematically dismantled and tossed in disarray, President Bush's dream of 'peace' cannot materialize. **Who would be the next victim in this procession? One cannot say with certainty whether it would be Pakistan or Syria.** Pakistan is also allegedly aspiring to become a nuclear power. Whether or not it has already acquired this capacity is debatable, but there are many options at their disposal which they can invoke to destroy Pakistan, e.g., the unresolved dispute in Kashmir or the Sikh unrest in the Punjab. So India can easily be prompted for developing such a situation. Or suspension of defence and economic aid from the Western powers can be used to render Pakistan weak and defenceless against India. **But Syria is in real danger and may likely be the next victim of their designs.** This country has recently emerged as a military power. It would be a colossal misconception, indeed a folly, on the part of Syria if it thinks that it would be spared because of its alignment with the Western powers in the current war against Iraq. As long as Israel stands as a power at its borders, Syria cannot be secure.

Then Iran also faces a similar danger, and so does Turkey. As to how this dream can be realized in the case of these two countries I can very well visualize. First, a rift that already exists between the two countries can be further aggravated. This can subsequently be fanned until it develops into a full scale war. The example of Iraq is a case in point. Iraq was strengthened through covert support of the U.S. and its allies, and then incited by them to attack Iran. The Arab as well as the European allies of the U.S. had been covertly supporting Iraq by selling war equipment and weapons of mass destruction. The dream of President Bush should be interpreted in the light of these events. As this dream progresses and unfolds itself, the hideous background of this **"Dream of Peace"** would help us become increasingly aware of its line of advance.

The methodology employed so far by these powers for the accomplishment of their designs is clear. In the first place, they inflate the military strength of a Muslim country, and then by creating discord with its Muslim neighbour, incite it to belligerence. Both the nations are then given an ample supply of weapons. This is how they are destroying Muslim states, piecemeal. In fact it is a dream of death and destruction of the Muslim countries, and a scheme of promoting the interest of Israel, which President Bush wrongly dubs as a "Plan of peace".

<u>HANDS STAINED WITH THE BLOOD OF THE OPPRESSED</u>

This takes my mind to a Shakespearean play called **"Macbeth"**. Lady Macbeth instigated her husband to murder the king while he was asleep. He carried out the murder, but it created a psychological reaction in lady Macbeth. She perceived herself to be the real

murderer and, under psychological stress, she kept washing her hands, repeatedly, saying that her hands smell of blood. In her own words:
"Here's the smell of the blood still, all the perfumes of Arabia will not sweeten this little hand"
However the case of President Bush is a little different. His hands are stained with the blood of Muslim Arabs. I assure him that the stench on his hands would continue to haunt the U.S. and its allies forever. **All the perfume of the world would neither be enough to transform this bitter odour into fragrance.** As to his **"Dream of Peace"** which he proclaims so loudly, is nothing but a reflection of Macbeth's soliloquy. Macbeth tries to sleep but his sleep has vanished due to the pricks of his conscience. He considers his crime so unpardonable that, in his agitated state of mind, he cannot sleep any more. He imagines that he has heard a voice saying:
Methought I heard a voice cry, " sleep no more, Macbeth does murther sleep"
In Scottish accent murder is spoken as murther. This, in fact, was a psychological reaction of strain on his nerves. His pitiable state of mind cannot be expressed in better words. He thinks that he had murdered his own sleep, so how could sleep come to him now? With a little modification this may well be applied to the dream of President Bush,

"Me thought I heard a cry, peace no more, America does murder peace"
I, too, hear the voice of a crier who is saying that this planet will never see peace again. If his dream materializes then I can say with certainty that peace would never return to this continent. The United States has massacred PEACE forever!

What would happen in its aftermath? What can we do about it? What advice can we render to those nations who have advanced so far towards destruction? How can we get them back? I will address this topic in my future sermon. I want to complete this subject as quickly as possible, so that I may revert to my real and lasting subject of educating the Ahmadis about how they can stay focused in their prayers so that they may achieve an eternal pleasure in their prostrations before the Almighty God.

In the name of Allah, the Gracious, the Merciful

THIRTEENTH FRIDAY SERMON

FEBRUARY 15, 1991

LATEST SITUATION OF THE GULF WAR

After reciting the Opening Chapter of the Holy Quran, Al-Fatiha, Hazoor said:

I revert to my continued commentary on the ongoing war in the Middle East. Unless we understand its background - what caused the conflagration - why did it spark off - i.e. unless we are fully cognisant of its total perspective, we would be unable to redraw the map of a new world. Presently, a flurry of peace making activities is being observed which is motivated by two advantages that the U.S. could possibly gain, but before stating these, let me mention what is happening. The U.S. created an impression for the rest of the world, prior to their aerial bombardment spree that the U.S. desired peace and it had repeatedly presented reasonable peace proposals to Saddam Hussein which had been repeatedly rejected by him. Now in this second phase of the war the U.S. has re-initiated the same peace making campaign. This is motivated by the fact that even though the U.S. has much greater military superiority and can inflict greater damages on Iraq, yet the U.S. casualties would be sizable. The advantages sought by this U.S. led peace initiative may be summed up as follows: To get Saddam Hussein to visualise his potential losses and vacate Kuwait under duress. To mobilize the Iraqi public opinion against him on the assumption that the entire catastrophe could have been averted by just withdrawing from Kuwait. This would have solved all objectives, i.e. the evacuation of Kuwait, the disintegration of Iraq and the saving of American lives: the last being of utmost importance to them. Emissaries were repeatedly sent to Baghdad, whether these were from Pakistan or from elsewhere. They all had instructions to present the issue in such a way as if the entire crisis could be resolved and the war everted by simply withdrawing from

Thirteenth Friday Sermon Feb 15, 1991

Kuwait and that Iraq should not show intransigence over such a trifle, especially in view of the heavy losses it had already sustained.

But this is far from the reality. I had exposed this total falsehood and deception in an earlier sermon. Saddam's stand has always been that although his occupation of Kuwait is an act of aggression, but similar aggression has, in the past been directed against the Muslim countries by the state of Israel and these illegal occupations still persist. Moreover, this state of affairs has continued despite the numerous resolutions of the Security Council of the United Nations. So, if you crave for genuine peace then do not look at the Kuwaiti situation in isolation. Consider both issues in tandem, so that unlawful occupation may end, not only in kuwait but also in the other neighbouring lands and this protracted phenomenon of infringement in the region may come to an end - once and for all.

The U.S. has strongly rejected this view of linkage of issues. All emissaries sent to Iraq from various countries including the U.N. Secretary General were told explicitly by the U.S. to refrain from discussing the **"issue of linkage"** - in other words, the symmetric approach to the occupation of Kuwait as well as that of Palestine. A mere consent of any country's envoy to consider the "linkage" as part of the agenda would have been enough to expose the U.S. deception and create a psychological problem for those Muslim Arab States which are siding with the U.S. **The U.S is demanding that Iraq withdraws from Kuwait while allowing Israel to retain its occupied territories.** This is such an overt act of double dealing that it makes it very difficult for the Muslim states to continue to side with the U.S. This however is all together a different matter as to the real motives of Muslim States to adopt a pro-U.S. posture. I will speak about that later.

According to today's news, Saddam Hussein, who has out manoeuvred the West in political shrewdness and diplomacy on numerous occasions in the past, has added yet another point to the tally, by successfully persuading the USSR and some other countries for calling a meeting of U.N. Security Council. So the issue that was deliberately being kept away from the table of diplomatic negotiations will now, after all, be considered by the Security Council. Saddam Hussein has said that he is ready and willing to withdraw from Kuwait, provided the Security Council takes up all the issues together and explain to the world why its own resolution No. 242 has never been implemented. This resolution stipulates that all the Arab lands that had been occupied as a result of Israeli aggression be vacated. So this is the phase at which the war is currently being waged.

DETERMINING THE RESPONSIBILITY FOR WAR

As for the laying of blame for this state of affairs, we cannot put the entire blame squarely on any single party. This is a protracted topic demanding much more time to do justice to it. It is only Allah who knows when this war would come to an end and what that end would be. But I can say with certainty, that this war would not solve any problems - rather the problems would multiply. This war has demonstrated that the Quranic description:

$$وَأَخْرَجَتِ الْأَرْضُ أَثْقَالَهَا$$

"**And the earth brings forth her burdens**" (Chapter 99:3) is writ large on the horizon. Not only has the planet earth coughed up the Middle Eastern issues but so have similar issues in other parts of the world come to the surface. Questions such as, what would be the parameters of the "new world" have arisen. What would be the nature of the diplomatic relations between the big powers and the smaller states? What role would be assigned to the United Nations? Is the U.N. even capable of performing that role? All these questions and many more are being considered by the whole world. So, **regardless of whether the war grinds to a quick halt or whether it drags on much longer, my subject matter will continue to have an enduring relevance, for it is tied to the long standing international issues including such issues as, who would have control over the oil wealth and how it should be managed.**

As far as the laying of responsibility for this war, I believe that the responsibility for this certainly rests on Saddam Hussein. He was too hasty in invading Kuwait, and as a result of that, he not only damaged his own reputation as a leader but he also damaged the reputation of Iraq. **The worst damage being that he was caught in the enemy's trap.** Now that the matter of responsibility for this war is being debated in the whole world, many U.S. intellectuals and scholars have openly admitted that the greatest share of responsibility lies with U.S. Whatever mischievous plot was laid down by the U.S., Saddam

Thirteenth Friday Sermon Feb 15, 1991

Hussein got caught in that trap and that was a great misdeed. Saddam is therefore, responsible on this account. As far as the U.S. role is concerned, let me draw your attention to the statement of James Atkins[1] - a former Ambassador of the U.S. in Iraq:

"An anonymous defence consultant, using the pseudonym of *Miles Ignotum* (unknown soldier), wrote an article in 'Harper's' to this affect. Ignotum even developed a plan to send U.S. forces to Saudi Arabia in numbers close to those of early August, less than one week after the invasion of Kuwait. James Atkins, former U.S. ambassador to Iraq, has gone further. He believes the U.S. **'suckered'** Saddam Hussein into the invasion by persuading the present U.S. Ambassador, **April Glaspie**, to give him the go-ahead. A week before the invasion, Glaspie assured Saddam Hussein that the U.S. would have 'no position' on such an act and treat it purely as an Arab to Arab affair."

Then there is the statement by **General Michael Dugan**. This General was the Chief of the U.S. Air staff but he was relieved of his duties for talking to journalists and revealing that the real design of the U.S. action is to launch an attack on President Saddam Hussein with the purpose of killing him, his coterie, his entire family and thus resolving the whole matter, and that the Air Force stood ready to achieve this objective. He further hinted that this suggestion emanated from Israel. Subsequently the media took up the matter and wrote[2]:-

"Defence Secretary Richard B. Cheney dismissed Air Force Chief of Staff Gen. Michael J.Dugan last week for showing 'lack of judgement' in discussing contingency plans for war against Iraq, including targeting Saddam Hussein and his family and the decapitation of the Iraqi leadership."

---

[1] Canadian Ecumenical News Jan/Feb 1991: Page 3
[2] Aviation Week & Space Technology / September 24, 1990

[3]"But Dugan's biggest sin, in Cheney's eyes was references to Israel's contribution to the U.S. military effort. Dugan said that **Israel had supplied the U.S. with its latest high-tech, super accurate missiles,** and that based on Jerusalem's advice that Saddam is a 'one man show', the U.S. had advised a plan to decapitate the Iraqi leadership -beginning with Saddam, his family, his personal guard and his mistress. Such targeting, Cheney was quick to point out, not only is political dynamite but also 'is potentially a violation' of a 1981 Executive Order signed by President Ronald Reagan flatly banning any U.S. involvement in assassinations"

This is not a statement made by an outside observer that there was a plan to kill President Saddam Hussein, his friends, family and other notables and that this is how they intended to *solve* this entire problem; but it was a statement from the U.S. Chief of Air Staff which does carry a lot of weight. The reaction of the U.S. administration following the statement, to release the General of all duties, is quite extreme. However, there is no justification for such extreme reaction on this statement by the General. As a matter of fact, the whole world is aware that the U.S. has already invaded Libya and the prime target was the person of President Gaddafi. It is widely known that the U.S. law does not empower the American President to get somebody killed in another country, though such assassinations have been carried out as a common routine in the past. They call such murders as "covert operations" but when such covert actions become explicit and known to the public then it becomes a big crime. If the plans to kill foreign Heads of States is a crime, then the U.S. shoulders the greatest responsibility for that.

Another element is that this entire operation is being conducted in the name of the United Nations, whereas, the fact of the matter is that the votes of many countries have been purchased. Many countries have been subjected to immense political pressure while others have been tempted for future U.S favours. Actually this is entirely a U.S. stage drama.

---

[3] The Time October 1, 1990

President Saddam Hussein has always considered that it is a joke to call this body as the "United Nations". In reality it is the U.S. that is operating the U.N. Recently, when the Secretary General of United Nations[4] went to President Saddam Hussein for holding talks with him, the President expressed his opinion that this entire action is being taken to deceive the world, and this is an American ploy. To call such a body as the U.N., which sponsors such unjust resolutions was a misnomer. The Secretary General responded that as far as his personal opinion was concerned he entirely agreed with him, since this is exactly what happened. But as far as formally admitting this in public, he was not in a position to do that... The U.S. administration did its best to black-out this part of his statement, because when the Secretary General went back and submitted his report it did contain this and certain other admissions. However, President Saddam Hussein has publicised these matters and laid them bare before the whole world.

The prime responsibility of this war thus lies with the U.S., although Saddam has only been made a tool. As for Saddam's share of responsibility for this war, there are certain elements in view of which we are obliged to admit that he had little or no other choice. The responsibility of the allies is quite obvious, and the worst part of it is that this has been done to achieve certain petty objectives. All the allies had a vested interest in this war.

The Israeli part of responsibility for this war is that the entire plot was hatched by Israel, and as I have pointed earlier, from the Israeli point of view, there couldn't possibly have been a better time. A rapidly expanding Muslim force which could have proven a great threat to Israeli interests during war was intended to be pulverised in such a classic manner that the instruments of destruction were partly financed by Muslim countries and partly by some allies. The manpower being happily provided by the Americans, the British or the Arabs - all this to achieve the objectives of Israel. As a by-product of this War, Israel may also have the excuse to occupy certain other parts or parcels of land and later collect a "booty" of many billions of dollars. Israel further reserves the right to target a

---

[4] The Guardian London U.K. February 12, 1991

half-dead Iraq, (God forbid) and extract vengeance at its convenience. So Israel has been the greatest beneficiary of this war and therefore it must assume the greatest responsibility.

The United Nations is also responsible for it. When members of Parliament were being purchased in Pakistan, then a political term gained currency, it was called **"horse-trading"**. What was happening was indeed horse-trading but one wondered what was the origin of this term which meant the purchasing of votes of the Members of Parliament to gain political advantage. But looking at the behaviour of the U.S. government one can easily see that the idea must have originated in America, for the way they have purchased votes in the United Nations is clearly horse-trading. They have indeed done a great deal of horse-trading. **So if the United Nations has degenerated into an Organization which can be easily bought by rich nations to serve their interests then it becomes a heinous crime. Indeed it is suicidal and it robs this Organization of International trust for ever.**

HISTORICAL PERSPECTIVE AND THE SAD INDIFFERENCE OF THE MUSLIMS

The historical perspective must be kept in mind. Historically, the British government had an important role to play in conjunction with the Jewish conspiracy which resulted in the establishment of the state of Israel. It is not necessary now to go into all the details. **Theodor Herzl** was the architect of this plan in 1897, and according to this plan many British scientists and intellectuals were appointed to diffuse into the Western countries. **Weizmann** was one of these scientists. He was an expert in Chemistry, a Polish national, educated in Germany and migrated to Britain just before the Second World War and later became a University professor. During the period of 1915 - 1918, he established contacts with influential people, specially Lord Balfour, who was then the Foreign Minister in the government of Lloyd George. It is no wonder that the greatest struggle for the establishment of the state of Israel was done by **Balfour**. So Britain would also be counted in the contemporary war as a nation that has responsibility, because this issue in itself is totally un-justified and should not have become an issue at all. You go into somebody's country and then impose another nation upon them and then, in total disregard to the wishes of the original people and of your own mandates and treaties you continue to commit one transgression after another. There can be absolutely no justification for this behaviour. The British nation came to play the greatest historical role in this issue, therefore the British would remain a party to this responsibility for all times to come. However let me also point out here that initially the entire British nation was not a party to this.

When we look at the struggle, spanning the period from 1917 to 1920, we discover that the Muslims, too, behaved in an extremely irresponsible way, right at the time when the Jewish people were throwing the web of conspiracies all around and were trying to sway the influential people. Muslims were totally oblivious to the implications of these happenings. Lord Curzon followed Lord Balfour as Foreign Minister. He supported the Muslims very strongly. He has revealed many amazing matters which makes one wonder as to why it is that while on the one hand the Jewish people were busy hatching conspiracies and doing their utmost to achieve their objectives, yet the Arabs, it appears, viewed all the happenings from a keyhole from outside. Either they were not allowed to enter the arena where their fate was being discussed or was it that they were completely oblivious and unconcerned of the happenings. At any rate, to say that the entire British nation was a party to this plan would be incorrect. **Lord Curzon**, for instance, vehemently opposed this matter. He understood the real reason for the establishment of Israel. The essence of what he said was that[5] he was repeatedly pressurized to accept the historical link of Israel with Palestine which he understood was a deep and dangerous plot that would have far reaching consequences. Once it was accepted, there would be no basis to check and stop the Jews "and the use of such words might be, and was, indeed, certain to be used as the basis of all sorts of political claims by the Zionist for the control of Palestinian administration in the future."

So, Lord Curzon remained adamant against the establishment of Israel until the very end, but the cabinet of Lloyd George due to some clandestine plans slowly passed into the Jewish sphere of influence and

---

[5] The Origins & Evolution of the Palestine Problem 1917 - 1989 Pages 21-28. Published by the United Nations. New York 1990

ultimately succeeded in having this issue passed as a bill in the parliament that the Jewish settlements in the Palestine area should be established on the ground that this has a "historical connection". The first phrase on which Lord Curzon had raised his strong objections was very cunningly substituted with the apparently harmless phrase **"historical connection"**. The rest of the quotation I cannot present at this time, but when you would read the entire text you would be surprised that extremely deceptive language has been used so that the Jews may achieve all their objectives. When this bill was presented to the British House of Lords they exhibited complete sense of justice, for which they deserve credit. And not only did they remain on the path of justice, but they issued a very stern warning to their own nation that they should not, as a nation, get involved in this conspiracy, otherwise, it would be a grave act of transgression; the ill effects and ramifications of which would continue to be felt for a very long time. We cannot say whether the evil consequences would ever come to an end. So the House of Lords rejected this bill. Later on it was presented to the House of Commons again and somehow they got it passed as a law. A member of the British House of Lords, **Lord Sydenham**[6] said in response to Balfour:

> "...the harm done by dumping down an alien population upon an Arab country - Arabs all around and in the hinterland may never be remedied. What we have done is, by concessions, not to the Jewish people but to a Zionist extreme section to start a running sore in the East and no one can tell how far that sore will extend".

So the British nation behaved in a just manner at that time, and it holds on to justice even now. Even today their notables and intellectuals have expressed their honest opinion on this issue very courageously, but since the conspiracies are running very deep, as I have pointed out, so the British have pretty much got entangled in the Jewish clutches. Today we blame the U.S. administration responsible, but at that time, even the U.S. was committed to justice. For instance,

---

[6] Ibid. Page 29

Thirteenth Friday Sermon Feb 15, 1991

the principles presented by U.S. President Woodrow Wilson in 1918 stated that the majority of a country has the right, and must be fully involved in any decision that is being contemplated regarding their destiny. If they do not agree, then it is not the right of anyone else in the world to impose any decision upon them. So this was the state of affairs in America at that time.

The U.S. in 1919 sent a Commission which was called **King Crane Commission**. This Commission also submitted a very detailed report which was based on justice and noted in that report that,...we assure you that Israel cannot be established without resorting to a huge force and a lot of bloodshed on a very large scale. And then why should this be done at all? Just because these people were living there two thousand years ago? The Commission further states that if this argument was to be accepted, then logic, wisdom and justice would be obliterated from the face of the earth. This proposal, they wrote, was so ridiculous that it should not even be considered.

Compare that glorious era with the current period when the entire American administration is playing in the hands of the Jews like a puppet. Completely devoid of justice, foresight or any moral values - Alas nothing seems to have survived! Muslims are to be blamed on account of the fact that they should have kept a watchful eye on the international developments with a view to safeguarding their own interests. And under those conditions they should have been vigilant and should have tried to penetrate influentially just as the Jews were spreading their influence around them. **But it appears that after the Muslims rejected the Promised Messiah**[as]**, they became devoid of any leadership that could have had a universal approach to solving the problems of the Muslim nation. That could have energized the Muslims and fused them into one body with a dynamic mind and a dynamic heart.**

As far as the reasons for this war, or in other words the objectives for which this war is being fought, the "Sunday Times" - newspaper writes:

"The reason why we will shortly have to go to war with Iraq is not to free Kuwait though that is to be desired, or to defend Saudi Arabia, though that is important, it is because President Saddam is a menace to vital Western interests in the Gulf, above all the free flow of oil at market prices, which is essential to the West's prosperity." (Sunday Times, London U.K. 12 August, 1990)

The newspaper has admitted the fact that these objectives are based on purely selfish grounds. In simpler words, it means that the West has rights over oil in the Gulf, and therefore it is going to war to protect those self-ascribed rights and cannot afford to allow Saddam Hussein to play with the market rise and fall of those prices. But in fact this is an incomplete admission. As a matter of fact, a part of these objectives is to safeguard Israel and to permanently insulate it from any potential threat from Iraq. Indeed the objective is to neutralise any future Muslim threat to Israel and to nullify any future challenge to the existence of Israel. So this was the primary objective, which of course is linked with the oil situation; because one of the purposes of establishment of Israel was to impose a sentry over Muslim countries so that it can be utilized in proxy, to punish those Muslim countries which are not conforming to the Western interests.

THE GAINS AND LOSSES OF THE WAR

Now I will say something of the Profit and Loss situation of this war. So far, the cost of this war has been 89.5 billion U.S. dollars. It is stated that one billion dollars per day is the expense of this war and up to now the war has gone on for 30 days, that makes it 30 billion dollars. It is also stated that before the outbreak of hostilities, the U.S. had spent 9 billion dollars, the British government had spent 2 billion dollars and their daily running expenditure is not known with certainty. On top of this, a lot of money has been spent on purchasing the support of other countries. That has also to be added to the cost of this war. **21 billion dollars loan to Egypt has been written off. You can well imagine the price tag for the bargain of Muslim support.** Israel has so far been promised 13 billion dollars as "prize money" for not taking immediate revenge for those few hundred of its citizens who were wounded in the scud missile attacks. Once Iraq has been weakened and demolished after the ravages of this war, then Israel could have a free hand to extract vengeance from Iraq. What a spectacle of "patience" Israel has presented to the world! And as a result of that, and in recognition of it, has been offered a gift of 13 billion dollars! A paper, published in Britain, called "Al-Arabia" has

Thirteenth Friday Sermon Feb 15, 1991

given a statement saying that Saudi Arabia has given 3 billion dollars to the Soviet Union. One billion dollars have been given by Kuwait, besides other miscellaneous expenses have also been incurred on Turkey and Syria. Several promises have also been made to these countries which have to be looked into, after the war. We have no knowledge of what they are.

The terrible disaster that has overtaken Kuwait and Iraq is on top of all these expenses. It is stated by the observers that 50 billion dollars would be spent on rebuilding Kuwait alone, and it is estimated that it would take at least 500 billion dollars to restore Iraq to its pre-war condition. So these expenses are on top of the war expenses or the expenses incurred upon bribing various countries. These expenses are simply astronomical.

Then the loss of life and the amount of misery to which humanity has been subjected are in addition to all this. The great economic loss that has been inflicted on the Third world is around 200 billion dollars up to this moment. Annalists estimate that this economic shock would continue to increase with the passage of time. So 200 billion dollars damage has been sustained by the poor countries of the Third world so far.

Another loss of this war has been the environmental pollution as well as the contamination of marine life. During the course of the war, an American General proudly admitted and boasted that they had successfully hit the oil wells and oil had started seeping out. The very next day, the whole story was retracted and Iraq was accused of not even sparing the birds in this war. Birds of the kind of coots, cormorant and other wild ducks were repeatedly shown on the T.V. dripping in oil slick. And this was supposed to project the tyranny of Saddam Hussein who was insensitive even of the plight of innocent birds. Repeated mention of the loss of marine life has been used by the West to indicate the great compassion they have for human, marine or other forms of life. But I would expose before you their "compassion" towards human suffering to uncover their duplicity. The Holy Prophet Muhammad[sas] used one word *"Dajjal"* **(The great deceptionist)** to encapsulate the entire history of this current historical epoch. This duplicity is so horrifying that you would be surprised to learn that the African continent is suffering from hunger for many years and millions of infants, women, men young and old have been reduced to mere skeletons and they are passing through their painful death in this manner but no attention is been given to them. Now you have heard the estimate of war expenses - five hundred fifty billion dollars would be needed to rebuild after the war and approximately One hundred billion dollar of miscellaneous expenses and two hundred billion dollars worth of losses sustained by the Third world countries. The grand total of all this comes to approximately one thousand billion dollars. As opposed to that, today, **twenty five million African people are on the brink of death, as a result of hunger**. And this is an estimate made by the United Nations. If it costs two dollars per day to provide food for one African person to keep him or her alive then only 1.5 billion dollars are needed to keep 25 million Africans alive for one whole year. **Now you imagine that those who have no mercy for 25 million people - those who are raining down death and destruction on 16 million Iraqis by spending tons of money are raising hue and cry at the death of a few birds! This is nothing but mere deception and mischief.** If the allies had an iota of human compassion, they would first attend to the human lives. They would have attended to the poor Africans and people of other countries who are dying of hunger and attempted to remove the economic imbalance. These 25 million starving Africans could have had two hearty meals for one complete year for only 1.5 billion dollars. But they continue to spend one billion dollars each day to rain down death and destruction upon human beings and cannot spend this one billion dollars for a period of nine months to promote life - and imagine that this amount will sustain the life of 25 million people!!

This reminds me of an anecdote narrated by **Sir Winston Churchill** in his book "Great Contemporaries": He says that once, when the then Prime Minister **Mr Lloyd George** was vexed with one of his ministers, **Mr Edward Gray**, because of his policies, he endeavoured to intercede on his behalf. Attempting to prove his loyalty to Britain he said that even if the Nazi Germans were here and they put a gun on the forehead of Mr Edward Gray to sign on a treaty of their choice, Mr Gray would never yield to such intimidations. To this the Prime Minister retorted that if the Germans were smart enough and knew the weak points of Edward Gray they would rather put it this way "If you don't sign this treaty, we will scrag all your squirrels at Fallodon" Mr Gray would then immediately append his signatures on the document!

They have lost the sense of balance of their values, and this has been going on for a long time. **They are willing to mortify human beings in favour of dogs. They are un-willing to sacrifice their petty self-interest for the welfare of humanity.** So they are completely and fully involved in the criminal responsibility of this war. If they would not be held accountable today, then definitely tomorrow would hold them to account.

According to some intelligent commentators one of the reasons why the U.S. jumped into this war is the so called **"Vietnam complex"** which haunts President Bush and the U.S. The situation in Vietnam had some parallels with the current situation. In Vietnam, the Americans had inflicted such heavy bombardment, that prior to the onslaught on Iraq, such horrifying bombardment had never rained on any other country. American bombardment obliterated towns after towns and disrupted life so much and destroyed the economy to such an extent that such unilateral tyranny is seldom seen in human history. The scale of this destruction was spread over a wide expanse of the country, but despite all that they could not break the spirit of the Vietnamese nation. They could not bring them to their knees. The nation continued to offer sacrifices of their lives and continued to fight, but simply refused to prostrate before the hegemony of the United States. The result was that eventually, the U.S. had to swallow their pride. Their stubbornness was softened and they had to make a hasty retreat from Vietnam without achieving their objective. When we hear about the anti-Vietnam war movement in the United States some people mistakenly believe that the American public opinion was against the Vietnam war because of their human compassion. The fact is that even if a million Vietnamese had died in the war, the American public opinion would not be bothered at all, it would not have bothered even to the extent to which it was concerned to see a few wild ducks die in the oil slick. But the prospect of American casualties and the challenge to American pride has become such a torment for them and such a bitter pill which they cannot swallow.

THE PSYCHOLOGICAL PERSPECTIVE OF THE WAR

So this is the psychological perspective of this war. The United States has been licking the wounds of its smashed pride up till now. This is the opportune moment when the U.S. is poised to extract the revenge of Vietnam from Iraq. They believe that it is only after breaking the will of Iraqis that the U.S. would be able to exorcise the ghost of Vietnam.

I remember that President Bush or one of his colleagues had said: "what are you talking about Vietnam? This war would not be allowed to become another Vietnam. It will not be years, it will not be months, it will not be weeks, it will be days".

Later on, we heard President Bush re-state his observations saying: "it will not be days, it will be weeks running into months." Today one month has passed and so far they have been unable to break the will of Iraq and whatever claims have so far been made by Saddam, have been proven true and whatever ill intensions they had boastfully harboured, have failed to materialise. So today is the day after which this prediction of running into months would be literally true, but this second stance of President Bush has falsified his previous utterances. It is a matter of fact that if the entire Iraqi population were killed - God forbid, the American public opinion would remain unchanged, but even if a thousand American coffins were shipped to the U.S. then the American public opinion would lose its equilibrium and start rattling. So this entire peace initiative is being propagated on account of these reasons. One should continue to pray to God that He should not allow false gods to be imposed upon humanity. The greatest calamity in the world is when the Oneness of God is threatened. O Allah, if such false dem-i-gods are allowed to function as 'god' then who would remain to worship the true God and where would they live in this world? There would not be any abode for them in this world ruled by such false gods. So the greatest threat is, to the "Unity of God" - to the Kaaba - to the Lord of the Holy Prophet Muhammad[sas] - to the sacred names of these precincts. The fact is that the "Oneness of God" would never be threatened - God Willing. The Holy Prophet of Islam also supplicated before God to invoke His Mercy by saying:

O' God if today in this battlefield of 'Badar', You did not come to the help of this handful of worshippers who are my

Thirteenth Friday Sermon Feb 15, 1991

companions, my devotees, and Your beloved - and if you would allow them to perish then O' my Lordthere would be none left to worship You"! لَنْ تَعْبُدُ فِي الْأَرْضِ اَبَدًا

So in like manner today, the question is that of the honour and glory of the Oneness of God and, Ahmadi Muslims are prepared to defend these values. I tell you with certainty that the Ahmadi Muslims of the entire world are standing shoulder to shoulder with one another. They are similar to the organs of the same body, ever ready to sacrifice every thing they have for the reverence of the **Unity and Oneness of God**. You would recall that the Third Successor to the Promised Messiah[as] used to say, that the next century would be the century of establishing the Oneness of God and implementing His glory. This is absolutely true. The dangers that seem to threaten the very concept of the Oneness of God are there to prop-up and prepare the Ahmadi Muslims for future greater sacrifices. They are there to remind us about the great responsibilities that would devolve upon our shoulders and for which we have been chosen.

THE HISTORICAL PERSPECTIVE

The military objectives of this war and the psychological factors motivating these have a very deep rooted connection with history. One perspective of this contemporary war or even that of the establishment of the state of Israel is a historical perspective that is connected to the history of wars that were fought between Muslims and Christians. You would recall that the **crusades** started around the year 1095. In the year 1190 or 1191 Sultan Salahuddin **(Saladin)** captured Palestine and after that nobody could snatch Palestine away from him. These wars between Muslims and Christians continued for approximately two centuries. Muslims never took the initiative in these wars by being the first to attack. However, it is an established fact that European nations joined hands as many as eight times and attacked Muslim Arabs. Many times they had an upper hand in the battles, but eventually the Muslim countries succeeded in safeguarding Palestine from the grab of the European invaders. The laceration of those historical defeats is still fresh in their memory. They harbour a deep resentment to this historical fact that such great European powers acting in unison were still unable to defeat the Muslims. Richard - the

Lion-hearted also took part in these invasions and was defeated; so were some powerful monarchs of France. Germany and Belgium also participated but nobody could turn the tide. So these wounds are still bleeding and their painful memories still alive. Secondly, they had to bite the dust at the hands of the Ottoman Empire and the Ottoman government occupied a substantial portion of Europe. So this has also been a running sore for these powers.

At any rate the long and short of this is that the crusades and the ascendancy of the Ottoman Empire is spread over a very long period of time. Particularly during the time of Solomon - the Magnificent, these powers were repeatedly routed. This forced them to regard Islam as their greatest threat. In their psychological perspective this matter is always alive that just as once before in history, Muslims countered their aggressive moves in the strongest terms, they must never be allowed to repeat that performance and thus protect their interests.

JEWS - VICTIMS TO TYRANNY AND PERSECUTION IN EUROPE

There is another very interesting dimension to this perspective, very profound and very painful as well. When Theodore Herzl introduced the plan of establishing a Jewish state, the reason he presented was that they were being oppressed and terrorised for over a thousand years in Europe. There was an incident of repression in France, when a Jew was wrongfully indicted and later convicted. Herzl travelled to France from Austria and was so moved by this act of injustice that he started a movement for the establishment of Israel. So this was the reason that triggered the movement for the establishment of an Israeli state in the land of Palestine. No one cared to ask them as to how the cruelties perpetuated against the Jews by Europeans could be rectified by taking revenge from Palestinians. How would these cruelties taper off by their entry into Palestinian lands. **But the fact remains that the Jews were certainly justified in saying that the Christian Western world subjected the Jews to such sustained horrifying cruelties that have no parallel in history.** Let me draw your attention to some pertinent details in this context. The crusades which began in the year 1095 started from France and it was probably **Lord Godfrey of Bouillon** who took the lead. When he and other French monarchs embarked on this campaign or the first

Thirteenth Friday Sermon Feb 15, 1991

crusade they thought of performing an act of "charity" before embarking upon such a momentous task. So Godfrey of Bouillon put forward the idea that the best charity is to avenge the crucifixion of Jesus Christ[as] by slaughtering all the Jews. Just as the Muslims have an institution of offering animal sacrifice or charity before they proceed to accomplish important tasks, similarly their idea took the form of a Jewish genocide in France. We do not find many examples of an unarmed nation being subjected to such extreme cruelties in the entire human history. So this was the so called "act of charity" that they performed before embarking upon the first crusade. Then this became a common practice, and for the next two hundred years that before embarking on each crusade, the Jews would be randomly slain as an act of "charity"! Another occasion when the Jews were slaughtered in cold blood was to ward off any impending evil. You might have heard the historical reference to 'black death' over the period of 1347 to 1352. This was a terrifying epidemic of plague which had engulfed Europe. It was said to have originated in China then passed through Eastern Europe to end up in Western Europe. To ward off the evil of this disease they started sacrificing the Jews and spread many false myths about them. One of these being that it was indeed the ill premonition of the Jews in their midst and their mischief that brought this calamity upon them. So the annihilation of the Jews would be an act of virtue and that this would ward off their afflictions. You would be shocked to hear that countless Jews were killed or incinerated alive in their own homes. The number is stupendous and no definite estimates exist. According to some rough estimates, Jews were completely annihilated from sixty large towns and from 140 small towns. So this was the second vengeance that the Christian world took from the Jews. There were many others, but the third main revenge from the Jews was by Nazi - Germany. Although the facts and figures regarding this revenge - better known as the **holocaust** are not acceptable to all researchers but the Jews do insist that **6 million Jews** were Killed in gas chambers. This happened over a period of ten years. So the argument was that in view of these horrifying cruelties to the Jews, they must be appeased and given their own home. It is a historical fact that many Jews would escape from these brutalities and take refuge with the Muslims in Palestine.

History stands as a witness that even during the period when the Muslims were at the zenith of their power, the Jews were never maltreated. Muslims twice occupied Palestine. They proclaimed a general amnesty regarding liberty, life and property, and did not persecute any Jew or Christian. The first occupation of Palestine was during the Caliphate of Hazrat Umar while Sultan Salahuddin occupied Palestine for the second time. The historians agree that with these two exceptions of Muslim occupation of Palestine, there was never a time when Palestine was occupied by any alien army which did not conduct a massacre. For instance, when Richard- the Lion-hearted who was a British King, occupied a part of Palestine, he carried out a genocide of all Jewish men, women, children, as well as Muslims. None was left alive. So this is the history of justice, human values and mercy of this nation which forced the Jews and led Herzl to consider that they were not in peace and should therefore have a separate state. This is strange that if they were not in peace in Europe, then there should have been an en-block exodus of all Jews, but what is this unusual solution that they continue to inhabit Europe and in fact have increased their grip and influence on that continent and then went on to carve a niche in the heart of Muslim lands. This is no solution at all. This is like the case of someone who gets kicked by a donkey, and in his anger, would go and hamstring a camel. This is like a person getting flogged by someone and his taking revenge from somebody else. This is great transgression and there is no logic in it.

I think that in the current decisions regarding waging this war in the Middle East this has become a psychological perspective for the Christian powers, but one must try to find out as to why the Jews were repeatedly and so frequently subjected to these cruelties. It appears that the historical heritage of an **"eye for an eye"** exists in Jewish tradition, therefore it may be that as a result of these cruelties against them they may have resorted to taking revenge in some secret way. It is not possible for them to have forsaken their history and heritage for two thousand years and abandon this revengeful aspect of their attitude out of their nature. It just cannot be. Although that part of history is not preserved for us to look at, and we don't know, but what we do know is that certain allegations and charges were made against them and as a result of that they were subjected to cruelties.

Thirteenth Friday Sermon Feb 15, 1991

The cruelties exercised against the Jews are fresh in the memory of the Christian West and the West is fully aware of the Jewish legacy of revenge. The character of **Shylock** in Shakespeare's famous drama, **The Merchant of Venice** has immortalized the literary portrait of the Jewish revenge. Under these circumstances, perhaps they did not think of it initially, but it appears that subsequently their thoughts were guided to this idea that **why should we not divert this threat of a potential Jewish revenge from ourselves to the world of Islam. This would kill two birds with one stone. There is a silly joke which illustrates this case:** They say that there were three suitors of a women. One of them was very smart. While the other two were fighting to lay claim on the woman, this third man stood as a silent spectator. Someone asked this third fellow that although you seem to be quite clever yet it is strange that you are not taking any part in the bidding. He replied "don't you worry, I am instigating one to fight with the other and my intention is that when one of them kills the other then I will become the prosecution's witness against the murderer. Thus one would get murdered, the other would go to the gallows and I will carry the day". Although this is a silly joke but in reality, the same crime is being enacted in front of our very eyes.

This is the ultimate conspiracy of the West according to which they are trying to use the Jews to take revenge from Muslims and thus subjugate them. Secondly, they are attempting to deflect the Jewish wrath against the Christians towards Muslims. But I would explain later that this is the height of folly of the West. They would only learn after falling victim to this deception and then would they realize what blunders they had committed. That would be the time when the Jews would be completely out of their control.

<u>PROMISE TO OFFER ADVICE</u>
In future I will give some advice to the Western powers in this context and particularly with a view to getting out of this mess in which they find themselves and focus on what policy they should adopt to bring about a lasting peace in the world - what changes in their attitude are required. Then I would advise the Jews that if they do not correct their ways they must be aware of the ultimate destiny that the Holy Quran has spelt out for them. If they do not take

advantage of this advice then they will not be able to elude this destiny. Thirdly, I would advise the Arabs and Muslims as to the role they should play in this ever changing world. I would tell them of their mistakes which should not be repeated, and propose their future line of action. Fourthly, I would advise various nations of the world as to how they should shake off the yoke of false gods and how they should embark upon a peaceful struggle to gain this objective.

It is sheer emotionalism and ignorance that you should hate the British or hate the Americans. These are only the ravings of madmen. Hate can never triumph in this world. It is the high virtues which eventually emerge as victorious. The code of conduct of the Holy Prophet[sas] succeeds, because that is the conduct of the best behaviour. If the Muslims were to adopt that code of conduct it would be an exemplary charter for the whole world. Such a code of conduct is invincible. No power on earth can eclipse the code of conduct of the Holy Prophet Muhammad[sas]. So revert to that code of justice and adopt that precept, then the entire problems of this world can be resolved, and that genuine new revolution can start, creating a heaven on earth! If you do not accept that, then you would continue to fight and this world would continue to face trials and tribulations.

In the name of Allah, the Gracious, the Merciful

FOURTEENTH FRIDAY SERMON

FEBRUARY 22, 1991

OPTIMISM OF THE UNITED STATES AND ITS ALLIES

After reciting the Opening Chapter of the Holy Quran, Al-Fatiha, Hazoor said:

In my previous sermon I had said that *Insha Allah* God willing, I would give certain suggestions to the world from different aspects. I will begin this by advising the U.S. that it should attempt to perceive itself through the eyes of others.

In the euphoric atmosphere generated by the lofty praises heaped on President Bush, he psychologically seems to have been blinded as to what is being thought of his policies by others and what image he presents to the outside world.

THE WRONG THINKING OF THE U.S. AND ITS ALLIES

President Bush is convinced that the whole world is following his lead like a pack of hunting dogs following the heel of a hunter. This act, in the hunter's terminology, is called "**to heel**". He thinks he has brought England to heel along with other allies. Such nations may feel that after the hunt is over they would be rewarded with some of the left-over scraps. This is the aim of President Bush in crushing Iraq and the Muslim world under the pretence of liberating Kuwait.

From another angle it would be more accurate to say that Israel, and not President Bush brought the world to heel, and that the United States itself has joined the pack, at the heel of the hunter. This gives a more accurate picture and the world views the recent events in this perspective.

Things look different when viewed from a different angle. So the U.S. has its angle of view, but there is another angle of view as well, which I will illustrate by presenting you with a few examples. The United States and her allies believe that Israel will protect their oil and

Fourteenth Friday Sermon Feb 22, 1991

other interests in the Middle East, hence they have to pamper and please Israel at all cost, even at the risk of alienating the rest of the world. On the other hand, Israel believes it is to its advantage to incur the hostility of the entire Asiatic world if such sacrifice is necessary to have the unreserved backing of a Western Super Power.

Thus the United States and the Western allies think that they need Israel in the same way as Israel thinks it needs the West. Why is this game being played? And to what lengths will it go? On this point I shall address you later.

As regards the oil interests, the West has failed to make a deep study of the inherent nature of Israel. Temperamentally, Israel is such that being so near the oil fields, it will not refrain, in the course of time, from attacking and acquiring the oil fields. Making Israel the protector of the oil is like the *Punjabi anecdote of expecting a cat to guard a bowl of milk or a goat to protect grain.* It is a simple but profoundly wise illustration, for there could not be greater stupidity than entrusting the crops to the goats and milk to the cats. The interests which Israel is supposed to safeguard stand in the greatest danger from Israel itself. If the world does not take notice of this fact now, the consequences will be the same as I have hinted. But I shall talk at length about it a little later.

HATE ALWAYS BEGETS HATE

Israel has succeeded in delivering this message to its Western allies, especially the United States, that peace in the region can only be achieved by preventing the emergence of **Nassers and Saddams** and that for as long as people of this type continue to surface, the region will never be at peace. An obvious corollary of this message is that the Arab spirit and its yearning for emancipation be crushed; the concept of support of the Palestinian cause be smashed. Practically, the West has already accepted this concept. The West fails to realize that, in fact, the reverse is true. It is the atrocities committed by the West which gave birth to "Nassers and Saddams". Saddam was born as a result of the excesses committed by the West on Muslim countries, specially in Egypt to eliminate Nasser. That action created hatred, and hate always begets hate. A sour tree never bears sweet fruit. **So long as excesses are committed against the Arabs and so long as they are not redressed with justice and** fairplay, one Nasser after another and one Saddam after another will continue to emerge. **This is the decree of God and it remains immutable!**

The bombardment on Iraq has been so dreadful and on such a gigantic scale that the bombardment carried out in the entire Second World War pales into insignificance. In the Second World War 2,700,000 tons of bombs were dropped in six years. In Iraq, 150,000 tons of bombs were dropped in less than five weeks. From these figures you can imagine the fury with which Iraq is being smashed. The West makes no attempt to comprehend human nature. The West fails to realize that such a bombardment creates the climate for the germination of more Saddams, not only among young Arabs but also among other non-Arab Muslims. There are many among the younger generation who are watching the situation and as a reaction, have made up their mind about their future actions. **So to expect the sweet fruit of peace from such bombardment is the height of ignorance.** Hate always begets hate. What is cause of this hatred? So long as the root cause of what it is which creates people like Saddams and Nassers is not determined, and so long as the seed of hated is not uprooted, no peace can exist in this region.

<u>ISRAELI MOTIVES</u>

As far as I have observed, and facts bear me out that the establishment of Israel is indeed the root cause of the beginning of all this strife and hate. The waging of wars is among the aims in the concept and creation of Israel. I am not saying this on my own; David Ben Gurion, the founding father of Israel, also claims so. I will read to you from 'The Making of Israel' by James Cameron: On page 55 he writes:

> "For Ben Gurion the word state, had now no meaning other than an instrument of war. I can think of no other meaning now, he said...I feel that the wisdom of Israel now is that to wage war, that and nothing else, that and only that."

This reminds me of two lines by **Coleridge in Kubla Khan**, when he writes: "And amid this tumult Kubla heard from far ancestral voices prophesying War!"

Fourteenth Friday Sermon Feb 22, 1991

Whether or not Kubla Khan heard ancestral voices coming from afar, but Ben Gurion certainly heard the loud rallying cry from Zion Hall calling out on Israel; as if saying 'From today onwards the aim of your existence is only one and only one, to keep waging wars and keep involving the world in these wars. Now there is no other aim of Israel except this.'

How can the U.S. and its allies in supporting an Israel with such motives, conceive of peace. They may deceive themselves in their objectives and aims, but by supporting Israel, the possibility of peace completely disappears. It is inherent in Israel's nature and in its national ideology that it would implicate the whole world in conflict and wars. Why does it do that? Towards the conclusion, I will reveal this secret, which in fact is an open secret.

SADDAM - PICTURED AS A NEW HITLER

America and its allies have been attempting to convince the world that Iraq is as great a danger to the world as Hitler was. Saddam is pictured as a Nazi, a Nazi with a new face. Yet one Western commentator has said that you call this man a Hitler while he has not been able to conquer Iran in eight years. Hitler, all of a sudden created havoc and panic in the whole world. The West trembled at the mention of his name. He marched from Berlin and knocked at the door of Leningrad. His rockets were falling over London. How can you call Saddam a Hitler when **your** bombs are raining relentlessly on him? What ignorance! He cannot even manufacture one scud missile, and you are keeping the count of his remaining scud missiles. The modification he attempted to make to extend the range of his scud missile is so crude as if it was the tinkering of a bazaar tin-smith. Examining the debris of the scuds with its clumsy modification, people were joking that this was the level of technology of Iraq who was challenging the West. ***This is the man you call Hitler!***

Israeli Generals have claimed[1]:

"Israeli Generals have often boasted that they could take on all

---

[1] Dispossessed The Ordeal of the Palestinians: By David Gilmour Page 224

the Arab armies at the same time and still destroy them and the chief of staff has even claimed that he could defeat the armed forces of the Soviet Union"

Thus in destroying an imaginary Hitler in Saddam, the Americans and their allies are in fact fostering the state of Israel which has assumed the posture of a real Hitler. How ignorant and devoid of inner vision is the West? Does it not realize that it was Israel which in the first place called Saddam and the Palestinians as Hitler? By raising the Hitler-bogey, the West is patronizing a "Hitler" and if they do not realize, the future will reveal what Israel's motives are and how Israel will treat the United States and the West.

WHAT IS HAPPENING & WHY IT IS HAPPENING

Against this background, the Muslims note that Israel is inflicting on them one cruelty after the other and that it is being backed and supported by the West. They are astounded, unable to comprehend all that which is happening to them. Israel repeatedly speaks of Muslim "terrorism". One is sick of reading that Muslims are "terrorists" and Palestinians are "terrorists". Israel and the Western media paint Islam as if it is synonymous with terrorism and equate a Muslim with a terrorist. In fact, it was Israel which first initiated and practised terrorism. Now I will mention briefly the barbaric and dreadful acts of terrorism perpetuated by Israel. **The ruined Muslim cities of Der Yasin, Jaffa, Kabia, West Beirut, Sabra and Shatila all bear testimony to this terrorism.** These cities were devastated and the inhabitants, men, women and children were indiscriminately and mercilessly slaughtered in cold blood in broad daylight. Most mercilessly, their bodies were pierced through by lances and then other cruel methods were used to inflict death, which resulted in wiping off the entire population in those areas. Hundreds, if not thousands of villages are in ruins - not a single structure was spared. **In 1977, just in one raid, 250,000 Palestinians were rendered homeless. The West is aware of all this but it has remained mute and preferred to look the other way.** Muslims, whether Arabs or non-Arabs, are astounded at to what is happening. On the one hand, one atrocity after another is being committed in the name of justice but no one has the courage to caution Israel that the atrocities it commits and its reign of terror will add a shameful chapter of cruelty and terrorism to world history. In fact, the West and the United States close their eyes to these shocking and horrible events.

There are many other examples, but because of lack of time I cannot recount them all. The darkest chapter in the history of terrorism was written by Israel in 1982 when it plotted against Lebanon and code named this as *"Operation Peace for Galilee"*. In his book 'Dispossessed', David Gilmour thus sums up the topic[2]. It is Israel's contention that "Operation Peace for Galilee" was to secure its own safety and to prevent itself from being constantly attacked by Palestinians. The author, Gilmour says the truth of the matter is that in 1981 a peace pack was made between the Palestinians and the Israelis. The Palestinians, never even once, violated the terms of this agreement, but in May 1982, the Israelis, suddenly, and without provocation attacked them. He says that Lebanon has never posed a threat to Galilee and it has been established that long before 1982, Israel had completed battle plans against the Palestinians. Israel subsequently attempted to concoct false excuses for its aggression. The author further states that in 1982, Beirut was subjected to intensive bombardment by day as well as by night. Big guns from the ships at sea pounded Beirut, and people were dying all over... No voice was raised in protest at the atrocities against the Palestinians. Not a bleep of protest came from Western powers, and how unfortunate that, even the Arab world was cowed into silence having been awed by the terrorism of Israel. [3]**In that savage attack and bombardment 14,000 people died, more than 20,000 were injured and many were made homeless.**

Some newspapers published accounts of this bombardment. You would recall that towards the end of World War II, Germany had bombarded England and Belgium with V-2 rockets. This was considered the most horrible period in the war. In England the V-2 bombardment was discussed and written about in the media and the pictures of damage and injuries were repeatedly shown on T.V

---

[2] Ibid Page 223, 224
[3] Ibid Page 223

programmes and through other media. The propaganda machine went into full gear and the press did not allow anybody to forget the savagery of the attacks. You will be surprised to learn that during the aerial bombardment only 7000 people were killed in Belgium and Britain, while in the bombardment in Beirut 14,000 people were killed. No one has given any importance to this act of terrorism and no Western power has protested or raised its voice against Israel.

THE STATUS OF ISRAELI PROMISES

As far as the promises of Israel are concerned it is said that if the Arabs resolve their differences with Israel, they have nothing to fear. That is a white lie, a lie unequalled in it's enormity. I will present statistics to show that Israel's promises cannot be trusted and that the Israeli lie is greater than all the lies in the world put together.

In the 1967 war, which was forced upon the Arabs by Israel, the Arabs lost a good amount of territory to Israel. Before the War, Israel promised and made the Western powers to believe that it would not annex any Arab land and that it would not dispossess the Arabs of **even one foot** of their territory. Israel alleged that it only occupied the land to teach the Palestinians and its supporters a lesson and as a warning that any attack on Israel would merit punishment. **Levi Eshkol**[4] was the Prime Minister of Israel just before the 1967 war. **"Israel", said the Prime Minister, "had no intention of annexing even one foot of Arab territory."**

After the 1967 war, if one were to count the number of feet of land that had been annexed by Israel it would run to **73 trillion feet!** You have heard of a billion, one thousand million equals one billion and 1,000 billion is one trillion, that is 73 thousand million square feet of Arab land has been annexed.

This reminds me of a Western writer who once, talking about the atrocities committed by Israel, said: **"An eye for an eye, I understand, is their religious belief. And a tooth for a tooth. But 20 eyes for one eye is something beyond me."**

What this Western writer did not realize is that the Israelis are prepared to break trillions of promises, not one promise. Israel's

---

[4] Ibid Page 225

word is worthless and it has totally lost all credibility. It is not a coincidence that when Israel attacked Lebanon in 1982, it had likewise said:[5]

"**We have no intention of taking even an inch of Lebanon.**"

After Israel attacked and subdued Lebanon, apart from committing appalling atrocities there, before leaving Lebanon, it annexed all the land south of the Litani River, which was a part of its original plan[6]. **If that portion of land were surveyed in terms of inches it would be 8 trillion inches and 830 billion square inches.** So when Israel states that she does not want even a single inch of land, in reality, she means to grab 8 trillion and 830 billion square inches.

This made me think of Israel's history, and wonder when this principle "an eye for an eye and a tooth for a tooth" was first preached. How long ago was that? If the interval of time that has elapsed were counted in seconds then on gets an idea as to how much Israel has intensified in its scope and scale of revenge. I was amazed to find that if one calculated the time span between the revelation of the *Torah* and the present time, in terms of seconds, then it would amount to 6 trillion, 244 billion, 128 million seconds. You can well imagine that from the time of Moses[as] to the present day 6 trillion 244 billion and 128 million seconds have passed and during this time, Israel's broken promises have mounted to astronomical figures; indeed Israel has been telling lies at a faster rate than the passage of time. Similarly the scale of its retaliatory action has soared in the same proportion.

As regards the appalling destruction to Lebanon caused by Israel, I will quote a comment from a diplomat **Mr Theodore Arcand** who was then the Canadian Ambassador in Lebanon. In describing the bombardment of Lebanon, he said[7] that compared to it the **bombing of Berlin was a tea party.**

---

[5] Ibid Page 125
[6] Ibid see pages 220, 221, 225
[7] Ibid 224

HORRENDOUS CRUELTIES INFLICTED ON PALESTINIANS

Some observers who had analyzed the situation state that Israel only intends to decimate the Palestinians but also to totally strip them of their dignity, humanity and self respect. Dr. Nahun Goldman, the founder of Zionism and President of World Zionist Organisation, as well as the Head of the World Jewish Congress for many years, writes[8] **"The apparent aim is to liquidate the Palestinian people."**

The Israelis also indulge in character assassination of the Palestinians by slandering them and to this aspect they attach great importance. A Western observer has written that the Israelis use abusive language for the Palestinians and their leaders, so much so, that when a Palestinian is mentioned, the name is always prefixed with a scurrilous epithet, a so and so terrorist, an animal or bastard... Referring to the presence of Yassar Arafat in Beirut, they say[9] 'the man who sits in Hitler's bunker'.

At one stage the Israelis said that the reason they hated the Palestinians was because they refused to accept the existence of the State of Israel and threatened to drown them in the sea. Yassar Arafat tried unsuccessfully to alley Israel's expressed, though unfounded fears, and at the United Nations he openly and officially declared, on behalf of all Palestinians, that the PLO accepted and recognised the right of the State of Israel and its people to freely exist. In reply, Israel announced[10]:

"The only useful thing the PLO could do, said the spokesman of Israeli Foreign Ministry, was to disappear. Palestinians no longer existed and therefore there was no point in having a liberation movement"

Israel has perpetrated great cruelties on the poor Palestinians, has heaped scorn, victimised and ridiculed them. It has taken all Palestinian land and rendered them stateless. It oppresses and inflicts cruel punishments on them each day and night. Palestinians have been slaughtered and their settlements destroyed. They have been rendered homeless.

---

[8] Ibid Page 226
[9] Ibid see Pages 224, 226, 227
[10] Ibid Page 227

Fourteenth Friday Sermon Feb 22, 1991

Four million Palestinians are wandering about listlessly, stateless, without a country, like lost souls. The Jews have been grafted in the land of the Palestinians. Day by day their numbers have been made to increase. Despite all these upheavals it is said that today there are still 1,500,000 Palestinians to the 2,500,000 Jews in Palestine and their number is increasing. It is Israel's aim to populate the West Bank with more Jews and then claim more land. Their strategy is that first they settle down, then add to the population, then further expand residential facilities and thus further increase their strength. So Israel goes on increasing Jewish settlements and bringing in Jewish immigrants, pushing out the native Palestinians who have been living there, born and bred on that soil for centuries. The Palestinians have no right now to live and reside on their own ancestral land and are told that they have no land, no country. We refuse to recognize you, they say. In the face of this Israeli policy, it is difficult to understand what considerations still motivate the U.S. to carry on its flirtation with Israel. The action of the U.S. in allowing Israel a free hand in the Middle East is **similar to some one letting a bull loose in a crop field.** A bull only eats the crops in the field but Israel is sucking the blood and devouring the flesh of the people while there is none to stop this brutality.

<u>THE FATE OF THE UNITED NATIONS RESOLUTIONS AGAINST ISRAEL</u>
You have heard about the resolutions against Iraq. It was resolved that unless Iraq complies in full with the various Security Council resolutions, the bombing, destruction, and battering of Iraq will continue even after Iraq was driven out of Kuwait. The pounding of Iraq shall continue till it is made sure, that for scores of years none shall be able to muster the strength to challenge these powers. In contrast to this stern and implacable implementation of the Security Council resolutions by the United States of America and the West during the Gulf War, whenever the Security Council has proposed resolutions demanding that Israel should stop perpetrating cruelties, the U.S. vetoes such a resolution. It was **27 times** that the Security Council branded Israel as an aggressor and asked it to vacate the forcibly occupied territories and desist from acts of aggression. **All such resolutions were vetoed; in many cases the U.S. was the lone country that cast its negative vote to kill such resolutions.** I have

studied those resolutions which were passed against Israel, calling for cessation of all atrocities or to vacate Palestinian land. The representative of the U.S. always **abstained** from all such discussions and resolutions. That happened 27 times too. The strongly worded resolutions against Israel were never passed, but the U.S. representative kept away even from those that only condemned Israel in mild language.

You have heard a lot about **Resolution No. 242** in which Israel was required to return the land taken in 1967 war. The reason why it was passed was that it was so vaguely worded that Israel could, and does interpret it in its own way. That is the only resolution against Israel for which the United States of America voted in favour. Why is the U.S. pro-Israel, despite being fully aware of Israeli actions? One simply fails to comprehend why the U.S. is behaving in such a manner.

<u>THE DIFFERENCE BETWEEN THE RESOLUTIONS PASSED AGAINST ISRAEL AND THOSE PASSED AGAINST IRAQ</u>

There is an interesting point that I have noted between the resolutions passed against Israel and those passed against Iraq. There is a world of difference between the two. Iraq is not allowed to breathe, not given even a chance. The resolutions against Iraq provide for a total prohibition of food and medicine to be imported into Iraq, and nothing, not even a leaf is allowed through. The sanctions had just been imposed when Iraq was invaded. In fact, before the sanctions were allowed to have their effect it had been decided to attack Iraq. The reason for imposing the sanctions was to starve Iraq of all necessities and cripple it before the launching of the attack. Later, in fact, even the **children's milk plant** was deliberately bombed. Now look at the difference in the resolutions about Israel and the attitude that the Security Council adopted despite the intransigence of Israel. The mild language of the resolution against Israel may be interpreted as if saying: 'We have told you to vacate the Arab lands but you are still there. We don't look on it with favour. We don't like this.' Israel does nothing. Another resolution is passed and it states in effect, once again 'Oh Israel we told you, we did not like what you are doing. We told you, we would not like it and we don't like it.' Israel still does nothing. Then another resolution is passed and repeats once again,

Fourteenth Friday Sermon Feb 22, 1991

'We have told you twice that we do not like your attitude and we shall be compelled to take such steps as will make you believe that we do not like what you are doing.' Yet another resolution is passed which virtually means: 'We have been compelled, as we said, to tell you that we certainly resent your behaviour...' In short, no action was taken against Israel except the passing of a few resolutions of this type.

This reminds me of a joke about the people of U.P. (India). They are a submissive and peaceful lot. If a person from the U.P. is struck a blow the victim does not retaliate but says, 'If you hit me again you will see.' If he is struck a second time, he still will not retaliate but repeats the same once again. This goes on every time he is struck. This is just a joke against the people of U.P. for there are many people in U.P. who are brave, bold and aggressive and have often successfully subdued their enemies, but this is true of the United Nations. The United Nations resolutions have been ignored time and again by Israel, which, in other words, said rebelliously: 'Your resolutions are not worth the paper they are written upon. They should be tossed into the waste paper basket - I would trample over such resolutions...' Every time Israel ignores a United Nations resolution, the United Nations passes another one admonishing Israel saying in effect 'If you do this again, we will be annoyed.' No action is taken, only paper resolutions are passed. **Why is this lunatic scene being enacted? There is a limit to such absurdity. One can hardly believe this is happening in this world.**

THE UNITED NATIONS

I ask the Muslims, the Arabs and the world: What is the use of this United Nations? The United Nations only serves the interest of the rich and powerful nations. What is the use of such a U.N., the constitution of which permits the powerful nations to make others the victims of their cruelty and yet not allow them to raise their voice of protest. If they somehow manage to introduce such a resolution, it is vetoed and the big powers, through their tout, continue perpetrating cruelty. They virtually rule the world and govern the destinies of the nations. In the name of the United Nations, the rich and the strong punish the Arabs and Muslims with impunity and inflict cruelties and atrocities on them.

But when the friends of these powerful nations transgress, no punishment is meted out and only weak and ineffectual protest resolutions are passed.

When I was young, I was fond of raising chickens. I noted that some chickens have the habit of leaving droppings in their owners grounds while laying their eggs in the neighbour's compound. Similarly the United Nations leaves its droppings in the yard of the Arabs and Muslims, but lays its eggs in the West and in Israel. If that is the objective of the United Nations then it is necessary for the world to ponder over this matter. Later, God willing I will advise the world on this matter also.

DEEP ANIMOSITY OF THE WEST AGAINST THE WORLD OF ISLAM

One can only conclude that the West is fundamentally opposed to, and harbours a deep animosity toward the Islamic world. This enmity has historical roots. Moreover, some ignorant Muslim Mullahs have painted an ugly picture of Islam and have created the impression that, should Islam be resurgent and return to its former glory it would retaliate and wreak vengeance on the West. I will speak to the Muslims on this point later on. For the moment, I can tell you that if the West is supporting Israel in order to subdue and totally demoralise the Muslims, or is thinking that by so doing, they could divert the attention of Israel to forget the past atrocities committed by the West on the Jews, and instead, continue to extract revenge from the Muslims, then it is gravely mistaken. The Jews never forget the wrongs done to them. They have a very long memory. Their memory for revenge is never erased. On the other hand, Israel is prone to forgetting the favours and good deeds done to them. Such deeds are as if writ on water, forgotten as soon as they are done. If you are aware of Islamic history you will know that for 800 years Muslims ruled over Spain. In that period, you will be surprised to know, that no Israeli was ever persecuted. You will also know that during this period when the Muslims were all powerful, though fighting took place among Muslim factions and cruelties were committed by different sects of Muslims upon each other, due mainly to irresponsible Mullahs inciting one sect against the other, yet in the history of Islam you will not find any recorded injustice committed upon the Christians or the Jews.

Fourteenth Friday Sermon Feb 22, 1991

THE JEWISH TRIBES OF BANU QUNKAH, BANU NAZEER AND BANU QARIZA

There were three tribes well known in Islamic history who were treacherous and turned against the Holy Prophet time after time. These tribes violated treaties they had entered into and treacherously joined the enemies during the course of wars. They betrayed the Muslims. In the end the Muslims had to take strong action against them. The three tribes were Banu Qunkah, Banu Nazeer and Banu Qariza. In 1947 when the United Nations was debating the creation of Israel, the Israelis taunted the Muslims. They said,

"we have a right to a home and you are in the habit of banishing us from our home. We have still not forgotten what you did to the three tribes of Banu Qariza, Banu Nazeer and Banu Quanka."

It is indeed amazing how Israelis kept alive those imaginary atrocities of 1400 years earlier. But Israelis conveniently forget the good deeds the Muslims did to them. They are a peculiar people. They have little sense of gratitude. They forget the occasion in 1490 when **Isabella and Ferdinand** ordered their expulsion from Spain. Before that, for nearly 200 years the Jews were subjected to indignities and cruelties. The Jews nevertheless stayed on in Spain and in the end they were compelled to convert to Christianity. When large numbers of Jews became Christians, the clergy alleged they were not true Christians, but had converted merely as a convenience, and in deceit. They became very rich, and the clergy made efforts to discover ways of relieving them of their wealth. The Christian clergy strenuously tried to persuade Isabella and Ferdinand to distrust the Jews and to reject their purported conversion to Christianity. The clergy asked that the Jews be handed over to them and be subjected to the **"Inquisitions"**. The Inquisition was a method used by Christians to investigate heretics and those whose beliefs and doctrines were suspected or were opposed to the established Church. The punishments meted out were gruesome, and many victims were badly tortured. The struggle by the clergy to have the Jews investigated by the Inquisition went on for a long time.

Isabella was at odds with the then **Pope Sixtus IV**. The Pope did not appoint cardinals of her choice. Thus she refused to hand over the converted Jews to the Inquisitions in Spain. In the end, greed prevailed. The clergy put up a scheme to Ferdinand. If the converted Jews were handed over to be investigated by the Inquisition, the property of those condemned, would be handed over to Ferdinand. The clergy was only interested in punishing heretics for heresy.

In 1480 the Inquisition commenced its work and it wrought havoc on the converted Jews. That period of suffering has no parallel in human history. Even then the clergy's ferocity against them was not satiated and there was an order for the expulsion of the Jews in 1492.

You may remember the Black Death which plagued Europe from 1347 to 1352. People died in droves. At the same period the Jews were also being persecuted in Europe, especially in France. The Jews tried to flee from their tormentors to Europe and Spain. They could not find refuge anywhere in the world except in the Muslim ruled Palestine. This is a historical fact. The second occasion was when the Jews were persecuted by Nazi Germany. They again sought and obtained refuge in Muslim Palestine. Throughout Islamic history the Muslims treated the Jews with magnanimity and had given them sanctuary, refuge and asylum. The Jews progressed and advanced in their learning and erudition under the beneficence of the Muslims. Cruelties and atrocities committed on the Jews were by the Western Christian Nations and peoples. **It is ironic that now the Jews are avenging themselves on the Muslims for the wrong done to them by the Christians.** The U.S. and the West are happy with this proposition that the urge for revenge by Israel is diverted and let-loose against the hapless and vulnerable Muslims of the Middle East. That would kill two birds with one stone. What better policy could there be?

<u>THE JEWS NEVER FORGET TO AVENGE THEMSELVES</u>

But the West forgets that the Jews are not a race that forgets atrocities and wrongs done to them. That is against their very nature. It is inevitable that they will extract revenge from the West. It is just a matter of time. Today, they will gain strength by sucking the blood of Muslims but tomorrow they will savagely attack other nations. Even now, Israel is so powerful that one of its generals boasts openly that it is prepared to take on and defeat even the Soviet Union itself. In many fields, Israel's technical know-how to manufacture military

Fourteenth Friday Sermon Feb 22, 1991

hardware is far superior to that of the U.S. It has made the Atom bomb and other nuclear devices. Why is all this happening? Why is Israel bent upon becoming, militarily more and more powerful? It is a great blunder on the part of the U.S. and its allies to think that Israel is doing so because it is scared of any Muslim threat. How could it possibly be frightened of Muslims? Whenever there has been a clash between Israel and the poor Muslims, the Israelis have ignominiously defeated the Muslims. Muslims have often been so badly routed that the whole Muslim world hangs her head in shame. What fear can Israel possibly have from Muslims? The real reason for the huge military build-up is that it aims to conquer the world. First, it will acquire the oil, then when the uproar arising from that action has subsided and after the necessary interval of time, Israel will proceed to implement the next step. Again after the necessary pause, it will go on to the next step, and so on and so forth. That is why when I say **that Mecca and Medina and the Muslim religion are endangered, it is undoubtedly correct.** There is also no doubt that Israel's aim is eventually to take over and acquire the oil fields, unless God, through our fervent prayers and through His Grace prevents that from happening. Unless God frustrates their designs, there is no other way to avert that catastrophe.

When Israel has achieved those objectives then it will seek to avenge itself on the West for the long saga of atrocities and humiliations and slaughter the West had inflicted on the Jews throughout the ages. The revenge will be so furious and savage that the West would not have even dreamt of. The Israelis have long been geared for war and are used to sounding the bugle of war which David Ben Gurion has already sounded. The Jews had sounded trumpets of War 4,000 years ago, and that is now reverberating in their ears again and again. The sound, the Israelis now hear ringing in their ears constantly is: 'War-War and War, is the only justification for your existence.'

So if the U.S. and its allies believe they are fooling the Jews and Muslims, by setting them up to fight one another, they are gravely mistaken.

PSYCHOLOGICAL REPERCUSSIONS OF DEFEAT IN VIETNAM

I had once said that the U.S. had many psychological reasons for attacking Iraq. United States had wanted to wipe out the chagrin of defeat it experienced in Vietnam. That had been a motivating force in its attack on Iraq. It was an attempt to redeem its military honour and to rise from the ashes of its humiliation. Now let me tell you in brief how in Vietnam, the U.S.'s arrogance and honour was shattered and how the self esteem and pride of the world's greatest power was trampled to dust. **The Vietnam war started on August 4, 1964.** By a coincidence or twist of fate that conflict was also started by a "storm" The United States code-named it as **"Tropic Storm"**. During the war between South and North Vietnam when Communist Vietnam wanted to topple the government of South Vietnam, the United States looked for an opportunity to help South Vietnam in defeating North Vietnam. At that time, there were 2 U.S. warships in Vietnamese waters. One ship **'The Maddox'** entered Vietnamese territorial waters, in an area within the jurisdiction of North Vietnam. North Vietnam sent out some patrol boats to attack the Maddox but the patrol boats were destroyed or driven away. The Maddox sailed out of North Vietnamese zone and then assisted by another United States destroyer the **"Turner-Joy"** it returned safely after two or three days. They waited for the expected attack from North Vietnam, in reaction to the provocation by the Maddox; so that the United States could find an excuse to attack and invade North Vietnam in retaliation. However, on the fourth day a tropical storm broke out in that area. A tropical storm is very fierce and is as dangerous as a desert storm. In this tropical storm all the radio and electrical equipment was rendered unserviceable and all signals were jammed and the crew of both U.S. ships were completely cut-off from all communication. The crew at that time thought that they were under attack by North Vietnam. It was, indeed silly to think so. The storm was so obvious and visible that only a blockhead could have thought that the electrical disturbance was caused by a North Vietnam attack. Anyway, when one is looking for excuses then even the flimsy ones would suffice. So the U.S. commenced pounding and bombing North Vietnam heavily. The United States maintained the view that it was only retaliating in response to a North Vietnam attack. So North Vietnam was attacked with great vigour. During the year 1964, 200,000 United States

Fourteenth Friday Sermon Feb 22, 1991

servicemen were shipped to Vietnam; in 1967 the figure had risen to 540,000. North Vietnam was bombarded day and night for 8 years. Altogether 2,500,000 tons of bombs were dropped on it. During the six years of the World War II, the total tonnage of bombs dropped all over the world was the same as that dropped on North Vietnam in eight and a half years of war. You must realise that Vietnam is only as big as Florida, and much poorer and far less prosperous and less developed.

UNITED STATES WAS HUMBLED
The Vietnamese fought against the United States of America for eight and half years. It is a poor country but what superb courage and endurance was shown by its people! During the war the casualties in both North and South Vietnam amounted to about 2,500,000, almost equal to the Jewish population of Israel. The Vietnamese fought on bravely and met and withstood the full brunt of the U.S. military might. They never gave in. They fought until they defeated the armed forces of the United States of America. The defeat humbled the U.S. and broke the back of its arrogance. The U.S. had to admit defeat and flee from the battleground. There was an interesting situation at the time of this defeat. In France, a Peace Conference had been convened to end hostilities. During the conference, the North Vietnamese refused any cease fire and continued fighting. They said they were prepared to fight and talk peace at one and the same time. The United States is emulating that example. The United states of America is treating Iraq in the same way, carrying on with the war against it and talking peace at the same time.

U.S. SETS THE MOST DANGEROUS PRECEDENT IN THE HISTORY OF WARS
So in Vietnam, the greatest and strongest world power was humbled by a small and poor country which was a great psychological blow to this Super Power. **The United States was determined at any cost to redeem its honour and to restore its self respect and pride and its image as the world's greatest military power. But the truth is that a broken back seldom gets fully restored and cured.** To date, the U.S. has rained four times as many bombs upon Iraq as in Vietnam and the fight still goes on. United States has boasted that the

war would last two days, yet it is now in its 6th week and Iraq is still fighting.

The fact is that the world has changed. Man now has more pride in himself and is prepared to go to any length to defend his independence and his dignity. This has resulted in waves of freedom movements sweeping over the world. Allah's decree is changing man's outlook on life. This is no time now for false gods. The false gods have to pack-up, but they appear not to visualise their end. They continue with their oppression, tyranny and cruelty, without caring what image they project and what history will say of their deeds. Today they call Saddam a Hitler, portraying him as a tyrant, oppressor and dictator. Even if every thing alleged against Saddam were true, all his acts of torture and cruelty pale into insignificance when compared to what the United States did in Vietnam; it is like comparing a mustard seed to a mountain. The wrongs done by the United States of America in Vietnam in eight and half years, far exceed anything that Saddam could possibly be charged with.

What right had The United States to enter a country the way it did in Vietnam and deluge it with bombs? What right had it to interfere in the internal affairs of Vietnam and join in to support one part to fight against the other? What right had it to bomb innocent people on such a scale and with such severity that one shudders even to think of its horrendous consequences? The havoc wrought on the Vietnamese people was unimaginable. But the greatest cruelty that the United States commits is that it continues to slander, malign and assassinate the character and honour of the soldiers and people of North Vietnam. The United States alleges that when the North Vietnamese re-captured cities in the war, they committed numerous atrocities against those Vietnamese who had cooperated with United States troops. United States accuses North Vietnam of killing hundreds and thousands of these people and burying them in mass graves in those cities. In a war of such ferocity between unequal combatants, a traitor or collaborator deserves what he gets. There is no law in the world that protects the life of a traitor or a collaborator in the course of a war. The United States admits that the people so killed had been their sympathizers. The United States talks of these atrocities but does not talk about the atrocities that it had inflicted on the Vietnamese for eight and half

Fourteenth Friday Sermon Feb 22, 1991

years. I feel the United States is suffering from a psychological problem and thus poses a great danger to world peace.

MERCENARIES AND WAR

There is a new and dangerous element added to this war. A new precedent, which is unparalleled in the history of world wars has been set. You must have heard about mercenaries waging a war but a war so dreadful and on such a large scale was never fought before by hired personnel. **One good aspect of the U.S. in Vietnam war was that this time it did not go around with a begging bowl for financial support to wage a war. In Vietnam, the U.S. spent $120 billion to fight that war for eight and a half years, and for this it relied entirely on its own resources. $120 billion is a vast sum. But the present war is being waged entirely on foreign money - money collected from other parties.** When such an example has been set of waging a war that is entirely financed by others, there remains no guarantee of world peace. It is as if, the United States has leased out its armed forces. It smacks of a mercenary force. That could mean that the destiny of poor countries will be solely in the hands of the rich ones. The rich and the powerful nations can demand contributions and financial resources from the poor ones and hire mercenaries to wage war on them, killing, maiming and destroying them. This precedent is indeed dangerous. Besides, an element of greed is associated with this type of war. When its results are made known, the other European nations too, will be motivated to reap benefits by waging a similar war. Great havoc and damage has been inflicted on Iraq and Kuwait. The U.S. has been paid vast sums of money to bring about such destruction, and it will be paid huge sums of money for repairing the damage done by its forces. **The U.S. is paid to destroy and then paid to repair and re-construct. Thus the U.S. plays two roles, the demolisher as well as the restorer. Paid for destruction - and paid much more for restoration.** The one who demolishes is paid less than the one who restores, just as a killer is paid less than a surgeon who saves lives. If this takes root, it will bring about a new and destructive way of thinking. Rich and powerful nations would be encouraged to make wars on weak and poor nations, as it will be a profitable venture. After all, the poor nations will pay both ways, for their own destruction and then for their restoration.

THE LAND OF IRAQ: MINARETS OF DEATH, MADE OF HUMAN SCULL

Lastly, I will tell you that the land and soil of Iraq has been grossly abused and its people oppressed for centuries. That soil has witnessed great pain and sorrow. Great havoc and destruction had occurred and prolonged wars and wholesale slaughter had taken place on it. Tragic human dramas have been played out there. If one were to describe that tortured land, one could perhaps call it a land of minarets of death, made of human skull. History tells us that the first assault was by the Assyrians. When the Assyrians conquered that area, they committed gross atrocities and indulged in indiscriminate slaughter of the people. They wreaked such havoc that for 200 years the people of that area lived in terror and fear. In 879 B.C the victorious king and conqueror built a minaret in front of his palace. On the minaret was inscribed this legend[11],

> "I am the king who skins people. I skin those who dare to oppose me. This minaret that you see is covered all over with human skin and skeleton and stuck on top of the minaret is a human skeleton. Live human beings have been used as bricks in its construction. I am the king who has skinned people. I am the king of destruction and death." On the one hand he admitted that he was a king of destruction and death but at the same time he claimed: "I do this in the cause of virtue and in fact the Assyrians war is a war of good versus evil. We represent virtue and the rest of the world represents evil"

I do not know if President Bush has studied that history. However, his action in Iraq is similar to the erection of a minaret of human skulls, bearing the same kind of inscription. That inscription would read something like:

> "We crush the spirit and ego of those people who dare challenge our authority. We trample them underfoot. We have a right to destroy obstinate people who do not bow to our command. We

---

[11] Chronicle of the World. Page 73. Longman Group UK 1989

break the backs of those who have the audacity to defy us and we will erect a monument of human skulls as was done in ancient Iraq."

The second human skull minaret in Iraq was built in 1258 A.D. by Halaku Khan. The third human minaret was erected in 1401 A.D by Taimour Lang(Tamerlane) in Baghdad[12].

THE MOST CRITICAL TIME IN HUMAN HISTORY

This unfortunate land of Iraq has been abused not once, not twice but three times by the erection of minarets composed of human corpses, human skulls and human skins. Those minarets were constructed to terrorise the population and cow the people to submission by tyrants and conquerors. What is happening today is a repetition of that mournful tale of sordid history. I don't know what the future will bring or when the tide of history will turn and the arrogant and the mighty humbled, but I do know that Allah will in due course, humiliate and humble the arrogant. **I can assure the United States of America that it cannot restore its back that was broken in Vietnam by inflicting indignities and atrocities on Iraq.** The back of United States of America broken in Vietnam will remain broken. The United States can gouge great and deep craters in the earth by exploding 2,500,000 tons of explosives. In those deep craters and ditches the reputation and good name of United States of America will remain buried in disgrace for ever.

As time goes on, these barbaric deeds, committed by United States of America, will become more and more manifest and the reputation of United States will be sullied and stained beyond redemption. It may well be that because of the overwhelming might of United States of America at the present, few critics may venture to proclaim their misdeeds and atrocities for fear of reprisals. However, these acts against humanity will not disappear or fade, but with the passage of time these will become more obvious and pronounced, and **future generations will read with horror and abomination that a so-called civilised nation could commit and condone such dark and wicked**

---

[12] Cambridge History of Islam Volume I : Page 170

deeds. **The United States must see itself as others see it and take great care to avoid becoming the moral outcast of the 20th century.**

The United States must recall the reasons which gave it its birth and attempt to achieve those noble aims. Instead the U.S. seems to be acting at direct variance to those ideals. It is not making any effort to achieve and promote peace but is rather actively inciting nations to war.

The U.S. is clearly not prepared to listen to any voice but its own. It is so intoxicated with its power and arrogance that it appears to be sitting on top of an imaginary minaret propped up by atrocities, unconcerned with the sufferings it has unleashed in the world.

As to what will happen in the future and what Allah's decree will be, I will *Inshallah* address you on this point in the next sermon. In that sermon I will also give advice to the Jews, Muslims and the rest of the world.

We are going through the most critical juncture of human history. We have reached a sensitive and delicate stage. There is still time to turn away from the catastrophe facing us. The opportunity to salvage our future is still not completely lost. I have firm faith that if they will listen to and heed to my advice which I will give in the light of the teaching of Islam and the Quran, the approaching calamity could be averted.

OFFER PRAYERS

But we have no position or influence in the world. We are only humble worshippers of God. We pray, but we are confident we can achieve with our prayers what we cannot achieve with our efforts. Our efforts have no significance. Our address falls on deaf ears, and cannot even quiver a single hair of the people of the U.S. Despite all that, it was destined that in the latter days, if anything can change the direction or course of world history it is the prayers of the followers of the Promised Messiah[as] Hazrat Mirza Ghulam Ahmad, the founder of the Ahmadiyya Muslim Community. It will be accomplished through the prayers of the devout disciples of Muhammad the Messenger of Allah[sas]. The earnest supplications of the humble servants of God can change the course of history.

Fourteenth Friday Sermon Feb 22, 1991

In his **"Khutba Ilhamia"** (The Revealed Sermon) the Founder of the Ahmadiyya Muslim Jamat says:

"It was destined, and it is destined and it will surely come to pass that when the soul of the Messiah will melt at the Divine threshold, and when at nightfall sounds of agony will rise from his heart, then I swear by God, the Great powers of the world will begin to melt as ice melts in the sun. In this way the days of destruction of those powers shall begin and the days of the breaking of their arrogance will dawn."

The Promised Messiah[as] is no longer with us. But the spirit of the Promised Messiah[as] lives on in the Ahmadiyya Muslim Jamaat. So to all the Ahmadi Muslims who carry his spirit within them I say:

"Rise in the night and cry before Allah with all your heart, and with all your soul, in painful sobs and deep lamentations and supplicate to your God. Have faith that when your souls melt at the Divine threshold the day will surely come when the Great powers of the world will melt. And this is decreed and written and no power on earth can alter or change it."

In the name of Allah, the Gracious, the Merciful

FIFTEENTH FRIDAY SERMON

March 1, 1991

ADVICE TO THE WORLD OF ISLAM & TO THE THIRD WORLD COUNTRIES

After reciting the Opening Chapter of the Holy Quran, Al-Fatiha, Hazoor said:

THE CURRENT SITUATION OF THE GULF WAR AND ITS BACKGROUND
At the start of the Gulf War, under the influence of Western propaganda, it seemed as if we had stepped back into the era of Nazi Germany and that a new version of Churchills, Roosevelts and Stalins had been reborn. The whole world was horrified to watch this dreadful spectacle. Now as the war comes to an end, although the scene is the same, yet a new picture has emerged. The scenario is the same; there is no change in the reality, but this reality can be viewed from another angle.

As this war ended, it reminded me of a well known Spanish satirical comedy character, **Don Quixote**. It is said that this comedian knight used to create imaginary ghosts, demons and monsters and would then create imaginary knights to fight these giants. It is said that he once fought a similar comic battle with a windmill. If we make a slight change in that story to apply it to the present situation, the story may go like this: that Don Quixote and his general named **Sancho Panzo**, were going somewhere riding their mules. On their way, they saw a windmill. Don Quixote told his companion: "This is the most powerful and most dangerous monster in the world, let us attack it together". Then galloping and shouting war cries, they attacked it. The modified version of the story would be, that they defeated the windmill, and dismembered it to bits and pieces. **Having demolished it, they began to brag that, this day, the most distinguished knight of the world had routed the most powerful monster of the world!**

So you see, the reality remains the same, but how the scenes change with the changing times! Similarly, this scene changes as we see the incident from a different angle. If we view the present situation from the angle of observation of the U.S., it would look as one says in the hunter's parlance - "to heel" (i.e. to tame a dog to follow one's heels) that the U.S. succeeded in 'heeling' Britain and France. It also 'heeled' the Soviet Union and Germany. In short, the U.S. 'heeled' many allies, and then in their footsteps a host of other countries were 'heeled' with the hope that after the "kill", they would have their share in accordance with their ranking.

SHOUTS OF KUWAIT - KUWAIT - KUWAIT

This army on the march, comprising the hunters and their heeled allies, could be heard shouting "Kuwait-Kuwait-Kuwait"; while those who were following them were sharpening their teeth in preparation as to when, on the pretext of Kuwait, they would have the opportunity to hunt down Iraq! So this is *one* of the viewpoints of this scene. Let us see this war from the viewpoint of Israel. Israel would be thinking, and is justified to think so, that it had succeeded in heeling the U.S. and all its allies. **All the heeled creatures were following Israel, yet oblivious of the fact that this "hunter" was such that it would turn around and pounce upon each one of the heeled species in succession, to feast upon the carcass.** This is *another* spectacle of the same event viewed from another angle, yet the reality remains the same, but its interpretation changes according to ones understanding. It is only the future that will show as to who was heeled by whom! The human mind displays a wonderful phenomenon on sounds as well. Different interpretations are deduced from the same voice. **One voice which the world perceives is that the limbs of Iraq are being broken so that it could never dare again attack Kuwait. As if the ultimate objective of the entire world was to preserve the entity of Kuwait, while every country of the world was free to attack any other country at will!** It is only Kuwait which no one is allowed to attack. Thus the outcry of "Kuwait-Kuwait-Kuwait" is aimed at forming this picture in the minds of one part of the world. But if the same voice is heard through the ears of Israel, it means to her that Iraq is being dismembered so that it may never ever dream of posing a threat to Israel. It is a lesson not only for Iraq but for every country of the world, never to think of looking towards Israel with an evil eye. So you see the voice is the same, but as it falls differently on different ears, the mind deciphers it accordingly.

Another aspect worth mentioning in this scenario is that even carnivorous animals, not on a hunting spree or fighting an enemy, look gentle and have a particular tame behaviour. Their paws are soft and velvety. Their fangs are hooded under fluffy lips. They live peacefully among themselves and do not look at other animals with greedy eyes. But when the time for the hunt comes, or they have to fight an enemy, then out of the same velvety feet emerge fierce claws, and out of the same soft lips appear terrible fangs that know no mercy. Therefore we too should take into account those times when people are recognized in their true colours. An Urdu Poet has mentioned the same in a beautiful couplet, when he says:

اک ذرا سی بات پر برسوں کے یارانے گئے
لیکن اتنا تو ہوا ۔ کچھ لوگ پہچانے گئے

"Alas! as a result of a petty dispute, the love of decades melted away. But, at least I was able to recognize the true face of some friends"

Regarding the Arab friends of the Western world, we have to say with bitter anguish, that even if there is a hell let loose on the Islamic world, their friendships with the West remains unaffected and they do not recognize their true friends.

This in short, is a summary of the background, and in this perspective I intend to place before you some other facts and to offer advice to different nations:

<u>THREE BASIC PRINCIPLES OF SECULAR POLITICS</u>
Since ancient times, secular politics has adhered to three basic principles which are common to the East as well as the West. One cannot say that these are the basic principles of politics exclusive to the East or to the West but these principles are in vogue everywhere. They were the same in the past as they are today.

The **First Principle** of secular politics is that whenever the tribal, racial or national interests of a nation **clash** with the principles of **Justice**, then give priority and precedence to tribal, group or national

Fifteenth Friday Sermon Mar 01, 1991

interests even if the principle of Justice have to be totally torn to shreds!

As against this the principle of politics, the teachings of the Holy Quran are totally different and largely at variance to this principle. The Holy Quran states:

وَلَا يَجْرِمَنَّكُمْ شَنَآنُ قَوْمٍ عَلَى أَلَّا تَعْدِلُوْا اِعْدِلُوْا هُوَ اَقْرَبُ لِلتَّقْوٰى

(Al-Maida: Verse 9)
"O Muslims! Your politics is of a different nature. This is the politics which is based on the commands of Allah, which lays down the inviolable principle that even the bitterest enmity of a nation or people should not prompt you to treat them with Injustice. Always stand firm on the standards of **JUSTICE**, since justice is nearest to *Taqwa*, (righteousness)."

The Second governing Principle of Secular Politics is that if you possess power and strength, then you must attain your objective through this sheer superiority of strength, since, for them, **"might is right"**. As if apart from this belief there is no other principle of fidelity existent in the world. In this regard, the Holy Quran presents a completely different principle; as it states:

لِيَهْلِكَ مَنْ هَلَكَ عَنْ بَيِّنَةٍ وَّيَحْيٰى مَنْ حَيَّ عَنْ بَيِّنَةٍ

(Al-Anfal: Verse 43)
"Only, he, deserves to perish, against whom you are equipped with the criterion of **Truthfulness**, which should also stand open as your testimony. And only he, should survive, whose survival is supported by **Truth.**"

The Islamic principle, therefore advocates that "Right is might" as against "Might is right"!

The Third fundamental principle of irreligious secular politics is that in order to achieve your objective you should, without hesitation, indulge in **false Propaganda**. This is not only permitted, but the greater the deception or falsehood, the better it serves the interest of their objective. You must defeat the enemy not only in the battlefield but also project and depict him as defeated in the field of ideologies and concepts through persistent propagation of falsehood. Since the dawn of recorded history, these three principles have always been seen active everywhere, except in those short-lived periods when politics passed into the hands of upright people who honoured their religious and moral values, or during such times when Allah had granted temporal power to the world of religion.

Opposed to it, the Holy Quran presents this principle:

$$\text{فَاجْتَنِبُوا الرِّجْسَ مِنَ الْأَوْثَانِ وَاجْتَنِبُوا قَوْلَ الزُّورِ}$$

(Surah Al-Haj: Verse 31)
Then elsewhere the Holy Quran says:

$$\text{وَإِذَا قُلْتُمْ فَاعْدِلُوا وَلَوْ كَانَ ذَا قُرْبَىٰ}$$

(Surah Al-Annam: Verse 153)
That even during the war of words or during the "Jihad" of words, you must not forsake the **Principle of Truth**. To abandon Truth and to accept Falsehood instead, is as impure and abominable as polytheism!

Allah says:

$$\text{وَإِذَا قُلْتُمْ فَاعْدِلُوا}$$

When you speak, speak only that which is based upon Justice. You should have no concern that by so speaking you cause to impair the interests of your nearest of kin.

<u>THE GREATEST TRAGEDY OF THE MUSLIM WORLD</u>
The greatest tragedy of the Muslim world today is that while on the one hand they declare Jihad in the name of Allah and in the name

of Muhammad[sas], yet on the other hand their policies and politics have been derived from the principles of irreligious politics. They have, thus, discarded the guiding principles of politics as enunciated by the Quran. This is the reason, why up till now, whenever the Muslims clashed with the opponents of Islam, they always suffered (barring a few exceptions) with humiliating and horrible defeats!

This so happened, for disregarding the Divine principles, despite the fact that there was a very clear and firm promise in the Holy Quran:

وَإِنَّ اللهَ عَلَى نَصْرِهِمْ لَقَدِيرٌ

(Surah Al-Haj: Verse 40)

Beware O' those who set out upon 'Jihad' for My sake and in My name; Listen! You may be weak but I am not. I give you my promise and this promise is inexorable that:

وَإِنَّ اللهَ عَلَى نَصْرِهِمْ لَقَدِيرٌ

These weak people may be despicable in the sight of the world, but when they set out upon 'Jihad' (The holy struggle) they will be granted Divine help and they will be made to dominate over their enemies.

This is the question agitating the mind of Muslims, world-over and that is why I have given this question special prominence; so that I may console the grieving hearts of all Muslims of the East and the West that this defeat is not the defeat of Islam: rather it is the defeat of those "Muslims" who abandoned the principles of Islam and instead adopted the defeatist irreligious principles.

<u>THIS IS NOT A BATTLE BETWEEN TRUTH AND FALSEHOOD</u>

Therefore, this war ceased to be a war between Truth and Falsehood -it turned out to be a war between The Mighty and the Meek. God supported neither side in such a situation. Whenever there would be a war between The Mighty and the Weak; the Mighty would invariably win. And this is the true meaning of the phrase: "might is right".

So in this terrible incident of the Gulf, there are deep lessons to be learnt The greatest lesson is that the Muslims will have to return to their lofty, unshakable and invincible principles. If they would not do so then the Divine promise of the dominance of God's servants over 'The Promised Land' (*Al-Arz*), will not be fulfilled in their favour. *Al-Arz* may mean Palestine, or even the whole world. As long as such righteous men of God are not born who practice the pure, everlasting and victorious principles of the Holy Quran, no victory - not even a worldly victory would be destined for them.

The Muslim hearts are bleeding at their contention that as the allies were on the side of "Truth", therefore, the truth has triumphed over "Falsehood". This is certainly not true. In this context there is another thing which need to be brought to your notice. An American General kept on harping that their soldiers had 'white' hats while the Iraqis were wearing 'black' ones. This is an ignorant fictional notion of the West; that all expert pistol marksmen wear white hats, while the villains, who are always defeated are shown to wear black hats. The fact is that this was not a war between the white and the black. To strengthen their claim, they have said that Saddam Hussein was so cruel and heartless that he tortured and killed the Kurds with chemical weapons and then completely erased their village upon village by aerial bombardment. If this is true, and may be it is true, then this too is a heinous Crime. Whoever did it, will be answerable to God and posterity. But this is not the complete picture of events. We have to find out as to who is the real culprit and who prompted Saddam Hussein towards this foul play and how he was taught such an evil; we shall have to go back to the pages of history.

<u>THE REAL CULPRIT</u>

The British Policy in 1920 was to force the Kurds into subjugation of Iraq, to which they naturally revolted. At this, the British army of that time dropped chemical bombs on the weak and defenceless Kurds and mercilessly massacred them in the thousands! Even after that, they continued to bombard their villages for years. This massacre had such a terrible effect even on the conscience of the perpetrators that in 1923 a high ranking British Officer Air Commodore **Lionel Charlton** resigned as a mark of protest, saying that this was so cruel and that it was beyond his level of his tolerance. We hear that Saddam Hussein committed similar crimes in Iran. He dropped chemical bombs on the Iranian army and even on the civil population, thus killing a large number of soldiers and civilians. But the fact is

Fifteenth Friday Sermon Mar 01, 1991

that in those days the West had supplied him with the equipment to prepare these chemical bombs. They also provided him with long range guns. Then, his staunch financial supporters were the Kuwaitis and Saudis backed by the U.S. resolutely standing in his support. It is probably true that **Saddam Hussein committed atrocities against humanity and he is answerable for it, but this is not true that Saddam alone is the culprit in this gruesome game.** There were many others too involved in this heinous crime. There are many cruel and heartless among the allies, who are today being presented as 'innocent' and 'righteous', who openly backed the cause of torture and oppression, as long as it suited their interest. It should, therefore be understood that this was not at all a war between the Truth and Falsehood.

THE REMEDY FOR THE HEARTBREAK OF MUSLIMS

Young Muslims are terribly heartbroken. The news which I get from across the world is that it became unbearable for the youngsters to watch the barbarities perpetrated against the Iraqis. They were tormented by what they saw on the T.V. Some young boys and girls came to see me to express their bitterness with their voices choked with pain and emotion. They ask in desperation: "What is happening! **Why is our God not coming to our aid.."**

When the servants of God snap their relations with Him and with the divine attribute of His Unity, and instead of adopting chaste Islamic principles, follow the defiled principles of the enemies of Islam, then God stands neither on this side nor on that side. Then such a conflict ceases to remain a conflict between TRUTH and FALSEHOOD.

Secondly, as far as worldly conflicts are concerned, they should remember that with this defeat, **time** has not halted! History continues to change direction. Times do change. If today it is so, tomorrow it is completely different. Some nations spent centuries in oppression and then God granted them dominance over their tormentors. Therefore, develop your line of thinking in accordance with the time-frame of Allah. Do not get restive keeping in view your concept of a time frame.

History is a continuous dynamic process which does not stand still at one point. To further console you, I take you further back into history. Recall the year 1919 and the incidents happening in Europe at that time. This was the year when the victorious allied powers had gathered at **Versailles** to seal the fate of the vanquished **Germans**. Incidentally, that was as well the year of elections in England. Before proceeding to Versailles, the then Prime Minister of England, Mr. Lloyd George, issued a statement that he would squeeze the "German Lemon" so hard that even its seeds would crackle and voices of agony will be clearly audible. It was with such mal-intentions that he proceeded to Versailles. An observer writes that upon reaching Versailles, when he learned about the vengeful designs of the French, he thought that his plans, in comparison, could be classified as gestures of forgiveness and compassion. The French had prepared such terrible and vindictive designs as if they wanted to exterminate each German individual. Finally, after protracted deliberations, such severe sanctions were imposed on Germany that it was made impossible for it, ever to prepare for a war or be in a position to stand against any nation of the world. Today, you see the same picture of the Americans versus the Iraqis!

In 1928, to make these decisions yet more strict and mandatory against Germany, Mr. Frank Kellog, then American Secretary of State, visited France and met the President to convene a conference of fifteen European nations. The theme of the conference was to 'Outlaw war'. War should be treated as a "fugitive at large" whose murder was anybody's right. But apparently what they were claiming was that we will bury the war for good.

LESSONS OF HISTORY

At the conference, there were representatives of fifteen nations. When the German delegate rose to sign the instrument with his golden pen, the hall reverberated with the claps and cheers of the audience. Nobody ever imagined that in such a short period of hardly eleven years after that conference, the same corpse (Germany) would come back to life and will overrun not only one country, or one continent but its terror will be felt in the imperial mansions of the East and the West and that the sounds of bomb blast would block all other sounds to reach their ear.

So you see, from the point of view of history, how soon within a few years the scene was completely changed. Our Allah is a living God and will live forever. Generations come and generations go. I do not advise you to put your reliance on the 'chances of history'. I only ask of you to keep in mind the subject of the changing situations of history. **Be not disheartened. Put your trust in God who is eternal and upon whom no power of the world can prevail. He can overwhelm every power of the world. These temporal powers are of no match or relevance to Him. If you are the aggrieved and the oppressed, and you are groaning with agony, then divert these moans into supplications before Allah, I assure you , that by so doing, every single defeat of yours will be transformed into a magnificent success.**

ADVICE TO THE ALLIED POWERS

I advise the allied armies and the Leaders of allied countries that if you cherish the welfare of humanity and want a lasting peace, then you should realize that in the past, all your political strategies and principles have failed miserably and repeatedly, and could not grant **Peace** to the world. Therefore for God's sake would you not learn a lesson even now and adopt these principles of Islamic politics which are linked with *'Taqwa'* **(righteousness)**.

If you adopt those **three principles** which I have earlier mentioned then you would find that this is the *only* means through which the world can be given a surety of a lasting peace. If you ignore them, then remember; whether they be the forces of tyranny and oppression from the East, from the West, or may it be the U.S. dropping nuclear bombs on Nagasaki and Hiroshima, or it be Japan setting unparalleled records of horror and cruelty in Indonesia, I assure you that if the intentions remain the same, which have been the intentions of politicians at all times, based on selfishness as against high morals, then all their efforts will be futile and they will never be able to give Peace to the World! **It is incumbent upon the powerful nations of the world that at first they destroy the demons of deceit lurking in their intensions.** If they will not do so then elimination the elite forces of Saddam or for that matter any other force will give them no guarantee of a global peace. Even if they cut Iraq into pieces, there will be no surety of peace in the world!

MUSLIM COUNTRIES SHOULD ESTABLISH ISLAMIC SYSTEM OF JUSTICE

For the destruction of man, there are "wolves" hidden in his intentions. Until those wolves are destroyed, and until man does not resolve to stick to the principles of JUSTICE, the world can never be given any guarantee of PEACE! Here then arises a very pertinent question. As long as the Muslim world itself does not accept the Islamic concept of Justice, as stated in the Holy Quran, and does not demonstrate its implementation in their own countries; how can they be justified in inviting the world towards the principles of Islamic Justice! This is not possible. **So long as the Islamic world does not establish the system of Islamic Justice, it does not adopt the Quranic concept of Justice, it can neither present Justice to the world nor should** *expect* **Justice from the world!**

In this scenario, we observe some horrible traditions established in the Muslim world, which can be termed as "infidelity towards Islam." Instead of understanding the Islamic teachings of Justice and accepting and adopting it, Islam is being presented as a religion which has no relations with Justice. Here, the biggest culprit is the *Mullah*, with him is the politician, and their unholy alliance, is ruining the concept of Islamic system of Justice.

THREE VICIOUS VIEWPOINTS

There are three erroneous concepts attributed to Islam and these are being presented to the outside world. As a result, a horribly distorted and mutilated picture of Islam is being presented before the world. Consequently peace is disappearing from every Muslim country. The **first concept** so projected is that to propagate one's ideas, force is not only permitted but mandatory. The use of force to change an ideology has been wrongly termed as **"Islamic Jihad"**. But simultaneously, it is claimed that this right is the prerogative of the Muslims only. Christians, Jews, Hindus or Buddhists do not enjoy the right to use force to change a Muslim's view point. As if God had granted this privilege solely to Muslims! What an unjust and crude point of view, which erroneously is being presented in the name of Islam to the outside world.

Fifteenth Friday Sermon Mar 01, 1991

Another false view point is that if a non-Muslim enters the fold of Islam, nobody has the right to sentence him to death and anyone, anywhere, in the world may leave his religion and join Islam no one, from any other religion, has the right to impose any penalty on him, but on the other hand, if a Muslim abandons Islam, and joins any other faith, Muslims all over the world have the right to put him to death. This is another unjust principle, which these so called standard bearers of Islam present to the world in the name of God and in the name of the Holy Quran.

The Third distorted view point is that while it is the obligation of Muslim governments to impose laws of Islamic *Shariah* (Islamic Jurisprudence) even upon those subjects who do not believe in Islam, but non-Muslim governments do not enjoy this privilege to impose their religious laws on Muslims in their countries. Thus according to this false principle, Jews are not permitted to treat Muslims according to laws of the **Talmud**, and Hindus are not permitted to enforce laws of **Manu Smurti** on Muslims. Thus this is the third erroneous conception of Justice. I have just given three examples of such vicious principles. But if you go deeper into the matter, you will find several other principles attributed to Islam as propounded by the *Mullah* of today which clash with the clear and true principles of justice as presented by the Holy Quran. In today's world, the weapons most frequently used against Islam are these three notorious principles, which are manufactured in the factories installed in Muslim countries. Jews are successfully exploiting these so-called Islamic principles throughout the world which in fact is a concoction of the Mullah. They present these to the Western world and claim, that with these vicious principles, how can we ever expect peace from these people who hold such crazy principles of justice devoid of all reason and commonsense. **Muslims claim one set of rules for themselves and a completely different set of rules for non-Muslims. Superior rights are reserved for the Muslims while the non-Muslims are deprived of every such right! If God forbid, this is the Quranic principle, the whole world would naturally loathe it and would consider the Muslims as a threat to world peace.**

Therefore, it is not fair to blame only the others for their excesses on Muslims. We should look inwards as well and see why these excesses are being committed and see how a shrewd enemy is using the very weapons manufactured by Muslims themselves against them. It is a fact that factories of such lethal weapons are functioning in Muslim countries and are being run by the Mullahs. These weapons are being 'exported' in large quantities to other countries where in turn these are used against the Muslim countries.

THE OBLIGATION OF MUSLIM STATESMEN

I consider that Muslim statesmen have also faltered on this point. They did not make an effort to understand the true teachings of Islam. They entrusted this duty to the Mullah of their time and remained indifferent on whatever distorted picture he presented of Islam. Yet their conscience and right thinking continued to renounce the picture painted by the Mullah. Even after knowing that the views of the Mullahs were un-Islamic, they did not have the courage to turn them down. This psychological perplexity has made the Muslim politics a "sick man". It presents a two-faced image of Islam. The politicians handed over their masses to Mullahs who possess medieval thinking. They did not seek guidance from the bright era of the Holy Prophet[sas]. Now that the politicians have delivered the masses to the Mullah with their own hands, they are now getting scared of the growing influence of the Mullah and are hesitant to confront them and tell that their goals are wrong because the politicians themselves are under the wrong impression that those laws may indeed be Islamic laws (God forbid).

Therefore it is high time that Muslim states come to their senses. The Muslim world has been split apart. The world of politics is different from the theological world, and there is a collision between the two. This is the second dangerous aspect as a result of which the world of Islam is facing a danger from within. The annihilation of this danger is important and urgent. Otherwise Muslims will not be able to play any role in the carving of a New World Order.

It is imperative that Muslim governments should proclaim in unequivocal terms, that any command that clashes with the injunctions of the **Quranic concept of Justice** will not be accepted as an Islamic command. The religious clergy should be repeatedly challenged and confronted on this issue. We declare that the Quranic concept of justice is not vague and is crystal clear. Its scope is not just national but international. If it were not international, it could not have been called a concept of justice. It is certainly international and absolute. First it should be decided whether this concept is international or not. If it is, then you will have to accept that every concept that clashes with the concept of the Holy Quran is un-Islamic.

Secondly, it is also essential to proclaim that anyone who attributes unjust views towards the Holy Quran, will be considered as arrogant to the Divine Word. Further, it should also be made known that anyone who tries to attribute towards *Hadith* or the sayings of the Holy Prophet of Islam, any theory against the Holy Quran will also be considered as hostile to the Holy Prophet. This is the only course of action that can remove the internal paradox in the world of Islam. If today there is a statesman who is gifted with intelligence and possesses the attribute of righteousness (*Taqwa*) and holds fast to the principles of justice and has the courage to say what is right and say it in the right manner, and also loves his nation and the world of Islam, then it is important that he should first declare a holy-war (Jihad) in this field. If the battle is not won on this front - no other subsequent battle will ever be won.

Due to the presence of certain types of hypocrisies, some issues seem to have been temporarily solved yet this problem has not been completely surmounted. We repeatedly see this spectacle in the world of Islam that wherever there is danger to the Muslim world from any direction, **"Mullahism" or Muslim fanaticism** begins to thrive. Mullahism begins to seep extensively into the brains of Muslims. At such times an extremist revolution looms large on the horizon. This process is continuing and is on the increase. If this trend is not halted with wisdom, and harmony is not established in the minds of the masses regarding religious and political thinking, Muslim countries would for ever remain weak and would always continue to face quakes due to internal perils of paradoxes. They will never see any stability. Therefore, urgent and firm decisions are needed . These decisions must be made today! Time is rolling very fast and will not treat us with kindness and compassion. Which compassion? How many times have we been punished by the 'time'? How often have we been disgraced and humiliated in the world. If you will not rise today, you will never ever rise. Therefore, rise and take a decision by calling God as your witness that you will raise the "sword of truth" merely for the sake of truth and start that **ideological jihad** which is not only permitted by the Holy Quran but is mandatory upon you by Divine order.

THE REAL DANGER FOR THE MUSLIM COUNTRIES

These are the dangers which I have explained, and for this reason no genuine democracy can ever flourish in an Islamic state. If you talk about the masses, then there is no effective arrangement for the teaching and training of the democratic system to the ordinary masses. They are included, neither in the political, nor in religious thought. Instead, the ruling junta comes to power through their votes, then rises to take on a new identity and image. Countries where there is no concordance in the thinking of rulers and the masses, even if democracy ever comes, it will only produce dictators and not democratic rulers. **This has often happened that dictators have been produced as a result of a democratic procedure.** Another bigger danger is, that Muslim rulers have always feared that "Mullahism" might produce so much bad-blood in the masses against the rulers, that in the name of Islam they may eventually revolt against them. Therefore, the rulers start becoming even more dictatorial and start to use oppression to an ever greater extent. Because those who are thus persecuted are, according to the thinking of the masses, genuine sympathizers of Islam; thus sentiments continue to build up in favour of the clergy and against the politicians.

This is not a single issue. It has a number of offshoots. Its only remedy is that which I have already suggested. Hold the **Quranic System of Justice** as you will hold *Urwa-i-Wusqa* a strong ring which is destined never to break. **This is the Rope of Allah and the Rope of Justice which was lowered by the Holy Prophet to create peace among the nations of the world.** Without holding fast to this rope, you can never find peace anywhere in the world so hold fast to this ring and invite the whole world, which is yearning for PEACE to hold on to this ring!

Then there is another absurdity. Announcements and decrees of jihad (Holy-War) are made. Yet the above mentioned principles of the Mullah are also not recognized. This is the second folly of the politician that while he knows for certain that the Islamic system of justice does not permit such wars and conflicts to be branded as Jihad.

Fifteenth Friday Sermon Mar 01, 1991

Yet, whenever the country faces a danger and a war becomes imminent, politicians join hands with the Mullah in calling upon the masses to support the so-called Jihad. As a result of this, the world becomes even more disgusted with such nations and convinced that, outwardly they may say that Islamic Jihad does not call for the use of force to spread an ideology yet when the need arises they never hesitate to lean on this ideology. This is what is happening repeatedly, and has occurred on all occasions.

If you glance at the history of battles fought by Muslims after the blessed era of the Holy Prophet, you will be amazed to know that they wrongly labelled each and every battle a 'Blessed Jihad'. Not even a single battle is fought by Muslims which was not termed a 'Sacred Jihad'. These might be the battles with non-Muslims or with their own brethren. They may be battles of Sunnis against Sunnis or Shiite against Shiite or the Shiite against Sunnis: This is strange that all such battles were invariably termed as Sacred Jihad by the clergy and the politicians. They have never fought a single battle which was not termed a Sacred Jihad! Countries all over the world fight political battles but Muslims only have to fight Jihad! The greater number of these so called Holy Battles have been fought by Muslims against Muslims. In the name of Jihad, they slaughtered one another. This joke has assumed the proportion of a tragedy; a painful tragedy which must now end. If we observe this paradox from a purely worldly angle, it appears the biggest joke of our times; and it is being wrongly attributed to Islam. If we look at it through the eyes of a Muslim heart, it seems to be the most painful and terrible tragedy which we have not been able to dislodge and shake off for the last thirteen centuries! Therefore, if you want to change your fate, then make a pious change in your ideas, tendencies and conduct. As long as Muslims do not revolutionize their thoughts they will never be in a position to bring about any change in the world.

MEANINGLESS SHOUTS OF JIHAD WITHOUT ADEQUATE PREPARATION

And the height of the tragedy is that while believing in their brand of the ideology of jihad, they make no preparation for it. The divine teaching was:

$$\text{وَأَعِدُّوا لَهُمْ مَا اسْتَطَعْتُمْ مِنْ قُوَّةٍ وَمِنْ رِبَاطِ الْخَيْلِ تُرْهِبُونَ بِهِ عَدُوَّ اللَّهِ وَعَدُوَّكُمْ وَآخَرِينَ مِنْ دُونِهِمْ لَا تَعْلَمُونَهُمُ اللَّهُ يَعْلَمُهُمْ}$$

(Al-Anfal: Verse 61)
O ye Muslims, be prepared for your self defense and make the best preparation against any enemy who has the capacity to attack you at any time. Be prepared on every front with your cavalry and infantry that the enemy be scared of you. No one should dare to attack a well prepared people like you. Before they become your enemies, they were the enemies of Allah.

$$\text{عَدُوَّ اللَّهِ وَعَدُوَّكُمْ}$$

Therefore you may be oblivious of your enemies but God is not.

$$\text{لَا تَعْلَمُونَهُمُ اللَّهُ يَعْلَمُهُمْ}$$

At a time when you might be unaware of them, God will be watching them. Therefore, if you obey the Command of Preparation with your heart and soul, God gives you the glad-tiding, that even in your obliviousness, God will cover you and protect you from the onslaughts of your enemy.

These are the responsibilities of Muslims after they accept the teachings of jihad and the instructions to act upon them which have been laid down by the Holy Quran. Where are the Muslims who act upon them? **In fact, every Muslim country depends for arms and weapons on the very country against whom it declares jihad.** The Eastern or Western countries who are branded as polytheists, away from God, the enemies of God, idolaters, tyrants, cruel, and what not, about whom it is pronounced that you are ordered by God to fight against them are the very countries before whom we extend our begging hand for rockets, war planes and naval ships as well as guns and all other related paraphernalia. Simplicity has its limit!

Fifteenth Friday Sermon Mar 01, 1991

An Urdu poet has said:

اس سادگی پہ کون نہ مر جائے اے خدا
لڑتے ہیں اور ہاتھ میں تلوار بھی نہیں

"Who will not die on my beloved's naivety; he fights but fights without a sword"

But this naiveness may be understandable, it may be intelligible, it may be mere ingeniousness; but your simplicity reaches the very pinnacles of ignorance. People whom you call your arch enemies and to whom you throw the gauntlet and tell that your religion has enjoined you to suck every drop of their blood, and then you beg them to give you arms so that you can slit their throats!!

GOD DOES NOT CHANGE THE FATE OF THOSE WHO DO NOT ATTEMPT TO CHANGE THEMSELVES

Could there by any limit of ignorance? When the whole nation decides to commit suicide; who and how can someone come to their rescue? Even God does not help such people as He Himself says:

اِنَّ اللهَ لَا يُغَيِّرُ مَا بِقَوْمٍ حَتَّى يُغَيِّرُوْا مَا بِاَنْفُسِهِمْ

(Sura Al-Raad: Verse 12)
"Surely, Allah changes not the condition of a people until they change that which is in their hearts"

حَتَّى يُغَيِّرُوْا مَا بِاَنْفُسِهِمْ

God never decides to aid any people and does not come to help them or make a change for the better in them until they change themselves. This verse has a dual meanings. Firstly, He does not help them until they bring a change in themselves. Secondly in another verse it is implied that the nations that are callous of the blessings of God or decide to destroy those blessings with their own hands, Allah does not change their fate. This verse is open to interpretation which means that it can have more than one meaning. Firstly, that God will protect those blessings granted to them by Him as long as the people themselves do not squander them away.

Secondly, God will not alter the fate of such nations who do not initiate an earnest effort to change their situation.

ADVICE TO THE MUSLIM WORLD

Therefore, I advise the Muslims to return to Islamic values and to its eternal and universal principles and then they will behold the divine blessings showered upon them from every direction.

My second advice is that you pay attention towards the study of Arts and Sciences. How many centuries have you wasted in mere slogan mongering and have remained preoccupied by the world of poetic fantasy by making the robins clash with the eagles? The 'eagles' continued to pounce on you and you could make nothing for yourself. Other nations advanced in arts and sciences and remained dominant over you, and gained supremacy over you in every field. Now you talk of competing with such nations while ignoring all efforts to acquire the well-tested weapons which they had been successfully using against you. It is therefore very important that you pay earnest attention towards the learning of arts and sciences. Do not toy with the sentiments of Muslims by inciting them to fight in the streets, hurling profanities on others, thus ruining them morally as well as intellectually. Afterwards, you have them flogged or shot by the police. Thus, you not only injure them physically, but you also desecrate their self esteem!

This is the game you have been playing for quite long. You incite the youngsters and when these miserable people come out in the streets as a token of their love for Islam, then they are discredited and humiliated. They are clubbed down and bullets are rained upon them, while they remain bewildered as to why this is being done to them. Therefore, instead of playing with their sentiments, encourage them, teach them etiquettes, give them the teaching of restraint. Tell them that if they wish to find a respectable place in the comity of nations then they should excel in the field of arts and sciences as well as in other studies. Without this, they will never attain their rightful stature of respect and honour.

Fifteenth Friday Sermon Mar 01, 1991

THE NEED FOR SELF RELIANCE

From the economic point of view, the situation is such that except for a few oil producing countries that are gifted with extraordinary wealth, all other Muslim countries including the Third world nations are extending their begging hand towards those affluent countries, about whose excesses, they often complain. And they instill into the minds of their masses, hatred for these affluent nations, complaining that they have come here and enslaved us and eventually we have to extract retribution for these excesses. Paradoxes are thus created. The name of 'British' in Saudi Arabia and Kuwait is considered taboo and the word 'Americans' is an abuse. It is said that whoever will speak in favour of America or Britain will deserve the death penalty. Despite this the whole nation is virtually sold out to the Americans and the British by pledges of unqualified allegiance. Nobody realizes this. The poor nations have been reduced to paupers and the affluent nations are totally dependent upon their opponents for their very survival.

THERE IS ALWAYS HUMILIATION IN A BEGGAR'S LIFE

What a state of stark helplessness! You may be a rich or a poor nation, but your survival is totally dependent on your remaining a beggar. You cannot live and cannot breathe with dignity and freedom. Therefore, the biggest danger to Muslims and the Third world is their self-imposed humiliation. **Why don't they understand that a beggar can never be a free man?** If you accept the life of a pauper, you will always remain dishonoured and humiliated. Other nations could be excused since their religion gave no specific instruction to them in this direction. But on the day of Judgement how will you vindicate yourself before God and the Holy Prophet of Islam? Will this verse of the Holy Quran not stand as a witness against you?

كُنْتُمْ خَيْرَ اُمَّةٍ اُخْرِجَتْ لِلنَّاسِ

(Surah Al-Imran: verse 111)

'O you the servants of the most noble Prophet Muhammad[sas]! You were the best creation in the world, raised for service to humanity.' Then again, will this advice of Muhammad Mustafa[sas] not stand witness against you?

$$\text{اليد العليا خير من اليد السفلى}$$

(Al Muslim Kitab ul Zakat)
"The upper hand, i.e. the giving hand is always superior to the lower or the begging hand"

You handed over your good qualities to others with your own hands and became mendicants and beggars. Your politicians very proudly declare in front of the whole nation that the U.S. has agreed to grant us so much aid. And the aid which the U.S. has refused to approve has been granted to us by Saudi Arabia! If a medicant's blood is coursing through your veins, how will you walk with dignity with you head held high in the comity of nations? You are in the habit of living in a world of poetry. You are the fans of the poet **Iqbal**, who says:

$$\text{اے طائر لاہوتی اس رزق سے موت اچھی}$$
$$\text{جس رزق سے آتی ہو پرواز میں کوتاہی}$$

"O Heavenly bird, death is better than such sustenance; A sustenance which restricts your flight towards lofty heights."

Singers chant this verse on the Radio and T.V. most melodiously while the Muslims laud it by the rhythmical nodding of their heads and exclaiming that surely death is better than such sustenance. **But in actual practice, they prefer and readily accept such sustenance - yes that sustenance which binds them in shackles and slavery. What to say about the restriction of flight into the skies, now a leap for every grain, even below the net, is termed the ultimate flight of this bird.** No better politician could there be today, than one who would go to the U.S. with his beggar's bowl and return with alms, go to China and Russia and return with charity. This is, what is now considered the yardstick of successful politics. **This is the politics of wanton shamelessness!** Iqbal, the poet, was not wrong when he said that death is better than such sustenance that binds your hands and feet. By accepting such sustenance, you were disgraced. You betrayed the nations who accepted you as their leaders and you betrayed even your own people. You are responsible for making them the slaves of the Super Powers.

O Muslim politicians and leaders, come to your senses. Repent, otherwise tomorrow you will be presented in the criminals' dock in the court of history. More than that, you will stand in the criminal's dock on the "Day of Resurrection" before God and the Holy Prophet Muhammad[sas].

Another severe damage to such nations who become habitual beggars, is that they become incapable of improving their economic condition. The psychology of a nation is the same as that of an individual. Just have a look around you. You will see that those people who are in the habit of begging and who are accustomed to live a life of ease and luxury are always seen begging. **This is the reason that the Holy Prophet saw a vision that on the Day of Judgement those who beg, will be possessed of emaciated bodies with bare bones.** This meant that you can never fill your house by begging. A medicant always remains empty-handed and is never granted the resolve and temperament to improve his economic condition.

Therefore, until and unless, the nations decide to stand on their own feet, they can never prosper economically nor can they ever attain economic stability.

ADVICE TO THE THIRD WORLD

I appeal not only to the Muslim countries but to the Eastern world, Africans and South Americans, that after you have experienced all this, I implore you to please become aware and take a decision to change your own fate. The period of humiliation and degradation has been long. Now come out of this nightmare. For your enemies and the Super Powers there could be a cheerful conception of a New World Order, but for the Third world nations no other nightmare could be more dreadful. If you want to be the builders of the New World Order, then start caring for, and fashioning your own dreams. Try to learn the noble ways of transforming your dreams into deeds and actions. No nation can be free until it is economically free. The first step towards economic advancement is to safeguard your ego and self-respect. This will not be possible until and unless a campaign for austere lifestyle is adopted in the Third world countries. The difficulty is that the gulf between the rich and the poor is widening while it is narrowing in the countries you call 'capitalist'. If you observe the poor countries of Asia, Africa or south America, you will find that the gap between living standards of the upper and the lower class is becoming wider and wider each day generating many problems. In the first instance, this must be checked and narrowed down through suitable advice and good exhortation. Then, laws be enacted to further narrow this gap. If such a campaign starts from the top, it will succeed, otherwise it is doomed to failure. The people at the helm of affairs who hold the reigns of power should take a lead in this pioneering movement and demonstrate to the masses how to lead simple lives.

Therefore, in the achievement of economic stability and progress, this second important principle should be kept in view that the standard of living of the ordinary masses should be raised. You have to introduce two policies. You should raise the standard of living of the poor as much as possible by channelling the flow of wealth towards them while at the same time lowering the standard of living of the rich. **A point of wisdom must be remembered that the unfair distribution of wealth is less harmful than the unfair spending of wealth!**

<u>RAISING THE STANDARD OF LIVING OF THE LOWER CLASSES</u>

No movement of hatred can be carried out against such rich people who invest their money in erecting factories and who keep the wealth in circulation and have an austere lifestyle. Because practically, they are rendering a service to the country. Those who are in the habit of spending more than what they earn, result in ruining the fabric of their own moral structure, they ignite fires of hatred in many hearts. Industrialists and other rich businessmen may be in limited numbers but the greater majority of people in easy-going countries consist of such corrupt officials and politicians who thrive on bribes, and help spread this scourge of bribery. The politics of such corrupt politicians is eroded and eaten up just as a worm nibbles at a straw. They exploit politics to earn money and to form blocs and groups. Their politics is used to threaten the poor and to extract revenge from their opponents. The entire direction of their politics is focused towards matters for which politics was never meant. As a result, they become oblivious of national issues and have little time to meditate over them. Their line of thinking continuously flows only in one direction i.e., how to strengthen their own influence. How to seek revenge from their adversaries and how to amass as much wealth as possible. Such political life is short lived. They are apprehensive of their future and therefore want to amass as much wealth as they can, that very day. They may even barter their honour to buy or to sell votes. **When all such illicit maneuvers become legitimate in politics then how can such politicians protect the interests of a nation!**

The most damaging contribution to this problem is made by the inclination of a nation to an unrealistic and artificial standard of luxurious lifestyle which is unsustainable to the economics of that country. Such nations become beggars, their politics becomes stained, their economic structure is torn to bits and nothing is left of it.

WHO WILL DERIVE BENEFIT FROM THIS ADVICE

Which ears will listen to this advice? Which hearts will be moved and triggered into action? If the entire moral, economic and political foundation is unstable, if the very ideology is deteriorated, if the motives are rotten, no correct advice will produce healthy effects on anyone. I have given advice to affluent nations, that for the sake of God, they should safeguard their motives, which have demons and wolves lurking in their intentions. The decision on the fate of the world is decided by such motives. Their diplomatic craftiness cannot subjugate their motives, rather they stimulate them; so on the other hand **I advise Muslim countries and those of the Third world that for the sake of God, search into your motives**. If you have taken up **engineering** and from your childhood you think that you will get an excellent opportunity to collect bribes, you will build mansions, build palaces like those of your neighbours or of anyone else you saw, then mind you, that with this intention, you will not be able to make any positive contribution in the world. If you prefer to become a **doctor**, only to amass piles of gold and build huge and magnificent hospitals with which you will collect more money for yourself and would leave behind treasures of wealth for your children, then remember that you are a **Sick man**. Therefore, pay heed to the maxim **"physician, heal thyself"** and act upon it. It would have been better if you had not existed, instead of becoming a doctor of this type because he who does not study medicine for the service and betterment of his community, his profession will be devoid of the blessings of God.

If, before adopting a **career in politics** you were dreaming of becoming a politician like the one who was formerly a menial office employee, a simple police officer, or a petty officer of the government who resigned and entered politics and thereby became a multi-millionaire and a powerful person and you dream to be like him and become powerful, then remember that the very day you took this decision, that was the day when you strangulated the institution of politics. If you ever became the leader of a country the following Arabic verse will fit you:

$$اذا كان الغراب دليل قوم$$
$$سيديهم طريق الهالكين$$

"When ravens become the leaders of a community, they certainly lead them to destruction."

Therefore, reform your motives. Decide that by-gones are by-gones. Discharge the obligations of leadership just on the same lines on which the Holy Prophet of Islam discharged his obligations when he was given the leadership of the world. That is the only way to render obligations as a leader. Apart from that there is no other way. Let me remind you of the last prayer of Hazrat Umar when he was terminally ill, and death stared him in the face and he was very restless. At that time, he prayed, "O God, if there are any good deeds I may have done, let them go unrewarded. I do not request any recompense for them. But my humble request is that kindly overlook my faults and shortcomings. I find no strength to answer for my shortcomings." Today, this is the true spirit of Islamic politics which is required of Muslims and non Muslims. **The solution of all the problems of today is the revival of this spirit in politics. This will bring back to life a dying humanity. If this spirit survives, wars will be doomed.**

But if this spirit is allowed to die, fire of wars is sure to get rekindled, and then there will be no power on earth to extinguish them.

In the name of Allah, the Gracious, the Merciful

SIXTEENTH FRIDAY SERMON

MARCH 08, 1991

COMPREHENSIVE ADVICE TO TRANSFORM THE DREAM OF WORLD PEACE INTO REALITY

After reciting the Opening Chapter of the Holy Quran, Al-Fatiha, Hazoor said:

ANOTHER TALE OF HORRIFYING ATROCITIES

The Gulf War, which began on January 16, came to an end on the most horrifying night of February, 26. This was a night of such horrible atrocities that the like of it is not to be found in the history of man's modern warfare. The retreating Iraqi army and the city of Baghdad were made the target of so much bombardment throughout the night, that as far as I have studied the history of warfare, in no other country and in no other war have such horrific atrocities been committed and such one-sided bombardment been carried out. Observers say that the armies which were returning from Kuwait to Basra were made the target of such intensive bombing that the road from Kuwait to Basra was littered throughout with corpses, and that the shattered bits of trucks, cars, armoured personnel-carriers and many other kinds of transport were scattered everywhere. It was an unbearable scene of terrible destruction. This is the commentary of Western observers. The correspondent's voice broke and trembled repeatedly as he described the bombardment. He was saying that one could never imagine the horrifying bombing which was being carried out that night in Baghdad.

HUMILIATION IN VIETNAM

I have said this before that besides other factors, it is the ghost of the U.S. humiliation in Vietnam, transformed into inferiority complex, which keeps haunting them, and they want to get rid of this ignominy once and for all. That night seemed to be a night of uncommon intoxication when, drunk with the blood of the Iraqis, they wanted to drown their sorrows of Vietnam. This impression is further strengthened by the post-war remarks of President George Bush who stated[1]:

"By God we have kicked the Vietnam Syndrome once and for all!"

But the true state of affairs is not as they understand it. The fact is that they were being pursued by the demon of their horrifying atrocities in Vietnam and now they have created yet another such demon. So now it is no longer the case of just one demon but that of two. There are now two ghosts which will continue to haunt America. One is the ghost of Vietnam, the other is the ghost of their recently perpetrated atrocities on Iraq. They fail to see this because their analysis of this situation is completely different from that visualized by the rest of the world. The world does not see Vietnam as a place where 54,000 Americans were killed and their corpses were sent back home. The world views the story of Vietnam as the killing of two and a half million Vietnamese, and the reducing to dust of thousands of hitherto inhabited cities and villages. How things appear different when viewed from different angles! They thought that they had escaped the Vietnam humiliation because in comparison to the 54,000 Americans killed there, in this war their losses were negligible. But the truth of the matter is that history does not view things this way. **History's view of Vietnam has always been and shall always be that in this modern age, the United States of America, donning the cloak of civilization, unjustly attacked an extremely weak and poor nation, and continued raining death and destruction upon it for eight and a half years. Such hideous bombardment was rained down upon them, that village after village and entire regions were made desolate.** They cannot, therefore, ever erase the memory of Vietnam because the world will not permit them to forget it. And now to this, has been added the tyranny perpetrated upon Iraq.

---

[1] Harrisburg Patriot News. U.S.A. March 21, 1991

3,000 IRAQI VILLAGES TURNED TO DUST

Mr. Tom King, who is the Secretary of Defence of the British government, summarized of the destruction in Iraq in just one sentence that "in this short time, we have reduced to dust 3,000 villages of Iraq." Now just consider the initial claims that this war was being fought to liberate the oppressed Iraqis from the clutches of a cruel tyrant. These claimants now admit that they have turned to dust 3,000 Iraqi villages. It is not necessary to go into the other details here, as to how many Iraqi soldiers were killed or how much loss of other types of weapons occurred. But in this short period, the total and utter destruction of 3,000 villages is such an unparalleled event that nowhere in history an incident is to be found when so much destruction was wreaked in such a short time upon any nation such as has been perpetrated upon Iraq by these tyrants. **And despite this, the trumpets of victory are being sounded. This is baffling. This is the acme of disgrace and dishonour.**

It is as if a duel is scheduled between the Japanese wrestler *Anoki* and an American child; and upon pulverising the child to death, Anoki should start proclaiming the victory of Japan over America! Thirty nations joined together. All the powers of the world having superiority in every field and in every kind of modern weaponry, and in every way having the upper hand, united against Iraq and, as I mentioned in a previous Friday sermon, that after extracting its teeth, severing its limbs and dismembering it as one would dismember an animal - then they went on to finish Iraq off and boasted of having dealt a humiliating and exemplary defeat upon that country. This has to be the very height of despicable ignominy.

These matters have now become a part of history. It is in connection with the future repercussions of this war that I offered advice in my last sermon. Now, I wish to present some additional suggestions to the Arabs, to other Muslims, and in particular, to the nations of the Third world.

SOME VALUABLE SUGGESTIONS FOR THE ARAB NATIONS

The Arabs, as well as Iran, must urgently resolve their internal disputes. There are **three** such disputes which, if not resolved immediately, will forever divide the Arabs on the Palestinian issue.

Sixteenth Friday Sermon Mar 08, 1991

Firstly, Iran has had a historic rivalry with the Arabs, as a result of which Saudi Arabia and Kuwait had felt compelled to support Iraq in spite of their mutual differences. At no cost could they tolerate Iran coming close to them.

Secondly, there is the Shiite-Sunni issue about which Saudi Arabia is very sensitive. Saudi Arabia would never tolerate an increase in Shiite influence. **The third issue** is that of the Kurds.

So far as the enemy's strategy is concerned, Israel is most keen that all three of these issues explode simultaneously. For instance, when the war was about to end, Shiite rebellion was ignited in the south of Iraq, as a consequence of which the issue of old Iran-Arab rivalry would automatically have arisen. The Shiite Clergy of Iraq turned to Iran for help and it looks as if Saudi Arabia exerted pressure upon America to stop it from becoming a tool for this Jewish conspiracy. Although no such news has come out, yet this is a logical conclusion, otherwise, this matter was not such as to have naturally ended here. It is equally likely that Iran acted wisely since otherwise a seed for future bloody wars would have been sown. Nevertheless, this effort on the part of the enemy is continuing, and if it succeeds, the enemy will attain two important objectives. Firstly, the rivalry and antagonism between Iran and the Arabs will keep increasing. And secondly, the Shiite-Sunni issue will become inflamed. And these two divisions could then result in many other disputes, and even lead to wars. The Kurdish issue, too, has been fanned at the same time. But this issue has not developed further because although the Western nations talk of justice, yet in reality, they have in view their selfish interests. Stirring this issue at this particular moment did not serve their objectives. The reason for this is that the Kurdish issue does not pertain only to Iraq. It concerns four nations i.e the Iraqis, the Iranians, the Turks and the Russians. So if in the name of justice, the Kurds were roused and helped against the Iraqis, they would certainly have to be incited against the Turks as well. Otherwise their duplicitous stand on justice would have been exposed. In any case, rousing the Kurds would have sent a new wave of freedom movement among all the Kurds and difficulties would also have been created for Iran, Turkey and the Soviet Union.

So, for the time being, the decree of Allah has put off these problems, but it is most essential that all Muslim nations connected with these problems should put their heads together immediately and resolve these issues once and for all. Otherwise, these matters will continue to hang over their heads like a sword hung by a wire, the other end of which is in the hands of the Westerns powers, who, whenever they wish, can let it fall on their heads to injure them and use it to rip them apart from head to toe. This frightful possibility of the exploitation of these issues will forever hover over their heads. And the same is the case of the other issues facing the world. The Western powers always stir up some already simmering issues at will, then manipulate them to their benefit and in this way keep the nations of the Third world fighting and killing one another.

I wish to advise them on another important matter. **Apparently, it is being said that America is bringing pressure to bear upon Israel to vacate the West Bank of Jordan. But I am certain that this all is a charade. A drama is being enacted.** If the U.S. had been sincere about Israel vacating the West Bank of Jordan, then it would have accepted Saddam Hussein's first day's offer that these two issues be linked together: 'I vacate Kuwait, you get Israel to vacate the occupied territories' Then without shedding a single drop of blood, all of these issues could have been resolved.

Israel is rapidly establishing settlements in these areas and the major portion of money which Israel is currently receiving from the Western powers is being used to settle the **Russian Jewish immigrants** on the West Bank of Jordan. Therefore, one cannot find any logical reason whatsoever for accepting the notion that America is sincere in pressurising Israel or that Israel is yielding to this kind of demand.

Another danger is that leaving this issue aside, Syria may be compelled, just like Egypt, to enter into a bilateral peace agreement with Israel. If this happens, then none amongst the Arabs, except Iraq and Jordan shall remain to patronize and advocate the rights of the Palestinians. You are witnesses to the treatment meted out to Iraq, and Jordan does not even have this much strength. There is the possibility that Israel may continue its provocation and harassment against Jordan so as to have a pretext that Jordan's continued aggressive behaviour towards us or its providing assistance to our enemies, necessitates that we occupy it as well.

So from this point of view, it is of utmost importance that these three nations of the Middle East; namely, Iran, Iraq and Jordan, form a united front. They also need to reach an understanding with the other Arab nations so that these three do not become isolated into a completely distinct group but that they continue to receive the support of other Arab nations also.

Another issue which will now be raised, concerns the giving of charity by the oil-rich Arab nations such as Saudi Arabia and Kuwait to those Arab countries which have no oil. If such countries receive aid from the oil-rich countries on the basis of 'charity', it would be suicidal - that they have no legal right to it but are being given this aid just as giving alms to a beggar. This attitude would not only diminish but completely destroy forever any remaining chances of a resolution of the Palestinian problem. Therefore, the Arabs should adopt this stand that the oil wealth bestowed by God upon them, is their jointly owned wealth and they should all agree upon a formula that ensures their joint responsibility for its protection and fair and equitable distribution amongst the joint owners. Of course, the countries where this wealth has been discovered would receive one fifth share as is the Islamic rule concerning such bounties. Or where there is a difference of opinion between experts of Islamic jurisprudence (*Fuqaha*) some extra portion can be given to these countries. But it is necessary to get their agreement to this principle of "common ownership of oil-wealth", and it is necessary that this principle be strictly adhered to. Then whatever money the non oil-producing nations receive as a consequence of this agreement will not be at the cost of their self-esteem, but as their right. Indeed the truth is that initially, all the Arab world was one country. It was fragmented by the Western powers in contradiction of their own promises. The fact is that at the end of the First World War, the British had given a clear, binding, absolute and categorical promise that they would leave behind a united, free and independent Arabia. But that promise of a united, free and independent Arabia has not been fulfilled to this day. This means that, at that time it had been accepted that the wealth of all Arabia was jointly owned. They should hold fast to this principle and adhere to it strictly and should hold negotiations along these lines.

THE NEED OF ESTABLISHING AN ECONOMIC COMMONWEALTH

Another important matter is that an Economic Commonwealth must be established for the whole of this region. The concept which was presented earlier by President Nasser of Egypt was of a political union. It is not necessary that political union may precede economic and other forms of union. When the concept of political union gets priority, then sometimes the cause of economic and other unions is severely damaged. It was for this reason that when establishing the E.E.C., the sensible leaders of Europe first talked of economic union and then after attaining the objectives of economic cooperation piecemeal, they started taking the steps towards political union.

The concept of a **Pan Arabism movement**, advocated by President Gemal Nasser had actually been conceived much earlier by Jamaluddin Afghani and it was by adopting this philosophy of his that other movements flourished. Actually, this concept of Jamal-uddin Afghani that all Arabs should unite or rather that the whole Islamic world should become one country -is unacceptable to the Muslims in this form. **The Holy Quran has made no mention of this concept that all Muslim countries should be under one government.** In this form, even the attainment of total Arab unity seems impossible except that it be attained in various stages.

Therefore, the most important step is that of economic union in which there should be a common plan of action and common programmes, and this whole region should in particular develop plans to become self sufficient in food and industry. Only then can some surety be given of the independence and freedom of these countries.

DANGER FOR THE THIRD WORLD

In this connection, another important thing worth mentioning is that the issue of economic independence relates not just to this region, but rather to all the nations of the Third world, for they face a great danger which should be understood fully right away, and against which adopting preventive counter measures is most essential. That danger is the danger of neo-imperialism.

After the accord with the Soviet Union, the Eastern Communist world is abandoning this ideology and fast returning to the earlier times, and now the new rivalries will be with respect to imperialism. Once Russia has recovered from its current problems and has

Sixteenth Friday Sermon Mar 08, 1991

overcome them, the snatching away of markets from these countries shall be of paramount importance to Russia. Germany shall rise as a new economic power and many countries of Eastern Europe shall unite with Germany in this matter and their combined production shall demand new markets. Thus all countries of the Third world face frightening dangers. Europe is awake and so is America and their unified objectives are to economically dominate the Third world countries in such a way that they would gasp for life. There would remain no prospect for the nations of the Third world to survive with dignity, eating two decent meals a day. Some countries of Africa have already reached this state where it is difficult for them even to breathe with ease.

THE NEED FOR ECONOMIC COOPERATION AND FOR RESOLVING MUTUAL PROBLEMS

The establishment of Common markets for economic cooperation is, therefore, essential. Pakistan, India, Bangladesh and Sri Lanka, for example, are in a region where there is a natural possibility for the establishment of a common market for economic cooperation. But this is possible only if their regional problems can be resolved. If these internal issues remain unsettled, then neither can the economic markets be established nor can any other solution be found for their current painful state of affairs. By this, I mean that state of affairs in which all avenues for these countries of the Third world, leading to freedom from their problems are forever sealed off. All paths leading to their deliverance are blocked, and yet with eyes closed, they continue to follow the same incomprehensible lines of thought. The following are some of the problems:

There is the "Kashmir issue". As a consequence of this issue, the rivalries that have developed between India and Pakistan are such as to compel them to maintain such large armies which no country of the world can afford while continuing to exist as an economically independent country. A nation which spends more than 60% of its gross national product on maintaining an army can never lead a life of dignity. Such life is not destined for it. The reason for this is that the country which spends beyond its means on defence, must go a-begging.

THE CURSE OF BEGGING

From the economic point of view as well as for maintaining their military strength, such countries have no other alternative but to go begging for their survival. The final analysis is that India and Pakistan have been afflicted with the 'curse of begging'. On one pretext or the other, they reach out and extend their hands for 'alms' from the East as well as from the West.

Thus, an amicable solution of the "Kashmir dispute" and other similar disputes could result in a revolutionary progress in these areas. Besides these, there are other matters to be tackled. Not only India and Pakistan but many countries in Africa, Asia, South America and in the Third world face such problems. As a result of regional disputes, restlessness and lack of mutual trust, they are forced to spend a much higher percentage of their revenues on defence than that spent by the affluent countries. As compared to these poor Third world countries, the rich nations do not spend even one-tenth of their percentage. Many rich nations spend about 3% to 5% of their revenues on defence. If this percentage reaches 7, we hear heated debates and protests against such expenditure. Now imagine the luxury of the poor under-developed nations who spend 60% and even up to 70% on defence and still find it insufficient and then go out seeking military aid.

THE NEED FOR SELF-SUFFICIENCY

The economic condition of poor countries can never be rectified because economic aid has turned them into beggars. Every poor country is in this deplorable state. Any person who adopts the habit of clinging to a false standard of living or one who becomes habitual to begging to maintain that artificial standard, becomes psychologically unfit to make any improvement in his economic condition or to have any confidence and self reliance. Similar is the case of nations. You may never have seen beggars attaining prosperity. They beg and eat; their lives are deplorable. Their entire lives are spent in misery and want. In contrast to this, those who learn to live in contentment, sometimes progressively rise from extremely poor conditions and become very rich.

Thus unfortunately, the nations of the Third world are under another curse i.e. **lack of contentment, and the lack of self-respect** and the deplorable habit of begging to maintain a false standard of life. You may have observed that sometimes even a rich man will not spend so much money in hotels as a man accustomed to begging may spend. For such a man, money has no value at all. He begs and eats well, and that is that.... It is the safety of his hands that he wishes for, so that they can again be extended for begging. Such exactly becomes the psychological condition of these nations. They have adopted a false standard of life which bears no relation to reality. Outwardly, they appear prosperous, but their prosperity is based on begging. And this appearance of prosperity continues to beguile them. The hardships of poverty could have forced them to strive to stand on their own feet economically but they have done nothing. These hardships are only felt by that segment of the population which is helpless, and not at all by those who are in authority. That is to say, these nations are split into two sections. One section comprises of the few, called the 'upper class'. They are completely insensitive to the life of the poor and completely unaware of the plight of the poor languishing under their very eyes. Thus, those who suffer the agony and pain are powerless to cause any change for the better. They do not formulate the policies of the nation. While the brains and heads which make the policies are such that the perception of pain never penetrates them!

This is the deep nervous disorder. Just as in the case of a person with a broken spine; the brain loses all feeling of the lower part of the body and fails to feel anything even if the foot is burnt - this is exactly the frightening affliction which affects countries of the Third world as a consequence of their habit of begging.

THE CURSE OF MILITARY AID

Now let us examine the case of military aid. Once you purchase expensive weapons, then the economic situation which has been mentioned earlier will further deteriorate. Since your national economy does not allow large purchases, you are forced to beg. This is what is happening nowadays. When you buy weapons from other nations, then along with the weapons arrive their military training personnel or your military personnel have to go to their countries to receive such training. All the spy networks of these foreign powers in the Third world countries are functioning mainly as a result of the exchange of such personnel. Moreover, as a direct consequence of begging for military hardware, the possibilities are created whereby the control of the Armed Forces of a receiving country pass into the effective control of the donor country. And as far as I have observed the situation of the donors and receivers of Military Aid, openly admitted by the journalists of these countries as well, is that wherever military aid was given, a sizeable number of the military personnel were 'purchased' for covert operations. And this is occurring frequently in every country where military aid is being received.

Now the most dangerous aspect of this is that it is not only the U.S. which is enslaving countries through military aid but Israel also functioning as the right-hand of the U.S. is carrying out the same task. When the U.S. cannot directly give military aid, it assigns the task to Israel and there are some places where they both function in their own spheres and succeed in tightening the noose of slavery around such nations.

THE THIRD WORLD - A DUMPING GROUND OF OBSOLETE WEAPONRY OF THE WEST

It must be remembered that the Third world remains a ready market for the obsolete weaponry of the Western nations. Whenever new weaponry is made available, markets have to be found for disposing the obsolete models, the natural consequence of which is that in some poor countries the 'crops' become ripe for harvesting. Thus the conflicts of poor nations provide the market for these weapons.

So far only a trickle of the surplus American arms have been used up. There still remain for sale, mountains of Russian arms. It would not be of any surprise if other Western nations follow suit and join in this business.

SIMILARITIES BETWEEN MILITARY AID AND THE DISEASE 'AIDS'

So when I say that there is a similarity between military aid and AIDS - this is not a laughing matter. It is a deep truth. The world is terribly frightened today because of *AIDS*. And it appears from some estimates that **by 1997-98 it will cause widespread death among the Western nations.** It is not necessary at this time to go into the details of this as I have already discussed the matter on other occasions. A brief description of AIDS is that the germs of this disease enter into the bloodstream of man and settle in his defence or immune system and take control of it. Thus, the defensive mechanism, which God Almighty had created to combat disease, becomes a victim to the disease and the body becomes incapable of acting against an intruder. Military Aid is precisely similar to AIDS. Foreign nations take control of the defence systems of our poor nations and the greatest tragedy is, that there is no complete realization of this. Even the healthy parts are unaware of what is going on.

INSURGENCY AND COUNTER INSURGENCY MEASURES

In Pakistan, as well as in all the countries of the Third world the attention of the intelligence services are focused on internal strife. As a result, 'counter insurgency measures' are taken and organizations are set up which are ever ready to take steps against internal rebellion. And for learning the tricks of counter-insurgency measures, help is sought from America and in many cases from Israel. Now you can see that in Sri Lanka, Israel taught the authorities counter-insurgency methods and at the same time trained the rebels to take effective measures of mounting an insurgency!

Similarly in Liberia, Israel taught them how to confront a rebellion and now the commentators are writing that Israel protected the Head of State of Liberia in such an excellent manner that the true intensity of the rebellion was never allowed to reach him. This is how he was completely surrounded. The list of such countries is very long. There are many other African countries and some other Asian countries where not only America but also Israel is foremost in teaching them the ways of counter-insurgency. The fact is, that the real danger stems from those very people who have come to teach them. They succeed to have control over these poor countries through their own armies.

Thus, if there is any need, then the need is for gearing up such an intelligence system, which would look into the different kind of poisons that have been left behind, wherever, and whenever military contacts were established with Western or non Western powers. They should look into the type of contacts that have been established and a continuing surveillance should be maintained on those personnel who are involved in such contacts.

Dangers in most cases will be external. The likelihood of internal dangers is relatively small. If you can successfully confront the external dangers, then the internal dangers constitute little significance. Internal dangers do arise, but always as a consequence of oppression - otherwise it is improbable that our armies should face dangers from their own citizens or our politicians should face any danger from our own citizens. This is the second aspect which merits attention.

The advanced or developed nations, outwardly profess that dictatorship must be brought to an end. **But in reality it is dictatorship alone which suits them in enslaving the Third world countries** because wherever there is dictatorship, internal dangers start developing. To safeguard against such dangers external allies have to be found and these external allies are found just as I have already mentioned. Then, so long as things are done in accordance with their wishes, they provide the needed support. When something is done against their wishes, this 'support' crumbles by itself. This is the ignominy to which the Third world is prey. It is high time that we make use of our wits. Now that a new era of imperialism has started posing extreme dangers, it is essential for the preservation of our national independence, freedom, self respect and for leading a life of dignity amongst the comity of nations, that we reflect deeply on all such matters, and act with swiftness.

HARMFUL EFFECTS OF FOREIGN AID

In brief, the following are the dangers inherent in accepting aid in its current form from the rich countries:

Firstly, the aid giving country gives the aid by disgracing and humiliating the recipient country and adopting an arrogant attitude so much so that if the recipient country decides to exercise its right of freedom of conscience, it is threatened with termination of such aid. The treatment of Jordan and King Hussein is a recent example of this.

Secondly, strings are attached to such an aid or conditions which compromise national independence are laid down.

Thirdly, aid comes with a crippling burden of interest bearing conditions and is often accompanied by highly paid 'foreign instructors' who are a part and parcel of the aid-package. These instructors end up consuming the better part of this aid.

There have been many bitter experiences in Africa and Asia where in the name of aid - first generation technology was sold at exorbitant prices, and usually such plants were unable to compete with modern

Sixteenth Friday Sermon Mar 08, 1991

technology-based plants. Besides these, there are many other maladies which continue to afflict Third world industries as a consequence of which their ability to repay the loans continues to diminish while the burden of their debts continues to escalate. Almost all of South America has now been strangulated by the chains of debt. I do not know of a single country receiving aid from America or from some other rich country for which the burden of debt is becoming lighter. This is a burden which increases day by day till a large portion of the national income is consumed up in paying the interest on the loans. Thus the countries which accept aid or go begging for aid have never, ever been seen to stand on their own feet. The recipient nations receive humiliating treatment, and in the event of any policy differences, threats of termination of the aid follow, which in turn not only ruin the national economies of these countries, but also have a devastating affect on the national character.

ESTABLISHMENT OF A NEW ISLAMIC SYSTEM OF ASSISTANCE

Thus, not only the honour, but also other far-reaching interests demand most vehemently that the offers of aid from the major aid-giving countries be politely turned down. And those Muslim countries which have been blessed with the wealth of oil should join with those non-Muslim countries which are willing to participate in the spirit of the Quranic injunction:

تَعَاوَنُوْا عَلَى الْبِرِّ وَالتَّقْوٰى

"cooperate with one another in good works". So they should set up a new aid-providing system under Islamic rules in which priority should be given in the first instance, to help those poor countries of the Third world which are constantly threatened by severe starvation and famine, to attain self-sufficiency in food. Or they should be strengthened economically to such a degree that they become capable of purchasing food from abroad.

FOOD USED TO ENSLAVE POOR NATIONS

The present attitude of the world towards the famine-stricken African countries is most disgraceful as well as ineffective. Famines do not arise in countries as unexpected and sudden eruption of a volcano. Expert economists know years in advance, where and when famine is due to strike. But completely unmoved, they wait till the time when the nation, utterly overcome by famine can be bound in the shackles of slavery through political and ideological commitments in return for some food. Therefore an aid system must be set up in accordance with the teachings of the Holy Quran which liberates rather than enslaves.

If, for the sake of God and for the sake of humanity, the oil rich countries were to donate the Islamic levy of 2.5% *ZAKAT* on their oil revenues for this purpose, then the scourge of starvation could be removed from the majority of the poor countries. Japan too needs to be approached. The countries of the Third world should frankly discuss this matter with Japan and ask if it would like to remain as a country of the Third world or would opt to be counted amongst the Western countries. If it wishes to remain in the Third world, then it is essential that it cooperates fully by guiding and playing a leading role in resolving, in particular, the economic issues facing the Third world. Otherwise Japan shall neither remain a part of the Third world countries nor will it be counted among the Western nations.

THE NEED TO RESOLVE THE KASHMIR DISPUTE

Returning to the subject of the Indo-Pakistan issues, I feel that in the matter of Kashmir there are three solutions which merit further study. The current state of affairs is in no way acceptable. If the situation continues as it is, then both countries shall be ruined. **Basically, there are three solutions which should be explored:** The **first solution** could be that Azad Kashmir (Pakistan held), Jammu (Indian held) and the Valley of Kashmir (Indian held) become three independent states.

The second possibility is that all the three parts of this disputed territory unite and form an independent country.

The third solution could be that Azad Kashmir is amalgamated with Pakistan, Jammu is united with India, while the Valley of Kashmir (presently held by India) becomes an independent state.

This is not the time for a detailed discussion. These nations have to make this decision themselves. This is their right, but so far as I understand the situation, **I feel the third option would be the most appropriate and in the best interest of peace in the region.** All people of Azad Kashmir are similar in temperament which is quite

Sixteenth Friday Sermon Mar 08, 1991

different from that of the Kashmiris of the valley. The Kashmiris of the valley have a distinct personality and a well-defined identity. And the people of Jammu have an altogether separate identity, and from the religious point of view too, they are much closer to India. Thus if stability is desired, this solution would turn out to be the best. But, independence should be granted under the condition that the newly independent state give a firm commitment that it would not pose a threat to the security of India or Pakistan by entering into separate treaties with any powerful country.

All these issues can be settled by mutually acceptable accords. If this is not done and similarly if peace is not made with the Sikhs, and if other internal matters are not resolved, then peace can never be established in the region.

A HUMBLE ADVICE TO PAKISTAN

There are imbalances that need to be set right inside Pakistan. For example, issues related to the Sindhis, Punjabis, Pathans and the language and ethnic issues. Then there are the issues of religious differences - all these issues are like gunpowder or like an active volcano - they could explode at any time. And these are the very same issues which other nations exploit to their advantage. Thus before these nations get an opportunity to benefit from this, you must correct the internal condition of your country. Correct your internal situation and also correct your relations with your neighbours. The greatest benefit you will receive as a consequence is that your attention will become focused on improving your economic condition and with a united action in the Quranic spirit of:

(Al-Maida: Verse 3) تَعَاوَنُوْا عَلَى الْبِرِّ وَالتَّقْوٰى

"cooperation in all that is good", **without bringing religion into it**, the possibilities will arise for cooperation with every other nation in pursuing all noble goals. As a result, military expenditure will be curtailed thus boosting the economy. In this way the *possibility* of improving the condition of the poor will be enhanced.

I have intentionally used the word 'possibility' because to improve the lot of the poor, these things alone are not enough as long as the thinking of the ruling classes continues to be sick, insensitive and shameless. If expensive hotels and restaurants continue to be erected, and if there is a band of people of high society who take the rounds of these restaurants and hotels from early evening to late in the night, and continue to be submerged in a life of enjoyment and luxury as is seen in the glittering streets of Lahore and Karachi at night; and if this tendency continues and no one turns his attention to the fact that underneath these glittering lights there is such horrid darkness that if you peep into this darkness, you would behold such painful scenes of suffering humanity that it would make your hair stand on end. I shall give you one example. My daughter **Faiza** had gone to **Qadian** (India) for the Annual Conference of our Jamaat. On her way back, she was accompanied by two other children. While waiting at *Atari* railway station to catch the next train she decided to have her meals. As she did so, a horde of very young, poor hungry children gathered around her. She told me that it was apparent that they were hungry and were not professional beggars. So she distributed that food among them. Then, she took out some other items of food given to her by friends in Qadian, and distributed that as well. What I am trying to place before you is not the fact that she distributed these things. This was an act which any person with a humane heart would have done any way - but the special thing meriting attention is that even among the poor and the destitute, one finds humanitarianism of high degree. Indeed in these poor countries, one is more likely to experience humanitarianism at lower levels of society than in the higher levels. "When all this had been distributed", she went on, "I had a can of Coca Cola left with me which I gave to an older girl to share it with the other children. She took a sip and then turn by turn gave this drink to each child. After each child took his or her sip, one could notice the same contentment and satisfaction on this girl's face which descends on a mother's face upon satisfying her infant's cries for milk. And she looked towards the children as if to say 'see how much we are enjoying this'. All the children formed a line and one after the other they would take their sip and it seemed as if they had just drunk from the spring of eternal life! Then, as the train moved, despite the attempts by the police to stop them, these children felt so compelled to show their gratitude that they kept running alongside the train and offering their thanks and waving their hands and kept on doing so for as long as they could see the train..."

While she was recounting this incident to me, I could not decide whether I felt more love for this daughter of mine, or for those hungry children, who after my daughter's little act of kindness, reciprocated with so much love. And I thought that in life, there are times when one encounters such instances where human values supersede the ties of blood that bind man together. And in the history of man, the greatest display of the dominance of the human values over the demands of blood relationship was in the time of His Holiness, Hazrat Muhammad[sas]. Without doubt, that was a time when the obligations of every blood relationship had been demoted to a secondary position. The greatness of the Holy Prophet Muhammad[sas] was that he raised human values to their highest pinnacle. We need to bring back those times. These are the human values which will rescue the Third world. We need to bring back those times. These are the human values which will save the Third world.

THE RESULTS OF TRAMPLING UPON DESCENT HUMAN VALUES
But these are the human values which are being trampled upon under your feet and in consequence, the decree of God continues causing you to be trampled under the feet of the big nations. Why have you failed to understand this hint of God's decree? It is a pity that these two countries, in their greed to possess the paradise of Kashmir, have driven the poor of their countries into veritable hell.

Thus, no matter how many other solutions are tried in the Third world, the future of the Third world cannot be changed, the Third world cannot become free and independent until self respect, human dignity and the values of kindness and gratitude are re-established and a commitment is made to protect all human values. The advanced nations which are referred to, as the nations of the First world are not only free and independent, but are becoming even more poised to enslave you. As I have mentioned earlier, the economic development taking place there is such that in the future, irrespective of whether or not they desire it, they shall be compelled to further trample upon the poor nations of the Third world. The West cannot allow their standard of living to drop. Their political leadership is incapable of advising their nations to lower their standards of living. Whichever party attempts this, would lose the next elections. They are now caught in such an evil trap, that they are compelled to perpetrate one injustice after another. The nations of the Third world shall have to rise up for their own defence. Without this, they can neither gain freedom from their own armies, nor from their own ills and bad morals; nor from all those cursed things which I have mentioned. When nations become prey to such vices, then why lament that we are dying and that vultures are sitting next to us, awaiting our death. A disease develops from within you, for your death, and that disease invites bacteria. It is true that diseases develop from bacteria, but it is a fact that bacteria can do no harm to a healthy body. Therefore, a disease develops from within and not from the outside. When a body no longer has any power left to resist a disease then these bacteria thrive and take control of the body and when their control becomes complete, death becomes inevitable, and the flocking of vultures to chew upon the carcass is a natural sequence of events which has to happen afterwards. The truth of the matter is, that this is a law of nature from which no power can safeguard you, if you do not decide to change yourself today.

Thus, before you reach this stage, where your corpses are left in the open fields for others to draw lessons from, or are interred in graves, if you decide today that you will make the moral values and the teachings, as expounded by the Holy Master Hazrat Muhammad[sas], as your plan of action and you resolve to protect human values and strive to restore and re-establish those lost values, then this is the only way of salvation for you from a life of disgraceful enslavement by others. Besides this, there is no other way.

THE NEED OF A NEW ORGANISATION OF THE OIL PRODUCING COUNTRIES

Similarly, it is necessary that some oil producing countries lay the foundations of a new *OPEC* - that is to say an *OPEC* in which there is no place for the devout bondsmen of the U.S. Those who cooperate with the U.S. may without doubt, be included because we do not at all follow the rule that alliances be established solely for the sake of opposition. The Holy Quran has made no mention of any such principle. Alliances must be established on the basis of goodness and righteousness. But if a country has established an alliance with big powers on lawlessness and this poses a hinderance towards the establishment of justice, then the interests of poor nations will be

Sixteenth Friday Sermon Mar 08, 1991

compromised if such a country is included. Thus it is essential that oil-producing countries like Iran, Iraq, Nigeria, Indonesia and Malaysia establish a new alliance. Similarly, those countries which produce some oil, may also collaborate with those oil producing, countries to form an *OPEC* of their own. If the members of this *OPEC* cooperate and jointly formulate their policies, then the Western world would not be able to implement and impose its schemes, as was done in the case of Iraq compelling it to act in an extremely injudicious manner. Saudi Arabia and Kuwait etc. because of their oil powers, could, for a time, make life difficult for this new *OPEC*, but if the new organisation perseveres and holds fast to its principles then after a while, this game of applying pressure would end. Then you would see very beneficial results of this.

ASSOCIATION OF NON-OIL PRODUCING COUNTRIES

Those countries of the third world which produce no oil also must form a united association of non-oil producing countries, because whenever there are wars or political upheavals, these hapless countries are the ones who suffer the greatest damage. Thus, they must unite for their own protection and enter into some-long term agreements with the oil producing countries so that in the light of previous experiences they may work to shield themselves from the ill effects of any future crisis.

THE NEED TO PROTECT THE INTEREST OF THE WORKERS FROM OTHER COUNTRIES

In this regard, another small alliance also needs to be established. Those countries which provide labour to the oil producing countries have never paid attention as to how cruelly their citizens are disgraced and humiliated and how viciously they are maltreated in these countries. There is no one to look after their interests or enquire about their welfare. As a consequence, the national honour of these workers is crushed and shamelessness begins to take root. I have not had the opportunity to go there but the stories, which some travellers have recounted of what happens to these workers in the Gulf, starting immediately after they disembark at the airport, are such that a man of dignity and honour cannot even bear to listen. For example, when Pakistani planes arrive at the airport, the local police, armed with batons and sticks are already there awaiting their arrival. They strike them on their knees ordering them to stand erect and line up here or there. The humiliating treatment meted out to them is similar to the manner in which cattle are driven in cruel and oppressive countries. In the developed countries, even the cattle are treated with greater compassion. How long would they tolerate this kind of treatment? They are treated like slaves and even their earnings are not protected. This is grave injustice. These unfortunate people go there to work and earn a few thousand as a result of life long toiling. Their contracts are such that if their masters decide not to give them their wages, they have every right to do so. And even if they go to the courts, they are not given a hearing. So if the employer happens to be a heartless taskmaster, and is aware that he can do whatever he wishes, then an employee is sure to receive even more humiliating treatment than would a slave. Thus. countries such as India, Pakistan, the Philippines, etc. or all those countries which supply the workers, need to get together to guarantee the respect, honour and dignity of their workers and if their rights are denied to them, or if they are deprived of their rights or are maltreated, then all those countries which provide the labour force should unite to put pressure upon the employers of such countries to accord basic human rights to their workers.

EQUILIBRIUMS AND JUSTICE

This will result in an equilibrium and peace would follow as a consequence of such an equilibrium. Balance is another name for justice, which terminology the Holy Quran has also used. Peace is not established by the dictates of Kings, Dictators or Presidents of powerful nations. Peace will only be established as a consequence of equilibrium which is the outcome of justice. In fact both these words are synonymous. Thus, there is a dire need for the establishment of new equilibriums in politics of the world and a commitment is needed that every association and every alliance of ours will function on the principle of the supremacy of justice.

In all these groupings which I have mentioned, the main and fundamental criteria of a participating country should be its unqualified commitment to the principle of the acceptance and supremacy of **Justice** above all national interests. Furthermore, such arrangements must be made which would always ensure the attainment of the supremacy of the demands of justice. And whoever fails to respect the demands of justice would be expelled from the framework.

THE NEED OF A NEW UNITED NATIONS FOR THE THIRD WORLD

It is also worth mentioning that the Gulf War and the events that took place during it have taught the Third world nations another very important lesson, that the present system of the United Nations has become outdated. That is to say, as far as the interests of the Third world are concerned, the system within the United Nations has become completely outmoded and is worthy of being discarded. As long as Russia was opposed to the U.S. or had a rivalry with her, the U.N. was not capable of destroying the poor countries because America or Russia could use their power of veto to come to the rescue of the impoverished countries. Now, no one is left in the entire world to support a poor country. An accord has been reached, not for the doing of good but for perpetrating evil.

Thus when the Holy Quran says:

(Al-Maida: Verse 3) تَعَاوَنُوا عَلَى الْبِرِّ وَالتَّقْوَى

"Cooperate with each other for the doing of good and righteous deeds", it implies cooperating for good deeds and not for the perpetration of evil. But the political world's alliances and treaties of cooperation do not consider questions of goodness or evil; they talk of cooperation in doing whatever is of common benefit. These are the decisions which have already been made in the world. Russia and the U.S. between themselves have already made such resolutions. China at this time has been relegated to the sidelines for it lacks the strength to interfere in these matters and it will be weakened economically even further till it is forced to yield completely.

If this state of affairs continues unchanged, the United Nations and all agencies related to it, such as the Security Council, etc., would only be used to oppress the weaker nations and would never be used for their benefit. They will only be used for the benefit of those who accept the yolk of their enslavement and prostrate at their feet - for them, the U.N. will bring riches and create all kinds of facilities and grant them awards of honour and extend to them offers of friendship. Every kind of benefit attainable through disgrace, humiliation and meanness would be available for the Third world countries. But there is no possibility for these nations to live with honour and dignity, holding their heads high, while remaining affiliated with this United Nations.

One solution is, that as, just after the First World War, the "League of Nations" came into being in 1919, then after the Second World War in 1945, the "United Nations" was set up, therefore, after this tragic one-sided war, a new **"United Nations of the Third world"** must be established to include only the poor and the powerless countries. The non-aligned movement, which had been started earlier, has become outdated and meaningless now. It has no lifeblood left in it. Now a new movement must be started in which India, Pakistan, Iran and Iraq, etc. can play a very important role, but they will have to eliminate the religious prejudices from these discussions.

MUSLIMS AND NON MUSLIMS PITCHED AGAINST EACH OTHER

For this reason, another advice is that although the Muslim countries should maintain relations of love and affection between themselves and fulfil the responsibilities that fall upon them consequent to those brotherly relationships, yet they should not set the Muslim and the Non Muslim elements against each other. If this polarization continues, i.e. the pitching of Muslims and Non Muslims against each other, then even if by the word "Non Muslim" you only meant to refer to the Western powers, even then, all the nations will be alarmed and will feel threatened because Japan, Korea, Vietnam, India, which are all great Non Muslim powers, will think that this alarming message is meant for them also. So this policy of setting the Muslims against the Non Muslims is a suicidal policy born out of ignorance because nothing shall be achieved as a result; instead, they will lose even the little that they currently have.

Thus, unity amongst the Third world countries cannot be established unless and until we act on the Quranic teaching of:

تَعَاوَنُوْا عَلَى الْبِرِّ وَالتَّقْوٰى

"cooperation with each other for the doing of good and righteous things". In this command, there is no mention of religious differences. On the basis of this teaching, one can cooperate with a Polytheist, with a Jew, with a Christian or with an Atheist. There is no mention of religion here. Goodness and righteousness is the only yardstick for cooperation. Cooperate in every thing that is good! Operating on this principle of cooperation, and working on an extensive cooperation plan with nations, the establishment of new United Nations of the Poor Nations becomes all the more imperative.

Now, it is necessary that the poor nations of the world lay the foundations of a parallel United Nations whose charter should only include those laws which it will have the ability to enforce. Every country attached to this body would give a solemn pledge that in all circumstances, it would accept the supremacy of the demands of justice above every thing else.

An effective bi-lateral discussion mechanism based on justice must be established under the auspices of this body to resolve the entangled mess of Third world disputes. The participating nations must resolve that they would never invite the rich and powerful nations to interfere or intervene in an attempt to settle their disputes.

CONTRADICTIONS IN THE CHARTER OF THE U.N.

The existing United Nations Organization has many internal contradictions - these should be studied so that in the new associations such contradictions do not develop. As I have mentioned before, this is a strange and unjust rule that if, from among the whole world, America, Russia, China or any one of the five Permanent Members decided to perpetrate atrocities upon any country of their choice, then it could carry out this criminal attack with impunity. The rest of the world would remain powerless to take any counter measures as long as any one of the permanent members of the Security Council continues to brandish its Veto power. The exact status of the United Nations or of the security council has still not been determined till today. Is it a court of justice? If it is a court of justice, then what is the need for the International Court of Justice? If it is not a court of law, then while determining or settling disputes what kind of decisions can it make? And further, not being a court of law, it implies that it does not have the power to have its decisions imposed forcefully. And if it is a court of law, then to what exact limits would its authority extend? Would those nations that are not members of the Security Council be affected or not? This is another question which arises as a consequence of this anomaly.

Then if it is just a consultative body, the question of forcefully imposing its decisions does not arise. In such a situation, a code ought to be established of such moral pressure which can be applied against all nations with equity. But if it is merely a body set up for the purpose of mutual cooperation then it must be decided as to how cooperation may be obtained and which means ought to be adopted for this purpose and if cooperation is not forthcoming, then what ought to be done. These are all pertinent questions and contradictions which have yet to be resolved.

Similarly, if it is a body established solely for the welfare and prosperity of the poor nations, then from this point of view also, the status of the U.N. ought to be clearly defined. Without reference to politics, colour or race; a plan of action must be prepared to assist the poor nations or the disaster stricken regions. Ways should be found whereby administration of the U.N. could, not only take independent decisions for assistance, but also have the capacity for critical evaluation of the issues.

It should also be determined, how the decisions of the U.N. International Court of Justice can be enforced with certainty so that even the big powers feel compelled to comply with them. As long as no satisfactory answers are given to these questions which would guarantee and protect the rights of the poor and weak nations - as long as this does not happen, this body shall continue to be merely a deceitful instrument in the hands and in the monopoly of Super Powers. If it is a court of justice, then the most important question would be of enforcing its decisions. Take the case of a poor country deprived of the support of America, Russia, China, France or Britain in whose favour the U.N. decides, say by a two thirds majority saying that this is an oppressed country which deserves to be helped at all costs. The question arises how would this decision be enforced? What kind of a court of justice is it that does not have the cooperation of the enforcing powers available to it and lacks a definite mechanism for obtaining such a cooperation?

<u>U.N. TAKES DECISIONS WHICH IT CANNOT IMPLEMENT</u>

This is exactly like the case of the Red Indians of America, who once appealed against the U.S. government to the Supreme Court of America, and placed the matter before it that the government repeatedly made treaties with them, but then, time and again, it has violated them. Repeatedly they gave false assurances and just as often forced the Red Indians to vacate those very areas concerning which they had been given clear, unequivocal guarantees, that these were their lands and that they would no longer interfere with them. They complained that they had been continuously squeezed from their lands, so much so that now they find themselves in such a state that their very survival is at stake. Now it is a question of life or death. Upon this, the Supreme Court of America gave its decision in their favour. They said that this is an absolutely valid complaint. In all those matters brought before us, the government had adopted an unjust stance and the Red Indians were right. Therefore all earlier decisions to the contrary be cancelled and their previous rights be restored. When this decision was handed down, the President of America welcomed the decision most heartily, but added that the Supreme Court should now also arrange for its implementation. This is exactly the situation of the United Nations today. If even one member among these five permanent members decides that a particular decision must not be implemented, then that decision stands nowhere.

What a strange institution of justice! If the Super Powers unite to perpetrate aggression or injustice on any country, then in that case, everything can be enforced and implemented, but when, once it is decided not to implement or enforce a resolution, then no country of the world, separately, or even collectively can do anything against the wishes of just one permanent member country.

Even if these powers reach a consensus as they did in the case of Palestine, when in many resolutions all five permanent members arrived at a common accord in the Security Council that Israel shall vacate those occupied territories even then the decision cannot be implemented or enforced. This is truly a strange kind of institution for 'world peace' and a strange kind of United Nations. It has the power to take decisions, but it does not have the power to enforce decisions. The power to enforce decisions is in the hands of the Super Powers, and all other nations are at their mercy. This institution does not merit continued existence. It is an institution for perpetrating and protecting slavery. It is not a body established to protect freedom.

So, if today, the nations of the Third world do not hoist the emblem of rebellion against this institution - or rather we should say that if today the nations of the Third world do not compel them to cooperate in administering justice and changing the rules then these nations can never become free and independent, and this institution shall give rise to further dangers for the world and it shall be used repeatedly to fulfil horrifying objectives. It is not necessary to go into the details of this here.

AN IMPORTANT ADVICE TO ISRAEL

I wish now to put one last matter in front of you. Addressing myself to Israel, I wish also to give them a suggestion. Generally, the impression among the Muslims is that Israel was established consequent to a conspiracy of the West, and by the intrigue of the Israelis. This is correct in its own domain. But if the decree of God had not so desired, this could never have come to pass. This must be understood. Which dictum of Allah has created this issue of Israel today? We need to turn to this very dictum to find the solution of this problem. So, basing my conclusions on the Quran and the Hadith, I wish to unwrap this issue before you and want to give some advice to Israel, because today the peace of the world depends on Israel and on the decisions it makes. This is precisely what we learn from the Holy Quran.

In *Sura Al-Isra* of the Holy Quran, which is also called *Sura Bani Israel*, some verses address this issue, and I wish to place them before you. In verse 5, God says that we had decreed for the Bani Israel in the book (the Psalms of David are likely meant here)

وَقَضَيْنَآ إِلَىٰ بَنِىٓ إِسْرَآءِيلَ فِى ٱلْكِتَٰبِ لَتُفْسِدُنَّ فِى ٱلْأَرْضِ مَرَّتَيْنِ وَلَتَعْلُنَّ عُلُوًّا كَبِيرًا

"That you would surely cause mischief in the earth twice, and you will cause great rebellions."

The verse 6, states:

فَإِذَا جَآءَ وَعْدُ أُولَىٰهُمَا بَعَثْنَا عَلَيْكُمْ عِبَادًا لَّنَآ أُولِى بَأْسٍ شَدِيدٍ فَجَاسُوا۟ خِلَٰلَ ٱلدِّيَارِ وَكَانَ وَعْدًا مَّفْعُولًا

"So when the time for the fulfilment of the first of the two promises came, We sent against you some servants of Ours possessed of great might in war, and they penetrated the innermost parts of your houses, and it was a warning that was bound to be carried out and non could avert this decree."

$$ثُمَّ رَدَدْنَا لَكُمُ الْكَرَّةَ عَلَيْهِمْ وَ اَمْدَدْنٰكُمْ بِاَمْوَالٍ وَّ بَنِيْنَ وَ جَعَلْنٰكُمْ اَكْثَرَ نَفِيْرًا$$

"Then We gave you back the power against them and dominance and aided you with wealth and children, and caused you to grow into a great power." (Verse 7)

$$اِنْ اَحْسَنْتُمْ اَحْسَنْتُمْ لِاَنْفُسِكُمْ وَ اِنْ اَسَاْتُمْ فَلَهَا$$

"But with the condition that if you will now practice goodness and give up your old evil ways, then in reality you would be doing good to your own selves, but if you revert to your same old misdeeds which you had done before, then those misdeeds too will backfire upon you, i.e., in reality you would be perpetrating those misdeeds against your own selves. God says:

$$فَاِذَا جَآءَ وَعْدُ الْاٰخِرَةِ لِيَسُوْٓءا وُجُوْهَكُمْ$$

"Then the time came for the fulfilment of the **second promise** so that the decree may be fulfilled that you would again do evil and would taste its consequences and your faces would be disgraced and darkened."

$$وَلِيَدْخُلُوا الْمَسْجِدَ كَمَا دَخَلُوْهُ اَوَّلَ مَرَّةٍ وَّ لِيُتَبِّرُوْا مَا عَلَوْا تَتْبِيْرًا$$

(Verse 8)
"So they may again enter the Mosque as they had entered it before and destroy it" - meaning the Temple of Solomon. These two promises have been fulfilled and recorded in history. But there is a third mention which is also to be found in this same Chapter of the Holy Quran. As we read in the next verse:

عَسَىٰ رَبُّكُمْ أَن يَرْحَمَكُمْ وَإِنْ عُدتُّمْ عُدْنَا وَجَعَلْنَا جَهَنَّمَ لِلْكَافِرِينَ حَصِيرًا

that after this again when God would so wish or it would also mean that it is quite possible that God would so desire that once again He should show mercy upon you - but remember that when mercy is shown to you, you should not forget that if again you repeat your earlier misdeeds and persist in them, then we too will most certainly repeat the punishments which you have already tasted twice before.

After this, it appears that **no fourth occurrence** would come to pass in the world, because then mention is made of hell. After this, the matters pertaining to this world would come to an end. Then the final decisions would be taken after the Day of Judgement and punishment would be meted out by way of hell.

I want to mention briefly how the first two promises were fulfilled. The first promise began to be fulfilled in 721 B.C. when the **Assyrians** devastated the northern of the two Jewish empires and occupied it. This was the empire which was linked to the city of Samara which was also referred to as Israel. Thus this event began in 721 B.C. The second phase of the campaign to destroy the two Jewish empires began 124 years after it was started by the Assyrians. This time the Babylonians, led by Nebuchadnezzar, attacked the remaining empire of the Jews which was called Judea, of which Jerusalem was the capital.

Thus remember that in accordance with the promise, the first attack to break Israel, that is to say, to break the empire of the Jews in the land of Canaan occurred in 721 B.C. and was started by the Assyrians. The second phase was begun by Nebuchadnezzar in 597 B.C. and was completed in 587 B.C. During both the phases, the Jewish power suffered tremendous blows but during the second phase, it was truly and utterly destroyed and annihilated. Innumerable Jews were made prisoners and taken away by Nebuchadnezzar. The Prophet Ezekiel was amongst them. We learn from the Book of Ezekiel that the punishment which was meted out to the Jews was given them because - to use the divine terminology employed in this book - the example of the two cities had become that of two prostitutes who sold themselves and continuously exceeded all limits of shamelessness by eloping with strangers and abandoning friendship with God. A most frightening sketch is presented and then it says that the punishment

Sixteenth Friday Sermon Mar 08, 1991

that was destined came and God broke off His connection with them and said:

"O ye prostitutes, become ye verily of those to whom you belong." So actually Nebuchadnezzar took them away from their country and razed the Temple of Solomon to the ground.

After that, in 551 - 553 or thereabouts, with the help of the Prophet Ezekiel[as], a series of contacts was started with the people of Persia and their help secured. The accounts of Haroot and Maroot that we read in the Holy Quran relate to this period. Although ultimately, this change occurred many years later, but the process was started in the time of the Prophet Ezekiel[as].

Consequently, 48 years after the devastating attack of Nebuchadnezzar on Jerusalem when he completely destroyed the city of Jerusalem and Palestine, the Jews regained control of the Promised Land through the help of the people of Persia. This occurred in 539 B.C. when, with the help of King Cyrus, the Jews were taken back to Jerusalem and settled there. After this, they were able to live there for several hundred years. And, as recorded in some other books in the form of a prophecy, both these towns would again become prostitutes and would again adopt evil ways and would again receive punishment.

So, exactly in accordance with the sketch drawn out in the Holy Quran, that it was decreed, that twice you would create disorder in the earth, and twice you would become rebellious -it happened exactly like this for first they created disorder in the land, then other nations came and they rebelled against them and were crushed after their rebellion. So the second time when the phase of punishment began, the Roman King Pompeii captured Judah in 63 B.C. and started the campaign of their destruction from there. But despite this, this phase of destruction did not end till 132 A.D.

Hadrian was a great Roman Emperor. He occupies an extraordinary position amongst the history of the Roman Emperors. He is the same King whose empire extended from England to Africa and reached to the banks of the Euphrates River. He happened to visit England also. Here in the north there is a wall much like the wall of China. Some say that this wall is 80 miles long, while others say that it is only about 74 to 76 miles in length. This is a great wall which still stands today. It was erected by this same King Hadrian.

When the Jews again rebelled there, Hadrian recalled that general of his who was ruling over England at that time and sent him to crush this rebellion. He was a most capable general. This incident took place around 132 A.D. The historians do not fully agree on this though, and some say it took from 132 A.D. to 133/134 A.D. by which time the task was completed. He taught them such a terrible lesson for having rebelled that historians say that over 500,000 Jews were put to the sword. First I thought this could be an exaggeration, but then when I read the Holy Quran's prophecy that He would bless the Jews with many children and would bless their numbers greatly, then I understood that this was precisely a true historical fact. Truly, in those days over 500,000 Jews were killed there and the Temple was destroyed. Thus, twice the Temple of Solomon was built and twice it was destroyed. After all this had happened, God Almighty says:

عَسَىٰ رَبُّكُمْ أَنْ يَرْحَمَكُمْ وَإِنْ عُدْتُمْ عُدْنَا وَجَعَلْنَا جَهَنَّمَ لِلْكَافِرِينَ حَصِيرًا

That even now it could happen that God may turn to you with mercy. That is to say upon the fulfilment of these two prophecies and these two destructions. Even then it could happen that God may turn to you with mercy.

The question of when and how this is to happen is addressed in a verse towards the end of this Chapter (Sura). This verse pertains to the period of the Holy Prophet Muhammad[sas] and is surrounded by discussions of these very topics of the Holy Prophet's life. It means that this event of mercy was to occur in the latter part of the era of Hazrat Muhammad[sas] and in the time of his followers so it is said:

وَقُلْنَا مِنْ بَعْدِهِ لِبَنِي إِسْرَآئِيلَ اسْكُنُوا الْأَرْضَ فَإِذَا جَاءَ وَعْدُ الْآخِرَةِ جِئْنَا بِكُمْ لَفِيفًا

(Verse 105)
that when the time for the fulfilment of that last promise arrives, when you would be gathered together from all parts of the world and brought to this land - then the decree of God would so arrange that all of you would be gathered together. Indeed this has occurred for the very first time. Previously, the Jews repeatedly settled in Palestine,

Sixteenth Friday Sermon Mar 08, 1991

but never once did it happen that the Jews of the *Diaspora* or the area where the Jews had scattered were all again gathered together. This is the first such instance in the history of the world. Observe how clearly and with what amazing brilliance the prophecies of the Holy Quran have been fulfilled and will continue to be fulfilled in the future.

Thus, I wish to inform the Jews that God's decree, in keeping with these prophecies, has decided to have mercy on you and as a result of the extreme injustices perpetrated upon you by Nazi Germany, has decided that enough is enough. Maybe now you have learnt your lessons. You have been forgiven and again been granted domination in the land. The Muslim powers will not have the strength to break this dominance for we learn from the sayings of the Holy Prophet of Islam that a great mischief will rise up from that narrow sea between Iraq and Syria which will drink up all its water. This sea which is mentioned in the sayings of the Holy Prophet is in Israel and is called the Sea of *Tabriyya*. It is a small sea through which the Jordan River passes. There a great army shall be gathered together there and will emerge from there and a very great power it will be which shall issue forth from there for the attack. Thus if Israel fails to learn from the lessons of the last two destructions then a disturbance will rise from Israel to destroy the peace and security of the entire world. This has been destined and cannot be changed by any worldly power.

Then, God Almighty, says we shall destroy it and shall so arrange that they and all the powers that have joined them and are helping them are blown to pieces and made a sign of warning for posterity. The last message which is in this saying of the Prophet Muhammad[sas] is that God would cause to grow such carbuncles (boils) in their throats and will inflict such diseases on them that they would be killed on a wide scale and in a most horrible manner.

PROPHECY ABOUT THE AFFLICTION OF "AIDS"

This is that same disease, resembling AIDS which I have already mentioned. This estimation of mine is based on the following prophetic sayings of Hazrat Muhammad[sas]. It is related that one day the Holy Prophet Muhammad[sas] made mention of the **Dajjal** (anti-Christ) and while mentioning in great detail the circumstances surrounding him, he said: (I shall present only a few sentences from the detailed account)

$$اِنَّهٗ خَارِجٌ خَلَّةً بَيْنَ الشَّامِ وَالْعِرَاقِ$$

"the Anti-Christ shall appear from the area between Syria and Iraq. Right, left, or which ever direction he shall turn to, he shall go on causing death and destruction. It shall move with the swiftness of a rain-laden cloud which is being propelled from the rear by fast winds" (just like the jets of today)
He went on to say that:
"in such circumstances, Allah, the Exalted shall raise the Promised Messiah[as] and shall inform him through revelation:

$$اِنِّىْ قَدْ اَخْرَجْتُ عِبَادًا لِّىْ لَا يَدَانِ لِاَحَدٍ بِقِتَالِهِمْ$$

that I have now created such people against whom no one shall have the power to wage war." Then he further said:
"Allah shall raise Gog and Magog and they shall leave behind every height leaping over them rapidly." He said "the first parts of this locust-like army of Gog and Magog, shall pass by

$$فَيَمُرُّ اَوَائِلُهُمْ عَلٰى بُحَيْرَةِ طَبَرِيَّةَ فَيَشْرَبُوْنَ مَا فِيْهَا$$

the Sea of *Tabriyya* drinking up all its water so that when the latter parts of the army arrives, it shall say that once there used to be water here, where has it gone? In these heart-rending times, the Prophet of Allah i.e. the Promised Messiah[as], and his companions, will pray to Allah and Allah shall accept their prayers.

$$فَيُرْسِلُ اللّٰهُ تَعَالٰى عَلَيْهِمُ النَّغَفَ فِىْ رِقَابِهِمْ$$

And He will cause to develop such germs in the necks of Gog and Magog which would result rapidly in their death on a large scale." (*Sahih Muslim, Kitabul Fitan, Chapter: Zikr-ud-Dajjal*).

Sixteenth Friday Sermon Mar 08, 1991

Then in another Hadith, His Holiness, Hazrat Muhammad[sas] says:

لَمْ تَظْهَرِ الْفَاحِشَةُ فِى قَوْمٍ قَطُّ حَتَّى يُعْلِنُوْا بِهَا اِلَّا فَشَافِيْهِمُ الطَّاعُوْنُ وَالْاَوْجَاعُ الَّتِىْ لَمْ تَكُنْ مَضَتْ فِىْ اَسْلَافِهِمُ الَّذِيْنَ مَضَوْا

(Sanan Ibne Maaja, Kitabul Fitan, Chapter Al Aqubat)
"if a nation becomes afflicted with sexual shamelessness and makes open display of it, then a kind of plague-like affliction spreads amongst it which has never spread in any earlier generations." (Sunan Ibn Maaja Kitaab al fatan Chapter al-aqobaat)

This is that saying of the Holy Prophet (Hadith) which specifically points to the Aids disease in very clear terms. And this Aids is what has been referred to as a plague-like disease and about which it has been said that it has never spread in the world before.

It is interesting to note that the Holy Founder of the Ahmadiyya Muslim Community, **Hazrat Mirza Ghulam Ahmad**, too was given the news of the spreading of a new kind of plague. This is a revelation of **March 13, 1907**. He says:

"A type of plague will spread in Europe and other Christian countries which would be very severe" (Tazkirah p. 705).

Thus this is a catastrophe which is destined for them either today or in the future. If these nations do not reform themselves then the most dreadful calamities shall befall them as a consequence of their misdeeds. It is important at this point to clarify that all ominous prophecies, i.e. prophecies predicting evil consequences are always conditional even if the conditions are not spelled out in clear words. A clear example of this is found in the incident of the Prophet Hazrat Jonah[as] - that a categorical prophecy was averted through the repentance of his nation.

COMPASSION FOR THE JEWS, IF THEY CHANGE THEIR WAYS
Thus, although the issue of Israel's destruction or continued existence shall be decided in the heavens, yet if the moderate and

peace loving elements among the Jews succeed in prevailing upon the extremist Zionist elements by clipping the claws of their vengeance-seeking nature, and if as a nation they take this revolutionary decision that be it Muslim or Christian, they would deal with every nation on the basis of justice or better still, on the basis of Beneficence, then I assure them that as promised in the Holy Quran, Allah shall deal with them on the basis of Beneficence. And the Muslims, too, will treat them in a just and beneficent manner. They should remember that the nature, disposition or temperament of the Mullah, is not that of Islam. The nature which the Quran and the excellent example of the Holy Prophet has bestowed upon a Muslim does not conceive of vengeance but rather leans towards forgiveness and mercy.

ADVICE TO WESTERN CHRISTIAN NATIONS

I also sincerely wish to make the Western Christian nations understand that they should not view with contempt, the admonitory punishments in store for them as mentioned in the Quran and the Sayings of the Holy Prophet of Islam.

Divine epistles cannot ever be averted by human ingeniousness. If they can ever be averted then it is only through true repentance and seeking forgiveness of God and affecting a blessed change. If this is done then the forgiveness of Allah, which overcomes His wrath, is capable of averting or putting off forever any decreed punishment.

Thus it is important that you effect a fundamental change in your political, economic, moral and social mode of thinking. In every field, without exception, give preference to the demands of justice over the demands of national or racial interests. Treat the poor and weak nations with beneficence. If you cannot accept Islam, then at least return to the holy and pure teachings of the Torah and the Gospels and purify your civilization of the ever-increasing shamelessness.

If you accomplish this, then your diabolic destiny will be transformed into a fortune of bliss. And then uniting with the world of Islam and with other nations, you will be granted the opportunity to fashion and carve a New World Order and man's dream of global peace shall be realized. If you do not do this, then along with the old order which is sure to be destroyed, many great nations, too, shall be humbled. And their high rank and dignity will be reduced to dust.

MY HUMBLE SUPPLICATIONS

But my only wish and only prayer is that the New World Order should be constructed from the clay and water of the changed and reformed nations rather than upon the ruins of destroyed nations. As far as we are concerned, we have already been told by our God that we are frail. Over 1400 years ago, Muhammad[sas], the Messenger of Allah, had forewarned that God was going to establish such great nations that none would have the strength to oppose them. So you should never even think of opposing them with worldly weapons. This is a saying (Hadith) in a Chapter of "Muslim's book Kitab ul Fitan". Anyone can read it from there. The Prophet said: "Whatever will happen will happen through prayers." God's decree shall destroy these powerful nations when they decide to perpetrate iniquity in the world. If God has kept the world unarmed and helpless and granted these powerful nations unlimited powers to commit evil and vice then the ultimate responsibility of protecting His weak servants also rests on Him.

TERRORISM SHOULD BE ERASED FROM THE DICTIONARY OF MUSLIMS

Thus there is just one way to obtain this heavenly sustenance and that is, that a bond be established with God and that we reform our own selves as far as possible. No evil should ever be perpetrated in the name of Islam in the future. The concept of terrorism should be removed from the vocabulary of the Muslims. To do mischief and to cause pain to others just to keep some issues alive is a despicable act. These things have nothing to do with Islam. Become peaceful yourselves. Rectify your own relations first. Build up your relationships with the other nations and wait with patience. Then you will see how the plans of God will frustrate the evil designs of every other nation.

During the second part of his sermon, Hazrat Khalifa tul Massih IV said:

Today, I have taken longer to conclude this subject which I was constrained to discuss. However my heart desires quickly to revert to the subject I was discussing earlier - i.e. What is worship - what pleasures can be derived from worship - how to enrich that pleasure and what the opening chapter of the Holy Quran (Al Fatiha) teaches us regarding this subject.

That is why, I had decided somehow to free myself from this subject today so that I could return to the eternal subject of the "Greater Jihad" of worship.

In the next sermon, Insha Allah (God willing), I will revert to the subject of "Worship" again.

In the name of Allah, the Gracious, the Merciful

SEVENTEENTH FRIDAY SERMON (EXTRACT)

March 15, 1991

A SPECIAL APPEAL FOR PRAYERS FOR PEACE IN THE MUSLIM WORLD

After reciting the Opening Chapter of the Holy Quran, Al-Fatiha, Hazoor said:

During the current month of *Ramazan*, special prayers need to be offered for the welfare of Muslims all over the world. In this context, I had discussed in detail a number of issues in my earlier sermons. But I still foresee a multitude of problems endangering mankind which I could not touch upon, except in passing, because of the scarcity of time. I have already concluded this subject and have no desire of discussing it further except to caution you that in the next few months, certain dreadful decisions may be taken which may not only be detrimental to the Muslim world but may also engulf the entire world in a century-long era of misery and misfortune. It is also possible that as a result of certain other decisions, man, and indeed the Muslims may have the opportunity to withstand the final onslaught of all the satanic forces. If the Muslims withstand and endure this attack, the whole world, as a result would be shielded. The Ahmadiyya Muslim Jamaat must shoulder the greatest responsibility for the defence of the Muslims. I base this conviction on a particular saying of the Holy Prophet Muhammad[sas] in which he predicted that in the later part of the life of this world when the world would be engulfed in calamities and misfortunes, it would be the exclusive prayers of the Promised Messiah[as] that would rescue the Muslims and the world from this ordeal. Under the circumstances, the month of *Ramazan* could not have come at a better time when all such calamities have become quite evident. There are other covert plans still unveiled which may prove to be even more disastrous than the overt ones.

Seventeenth Friday Sermon (extract) Mar 15, 1991

But we can speculate, that following this catastrophe in the Gulf there may be other calamities in the offing. As we enter into the *blessed month of Ramazan*, when we would have special opportunity for prayer, I would urge you to dedicate the prayers in this month for the protection and defence of the Muslims, the defence of Islam and indeed for the defence of humanity. We should thus pray:

"O Allah, despite our utmost efforts we cannot match the enormous forces which You have created as foretold by the most truthful Holy Prophet Hazrat Muhammad[sas], fourteen hundred years ago. While we are weak, empty-handed, and powerless, our adversaries have been granted extra-ordinary material grandeur rendering us totally impotent before them. So we turn to Thee, seek Thy shelter and beseech Thee to accept the prayers of the Promised Messiah[as] and his humble followers by fulfilling the second part of the prophecy. The mighty worldly powers are possessed with such enormous wealth that comparatively, we are not even worth a penny. Because of their huge accumulation of wealth, they continue to barter the faith of humanity. Save humanity from the evil consequences of their material wealth. They have stockpiled mounts of destructive and lethal weapons. Their own scientists admit that the atomic arsenal of the U.S.A. and Soviet Union are so dreadful in their power of destruction that they are capable of destroying this world, scores of times. They are not only capable of destroying all human life but can also extinguish all traces of life on this planet."

Visualising this situation, we should pray, imploring God that:-

"Whereas You, in Your own wisdom has granted such enormous wealth to these wretched nations that even the combined wealth of all Muslim nations is of little significance not to mention the meagre resources of the Ahmadiyya Muslim Community. Their weapons possess such destructive capacity that even a fraction would wipe out the traces of nations from the surface of the earth. O Allah, to counter such powers You have raised this humble Community which possess nothing. But at the same time You gave us the glad tiding that You would listen to our prayers, bless our supplications and eventually tear to pieces these powerful nations."

The Holy Prophet Muhammad[sas] has illustrated this phenomenon by giving the similitude of salt, capable of melting a block of ice. Thus all deceptive and satanic powers, antagonistic to mankind and inimical to truth would melt away as if they never existed.

Thus O' Ahmadis - you possess the power of prayer. Recognise its magnificence which lies in your humility. Never forget the basic difference between worldly powers and spiritual powers. Worldly powers are based upon pomp and pride, while spiritual powers have the hallmark of absolute humility. Thus the amplitude of your prayer is dependent upon your mode of humility before God. The greater the recognition of your helplessness in prayers, the greater will be the strength in your supplications. Your prayers will be granted effectiveness as a result of your helplessness. Therefore fully comprehend the essence of this subject and derive the optimum benefit from this month of Ramazan. Prostrate before God in meekness, humility and desperation pleading that O' Allah, frustrate the evil designs of these great powers. Preserve whatever virtue is left in these nations. **Ahmadis are not allowed to hate any particular group of people or a nation. We have not been fermented with the enzyme of hatred. Therefore we cannot, like certain misguided nations, indulge in prayers against the Western powers or harbour any intrinsic hatred against anyone.** We simply detest evil. So, direct the focus of your prayers against vice. Do not pray for the destruction or annihilation of any nation out of prejudice and partiality. Instead pray to Allah saying:

"O' Allah eradicate the evil that is associated with some of your humble servants in the East. Also frustrate the evil designs of the powerful Western nations who dominate the world."

The evil associated with a powerful nation is always more dangerous since it has the potential of a rapid spread. The evil of the dominant power is more dangerous as it possesses the ability to wipe

Seventeenth Friday Sermon (extract) Mar 15, 1991

out values of virtue from the world.

We do not claim that the Third world nations are free of vice, neither do we advocate that the East is honourable while labelling the West as wholly corrupt. What we do say is that the inherent potential of the West in propagating vice is such, that the like of it has never been given to any nation in the past. In fact, the development of such a frightful situation was predicted by the Holy Prophet Muhammad[sas] when he said that towards the end of days, the emergence of the *Dajjal* (anti Christ) would cause so much evil and iniquity in the world that it would have no parallel in history. Since the creation of the world all Prophets were warned of the evil consequences at the appearance of the *Dajjal* and the subsequent emergence of a powerful nation which would spread iniquity. Therefore, your prayers must not be motivated by any latent prejudice, national or ethnic divisions, but should rather be sincerely prompted by the message contained in these prophecies. You should thus absorb yourself in fervent prayers by zeroing on the real target. If you do not do that, then it is possible that your prayers have been contaminated by the vice of your ill intentions, national prejudices or ethnic diversities. There are many evils of this type which secretly cling to our prayers thus poisoning them and rendering then ineffectual and unworthy of acceptance by Allah.

Thus, the need to deliberate on this subject in such depth arose out of my desire to explain to you that the acceptance of prayers are not solely dependent upon our weeping and wailing. For a prayer to be accepted by Allah, one would require a special level of purity of heart coupled with humility. Inculcate that pattern of prayers as exemplified and taught by the Holy Prophet Muhammad[sas].

Keep your conscience clear of your own vice and the multitude of other vices and then pray exclusively for the sake of Allah while shunning all types of national and racial prejudices. If you pray in this way, then I am certain that by the Grace of Allah your prayers are bound to be accepted. As we enter this unique historical juncture, the final equilibrium will eventually be in favour of Islam. *Insha Allah* We should pray and strive that we behold this inevitable triumph of Islam with our own eyes.

Amen.

A SAMPLING OF PUBLIC OPINION: COMMENTS ON THE GULF CRISIS
AND THE NEW WORLD ORDER OF PRESIDENT GEORGE BUSH

The intellectuals of the world collaborate and support the views expressed by His Holiness, Hazrat Mirza Tahir Ahmad.

His Holiness said:
"The stand taken by The Ahmadiyya Muslim Community in the present world situation has found favour and many voices of approval are heard rising from many countries. Just two days ago, an Ahmadi from a Western country informed me that a well known and influential commentator had expressed identical views on the present crisis as though he had read my sermons. He enquired if I, or some other Ahmadi was in communication with him. This was not an isolated letter. I have received similar letters from many places. Apparently it is a tribute to my sermons but I am not so naive as to accept this as personal praise. *Praise is not due to me but to Islam.* All praise belongs to God and to God's revealed religion and this is the proof of the truth and excellence of that teaching.

However, that was a clear indication that people are beginning to recognise truth; this gave me satisfaction in the sense that my confidence was strengthened. That made me believe that whatever comments I have made on this situation are in accordance with the teachings of Allah. Otherwise such comments would not have found support both verbally and in writing in various countries."
(January 25, 1991)

"Regardless of what the contemporary observers might say, to bamboozle the collaborating Muslim countries, the researchers and historians of tomorrow in the Western world, would say the same thing that I am saying today: that some Muslim countries joined hands with anti-Islamic powers, thus committing high treason against the Islamic interests, and tried to annihilate an up-and-coming Islamic country. Up to this moment we can only say that the future historian would record the fact that these Muslim countries fully collaborated

with the enemies of Islam to destroy a great Islamic nation, and that they did not display an iota of justice, compassion or even national pride."
(February 01, 1991)

"Do you think that the sounds emanating from the minarets of Mecca and Medina are those of Allah and His Prophet? The truth is that these minarets simply project the loudspeakers which are connected to the microphones located in Washington where Israel is the speaker using these microphones. This is such an obvious fact that no intricate debate is needed for it. Anyone who is even mildly aware of the contemporary situation knows this fact very well that Saudi Arabia is completely in the clutches of the U.S. and that the U.S. has completely capitulated to Israeli ascendancy and has practically incorporated Israeli primacy as part of its policy."
(February 01, 1991)

"The U.S. is paid to destroy and then paid to repair and reconstruct. Thus the U.S. plays two roles, the demolisher as well as the restorer. Paid for destruction - and paid much more for restoration."
(February 22, 1991)

"God alone knows how Iraq was lured into occupying Kuwait and then the whole sinister development ensued. But such incidents are seldom accidental. There are some underlying motives and some subterranean intrigues at work."
(August 17, 1990)

An Ahmadi Muslim telephoned and told me that he was being asked to give an interview on a T.V. channel or the BBC. He asked me what our stand was. He wanted my advice as to what comments or views he was to give on the present situation. I told him to say that his view is exactly the same as that expressed by **Tony Benn the British M.P.** I further advised him to give the following answer.**'If a fair-minded person is raising the true voice of my heart then what need have I to raise that voice myself, because if I raise it**

you will denounce me as a traitor, but if Tony Benn raises that voice, you will not dare to call him a traitor'
(January 25, 1991)

References:

David Omissi - Author of Book "Air power and Colonial Control" U.K. writes:

"The present Gulf war is not the first time Iraq has been visited by British bombers. When the RAF waged war in Iraq in the 1920s, it was not to liberate occupied territory: instead, British bombers were used against dissident tribemen. The work was not popular with RAF crews, and one senior officer (Air Commodore Lionel Evelyn Oswald Charlton) resigned his post rather than bomb villages in **Kurdistan**.........late in 1920, Charlton was appointed Senior Air Officer - in effect second-in-command of British forces in Iraq. He was shocked by what he found there.

The British military connection with Iraq had begun when it was taken from the Turks, in the First World War. In 1921 the British set up an Arab client state under King Faisal, son of Sheriff of Mecca. The New regime was not popular, especially among the Kurdish minority of the north-east so RAF bombers were brought in to force their integration into the mainly Arab state.

Winston Churchill, then Secretary of State for War and Air, urged the RAF to use mustard gas, which had already been employed by the army 'with excellent moral effect' against Shia rebels in 1920." For technical reasons gas bombs could not be used - but the campaign was brutal enough. Many villages were bombed simply because the tribesmen had not paid their taxes........

For a few months Charlton kept his doubts to himself and endured the anguish of carrying out a policy he believed to be barbaric. But in the autumn of 1923 he resigned, no longer able to 'maintain the policy of intimidation by bomb'.........

Other Air Force officers were unhappy that their bombers were being used to prop up an unpopular puppet king. 'Nobody really enjoyed bombing the Kurds,' one pilot later recalled, 'for their crime was merely to be rebels against the Iraqi government. Yet there were some who relished the thought of bringing Kurdish rebels to heel...'
(David Omissi is a research Fellow at Nuffield College, Oxford. His book 'Air power and colonial control' was recently published by Manchester University Press.)

Links Canada February 1991 (Winnipeg Coordinating Committee for Disarmament) states:

"Most of the Persian Gulf region was under the domination of the Turkish Ottoman Empire until the arrival of British naval power in the early part of the 19th century. The British conquered and took control over the coastal areas around the Gulf and some of the interior. When oil was discovered in Iran, the British took control over that valuable resource, too.

During the First World War, the British promised the Arabs independence (Hussein-McMahon treaty) in return for their support against the Ottoman Turks. But the British also signed the Sykes Picot Treaty with the French, which divided up the region among the two empires based on where each had built railway lines. As a token, the British gave Jordan and Iraq to two branches of the Hashemite family which had ruled Mecca, the holy city of Islam on the Red Sea.

Saudi Arabia

During this period, Sheikh Ibn Saud, the leader of Saudi family, conquered most of Arabian Peninsula with brutal military force (1902-1935), killing many men and confiscating flocks of sheep and goats which were the livelihood of the people of the region; the Saudis took no male prisoners. Ibn Saud married hundreds of women as a way of cementing his diverse kingdom. Today, Saudi Arabia is ruled by a royal family made up of a few thousand of Ibn Saud's descendants and relatives.

The Saudi conquest, which is still fresh in the memories of those who were conquered, engendered hatred for the Saudi family. The people also feel religious dissatisfaction with their rulers, since the

Saudis are not the traditional rulers of Mecca; the Saudis drove out the Hashemites. The Saudi family is further disliked because it has not used the country's oil wealth to benefit the people, who have no say in how the country is ruled. Dissent is ruthlessly and brutally suppressed.

In 1953, Ibn Saud died. His son and heir, Saud, tried to break the agreement with Aramco in favour of Greek shipping magnate Aristotle Onassis. Under strong American pressure, Saud was prevented from kicking out Aramco. In 1964 he was deposed in favour of his brother Faisal.

After the Second World War, Iran had a democratic government led by Mohammed Mossadegh, who nationalized Iranian oil production. A CIA organized coup in 1953 overthrew Mossadegh and installed the Shah in power.

U.S Pledges to Fight for Oil

U.S President Jimmy Carter's doctrine (1980) was the pledge to use U.S troops to keep the Saudi royal family in power and to intervene in the Gulf to protect what it considered "our" oil. There was no threat to Saudi Arabia from either Iraq or Iran at the time, so it was clear that the U.S government was pledged to protect the Saudi royal family from overthrow by its own citizens. Carter also pledged to intervene if U.S. oil companies were threatened with loss of control over oil production in the Gulf.

Iran-Iraq War

In the eight-year Iran-Iraq war (September, 1980 to August, 1988), Iraq was supported by the Gulf states and the U.S., who saw Iraq as opposing the spread of militant Islamic movements into the Arab countries. Once the war was fought to a stalemate, after more than a million people were killed, its former sponsors perceived Iraq as a treat......

Kuwait and the smaller Gulf states overproduced their alloted OPEC quotas to keep the oli price down and maintain pressure on Iraq. Kuwait is also alleged to have pumped oil from a large oil field which straddles the Kuwait-Iraq border."

(This article was sponsored by the Winnipeg (Canada) Co-ordinating Committee for Disarmament)

The Washington Post, June 23, 1991

"Meanwhile Bandar, a nephew of Saudi King Fahd and perhaps the most powerful Arab representative in Washington was also seeking support for the war from Jewish organizations and intellectuals. From August to the war's end, Bandar held meetings with representatives from the Simon Wiesenthal Centre in Los Angeles, the American Jewish congress and AIPAC. He consulted regularly with Jewish Democrats on Capitol Hill, including Solarz and Levine.

In January, he invited three well-known Jewish policy experts- Martin Indyk from the AIPAC-linked Washington Institute for Near East Policy, Michael Mandelbanm from the council on Foreign Relations, and Eliot Cohen from the Johns Hopkins School of Advanced International Studies- to inspect the Saudi military.

"It was a remarkable departure" Cohen said. "The Saudis had never looked favourably on Jewish intellectuals".

The Saudis were immediately interested in Jewish backing for war against Iraq, but they also wanted to neutralize opposition to future arms sales from the United States."

"What we are told by Prince Bandar was that as long as Saddam Hussein effected hegemony over the Mideast, no movement on the Palestinian issue was possible" said American Jewish Congress Director Henry Siegman. **Siegman said Bandar implied that if Saddam Hussein is no longer, most countries would then approach the issue on pragmatic terms."**

(Washington correspondent John Judis)

The Record: Sunday Feb 3, 1991
"ILLUSION OF DIPLOMACY MARCHED U.S. TO WAR. BUSH NEVER WANTED REAL NEGOTIATION."
By John E. Mack
and Jeffrey Z. Rubin
(Mack is professor of psychiatry at Harvard Medical School and Director of the Center for Psychological Studies in the Nuclear Age. Rubin is professor of psychology at Tufts University and executive director at Harvard Law School. They wrote this article for the Los Angeles Times:

"The actions and decisions taken by the United States after aug 2, while having the appearance of diplomacy for peace, were in fact the result of deliberate choices toward a very different end. It was three choices - the president's assertions notwithstanding - that moved us inexorably along the path of war.

We demonized and dehumanized our adversary.
We indulged in personal name calling, false analogies in past wars and demonic leaders of earlier times, then deliberately provoked Hussein through threats and insults, while lessening his incentive to respond to the pleas that were directed to him by so many individuals and nations.

We denied our own contribution to the problem.
By placing the blame entirely on the shoulders of our adversary, failing to acknowledge our own contribution - bolstering Iraq's war machine and **giving permissive signals before the conflict began,** for example - we put him on the defensive and further limited his ability to respond constructively.

We relied exclusively on the threatened use of force. ....
In an interview with ABC's Peter Jennings in November, Hussein asked that a dialogue be conducted between himself and President Bush "in which eyes could meet." What he got was not dialogue but preconditions for capitulation.

Having taken the position that only military power could "solve" the gulf crisis, we then shrouded our belligerent intent in the guise of collective will. Using the newly invigorated United Nations as a cover, we represented our determination to use force as being the result of a genuinely joint decision by the international community, rather than what it largely was: an American-engineered unilateral initiative.

We disregarded the other side's stated grievances and claims, while demanding unconditional surrender. Our original position was doomed to failure if what we sought was peace..........
We took no account of cultural differences. ....

We offered a response that was dispropriate to the problem.
We assembled an overwhelming destructive force in the gulf without adequately anticipating the circumstances of using it as threatened. We exaggerated the original problem by arguing **that international boundaries are inviolate - "sanctified"** declared Rep. Stephen Solarz, D- N.Y., one of the principal proponents of the war policy..... In fact Kuwait's boundaries were arbitrarily drawn in 1961 by the withdrawing of British colonialists.

We overcommitted ourselves to a course of action. By developing a U.N. deadline, to which we adhered with rigid insistence we lost room to manoeuvre and to explore peaceful methods of resolving the conflict.......

We used public presentation of conditions in order to intimidate the other side. Our public assertions - "no negotiations, no face saving, no linkage" - had the effect of hardening Hussein's response......

We paid lip service to efforts at diplomatic solutions. We indulged in a hypocritical pretence by announcing our "willingness to go the extra mile for peace" then refusing Hussein's demand that a meeting take place closer to Jan 15 than we liked. We were willing to talk only on our terms, which we knew Hussein would have to reject.

We derogated the other sides's conciliatory gesture........For example, Hussein's initiative in **releasing the hostages** was viewed not as a show of good faith, or a desire to move toward settlement, but as a cunning attempt to manipulate world opinion.

We insisted that the conflict be regarded as zero-sum.......
Consistently overlooked or dismissed were all alternative approaches that could turn a win-lose exchange into one with opportunities for both sides to do well. For example, we might have expressed a willingness to address the **Palestinian-Israeli conflict** while officially disclaiming linkage to the gulf crisis.

In conclusion, the Bush administration's approach to dealing with unjustifiable Iraqi invasion of Kuwait violated the principles of negotiating theory, political psychology, and the appropriate conduct of international relationships. **If our purpose was to destroy Iraq as a military and political power in the Middle East, which now seem apparent, the American people were never informed of such an intention."**

The Globe and Mail - Canada January 9, 1991

"Iraq is being portrayed as a monster compared to Hitler Germany, but only yesterday the United States was actively supporting Iraq in its war against Iran - a war Iraq also began. Washington's intentions in the Gulf are as great a source of apprehension among countries in the region as is Iraqi aggression.

The United States began deploying its forces against Iraq ostensibly to defend Saudi Arabia. But it has expanded its objectives to include liberation of Kuwait, dismantling Iraq's army and destroying its presumed nuclear potential, toppling Saddam Hussein and "kicking his ass."

Washington has patched together an international coalition by inducements, threats and bargains. Egyptian loans have been written off; Syria has been granted diplomatic respectability; China has received promises of renewed trade; Saudi king has been spooked into accepting U.S. troops; Soviet Union is offered aid.

The Americans have assumed the role of international judge and jury. It is an ominous situation."

(Mohammad Qadeer is director of the School of Urban and Regional Planning at Queen's University.)

Sunday Times: 9 Feb 1992

"Third World countries such as Libya and Pakistan could become targets of American strategic nuclear missiles under secret plans being drawn up by the Pentagon. The proposals are part of an American process to select **new targets** for its vast arsenal of nuclear weapons after the collapse of the soviet Union.

A report recommending the new target selection has been handed to General Lee Butler, head of the strategic air command, who will pass on his recommendations to President Bush"

The Toronto Star: January 12, 1992
Gulf War: One year later

Today, Bush has just completed the most humiliating trip abroad by a U.S leader in memory. Into the begging bowl that Bush took with him to Tokyo, the Japanese dropped only the odd coin, like a vague promise to buy more auto parts. Far more embarrassing, Bush also brought back the nightmarish image of himself, ashen-faced and vomiting on the floor at a state dinner, and of Japanese Prime Minister Kiichi Miyazawa's lecturing him that America's real problems are AIDS, homelessness, broken-down schools and incompetent corporations.

In the Middle East itself, the war today seem to have been like a real desert storm, creating havoc while it lasted but afterward leaving the sands humped and hollowed just as they were before. Saddam Hussein is still there in Baghdad. The Kurds, many of them, are still shivering in the mountains. The Middle East peace talks have slowed to a crawl and may soon halt entirely as Washington loses the will and interest to expand energy on anything except electing the next president. ....

It was a war about oil. We've got the oil again. the rest of the Middle East's problems are its own."

Why were Iraq's agricultural and water-treatment facilities destroyed, its electrical system crippled and air attacks carried out against clearly marked civilian vehicles on the highways and Bedouin tents in the desert? In a little noticed but exhaustively researched report titled *Needless Deaths in the Gulf War*, Middle East Watch calls a public investigation into all these points.

How much pro-war feeling in the United States (and Canada) was whipped up by a relentless public relations campaign, led by Hill and Knowlton, the American PR giant that was hired by *Citizens for a free Kuwait*? That group was financed by the Kuwaiti government.

Just one example surfaced last week. Harper's magazine publisher John MacArthur revealed in a New York Times article that **Nayirah**, the 15 year old Kuwaiti girl who had described to a stunned congressional hearing how occupying Iraqi troops has ripped Kuwaiti babies from incubators, is the **daughter of Saud Nasir Sabah, Kuwait's Ambassador to the United States and Canada.**

Her horrifying testimony had been critical in swaying public opinion in the days leading up to the war. Bush described it from the oval office. Seven senators cited her account in speeches before they voted to support the war in the Senate vote........

Imagine what would have happened if it had come out in November or December, before congress voted, that Nayirah was (the ambassador's) daughter and that Hill and Knowlton was paying for witnesses.

MacArthur believes that this story is the tip of the iceberg. He is writing a book, **Censorship and Propaganda in the Gulf War**, for release later this year.

"President Bush said that the people of Iraq weren't our enemy, but many of them died... even though it was a war in which Americans never really say anybody die... Saddam Hussein is still there entrenched in power, the Kuwaiti government is still at the top of the list of Amnesty International violators of human rights and President Hafez Assad and Syria are armed to the teeth. "It is difficult to see any new world order."

(By Richard Gwyn)

Toronto Globe and Mail: Feb 2, 1991

"Everyone involved in the Persian Gulf war is seeking divine help these days. Are they all talking to the same God?

King Fahd of Saudi Arabia, referred to by Saudis as "the guardian of the Holy places" in Mecca and Medina, said in December that he considered the foreign military forces opposing Saddam Hussein as "a blessing from God"

Just after hostilities started, Saudi Arabia's religious leaders issued a *fatwa* or religious decrees, describing the Iraqi leader as "the enemy of God" against whom a Jihad (holy war) was obligatory. The decree went so far as to authorize and bless any non-muslim party assisting in the cause."

(By Jock Ferguson)

Sampling of public opinion on the Gulf War

The New York Times: April 21, 1991

"Third, the Middle East and Persian Gulf region in now clearly an American sphere of preponderance. Pro-American Arab regimes feel more secure; so does Israel. U.S access to oil is now not in jeopardy."

Canadian Peace Alliance Toronto ONT.

"Oil or international law: What are we fighting for?

At present, our country, like its Western allies, can and should be accused of protecting its economic interest in oil-rich Kuwait, while ignoring the plight of other countries suffering from similar aggression"

The Guardian: March 2, 1991
"In the land of the deaf

But there is one lie the **lynch pin lie**- that has to be pulled out. This is the claim that the war in the Gulf had to be fought for the same reason as the war against Hitler and fascism in 1939. Nowhere in the world is there a poet who would back this comparison- for nobody in their heart of hearts actually believes it.

The comparison was made by the same politicians who three years before were protecting their "Hitler" and selling him arms. When Saddam Hussein gassed Kurdish villagers, George Bush opposed in congress the cutting off of aid to Iraq. What changed to make the same politician suddenly full of historical wisdom and righteous indignation? Instead of being fooled themselves, they now had to fool the public because their plan demanded hate. And to whip up hate quickly, you usually have to lie.

Picture editors of American journals trimmed Saddam Hussein's moustache so that it resembled Hitler's. And for this trompe L'oeil tens of thousands of civilian lives in Baghdad have been either physically or emotionally maimed, transformed into what spokesmen called **"collateral damage"**.

It would have been possible to liberate Kuwait and contain Saddam Hussein in many other ways. Every government in the world not on the U.S. payroll knows this. Germany in the thirties was a highly industrialised world power. Iraq was a small third world country, colonised well into this century, and armed only with weapons sold to it by Europe.

Nevertheless George Bush decided as long ago as last autumn, that the operations against Saddam Hussein was to be pursued in his way, so that the Middle East and its oil should be under U.S. control in the third millennium. This way involved colossal bribes, high speed, high technology and the high moral authority which accompanies **systematic deafness**. Deafness is both an aggressive and defensive weapon when imposing an order on distant populations who do not want to accept that order.

The onset of Washington's deafness concerning the Middle East began, however, decades before. **American power was deaf towards all the pleas of the Palestinian nation who had lost their land.** Had the Palestinians been heard Saddam Hussein could never have later claimed with any credibility the mantle of Arab honour. American power was deaf to the Iranian people, oppressed by the Shah, a US puppet, and by his secret police and by his wealth of trash. Had the Iranians been heard, there would have been no reason to arm Iraq against Iran.

Most recently, in 1988, American power remained deaf to Arafat's formal recognition of the right of Israel to exist as a state. Had they been heard there would have been no reason on earth for the PLO to place itself beside Saddam.

Since the crisis began, American power has also been deaf to the experience of the Arab people, deaf towards the suffering and pride of generations, deaf therefore to what lead them to find hope in the defiance of a pitiless tyrant - a hope which may become an article of faith, if he is turned into a martyr......

......deaf to a voice which might shout that the **"carpet bombing of a city suburb" (whatever the claimed target) is a step towards genocide:** deaf to a voice which might repeat that the cluster bombs being dropped on the cities contained 24 grenades, each one exploding into 2000 high velocity needle-fragments designed to cause the maximum untreatable wounds: deaf to a voice which might recall that Islamic culture has probably contributed as much to the human dream of Justice and reason as has Christianity.

Sampling of public opinion on the Gulf War

After the first day of the opening air offensive, a U.S. communique proudly announced that the tonnage of explosives already dropped on Iraq exceeded the explosive power of the A-bomb dropped on Hiroshima. To make such an announcement with pride is to be deaf to the word *Hiroshima*, as it is understood by most of those alive on this earth.

The deafness meant not hearing any voice raised to express any grief or claim which did not celebrate Desert Storm: and the code name already had a deafness at its centre.

The war over, is there reason to suppose that the victors will start listening? I am tempted to believe that only the defeat of the victors may one day bring back their hearing. When I say this, I am thinking of those with power, not of those for whom the pouches were prepared. The deafness of power is of course, the mother and father of all terrorist movements......."

(By John Berger)

The Daily Dawn Karachi Pakistan "New World Order"

Noam Chomsky, Professor of Modern languages and linguistic at Massachussetts Institute of Technology, looking towards the millennium, spell out the central message from the White House: **"We are the masters and you shine our shoes."**

"These are the admiring, words of the reporter who released the policy review, then quoting the hero himself: "By God, we've kicked the Vietnam syndrome once and for all."

The Turkish "peacemaker" were also authorised to intensify their repression of Kurds, in partial payments for their services.

Plainly, we have here a man who should be lauded for rare principle as he leads us to a New World Order.

The principles of the policy review were followed through out the Gulf crisis. In July, Bush indicated that he had no objections to Iraq's rectifying its border disputes with Kuwait by force, or intimidating its neighbours to raise the price of oil.

In such ways, the ground was prepared for the merciless slaughter that a leading Third World journal describes as **"the most cowardly ever fought on this planet."** The corpses have quickly disappeared form view, joining mounds of others that do not disturb the tranquillity of the civilised.

Much weaker enemies pose only one threat to the U.S: the threat of independence, always intolerable. The U.S. will support the most murderous tyrant as long as he plays along, and will labour to overthrow Third World democrats if they depart from their service function. The documentary and historical records are clear on this score.

In the Middle East, Bush supported Israel's harsh occupations, its savage invasion of Lebanon and its refusal to honour Security Council Resolution."

The Washington Post: USA
The Silence of the Diplomat:
"We have an ambassador who, on the instruction of the State Department, virtually gave a green light to Saddam Hussein, as Sen. Patrick Leahy (D-Vt) described it to National Public Radio.
Since August, she has been working quietly in the State Department. Despite repeated request by congress and the press, she has not spoken on the record about her critical meeting with Saddam one week before the invasion. For months the State Department prevented her from speaking: now, according to Deputy Spokesman Richard Boucher, it is up to **Glaspie.**

But Glaspie's critics say the overall tone of her response was too soft- instead of holding Saddam in check, she cleared the way for his advance into Kuwait.

One statement was singled out as sending an especially misleading signal to the Iraqi leader. **"We have no opinion on the Arab-Arab conflicts, like your border disagreement with Kuwait."**

The Toronto Star: January 27, 1991 B7
"The War against Iraq is insane and unjust"
If this war holds, as U.S. President George Bush believes, "the promise of a new world order," then God help us all.
Some order. Some world. Some morality!

Sampling of public opinion on the Gulf War

Morality and war are obviously and mutually contradictory. It has been the Church's greatest betrayal of Christ to have dropped his teachings on violence in favour of the theory of the so-called just war. Justice like truth, is among the first casualties of any war. **Certainly this insane gulf war is not just by any standards**.........

Yet, complete as the situation is, we desperately need to pierce the miasma of lies and propaganda that surrounds this present crisis to reveal some basic truths.

That's what one teacher at an American college has tried to do. Last fall, Michael Rivage-Seul, an associate professor at Berea Christian College, Berea, Ky; set his students a semester-long project to research the gulf conflict and the reasons behind it.

The result, summarized by him as the main feature in the Jan. 11 issue of the widely read **National Catholic Reporter, are worth repeating here.**

What the crisis is not about:

*The students found it is not about stopping "another Hitler". Saddam Hussein is not a world class threat. He's a regional dictator of a medium sized Third World country. **He is no more or less evil today than when he was the recipient of massive U.S. support against Iran in that eight year war. His much hyped "military machine" was unable to overwhelm Iran.**

*It's not about defending democracy. Neither Kuwait nor Saudi Arabia is a democracy; both are feudal oligarchies where enormous wealth has been monopolized for the benefit of the few at the top. They want to keep it that way.

*Clearly it's not about upholding the principle that larger countries must not invade smaller ones. The U.S. has never subscribed to that ethic. "History shows the U.S. has virtually written the book on shaping the destinies of weaker neighbours" one student wrote.

The student cited the 1983 U.S-led invasion of Grenada, the ravaging of Panama in December, 1989 (condemned as illegal by the U.N.), the 10-year war against Nicaragua, etc.

***Nor is the ear about maintaining "the international rule of law," they found. Indeed, the U.S has a very uneven track record in this area. "It supports U.N. and World court decisions only when these coincide with U.S. self-interest."**

The most glaring example of this is the way the U.S. along with

Israel, has simply ignored U.N. resolutions demanding the withdrawal of Israeli troops from their 23-year occupation of the West Bank and Gaza.

Similarly, in 1986, the U.S flatly refused to abide by the World Court's decision to stop its Contra war and to pay reparations to the Sandinista government.

*This conflict is not even about protecting innocent people from atrocities carried out by brutal military dictators or others. The students quickly realized the U.S. has never backed away from supporting leaders with the most abysmal of human rights records- Marcos in the Philippines, Samoza in Nicaragua, or Pinochet in Chile. The list is almost endless. Coalition members, President Hafez Assad, of Syria, is the latest embarrassment.

The students "discovered" as well that U.S. gulf policy has little to do with a consistent opposition to chemical weapons or nuclear proliferation. Over the years, the U.S has "staunchly opposed treaties controlling the production of chemical weapons"

The U.S has shown little if any concern about nations it approves of, such as Israel, having nuclear weapons. What's more, the U.S. has consistently and steadfastly refused to sign any treaty aimed at ending the testing of even more nuclear weapons. Its latest refusal came virtually on the eve of unleashing the present high-tech blitzkrieg against Iraq.

The student's research is correct. It highlights the abysmal hypocrisy of the loud claims to righteousness of the U.S. Canada and the rest.

In an interview in the Jan 7 issue of Time Magazine- the one with the remarkable double exposure shot of the two faces of George Bush on the cover under the, "Men of the Year" - Bush, speaking of his domestic policies, said: "We have the kinder, gentler approach. It is catching on. They used to laugh about the thousand points of light...."

There are 10,000 "points of light" raining down on the civilian population of Iraq every 24 hours from U.S and other coalition planes. They are bringing death and destruction to innocent people.

Sampling of public opinion on the Gulf War

We speak, rightly, of Saddam's "terrorism". But, nothing equals the terrorism now being used against the Iraqis in the cause of "peace." It's an outrage against our common humanity and must stop. In God's name.
(Tom Harper is a Toronto author and broadcaster.)

Toronto Star, July 21, 1991
"We know well what good came of the gulf war"

By Gerald Caplan.

And everybody praised the Duke
Who this great fight did win,
"But what good came of it at last?"
Quoth little Peterkin.
"Why, that I cannot tell," said he;
But 'twas a famous victory

Robert Southly asked the irrelevant question about the Battle of Blenheim nearly 200 years ago, but no such self doubt troubled our own leaders at last week's meeting of the Gang of 7. Clearly for them, the gulf war remains a famous victory.

Some terrible, mysterious illness seems frequently to befall those who reach elevated positions. It wraps their judgement, obliterates their faculties for common sense and reason. Any sane person, after all, would look at the consequences of that ghastly war and conclude that only a single objective that was claimed for it has been achieved, while the awful consequences remain overwhelming.

Yes, Iraq was kicked out of Kuwait, which matters. But that's the absolute end of the good news. Kuwait may be "liberated" but it's a hell hole, thanks in large part to the destruction inflicted on it by our side during the war and the horrors perpetrated since by the egregious Kuwaiti rulers to whom we have restored power.

There have been, writes one horrified observer, "mass executions of suspected Iraqi sympathizers, muzzling of the press, and harsh jail terms for suspected collaborators." Mass graves have been unearthed. And Kuwaitis have launched a "reign of terror" against those terrible fall guys, the Palestinians. Amnesty International - our era's Little Peterkin - reports torture of Palestinians using whips, knives, electric shocks, sexual assaults and - get this one - sulphuric acid.

You may recall an especially nauseating moment last January when an outraged George Bush cited Amnesty's description of Iraqi cruelty in Kuwait as justification enough for war to be launched against Saddam Hussein. Think his flacks have yet mentioned to the President that Amnesty's latest annual report, just published, includes a bitter attack on that kind of hypocrisy?

Amnesty had been documenting Saddam's "gross and widespread human rights abuses" in Iraq for years without eliciting any particular concern; small wonder, since the world was getting filthy rich supplying him with arms. Suddenly, with Saddam's entry into Kuwait, Amnesty's phone started ringing; suddenly, certain issues Amnesty had been raising in vain for years had become sexy.

But only certain issues, naturally. At the very same moment, the new report bitingly notes, "lengthy AI (Amnesty International) reports on grave human rights violations in countries such as Chad, Egypt, El Salvador, Iran, India, Mauritania, Myanmar, Sri Lanka, Sudan and Turkey were fortunate to be given reasonable space in the media, let alone be taken up at a high level by governments.

What a list. Half these countries are tried and true allies of the United states and the West. And I'm sure George Bush, crusader for human rights that he is, finds compelling reading in Amnesty's accounts of the state of human rights in the countries that fought shoulder to shoulder with the G-7 armies against Saddam. Check the entries for Egypt, Saudi Arabia, Syria, Turkey. Yes, as Richard Nixon said at the time, the war was "a highly moral enterprise".

It's true, alas, that the Washington Post revealed last month how the Americans deliberately lied to the world about their real targets during the war. Publicly, they never stopped insisting that Iraq's military capabilities were the coalition's sole targets. **Sorry, folks; it was a lie.** In fact the premeditated goal, as the Post shows, was to "disable Iraqi society at large."

"Damage to civilian structures and interests, invariably described by (U.S.) briefers during the war as 'collateral' and unintended was sometimes neither......(Coalition forces) deliberately did great harm to Iraq's ability to support itself as an industrial society."

"The worst civilian suffering," senior Pentagon officer told the Post, "resulted **not** from bombs that went astray but from precision-guided weapons that hit exactly where they were aimed - at electrical plants, oil refineries and transportation networks. Each of these targets was acknowledged during the war, but all the purposes and consequences of their destruction was not divulged."

Yet we persevere in our cruelty. As if the renewed horrors being committed by Saddam himself against Shia Muslims and Kurds within Iraq weren't enough; as if the devastation to the country from the kind of war "we" fought against the Iraqi people weren't enough; still the Gang of 7 insists on continuing sanctions against Iraq. The clear result? "The embargo doesn't touch Saddam or the people around him", one shopkeeper told a Canadian journalist. "All you are doing is starving us." Yes, the Iraqi war produced another famous victory. But this time we know precisely what good came of it.

* Gerald Caplan is a former national secretary of the New Democratic Party and a public affairs consultant.

The Calgary Sunday SUN
Sunday July 19, 1992

SADDAM HAUNTS U.S. ELECTIONS
By Eric Margolis in Washington

"......Earlier this month, the CIA apparently tried to stage a coup against Saddam using disgruntled Iraqi army officers. It failed miserably......

Democrats charge: Reagan secretly built up Saddam's power during the long Iran-Iraq war from 1980-1988. In the ensuing years up to Iraq's invasion of Kuwait, Bush knew about or covertly aided Saddam's secret nuclear and chemical programs. The administration was also aware of Iraq's genocide against the Kurds, massive human right violations, and illegal diversion of U.S. agricultural loans to buy arms.

The last accusation includes charges that Bush tried to cover up the loan diversions in violation of U.S. laws. And during this period, assert critics, the administration lied to Congress over its secret aid to Iraq and blocked efforts to impose sanctions on Baghdad........The U.S. originally urged Saddam to invade Iran in 1980. At the same time, the U.S. and Israel covertly sold $5 billion of arms to Iran. When Iraq appeared to be losing the war, the U.S. intervened massively to save Iraq and its then ally, Kuwait, from being overrun by Khomeini's armies. After the war, the U.S. continued to arm and finance Iraq as a counterweight to militant Iran........

The Bush administration knew well that desperate Iraq had a plan to seize part of Kuwait's oil fields along the Iraqi border. As tensions mounted between Iraq and Kuwait, the U.S. ambassador to Baghdad informed Saddam that Washington "took no position in Arab border disputes." The U.S. was clearly giving Saddam the green light to go ahead and grab part of Kuwait.......

The embarrassed administration now concedes its past policy towards Iraq was a mistake. But was it? America's long-term Mideast strategy is to prevent any state, except Israel, from becoming too powerful. So the U.S. aided and encouraged both Iraq and Iran to first fight one another to exhaustion, then finally helped Iraq to beat Iran. Saddam was built up until he got too strong. Then, he was undone by Desert Storm. In the end, the Mideast remained in pieces while the U.S. reigns supreme over the region.

The Democrats, smelling blood may manage to hit the administration with criminal charges - and before the elections. But they may not stick. After all, Bush was continuing the standard Mideast policies of his predecessors: **Divide, promote tumult - and rule.**"

Sampling of public opinion on the Gulf War

The Toronto Star Sunday, August 2, 1992
ETHICS
History will judge Bush guilty of monstrous crimes

George Bush uttering threats of renewed bombing against Iraq (hoping to regain momentum in his bid for a second term?), is still trying to pass off Operation Desert Storm as a victory for God, freedom and all that is noble and just. You can hear it in almost every speech. This rhetoric will increase as November election draws closer. It is near blasphemous cant.

Saddam Hussain may be a despicable, second-rate despot, but George Bush is no hero despite his posing. His war in the gulf was no victory for the forces of light over darkness. It was an unnecessary unmitigated disaster.

Until now, Bush and company - largely through a massive and wholly unprecedented manipulation of media coverage of the war itself - have been able to sustain the official mythology that the gulf war was a clear case of the good guys versus the bad guys. This is the familiar stance of the victors in any combat. But by now, even the most blind are beginning to see through the lies.

The truth is that Bush and those closest to him in the decision to pulverize Iraq will one day be judged by history as war criminals guilty of crimes more monstrous than those of Saddam Hussain himself.

Obviously this is not the accepted wisdom. But, in case anyone thinks I am alone in this view, let me tell you a story that all the major big-business media in the U.S. deliberately blanked out of coverage. It concerns the work and sessions of a 22 member War Crimes Tribunal which held public hearings in New York a few months ago. The panelists on the tribunal were distinguished citizens from five continents, including two from Canada, a labor leader from Ontario and a prominent jurist from Quebec. On Feb. 29, after five hours of hearing and viewing testimony gathered by the Commission of Enquiry during the previous 12 months, the panel read out their verdict. They found George Bush and others in his administration guilty of 19 charges of war crimes, crimes against peace and crimes against humanity for U.S. conduct before, during and after the war against Iraq.

This was not some hasty, far out event, the work of kooks, dreamers or subversive radicals. **The leader of the prosecution was a former attorney-general of the United States, Ramsey Clark,** who travelled extensively inside Iraq during the war itself. The evidence presented to the panel before and at the New York meeting (held in Marlin King Jr. Auditorium before 1,500 people) was meticulously gathered from Commission of Enquiry hearings held in 20 countries around the world and in 24 North American cities, including Toronto. In fact, it was the culmination of what was probably the largest independent global investigation into war crimes ever undertaken.

In addition to seeing footage shot by Clark and his team, the panel heard eye-witness testimony from such people as Mohammad Khader, a Palestinian living in Baghdad during the war. Khadar told how U.S. "smart bombs" killed thousands of civilians at the Ameriyah bomb shelter on the first night of the war, Feb 13, 1991. To the rest of the world, watching on TV, it looked like fireworks show. For him it was a torment of hell in which his wife and four of his daughters were killed in the slaughter.

Here are some of the charges sustained by the tribunal:

* The U.S. engaged in a pattern of conduct ... intended to lead Iraq into provocations justifying U.S. military action against Iraq and permanent U.S. military domination of the gulf.

* President Bush from August 2, 1990, intended and acted to prevent any interference with his plan to destroy Iraq economically and militarily.

* President Bush ordered the destruction of facilities essential to civilian life and economic productivity throughout Iraq.

* The U.S. intentionally bombed ... civilian life, commercial and business districts, schools, hospitals, mosques, churches, shelters, residential areas, historical sites, private vehicles and civilian government offices.

Sampling of public opinion on the Gulf War

* The U.S. intentionally bombed indiscriminately throughout Iraq.

* The U.S. ... used excessive force, killed soldiers seeking to surrender and in disorganized individual flight, often unarmed and far from any combat zones and randomly and wantonly killed Iraqi soldiers and destroyed material after the cease fire.

* The U.S. used prohibited weapons capable of mass destruction and inflicted indiscriminate death and unnecessary suffering...

The other crimes include corrupting and exploiting United Nations functions "as a means of securing power to commit crimes against peace and war crimes" war against the environment and a campaign of media control and misinformation.

Only by knowing the true nature of Operation Desert Storm can similar wars be prevented. You can learn more by sending for the video *Nowhere to hide*, with Ramsey Clark filmed on the ground during the bombing, or for other books, papers, videos and reports on the tribunal's findings. For information, write to International War Crimes Tribunal, 36 East 12 St. 6th floor, New York, N.Y. 10003 (212 254-5386)

* By: Tom Harper is a Toronto author and broadcaster.

PORTIONS OF THE VERDICT, FINDINGS AND RECOMMENDATIONS OF THE INTERNATIONAL WAR CRIMES TRIBUNAL NEW YORK, USA

"A 22-member War Crimes Tribunal representing the people of five continents concluded 12 months of gathering and reviewing evidence. Before a public meeting in New York Feb 29, 1992, they found George Bush and others in his administration guilty of 19 charges of war crimes, crimes against peace and crimes against humanity for U.S. conduct before, during and after the war against Iraq.

Some past tribunals have punished the losers in a war. Others have exposed aggression from afar. For the first time an international independent investigating commission brought charges from right within the country responsible for the war, and with the war-waging administration still in office."

Findings:
"The undermentioned (members of the International War Crimes Tribunal) find each of the names accused Guilty on the basis of the evidence against them and each of the nineteen separate crimes alleged in the initial Complaint, attached hereto, has been established to have been committed beyond reasonable doubt.

That the undersigned believe that it is imperative if there is ever to be peace that power be accountable for its criminal acts and we condemn in the strongest possible terms those found guilty of the charges herein. We urge the Commission in Inquiry and all people to act on recommendations developed by the Commissions to hold power accountable and to secure social justice on which lasting peace must be based."

Recommendations:
"The undersigned urge the immediate revocation of all embargoes, sanctions and penalties against Iraq because they constitute a continuing crime against humanity.

The undersigned urge public action to prevent new aggressions by the United States threatened against Iraq, Libya, Cuba. Haiti, North Korea, Pakistan and other countries and the Palestinian people. We encourage the fullest condemnation of any threat or use of military technology against life, both civilian and military, as was used by the United States against the people of Iraq.

The undersigned urge that the power of the United Nations Security Council, which was blatantly manipulated by the U.S. to authorize illegal military action and sanctions be vested in the General Assembly, that all permanent members be removed and that the right of veto be eliminated as undemocratic and contrary to the basic principles of the U.N. Charter.

The undermentioned urge the Commission to.....seek ways to provide the widest possible distribution of the truth about the U.S. assault on Iraq."
(Signed by all members: New York. 29th day of February 1992)
****End****

BIBLIOGRAPHY

*Abbott, G.F., Israel in Egypt, London, 1907.
*Amin Maaloof, The Crusades through Arab Eyes.
*Anwar G. Chejne, Muslim Spain, its History and Culture. University of Mannisota Press, 1974.
*Barbara W. Tuchman, Bible and Sword, How the British came to Palestine
*Benjamin Beit-Hallahmi, The Israeli Connection.
*Bermant, C., Israel, London 1967 P.15.
*Britain and the United Nations. Published by Her Majesty's Stationary Office, London 1970
*British Parliamentary Election Results. 1918-1949.
*Cambridge Medieval History, VII.
*Cambridge History of Islam, Vol.I Editors Holt, Lambton & Lewis, 1970.
*Chaim Bermant, Israel, London. 1967.
*Christopher Culpin, Making History.
*Chronicle of the World, by Longman Group U.K. 1989
*Churchill Winston, Thornton Butteworth Ltd. London
*Churchill Randolph Winston, The Six Day War.
*Clayton to Fo, Foreign Office Papers 3386, December 6, 1918.
*Colliers Encyclopedia.
*David Gilmour, Dispossessed The Ordeal of Palestine.
*Dictionary of 20th Century History, 1900-1982.
*Encyclopedia of Britannica, London (15th edition)
*Encyclopedia of Historic Places, Vol 1 A-L, by Courtlandt Canby.
*Europa Year Book, 1990.
*Garaudy R., The Case of Israel, London 1983.
*George, L., War Memoirs, London, 1933
*Graetz, H, History of the Jews, translation by Bella Lowy, Philadelphia. Vol III
*H. C. Armstrong, Gery Steel, London, 1939
*Hancock Smutts W,H., The Sanguine Years 1870-1919. London, 1962.
*Harold Wilson. The Chariots of Israel, Britain, America and The State of Israel London 1981.
*Heinemann book, 1967.
*James Cameron, Making of Israel, Secker & Warburg, London, 1976.
*Jean Plaidy, The Rise of the Spanish Inquisition, Published by, Robert Hall & Co, London.
*Jewish Encyclopedia, IX.

*John Connell, The Most Important Country (London, Cssel & Co)
*Joshua Prawer, The World of the Crusades.
*M. Lombard, The Golden Age of Islam, Elsevier Published by Oxford 1975.
*Mary & Sarge Bromberger, secrets of Suez (London, Panbooks)
*Michael Foot and Mervyn Jones, Guilty Men 1957 (New York Rinehast & Co 1957).
*Mohammed Heikal, Cutting the Lion's Tail Suez Though Egyptians eyes.
*Moshe Dayyan, a New Map... a New Relationship, Maariv, Tel Aviv, 1969.
*Nutting, No End of a Lesson.
*Origins and Devolution of the Palestine Problem, 1917-1988, By United Nations, New York 1990.
*Paul Harper, The Arab Israeli Issue, Wayland Ltd.; Hove East Sussex England. 1986
*Philip Ziegler, Black Death, London, 1969.
*Prados John Dr. The President's Secret Wars. William Morrow & Co. Inc., New York. USA 1986.
*Richie Ovendale, The Origins of the Arab-Israeli Wars.
*Robert Gotfried, Black Death, London, 1983.
*Roderic H. Davidson, Turkey, New Jersey, 1968.
*Simon Schama, Two Rothschilds and the Land of Israel, 1978.
*Statesman's Year Book 1990-91.
*Sydney D. Bailey, Four Arab Israeli Wars and the Peace Process, London, Macmillan 1990.
*Tabawi A.L. Anglo Arab Relations and the Question of Palestine, 1914-1921 London U.K.
*Treaties and Alliances of the World, Keesing's references publications, fourth edition.
*Victor Ostrovsky & Claire Hoy, By Way of Deception, The Making and Unmaking of a Mossad Officer, St. Martind Press, New York 1990.
*Walter Eytan, The First Ten Years, a Diplomatic History of Israel, London, Weiden Field, 1958
*Webster's Biographical Dictionary.
*Weizmann, C., Trial & Error, London, 1949
*William Prescott, History of the reign Of Ferdinand and Isabella the Catholic, London 1888
*World Book of the United Nations. 1970
*Yehoshafat Harkabi, Israel's Fateful Decisions.
*Zara Steiner, The Foreign Office and The War. London 1967

Newspapers & Periodicals
Al- Arab. London February 01, 1991
Aviation Week & Space Technology Sept 24, 1990
Calgary SUN July 19, 1992
Canadian Ecumenical News. Jan/Feb. 1991
Financial Times London January 14, 1991
Guardian February 12 & 16, 1991
Harrisburg Patriot News (USA) March 02, 1991
New York Times, March 31, 1957
New Canada Weekly, February 08, 1991
New York Times, November 05, 1956
New Scientist, February 02, 1991
Newsweek, October 23, 1990
The Socialist Standard
The Record, February 03, 1991
The Economist, January 26, 1991
The Plain Truth, October 1990
The Independent, December 20, 1990
The Sunday Times, February 03, 1991
Toronto Star, January 27, 1991; July 21, 1991; August 02, 1992
Toronto Sun, February 24, 1991
Washington Post, February 15 & 16, 1991

ARABIC BIBLIOGRAPHY

کتابیات

قرآن کریم

جامع صحیح بخاری

جامع صحیح مسلم

سنن ترمذی

سنن ابن ماجہ

سنن ابوداؤد

سنن النسائی

السیرۃ النبویہ ۔ الابن ہشام دارالجلیل بیروت

خطبہ الہامیہ تصنیف حضرت مرزا غلام احمد قادیانی علیہ السلام

حمامۃ البشری تصنیف حضرت مرزا غلام احمد قادیانی علیہ السلام

تذکرہ مجموعہ الہامات، کشوف و رویاء
تصنیف حضرت مرزا غلام احمد قادیانی علیہ السلام

بائبل عہدنامہ قدیم و جدید

مجموعہ الوثائق السیاسیہ العہد النبوی و الخلافۃ الراشدہ
مصنفہ داکتر محمد حمید اللہ دارالنفائس بیروت

INDEX & NOTES

A

Abraham[as]: never forget _ and Ishmael[as] 187
Abraham[as]: Mecca & Medina are holy because of _ 153
Abu Bakr Hazrat: Saud entered Mecca 1803 and demolished birthplace 144
Advice - Muslim nations 327
Advice - Oil-wealth to be considered jointly owned by Arabs 310
Advice - To Allied Powers 288
Advice - Western Christian Nations 339
Advice - Muslim World 297
Advice - Foundation of new OPEC 323
Advice - Need for protection of labour interests 324
Advice - Pakistan 320
Advice - Association of non-oil producing countries 324
Advice - Views on a new UNO for Third world 326
Advice - Israel 331
Advice - Follow teachings of Islam 137
Advice - Appeal 52, 53 Ahmadis 54
Advice - Muslim world 143
Advice - Charity for Africa 166
Advice - U.S. to recall its noble aims 277
Advice - Iraq 157
Advice - Politics 281
Advice - Third World 300
Advice - Who will benefit 302
African Continent: 92, 139, 166, 300
Ahmadi Muslims oppressed by the Mullah of Pakistan 97
Ahmadiyya Muslim Community: obligations to pray for human-race 149
Ahmadiyya Muslim Community: duty to make politicians aware 117
Ahmadiyya Muslim Community: our stand in this conflict 174
Ahmadiyya Muslim Community: pray for world peace 165
Ahmadiyya Muslim Community: responsibilities 69
Ahmadiyya Muslim Community: invitation 37
Ahmadiyya Muslim Community: did not support Iran for seizing hostages 115
Aids: similarities between military aid and the disease "AIDS" 315
Aids: prophecy about affliction of "AIDS" 336
Al-Mostasim: (Abbasid Caliph) 49
Alif Laam Meem Raa (Holy Quran) 49

Index - Notes

Allah: If you differ, revert to Allah and His Messenger 46
Allah: will destroy the arrogant & boastful 187
Allah: In His sight most honourable is he who is most righteous 73
Allah: How prayers are accepted 346
Allah: His forgiveness dominates His wrath 339
Allah: loves those who are just 36
Allah: collectively hold fast to "rope of Allah" 127
Allah: decreed that prayers would save world 70
Allah: Ka'ba - House of Allah 155
Allah: "My Allah" an excellent reply of Holy Prophet 102
America has murdered peace: 232
Amusing anecdote: peck on the wrestler's shiny head 123
Anglo-Iranian Oil Company 216
Animal-lovers: these _ savagely killed the Red Indians 139
Anthrax: used as instrument of war, was initiated by the West 87
Arab issue: it would be inherently wrong to approach this as _ 137
Arab League: may have considered this matter 33
Arabs: the West may even clothe its dogs yet would keep Arabs nude 59
Armenia: rivalries with Turkey and Azarbaijan 110
Arts and Sciences: my advice is that you study __ 297
Aslam Beg General: (Pakistan) against participation in war 194
Assets Freezing: they have no right to seal the assets of an adversary 64
Assyrians: committed gross atrocities in Baghdad 879 B.C. 275
Assyrians: in 721 B.C. devastated two Jewish empires 333
Aswan Dam: U.S. reneged agreement to give financial help for the _ 219
Atomic arsenal: Super Powers can destroy this world many times over 344
Australian Aborigines: British hunted, captured and castrated them 140
Azarbaijan: enmities exist between Armenia and Azarbaijan 110

B

Babar Emperor: the Hindus claim, he built the mosque at grave of Rama 95
Babri Mosque: Hindus of India attempting to demolish 95, 100
Babylonians: led by Nebuchadnezzar attacked Judea Jewish Empire 333
Badar: Battle of special prayer of the Holy Prophet 247
Baghdad: history of destructions 49
Bahrain: will be made to share the costs of the war 163
Balfour Lord: 1917, he made a commitment with the Jews 211
Balfour Lord: instrumental in establishment of Israel 239
Balfour Declaration: (1917) 221
Bangladesh: reaction against happenings in India 97
Bangladesh: common markets with Pakistan, India, Sri Lanka 312

Banu Qariza - Jewish tribe 268
Banu Qunkah - Jewish tribe 268
Banu Nazeer - Jewish tribe 268
Bavarian concept: (Germany) 83
Beggar with a Rod: (US) 206
Beggar: a life of humiliation - can never be a free man 298
Begging bowl: USA never begged with __ during war with Vietnam 274
Begin Menachem: commanded a terrorist group 215, 223
Believers: are like brothers 33
Ben Gurion David: sounded the bugle of war 270
Bevin: tried to stop illegal immigration of Jews into Palestine 223
Biological warfare: propaganda against Iraq 87
Black Americans: grim reminder of American record of slave trade 139
Blockade of Iraq: U.S. and U.K. indulging in wanton excesses 44
Blunder Greatest: Arabs show lack of awareness of situation 64
Bombardment of Iraq: 150,000 tons of bombs dropped in 5 weeks 257
Bombardment of Iraq: 4 times more bombs on Iraq than in Vietnam 272
Brahmins: 107
Britain: racial and religious prejudices remain active 109
Britain: double standards. South Africa 141
Britain: waged war to protect Western interests 216
British agents: in Iran 218
British agents: Saudis. Ahmadis were labelled as _ _ 193
Brothers: Muslims should stop fighting and murdering brothers 132
Buddhists: 289
Bull: Letting loose a bull in field of crops (Israel) 264
Burgis Anthony: British scholar, claiming knowledge of Islam 82

C

Caesar of Rome: in 272 A.H. had treaty with Baghdad 49
Career in politics: 303
Carpet bombing: of Iraq 160
Castrate: (Australian Aborigines) 140
Chad: (West Africa) famine 166
Chamberlain: UK advice to cabinet before World War II 213
Charitable donation: for famine victims in Africa 168
Charlton Lionel: (1923) resigned in protest for cruelties against Kurds 285
Chemical plants: the West gave technical know-how to Iraq 62
Chemical bombs: Saddam allegedly dropped on Iran 285
Children's milk plant: deliberately bombed in Baghdad 265
China: did not tolerate white coloured Communism 84

Index - Notes

China: Occupation of Tibet 114
Churchill Sir Winston: anecdote from book "Great Contemporaries" 245
Claim of Iraq: Kuwait was part of mainland, severed by British 90
Collective force of Muslims: 47
Colonialism by Czars: 77
Comments - our unprejudiced views: 185
Common markets: in Third world 312
Communism: concept on identical ideology 77
Congress: USA 152
Conspiracy of the Western powers: emergence of Jewish state in Palestine 215
Corpse of Iraq: U.S. will hand over corpse to Israel to hang 181
Coup d'etat: CIA busy in many countries 142
Covenant: with Allah 125
Covert operations: 237
Croatia: Yugoslavia 114
Crusades: (1095) 248
Curzon Lord: he rejected the "historical link" theory 240
Czars of Russia: 77

D

Dajjal: (anti-Christ) duplicity and deception 244, 336
David[as]: literature since _ that world would be under Jewish control 112
Deniability: by the President for covert operations 142
Der Yasin: Lebanon 259
Desert storm: real and dreadful storms are in hand of Allah 187
Destruction of civilian population: 209
Diagnosis of disease precedes prescription for its cure 210
Diaspora: area where Jews had scattered 336
Dictators: often produced as result of democratic procedure 293
Dictatorship: suites developed countries to enslave Third world 317
Diplomacy: British art of 205
Divine Leadership: invitation - accept the Promised Messiah 37
Doctor: If you want to adopt this profession 302
Don Quixote: Spanish comedy character 279
Dorab Patel Justice: (Pakistan) 118
Dream of Peace: 230-232
Dugan General Michael: relieved of duties because of disclosures 236
Duplicity: 45

E

East Pakistan (Bangladesh): 155
Eastern world: advice 300
Economic-boycott: 141
Economic Commonwealth: 311
Eden Anthony: 220
Edward Heath: endowed with foresight and political acumen 197
Egypt: loan written off. Price tag for Muslim support 243
Egypt: six day war with Israel 221
Egypt: peace with Israel on humiliating conditions 67,
Egypt: A Western satellite 192
Elders of Zion in Germany: 199
Elephant & Mosquito: US - Iraq 210
Engineering: If you choose this profession 302
Ethiopia: famine 166
Euphrates River: 334
Europe: Rising trend of racism 75
Expenses of this war: to be borne by Arabs 86
Eye for an eye: (Biblical) 251
Ezekiel[as]: two cities who turned as prostitutes 333-334

F

Fairness of Islam: Neither differentiates between East or West 119
Faiza: (daughter of author) 321
Falsehood: tool of politics 283
Famine: in Africa 244
Ferdinand: King of Spain (1490) 268
Fire: "war" 129, 130
Fish-pond illusion: inspired vision of a believer 46
Foreign instructors: end up consuming better part of aid 317
Foreign nationals: and diplomats are a trust 43, 52, 157
France: gave refuge and protection to Imam Khomenei 60
France: Joined Britain to attack Egypt for control of Suez canal 216
Frank Kellog: attempts to 'outlaw war' 287
Freemasons: will never be imposed on the world... 201

G

Gaddafi: President Libya U.S. bombed and targeted _ 237
Geographical boundaries: 91, 94
Geographical change: 95

George Bush: with Asad, a stunning change 194
George Bush: conceited arrogance 179
George Bush: "heeled" by Israel 255
George Bush: acting as a mercenary 152
George Bush: erection of a minaret of human skulls 275
Germany: 76, 82, 205
Ghalib: Urdu poet 117
Glaspie April: US Ambassador 236
Global peace: 289
Godfrey of Bouillon: (1095) leader of the "crusades" from France 249
Gog and magog: 68
Golan Heights: 194, 227
Goldman Nahun: founder of Zionism - President World Jewish Congress 263
Great Devil: weapon of hatred against the U.S. 60
Greece: 111

H

Hablel wareed: 126
Hablellah: 125
Hablen minannas: 126
Hablennas: 125
Hadith: (recorded sayings of the Prophet) 135, 292
Hadrian: great Roman Emperor whose empire extended Europe-Africa 334
Hafiz-al-Asad: Syria 194 .
Halaku Khan: destroyed Baghdad in 1258 A.D. 49, 161, 209, 276
Hamamatul Bushra: (book written by founder of Ahmadiyya Community) 55
Haroot and Maroot: 334
Hate always begets hate: 184, 256
Hate: never hate the British or Americans 253
Hazrat Mirza Ghulam Ahmad: 277, 338
Hazrat Safia: (wife of the Holy Prophet) 135
Hazrat Musleh Maood: 49, 123
Heel: 280
Herzl Theodor: World Zionist Congress 251
High moral standards: 138
High morals: 137
High moral ground: 181
Higher caste: 107
Hijaz: (Saudi Arabia) 143, 202
Hindi: language 108
Hindus: 97, 107, 289,

Hiroshima: Japan 160
His Messenger: 46
Historical perspective: establishment of Israel 248
Historical connection: Curzon used this apparently harmless phrase 241
Historical claims: India Babri Mosque 95
Hitler of this age?: 210
Hitler's era linked with Saddam: 58, 273
Holocaust: 250
Holy Prophet: 68, 118
Holy Quran: 46, 113, 168, 172
Holy-war: 118, 120
Honesty: Concept of 64, 174
Horse-trading: 239
Hostages: 44
Human shield: 157
Human psychology: 83
Humanity and high moral values: U.S. claim 140
Humiliation in Vietnam: 305
Hyderabad: Deccan 91
Imam of the Age: Hazrat Mirza Ghulam Ahmad 37

I

India: 43, 107, 114, 141, 312
Indo-Pakistan: Kashmir dispute. Its 3 possible solutions 319
Indonesia: 33, 35, 288
Injustice: Saddam is reflection of past _ of the West 60
Inquisitions: Jews massacred in Spain 268
Institution of Khilafat: 127
International Court of Justice: contradictions in U.N. charter 328
International plan: to win participation of Muslim countries 147
Iqbal Allama: (Pakistan) 78, 299
Iran - Iraq war: 129
Iran: occupation of US embassy 115
Iran: 53, 60, 156, 194, 231
Iraq should withdraw from Kuwait: 53
Iraq: 47, 115, 116, 141
Iraq's nuclear power-plants: 43, 180, 228
Ireland: 75, 109
Irish terrorists: 160
Isabella: Queen of Spain
Ishmael[as]: 187

Index - Notes

Islam: 131
Islam: 136
Islam: is not confined to any nationality 171
Islam: complete submission to will of Allah 122
Islam: 35
Islamic nationalism: 172
Islamic Jihad: 289
Islamic principle: 33, 40
Islamic issue: 137
Islamic problem: 35
Islamic Justice: 289
Islamic morality: 44, 52
Islamic politics: 105
Islamic values: 40
Islamic Terrorism: 224
Islamic Jihad: 184
Israel: root cause of restlessness 57
Israel: established on Palestinian territory 91
Israel: heeled all countries 280
Israel: PLO openly accepted and recognized Israel at UNO 263
Israel: threat to oil wealth 256
Israel: general claims they can even defeat Soviet Union 259
Israel: important advice 331
Israel: the primary beneficiary of this war 163
Israel: enjoys total immunity 223
Israel: 243
Israel: created by the U.N. 178
Israel: Bush can never afford to displease 227
Israel: speaks from microphones of Saudi Arabia 192
Israeli policy: of territorial & numerical expansion 229
Israeli promises: they continue to grab more and more territory 261
Israeli: lust for satisfaction of revenge 182

J

Jaffa: Palestinian Camp 259
Jamal-uddin Afghani: conception of Pan Arabism movement 311
James Atkins: former ambassador of U.S. in Iraq 236
Jamia Al-Azhar: Egypt 195
January 15 deadline: 151
Japan: plan to drag Japan into conflict 85
Jesus Christ[as]: if slapped on one cheek, offer the other 172

Jesus Christ[as]: Jews slaughtered as "charity" to avenge crucifixion 250
Jewish genocide in France: Godfrey of Bouillon's acts of "charity" 250
Jewish agents: the true identity of Jewish Agents apparent (Saudis) 193
Jewish Terrorism: terrorist activities of Jews never termed as _ _ 224
Jewish state in Palestine: 1948 Britain hurriedly left Palestine in chaos 215
Jewish racism: eliminating opposition to Jewish racism 74
Jews subjected to atrocities by West: 249
Jews: have the right to defy Security Council resolutions 224
Jihad: wrong concept of Jihad presented by the Mullah 293
Jihad: 65, 175, 182, 284, 295
Jihad: the Mullah wrongly label every battle as a "blessed Jihad" 294
John Brados: author of book "Secret wars of the President" 142
Jonah[as]: true repentance can avert categorical prophecy 338
Jordan: East 229
Jordan: 45, 67, 141, 221
Jordan's West Bank: 42
Junagharh: occupied by India 91
Justice and fairness Concept: Islamic teachings based on justice 119
Justice J.Dechene of Canada: his impartiality is beyond question 118
Justice: 40, 108, 118, 180, 183, 192
Justice: Principle of 282

K

Kaaba: Mecca 161, 186, 247
Kabia: Palestinian Camp 259
Kalima: (declaration of Unity of God) 97
Kashmir: 43, 91, 95, 230, 312, 319
Kerbala-e-Mo'alla: 144
Khawaneen: 77
Khilafat: 127, 132, 133
Khomenei: 60
Khutba Ilhamia: (revealed sermon of Founder of Community) 278
Khyber: Battle of 135
King Crane Commission: U.S. (1919) it was based on Justice 242
King of Spain: (1490) 268
King David Hotel: bombed in Jerusalem 223
King Hussein of Jordan: 41, 229
Kingdom of David[as]: 178, 198
Kosoro Metohija: province in Yugoslavia 114
Kubla Khan: By Coleridge 257
Kurds: 76, Bombardment by British (1920) 285

Kuwait: 40, 86, 115, 135, 156, 163, 280

L

Latter days: 68, 166
Law-bearing Prophet: 126
League of Nations: 210, 211
Lebanese camp: the horrors of a Lebanese camp 43
Lebanon: "we have no intention of taking an inch of Lebanon" 262
Levi Eshkol: "Israel has no intention of annexing even one foot..."   261
Liberia: 93, 111, 316
Linkage of the issues: 204, 234
Litani River: 262
Lloyd George: 239, 245
Lower caste Hindus: 108

M

Macbeth's soliloquy: 232
Maddox, Turner-Joy (Vietnam) American naval vessels: 271
Mandate for Palestine: 1920 League of Nations gave Britain _   211
Martyrs: Iran & Iraq both claim their dead as martyrs 130
McMahon: letter to sheriff of mecca and medina 202
Mecca & Medina endangered: 270
Mecca and Medina: 39, 143, 144
Mercenaries: 95, 274
Merchant of Venice: 252
Middle East: 39, 138
Might is right: 282
Miles Ignotum: (unknown soldier) an anonymous defence consultant 236
Military aid: the vicious cycle of military aid 314
Minarets of Mecca and Medina: 192
Minarets Of death and Human scull: Iraq 275
Mischievous lacuna in UN resolutions: 222
Misinterpretation of Jihad: 177
Missiles: supply of super high-tech _ by Israel 237
Mosques: of Ahmadi Muslims demolished in Pakistan 98
Mosquito & Elephant: Iraq-USA 210
Mossadeq Dr.: faithful and loyal to interests of Iran 217
Muhammad Ali Pasha: of Egypt who purged Hijaz of Saudis (1813) 144
Muhammad[sas]: 36, 113, 117, 186, 188, 322
Mullah: the temperament of the Mullah is not that of Islam 339

Mullah: the culprit is the Mullah - ruining concept of Justice 289
Mullah: The Mullah is the real culprit. He will be apprehended 98
Mullah: Pakistani Mullah gone a step further 97
Mullahism: bears no connection with the Holy Quran 164
Murder in the Name of Allah: A book by the author 116
Muslim statesmen: have faltered. Did not understand Islamic teachings 291
Muslim rule: Spain. in 800 years of _ _ no injustice was done to Jews 267
Muslim Khawaneen: 77
Muslim Heads of State: sent messages of advice 46
Muslim clergy: have no right to declare political wars as "Jihad" 184
Muslim world: as if it stands ready to defend Israeli interests 51
Muslim "terrorism": media paint Islam synonymous with terrorism 259
Muslim brethren: the true picture of Muslim brotherhood 130
Muslim countries: fully collaborated with the enemies of Islam 192
Muslims of India: undertook great struggle for creation of Pakistan 77
Mutual disputes: guidelines in the Quran for settlement of _ _ 33

N

Nagasaki and Hiroshima: 288
Nasser Gemal Abdul: 58, 218
Nasserism: 58, 59
Nassers: 256
National ideologies: 80
Nationalism: 74, 174
NATO: suppressed old enmity between Greece and Turkey 111
Nazi Germany: extreme injustices perpetrated on Jews by _ _ 336
Nazi era: race-oriented atrocities of the Nazi era 74
Nazi concept of Hitler: concept of superiority of Jews similar to _ _ 112
Nebuchadnezzar: Babylonians, led by _ attacked Jews in Judea 333
Neo-imperialism: a rising dander of _ _ to the Third world 311
Nest of the Islamic world: Saudi Arabia & Egypt 196
New World Order: features of Bush's dream of _ 228, 230
New world: question of new parameters of the world arisen 235
New World Order: role of Muslims in carving New World Order 291
New World Order: the spiritual dominance of Ahmadiyyat 202
New World Order: if based on justice, the West can fashion _ 339
New World Order: pray _ is not founded on ruins of destroyed nations 340
Non-Muslims by law: Pakistan Ahmadis 97
Non-aligned movement: is now outdated and meaningless 327
North Vietnam: (1964) how the US started the bombardment 271
Nuclear & Biological war: propaganda that Iraq possesses capability 86

Index - Notes

Nutting' book: "to knock Nasser off his perch" 220

O

Occupied territories: US vetoed resolutions calling for vacation of _ 138
Oil-wealth: diverted attention of Muslims towards materialism 31
Oil wealth: least defended - a puzzle 204
OPEC new: which would not consist of "bondmen" of US 323
OPEC oil production quota: dishonesty and breach of faith 35
Operation Peace for Galilee: savage attack kills thousands 260
Ottoman Empire: occupation of substantial portion of Europe 249
Ottoman Empire: concept bound to be resurrected 76
Ottoman Empire: Russia, Britain, France conspired to divide up _ 203

P

Pakistan: attention of intelligence services focused on internal strife 316
Pakistan: Kashmir issue compels India/Pakistan to maintain large armies 312
Pakistan: or Syria may be next targets 230
Pakistan: sending troops to "protect" the Holy Land 143
Pakistan: unexpected action to join coalition forces 193
Pakistan: took position that Muslims exert collective force 137
Pakistan: has touched limits of folly in sending its forces 47
Pakistan: ousted leaders complained that CIA never warned them... 61
Pakistan: "horse-trading" purchasing members of Parliament 239
Pakistan: "Two Nation Theory" of Allama Iqbal 77
Pakistan: advice 320
Pakistan: happenings in India are reaction of happenings in _ 97
Palestine & Palestinian problem: 91, 141, 180, 211, 263, 285
Palestinians: 4 million _ wandering, stateless, lost souls 264
Pan Arabism movement: 311
Pawns in a game of chess: world toys with Muslim countries as if _ _ 34
Peace: three principles to guarantee lasting peace 288, 289
Persecution of Jews: avenging on Muslims for wrong done by Christians 269
Physician, heal thyself: 302
Pir of Pagara: (Pakistani politician) 155
Plague: will spread in Europe 338
PLO: accepts existence of state of Israel 263
Politics: three Basic principles of secular politics 281
Politics: devoid of Justice and piety 40
Polytheism: to abandon truth and adopt falsehood is abominable as _ 283

Poor: Muhammad[sas] said "find me with the poor on day of Judgement" 167
Pope Sixtus: IV Isabella at odds with _ inquisitions in Spain 268
Pope: Muslims of Spain conspired with Pope to demolish Baghdad 49
Portugal: meeting with a retired judge from Portugal 119
Prayers: pray for welfare of world 89, 340, 344
Prejudices: 105, 108
President Bush's dream of peace: 225
Problems recurring - cause: 37
Profit and Loss: situation of the war 243
Promised Land: (Al Arz) may mean Palestine or the whole world 285
Promised Messiah[as]: consequences of his rejection by the Muslims 242
Promised Messiah[as]: "My God has given me glad-tiding about Arabs" 55
Promised Messiah[as]: Hazrat Mirza Ghulam Ahmad 36
Promised Messiah[as]: "The path of righteousness has been lost..." 36
Promised Messiah[as]: 1901 revelation regarding Freemasons" 201
Promised Messiah[as]: Allah will accept his prayers 337
Propaganda campaign: against Saddam Hussein 182
Propaganda: The West carries out _ which has semblance of rationality 46
Propaganda: that Iraq possesses chemicals for which there is no antidote 87
Propaganda: fundamental principle of irreligious politics 283
Propaganda: that Saddam will use nerve gases against adversaries 62
Protocols of the Elders of Zion: 198

Q

Qadian: (India The birth place of the founder of Community) 201, 321
Qibla: direction of prostration by Muslims 155
Quayle: Dan USA (Vice President) 206
Queen of Spain: 268
Quranic procedure of settlement of conflicts: 31
Quranic System of Justice: 293
Quranic principle: 33

R

Racial superiority: concept of _ _ 112
Racial prejudices: 74, 109, 110, 112, 136
Racial dangers: 106
Racism: 74, 83
Rajputs: 108
Ramazan: month of fasting prescribed by Islam 343
Red Indians: 113, 138, 329

Responsibility of war: 235, 238
Restlessness - cause: 57
Revenge: is similar to a flood which does not see balanced reaction 116
Richard B. Cheney: 236
Richard- the Lion-hearted: British King who occupied Palestine 251
Richest part of the globe: without proper defence 203
Righteousness (Taqwa): 31, 35, 71, 73, 81, 90, 100
Rightly guided Khilafat: 127
Roohani Khazain: (Books of the Promised Messiah[as]) 55
Roosevelt Kim: USA 217, 279
Root cause which creates Saddams and Nassers: 257
Rope of Allah: 127, 129, 293
Rothschild Lord: distinguished Jewish banker from France 211
Rushdie: Salman threats 142
Russia - China: differences based on colour prejudice 84
Russian woman: (1897?) who smuggled the "protocols" to Russia 199
Russian Jewish immigrants settlements: 309
Russian Empire: on the verge of disintegration 77

S

Sabra: Palestinian camp 259
Saddam Hussein: 42, 58, 147, 182, 209, 256, 286
Saddam Hussein: 209
Saddam: pictured as a "Hitler" 258
Saddamism: 59
Salahuddin (saladin): 157, 159, 248
Sancho Panzo: 279
Sanskrit: 108
Saud: - son of Abdul Aziz 144
Saudi Arabia: 45, 86, 116, 156, 163, 192
Saudi security: 48
Saudi Dynasty: 144
Scotland: 75
Scud missiles: 160, 163, 180
Scud missiles at Israel: 227
Second World War: 257
Secretary General: Mr Perez De Cuellar 147
Secular politics: 281
Security Council: 264, 326
Selfishness: 75, 105, 115

Serbia: Yugoslavia 114
Shah of Iran: 60, 218
Shakespearean play called "Macbeth": 231
Shariah: imposition of Islamic Law even on non-Muslims 290
Shatila: camp 259
Sheikhdom Arab: 163
Sheriff Hussein of Mecca and Medina: 202
Shiite Muslims: 76, 79
Shylock: (Merchant of Venice) 252
Sikh nation: 107
Sikh: unrest in India 230
Similitude of salt: 345
Sinai desert: 67
Slaughter: of over 3,000 Muslim men 223
Slaves: Africans slaves sold as chattel 139
Slovenia: Yugoslavia 114
Solomon - the Magnificent: 249
Somalia: famine 166
South America: 113, 300, 318
South African government: sanctions 141
Soviet Union: dangers looming 109
Soviet Union: that countries are created on ideology..... 77
Soviet Union: 74,
Soviet Union: asks for drilling rights in Iran 216
Soviet Union: Saudi Arabia gave 3 billion dollars aid to _ 244
Spain: 49, 110
Spiritual battles: the weapon prescribed by Jesus Christ[as] 172
Square-one: Saudi Arabia will never go back to its past 152
Sri Lanka: common market with Pakistan, India, Bangladesh 312
Sri Lanka: linguistic and national differences 112
Standard bearer of humanity: 181
Stench of dead bodies: 181
Submission (Islam): 126
Sudan: 164, 166
Suez Canal: 218, 219
Sunnah: 46
Sunni Muslims: 76, 79
Sydenham Lord: "...to start a running sore in the East...) 241
Synagogues: Jews built synagogues in Jerusalem 91
Syria: 42, 194, 221, 230, 244

Index - Notes

T

Tabriyya: small sea in Israel through which river Jordan passes 336-337
Tafseer-e-Kabeer: (larger commentary of Holy Quran) 49
Taif: (Saudi Arabia) 144
Taimour Lang:(Tamerlane) 50, 276
Tale of a sick horse: 225
Tamerlane: 50, 276
Taqwa (righteousness): 52, 81, 121, 124, 292
Teaching of Islam: 34
Technology: 269
Temple of Rama: 95
Temple of Solomon: 332, 335
Territorial boundaries: 171
Terrorism: 340
Theodor Herzl: 239, 249
Theodore Arcand: 262
Third world: 302, 313, 315, 322
Third Successor to the Promised Messiah[aa]: 248
Tibet: occupation by China 114
Tony Benn: the British M.P. 183
Tribes: "We made you into tribes and Sub-tribes for recognition" 73
Tropic Storm: code name for war with North Vietnam 271
Trumpets of victory: after crippling Iraq 307
Truth: Principle of 283
Truthfulness: 282
Turkey: 76, 109-111, 194, 231, 244
Turkish nation: 109
Turkman: 76
Two Nation Theory: 77

U

U.N. Resolution No. 242: 221, 235, 265
U.N. serves only the interest of the rich: 266
U.S. & the West: their actions speak louder than their words 182
U.S. dilemma in Iran: 61
U.S. defeat: 271
Umar bin Abdul Aziz: 159
United Kingdom: 75
United Nations: 118, 326
United Nations of the Third world: 327

United States has massacred PEACE forever: 232
United Nations role: 235
Unity of God: 185, 247
UNO: US operating UNO   238
Untouchables of India: 99
Uzbekistan: 110

V

V.P. Singh: the former Prime Minister of India   99, 108
Versailles: 287
Veto: 138, 179, 328
Vetoed: 27 resolutions (US)   264
Victory of numbers: Ahmadis do not require ___   113
Vietnam war: 161, 229
Vietnam Syndrome: 306
Vietnam complex: 246

W

Wahabiyya sect: 50, 192, 203
War of Yom Kippur: 221
War-expenses: 163
Washington: Saudi microphones located in Washington   192
Weapon of prayer: 88
Weizmann: a Polish scientist - contacts with Balfour (1915-1918)   239
West Bank of the Jordan River: 141, 227
West Beirut: 259
Western Christian nations: advice   339
Western diplomacy: 142
White Paper: British _ _ that spelled changes in its foreign policy   213
Wisdom: righteousness begets wisdom. Divine illumination   71
Woodrow Wilson: U.S. President committed to justice (1918)   242
World War II: 161
World Zionist Organisation: 263
World peace: 118

Y

Yardstick: U.S. & U.K. must use same _ for measuring problems   138
Yassar Arafat: 263
Yugoslavia: 113

Z

Zakat: appeal to oil-rich countries to donate 2.5% charity Africa 319
Zia-ul-Haq: Pakistani dictator 103
Zionism: Expansion of 212, 220-221
Zoo: surviving tribes in Australia are in settlements like animals in _ 140